Q2/MAY JO

T
27

£65.00

5199

TECHNOLOGY, COMPETITIVENESS AND THE STATE

Over the last decade Malaysia's remarkable economic performance has attracted attention around the world and been subject to much study and enthusiastic acclaim. However, in the wake of the present financial crisis, the debate has centred on whether this impressive growth rate can be sustained. As the economy moves beyond growth based on low labour costs and other factor-endowed advantages, industrial technology development becomes increasingly critical to continued growth.

This volume, and its companion, *Industrial Technology Development in Malaysia*, examine and evaluate Malaysian industrialisation in terms of its experience of and prospects for industrial technology development. The focus is on the role played by state-sponsored innovation in the process of economic development and in the context of national development strategies. *Technology, Competitiveness and the State* provides a valuable analysis of the technological development of a Newly Industrialising Country and reflects on whether existing development strategies can be maintained in the wake of the financial crises sweeping the East Asian economies.

Jomo K.S. is Professor in the Faculty of Economics and Administration at the University of Malaya, Kuala Lumpur and is the author of many works on the political economy of Malaysian development, including *Industrializing Malaysia* (Routledge 1993). **Greg Felker** is Assistant Professor in the Division of Social Science at Hong Kong University of Science and Technology.

ROUTLEDGE STUDIES IN THE GROWTH ECONOMIES OF ASIA

TECHNOLOGY, COMPETITIVENESS AND THE STATE

Malaysia's industrial technology policies

Edited by Jomo K.S. and Greg Felker

London and New York

First published 1999
by Routledge
11 New Fetter Lane, London EC4P 4EE

Simultaneously published in the USA and Canada
by Routledge
29 West 35th Street, New York, NY 10001
Routledge is an imprint of the Taylor & Francis Group

Typeset in Baskerville by
M Rules
Printed and bound in Great Britain by
Mackays of Chatham plc, Chatham, Kent

British Library Cataloguing in Publication Data
A catalogue record for this book is available from the British Library

Library of Congress Cataloguing in Publication Data
Technology, competitiveness, and the state: Malaysia's industrial technology policies/
K.S. Jomo, Greg Felker, [editors].
p. cm.
Includes bibliographical references (p.) and index.
1. Technology and state – Malaysia. 2. Industrial policy – Malaysia.
I. Jomo K.S. (Jomo Kwame Sundaram) II. Felker, Greg.
T27.M4T43 1999
338.959507—dc21
98–38050
CIP

ISBN 0 415 19765 1

CONTENTS

CONTENTS

FIGURES

TABLES

CONTRIBUTORS

Chris Edwards recently retired as Senior Lecturer at the School of Development Studies, University of East Anglia, Norwich. He has worked on the Malaysian economy since the late 1960s and has published extensively on industrialisation and industry policy issues.

Greg Felker is Assistant Professor in the Social Science Division at the Hong Kong University of Science and Technology, and has studied technology policy issues in Malaysia and Thailand.

Jomo K.S. is Professor in the Faculty of Economics and Administration, University of Malaya, Kuala Lumpur. He is the author and editor of various works on the political economy of Malaysian development.

Masayuki Kondo is Director, Research and Statistics Planning Office, Ministry of International Trade and Industry (MITI), Tokyo; while at the World Bank he studied Malaysia's industrial development strategy.

Sanjaya Lall is Professor at Oxford University on leave at the World Bank, and is the author of many influential books, articles and reports, most recently in the areas of industrial and technology policy.

Kit G. Machado is Professor of Political Science at California State University, Northridge. He has written extensively on the political economy of East Asia, with some focus on Japan–Malaysia relations.

Jörg Meyer-Stamer is with the German Development Institute at Berlin. He has written extensively on technology development issues, especially in Brazil.

Rajah Rasiah is Associate Professor in the Institute of Malaysian and International Studies (IKMAS) at the National University of Malaysia (UKM), Bangi, Selangor. He is author of *Foreign Capital and Industrialisation in Malaysia* (Macmillan, 1995).

K. Thiruchelvam has a PhD from the Science Policy Research Unit (SPRU) at the University of Sussex and works at the Malaysian Ministry of Science, Technology and the Environment.

Wong Poh Kam is Head of the Technology Management Centre at the School of Business Administration, National University of Singapore, and has published extensively in various areas, especially on industrial technology development in East, including Southeast, Asia.

PREFACE

A decade of rapid export-led growth thrust Malaysia to the forefront of the development debate in the 1990s. Malaysia's remarkable economic performance raised its global profile at a time when the neo-liberal 'Washington consensus' faced a vigorous heterodox challenge inspired by the rise of East Asian newly industrialised economies (NIEs). Was rapid industrial transformation in Asia explained by governments' adherence to free domestic and international markets, or by intentional strategies, discretionary interventions, and unique economic institutions?

Earlier accounts, such as the World Bank's 1993 *East Asian Miracle* study, argued that Malaysia and its fellow Southeast Asian 'tiger economies' differed from the first-tier or first-generation East Asian NIEs in their minimal state role and open embrace of international investment and trade. Malaysia's success thus seemed to vindicate the neo-liberal approach to growth.

Critical observers raised several questions about this interpretation. Was Malaysia's success in fact comparable to the NIEs' earlier transition to a self-sustaining industrial dynamism? Or, as some suggested, was it a transitory phenomenon produced by broader regional trends, namely the internationalisation of Japanese and East Asian NIE capital through foreign direct investment (FDI)? Finally, was the assessment of Malaysian growth as market-driven an accurate one, or were policy and institutional factors more important than previously recognised?

Motivated by these comparative concerns, a number of Malaysian and foreign scholars began to probe the Malaysian miracle through in-depth fieldwork during the early and mid-1990s. Though coming from a variety of disciplines, a remarkable number identified issues of technological change at the heart of their research questions. Technological development is widely recognised to be the foundation of sustained growth, but was long treated either as a 'black box' – a wholly exogenous process driven by scientific advances – or as an automatic response to changing factor endowments or consumer tastes. In the past two decades, however, research has shown technological change to be endogenous to broader development problems and outcomes. Technological innovation is a distinct process with specific determinants, but one that interacts closely with economic, social and institutional dynamics.

Researchers seeking to fathom the nature of Malaysia's industrial take-off thus employed new frameworks from economics, political science and management studies to assess its technological dimension. Often encountering each other in the field, they recognised an opportunity to bring together their research results in order to fill a crucial empirical gap in the study of Malaysia's ongoing transformation. Initial proposals for an international conference did not bear fruit, though the National University of Malaysia held a similar conference in 1995 attended by several contributors to these volumes. Instead, various studies were assembled through informal networks and contacts made in the course of research in Malaysia.

This collection of papers embraces a variety of disciplinary approaches and levels of analysis, a diversity that captures the multiple facets and determinants of technological change. Some studies analyse the technology development process at the national or policy level, while others focus on industry- or firm-level questions, and the studies were organised into two volumes according to this distinction. The two volumes must be viewed as complementary, however, since technological and other patterns of economic change reflect an interaction of micro- and macro-level influences, a point which these studies demonstrate well. This 'embeddedness' of firms' investment decisions explains the apparent paradox that, in an age of global economic integration, national differences in economic institutions become ever more apparent and consequential. As these studies make clear, the determinants of technological change include not only market incentives, but institutional and strategic factors at the firm, industry and national levels.

The editing of these volumes was a protracted effort, made more difficult by our inability to raise sorely needed financial support, and the consequent need to rely almost entirely on e-mail and postal communication and the goodwill of all concerned. The editors would like to thank the contributors for their willingness to submit their research findings for joint publication and for their patience in seeing the project to an end.

As usual, Foo Ah Hiang provided sterling help for much of the editorial work, for which we are most grateful. Working on this volume put an inevitable toll on our families to whom we are most appreciative for their understanding patience.

1

INTRODUCTION

Greg Felker with Jomo K.S.

Malaysia's striking economic performance during the last decade attracted great interest in policy and academic circles around the world. Sustained high growth rates involved profound structural change. Malaysia was transformed in a single generation from its post-colonial status as a primary product exporter into an industrially oriented economy and leading global manufactures exporter.[1] Real GDP grew by an average 5.2 per cent per year during 1980–90, and accelerated to a remarkable 8.7 per cent per year during 1990–95. Manufacturing output rose even more swiftly, averaging 8.9 per cent and 13.2 per cent per year during the same two periods. Malaysia's merchandise exports grew by 11.5 per cent annually during 1980–90 and by 17.8 per cent in 1990–95. Manufactured goods made up only 19 per cent of exports in 1980, yet by 1995 they accounted for 77.4 per cent of a vastly larger total.[2]

Even before the East Asian economic crisis erupted in 1997, however, notes of concern were often sounded amidst the chorus of acclaim for Malaysia's industrial achievements. Malaysia's economic 'miracle' presented a curious mixture of manifest dynamism and chronic structural weaknesses, giving rise to conflicting views as to whether rapid industrialisation was based on durable strengths or transient factors. On the one hand, continued inflows of foreign direct investment (FDI) and the partial diversification of manufactured exports seemed to dispel fears that rising wages would erode the country's competitiveness and cause foreign firms to divert their investments to lower-cost countries. At the same time, locally-owned firms' minimal participation in export industries, limited inter-industry linkages, and lagging productivity growth remained conspicuous problems. One leading Malaysian economist avowed a widely-shared optimism that 'There is always room at the top for a country that aims high and is prepared to work hard at it. It appears that Malaysia has the courage and the means to do just that' (Ariff 1991: 194). Other observers argued that the country's remarkable economic performance resulted from external factors like FDI and hence that 'There is an inherent fragility in the current Malaysian industrial "take-off"' (Bowie 1994: 191).

East Asia's financial crisis in the late 1990s makes this debate more urgent than ever before, as Malaysia struggles to preserve its industrial gains in the face of the regional economic collapse. Does the slump reveal the Malaysian industrial miracle to have been little more than a mirage based on foreign capital injections and 'irrational exuberance'? Or were real industrial and technological capabilities built up during the boom years, strengths that will revive the economy's upward trajectory once the turmoil subsides? The crisis in Malaysian and other Asian economies was first and foremost a matter of currency and financial markets. A complex set of international and domestic factors, including a 'virtual peg' of regional currencies against the strengthening US dollar, encouraged a binge of short-term foreign borrowing in the mid-1990s, much of which financed speculative investments in real estate and corporate equities. When the Southeast Asian pegs fell to attacks by currency traders in the first half of July 1997, rapid withdrawal of foreign and local capital snowballed into a general meltdown of investor confidence, which in turn produced a self-reinforcing decline in currency and equity values. Collapsing asset values imperilled entire financial systems and caused an acute liquidity crisis affecting virtually all sectors and firms.

While the crisis thus stemmed primarily from problems and dynamics internal to financial markets and non-manufacturing sectors, the real economy's structural dynamism was also at issue. The current account deficits financed by short-term borrowing stemmed primarily from over-investment in non-tradable sectors, but a slow-down in manufactured export growth, which began in 1996, had also contributed. The competitiveness of Malaysian manufacturing was less important in explaining the financial crisis, however, than in determining the prospects for recovery. According to conventional analysis, currency devaluation would enhance the cost competitiveness of industries in Malaysia and stimulate exports, offering a silver lining amidst the dark clouds of financial havoc. The actual picture has been far more complex. Malaysia's manufacturing industries, including exporters whose competitiveness is not in doubt, face a severe liquidity squeeze. Currency depreciation itself has been a mixed blessing for export industries, since non-resource based manufacturing relies heavily on imported inputs and technology, the costs of which have suddenly skyrocketed. Slow growth in key markets and devaluations in other exporting countries, make vigorous export growth anything but automatic for Malaysia. At most, devaluation would do little more than temporarily extend industrial and export competitiveness based on relatively lower production, especially labour, costs. While the crisis does not constitute evidence that Malaysia's industrial boom is exhausted, therefore, neither does it postpone the need to grapple with the challenges of fostering dynamic industrial change. The question thus remains – what are the underlying strengths and prospects of Malaysia's industrial sector?

The ongoing debate about the nature of Malaysia's industrialisation stems from an awareness that years of double-digit manufacturing growth had, by the early 1990s, brought the country to a new stage of development. The economy confronted a pivotal transition from labour-intensive manufacturing to an industrial structure based on higher-value-added, technology-intensive production. It is increasingly understood that technological change and the factors that shape it are the key issues in long-run industrial success. As an economy moves beyond growth based on low labour costs and other factor-endowment advantages, industrial technology development becomes ever more critical to sustaining development momentum (World Bank 1993: 87–90; Dosi *et al.* 1988). Contrary to orthodox theory, technological development involves far more than an automatic response to changing factor prices. Observers and policy makers in Southeast Asia, and in Malaysia particularly, recognise that the region's 'near-NICs' must spur the process of technological development if they are to recover and maintain their economic dynamism (Anuwar 1992; Ng *et al.* 1986; Osman-Rani *et al.* 1986). At its core, then, critical evaluation of Malaysian industrialisation involves an examination of its experience and prospects in industrial technology development. Has rapid growth in output and exports been accompanied by the development of capabilities to acquire, adapt and improve important technologies? Or has the deepening reliance on the production decisions of multinational corporations signified an externally driven, or even 'technology-less' form of industrialisation (Yoshihara 1988)?

Government intervention is often needed to remedy failures in markets for finance, skills and information. These market failures are particularly acute in technology development, providing a rationale for government to create special incentives for investments that build technological capabilities. Any such interventions require good policy design and careful implementation, which in turn depend on adequate administrative capabilities and information. If the government lacks these capabilities, policies to encourage technological capability-building must be correspondingly modest in scope to minimise the likelihood of government policy failure. Lall (1996: 39) notes that the infant industry argument has often been discredited by policies which invoke its logic while ignoring its requirements. He emphasises that such examples of government failure do not invalidate the case for judicious, selective interventions to address problems which impede technological capability development. Instead, he draws the following policy implications:

- industries selected for promotion must be realistically capable of achieving world efficiency levels in the foreseeable future;
- since resources are generally limited, efforts should be focused on a few industries at any one time, while performance should be strictly monitored and improved;
- as protection reduces the incentive to invest in technology capability development, countervailing measures are necessary, e.g. strong requirements to export early tend to enhance technical efficiency;
- as firms are often linked to other firms in the national economy, protection itself cannot ensure competitiveness unless related problems are adequately addressed, i.e. protection has to be coupled with complementary measures to develop capabilities.

If economic arguments about industrial and technology policies are inseparable from the question of the government's policy capacities, this in turn points to debates about the political foundations of successful 'late' industrialisation. What sort of institutional and political arrangements enable governments to intervene in a disciplined fashion and avoid policy failure? This question is crucial whatever mix of markets and state intervention prevails, since even a market-based strategy requires a neutral administration capable of resisting egregious rent-seeking and reconciling broader distributional pressures with the demands of market competitiveness. One popular but contentious argument draws on the East Asian NIC examples to suggest that only a politically insulated 'strong' state can implement strategic industrial policies without having them fall prey to rent-seeking pressures (Johnson 1987; Haggard 1990; Wade 1990; Onis 1991).

Malaysia's dramatic transformation makes it a critical case in these ongoing controversies. It has featured assertive state efforts to guide industrialisation, but strategic policies' actual contribution to development is strongly disputed (Lall 1995). Throughout the 1970s, government industrial policies sought to diversify the economy, diminish its reliance on primary commodities, and encourage manufacturing. The government became even more interventionist in the early 1980s, and launched a comprehensive strategy that set specific sectoral priorities to accelerate and deepen industrial growth. Strategic industrial policies initially focused on a state-led second round of import-substitution. The state's ambitious thrust into heavy industries resulted in several costly failures and contributed to fiscal and macro-economic crises in the early 1980s.

In the wake of the 1985–86 recession, the political leadership changed course and began an ongoing effort to streamline and rationalise industrial policies. Most importantly, the government embraced private-sector-led industrialisation and turned once again towards export-oriented growth. Yet it also persisted in attempts to influence structural change through indicative strategic guidance (Lall 1995). As the economy swung from recession to hyper-growth with full employment, the industrial policy framework focused on issues of export competitiveness, productivity growth and technological development. The success or failure of Malaysia's efforts to promote technology-based industrialisation holds unique significance for the political economy of late industrialisation – it is precisely this transition, in which an economy moves beyond traditional, factor-endowment sources of comparative advantage, which throws contending hypotheses about the roles of state and market in industrialisation into sharpest relief.

The export-led growth boom and the new approach to industrial policy have now lasted over a decade. Though the economic crisis has made the ultimate goal – transition to technology-based industrialisation – even more uncertain, the time is nonetheless ripe for an assessment of the character of Malaysia's industrial technology development and the role of technology policy and institutions. The next section of this introduction identifies the developmental goals and challenges which have inspired Malaysia's ambitious technology policies. The third section discusses recent theoretical perspectives on technological change in developing countries and highlights their policy implications. The fourth section details the evolution of Malaysian technology policy and institutions, identifying key trends in government and corporate technology strategies. The volume's individual chapters are introduced in the conclusion.

National innovation systems and the case of Malaysia

Firms create industrial technological development through their investment and production decisions, but they do not do so in isolation. Policies and institutions powerfully shape the incentives for firms to invest in technology, and also provide vital complementary resources, information, skills, and specialised technical services. In their efforts to develop technological capabilities, firms draw heavily upon such external technological resources through both market and non-market linkages. Furthermore, private investments in technological development confront various types of market failure. Many aspects of technological learning are highly interdependent or involve pervasive externalities. For example, one firm's investments in developing its workers' technical skills might easily benefit its competitors if trained staff switch companies. Another well-known example is the interdependence of technical progress in capital goods (or other supplier industries) and in downstream machine-based industries. As a result, there are significant areas in which some degree of co-operation among firms and public institutions may result in more rapid technological development. Conversely, a lack of institutions or policies for co-ordination may inhibit the rapid accumulation of technological capabilities, because individual firms will under-invest in them.

Awareness that an economy's technology development performance depends, to some significant degree, on investments and capabilities developed at a broader level than the individual enterprise has stimulated growing interest in 'national innovation systems' (see Nelson 1993; Lundvall 1992). Dahlman (1994: 541) defines a national innovation system as

> the network of agents and set of policies and institutions that affect the introduction of technology that is new to the economy . . . [including] policies toward foreign direct investment, arm's-length technology transfer, intellectual property rights, and importation of capital goods. The innovation system also comprises the network of public and private institutions and agents supporting or undertaking scientific and technological activities, including research and development, technology diffusion, and creation of technical human capital.

This definition suggests that general macro-economic, trade, industrial, and labour-market policies, and not only explicit technology policies, powerfully influence firms' incentives and abilities to seek improved technology. Technology development is nonetheless a distinct process which, while integral to broader industrialisation, has its own specific determinants and dynamics.

Studies of successful late industrialisation, particularly in Japan and the East

Asian newly industrialised countries (NICs – South Korea, Taiwan, Hong Kong and Singapore), draw attention to the role of innovation systems in supporting technological catch-up in leading industries (Freeman 1987; Dahlman 1989; Samuels 1994). Governments in both the advanced industrial countries and the developing world have recently sought to create or reform innovation systems to boost industrial growth and national competitiveness. Indeed, as global economic integration undermines their ability to use trade, macro-economic and state-enterprise policies to promote national industrialisation, governments have become increasingly interested in directly influencing micro-economic dynamics such as productivity growth and technical change. Nelson (1993: 3) observes 'There is clearly a new spirit of what might be called "techno-nationalism" in the air', while also cautioning that 'the belief that these [technological] capabilities are in a sense national, and can be built by national action' may in fact be misleading. This, then, is the critical issue. Where do national innovation systems come from? To what extent do they reflect strategic development priorities set by political actors, or rather emerge 'naturally' as demand for technology support increases among firms in the market place?

Malaysia is especially important in answering these questions, because few countries have pursued technology development as consistently and self-consciously over the past several years. The national philosophy, the Rukunegara, commits Malaysia 'to building a progressive society which shall be oriented to modern science and technology'. Explicit policies and institutions to promote technology development arose in the mid-1980s as a natural corollary to the programme of accelerated industrialisation and, in large part, as a response to the weaknesses threatening its achievement. In seeking to emulate the development models of first-generation newly industrialised countries like South Korea, Malaysian officials noted that explicit technology policies were important in the transition from labour-intensive assembly to a deeper and higher-value-added industrial structure. The cardinal industrial strategy document of the 1980s, the Industrial Master Plan (1985–95), therefore spotlighted technology development as a key weakness and object of policy intervention. Prime Minister Mahathir's 1991 'Vision 2020' manifesto, entitled 'The Way Forward' amplified the priority on technology development by declaring it one among nine strategic challenges facing the nation. It claimed, 'There is inadequate development of indigenous technology. There is too little value-added, too much simple assembly and production' and asserted the goal of creating 'an economy that is technologically proficient, fully able to adapt, innovate and invent, that is increasingly technology-intensive, moving in the direction of higher and higher levels of technology'. As the economy grew ever more dependent upon foreign manufacturing investment and exports in the 1990s, technology came to be viewed as crucial to continued prosperity in the increasingly competitive and technology-driven international economy. The need to promote technology development became a central feature of the growing discourse on national 'competitiveness'. For example, policy makers widely discuss the annual World Competitiveness Report issued by a Swiss consulting firm, which ranks countries according to their technology development levels and several other factors.

Malaysia shares these developmental motives with other so-called 'second-tier' NICs, such as Thailand, Indonesia, and (latterly) the Philippines. Yet, it is distinctive in the scope and ambition of its effort to deploy strategic technology policies to engineer the transformation of its industrial structure. At a rhetorical level, the Prime Minister and top government officials constantly emphasise the challenges and goals of national technology development in policy and public forums. Beginning with the Fifth Malaysia Plan (1986–90), each five-year development plan includes a chapter that identifies technology development goals and allocations. Public R&D and technology budgets have grown sharply, while new technology planning systems seek to guide investments into priority areas. Along with increased funding, officials have mounted a decade-long effort to expand and reform the nation's system of technology support institutions, including public R&D laboratories and university consultancy units. To encourage private-sector technology development, the government has offered new incentives for R&D and high-technology investments, even while gradually curtailing other discretionary investment incentives. Other policy efforts established specialised technology finance mechanisms and built new science parks to attract high-tech industries. Technology transfer and development became central issues in negotiations with the foreign investors who led the economy's recent industrial surge. Taken together, these initiatives add up to a fairly comprehensive programme to build a national technology development system and harness it to strategic industrialisation goals through increased investment, coherent central planning, and intensified consultation with the private sector.

Despite its high policy priority, however, Malaysia's attempt to orchestrate a technological transformation in industry remains a difficult and uncertain enterprise. First, while national institutions and policies may affect technology development, the extent to which public policies can accelerate and guide technological development in line with explicit strategies is far from clear, as suggested above. Nelson and Rosenberg's (1993: 4) overview of several case studies of national innovation systems cautions, 'There is no presumption that the [national innovation] system was . . . consciously designed, or even that the set of institutions involved works together smoothly and coherently.' Accepting the premise that national policies and institutions significantly affect the course of industrial technology development, one is left with the formidable challenge of defining what constitutes good technology strategy, policy and practice.

Several other obstacles give pause to easy predictions of success. Malaysia began its technology development programme with a deficit of pre-existing public and private institutions for industrial technology, and measurable technology development within the private sector was negligible until very recently. While its export structure is concentrated in relatively sophisticated products such as component and consumer electronics, for example, the industrial structure in the 1980s was remarkably 'shallow', with poor inter-industry linkages and an underdeveloped capital goods sector. Specialised technology infrastructure for industry was lacking, with few engineering consultancy firms, sources of finance for innovation, advanced skills training institutes, and commercial or public providers of industrial technical services and R&D. In short, Malaysia presented a curious picture of burgeoning high-technology exports with little local innovation activity.

Other obstacles are legacies of Malaysia's history as a resource-rich exporter of primary products or of previous industrial policies. An elusive though fundamental issue is the absence of an 'innovation culture' or tradition within local industry, in turn reflecting local private business groups' historic orientation towards commodities, commerce and other tertiary sectors. Throughout Southeast Asia, leading private business groups originated in trade and banking, but large-scale diversification into industry took place in the 1970s in countries such as Thailand and Indonesia. In Malaysia, attempts to promote industrialisation came relatively late, and the business groups which emerged under state patronage during the 1970s under the New Economic Policy (NEP) were largely outside manufacturing (Lim 1981; Heng 1992). Even after the government shifted its stance in the late 1980s to promote manufacturing development under private-sector auspices, the dearth of locally owned enterprises with distinct, long-run industrial orientations has frustrated efforts to jump-start indigenous technological development. Annual surveys by the Federation of Malaysian Manufacturers (FMM) indicate that, outside of the foreign investment sector, business awareness of and interest in R&D and other technology issues is generally poor.

A related concern is Malaysia's industrial structure, which was long characterised by a 'missing middle' of dynamic and technologically progressive medium- to large-scale indigenous enterprises. Small-scale, family-run ethnic-Chinese businesses dominated local manufacturing production until quite recently, and the majority of these employ obsolete production techniques and non-professional management systems (Ismail 1990). The gap in scale and technology between these firms and the leading MNCs has hampered efforts to build linkages between foreign-dominated export industries and the local economy.

A third issue is the historically dominant role played by multinational corporations (MNCs) in Malaysia's leading manufacturing industries. The deepening MNC presence has effected profound structural change in the Malaysian economy. Policy makers and observers are nonetheless concerned that passive reliance on foreign direct investment (FDI) results in a truncated form of technology transfer, whereby deeper design and research capabilities are not developed and the primary impetus for growth continues to lie in external factors (i.e. MNCs' international decision-making) rather than in locally driven productivity growth.[3]

Finally, the transition to technology-based industrialisation is threatened by the acute scarcity of technically skilled human resources. This weakness crucially distinguishes Malaysian development from the East Asian NICs, where massive investments in human capital anticipated rapid industrial growth. Nowhere is the paradoxical mixture of high-technology exports with weak local technology inputs more evident. Malaysia's manufactured exports have evolved rapidly towards products which usually require higher skill levels, yet some recent scholarship has indicated a *decline* in the skill content of manufacturing (World Bank 1997) and exports (Lee 1996). This paradox is largely explained by high-technology MNCs' capacity to subdivide and distribute the production process internationally to match host countries' differing skill levels and capabilities. A crucial question is the extent to which foreign firms in Malaysia have 'adapted down' to skills deficits by focusing on less skill-intensive production activities or by implementing skill-substituting automation, or, instead, 'adapted up' by absorbing the costs and limiting or ignoring the externalities (e.g. job-hopping) of genuine skills upgrading through in-house training. Many recent studies have indicated that MNCs have invested large and growing amounts in workforce training in conjunction with automation and other technological improvements (Rasiah 1995; Lall *et al.* 1994). A bleaker interpretation is that, more than enlarging the pool of skilled labour through their training activities, large MNCs have upgraded their own human capital by crowding out other firms in the skilled-labour market, offering superior salaries and benefits. In this view, MNC responses to skills deficits might exacerbate the general market failures confronting private investments in human capital. The result might be a growing technological dualism dividing large MNCs, for whom investments in skills development yield positive returns despite some spill-overs, from other smaller foreign and local firms struggling to maintain low-cost, low-skill production strategies. Thus far, the skills deficit has not appeared to prevent FDI-led industrial upgrading. Yet, even favourable analyses question whether such progress will be sustained in the absence of swift efforts to dramatically increase human capital stocks through expanded training and education infrastructure.

These cautions imply that local public and private institutions might be inadequate to overcome difficult challenges facing Malaysia's ambitious technology development programme. Other questions about the prospects for success start from the opposite premise, namely that national-level technology strategies and institutions have themselves become obsolete. The flow of technology in capital equipment, foreign investment and human skills is increasingly transnational, and Malaysian industry relies particularly heavily on international linkages for technological information and resources. As FDI creates intra-industry and intra-firm divisions of labour across national borders, the goal of guiding industry to develop specific self-contained technological competencies within national borders appears unrealistic to many observers (Simon 1995a). At the same time, national institutions and policies appear overly broad in light of recent work on flexible specialisation and regional development in industry, in which inter-firm networks, often in particular geographic clusters, figure as the most important type of institution nurturing technological learning (Storper and Scott 1992; Ohmae 1995). Firms' needs for skills and technical support vary widely not only across industries, but also by individual networks of co-operating firms which develop distinctive technology 'codes', or standards and protocols for skills, design and inter-firm communication.

In the context of these twin trends towards global integration and sectoral, regional and network differentiation, therefore, many argue that the scope for national policies has become more strictly limited to broad investments in basic education and infrastructure development. The Malaysian government's effort to target specific technologies is unlikely to influence industry's accumulation of capabilities, and, worse, might divert scarce human and financial resources towards non-productive investments. From this standpoint, the best which central governments can do is to accommodate global trends and support local initiatives through decentralising decision making and resources to regions, cities and non-state actors. The recent popularity of regional trans-border 'growth triangles' in Southeast Asia is an example of such an approach.

Finally, quite apart from the economic challenges to national technology strategies is the question of the administrative and political conditions necessary for effective implementation. A large literature addresses the political factors behind the successful use of strategic trade and industrial policies in the East Asian NIEs, asking why and how policy-generated rents (or subsidies) were deployed to reward infant-industry learning rather than the wasteful rent-seeking evident in many political economies (Amsden 1989). As noted above, one strand of argument emphasises the importance of a politically autonomous 'strong state', which insulates economic policy making from distributional demands, permits technically proficient bureaucrats to allocate rents towards developmental objectives, and holds private business accountable to performance measures (see Haggard 1990; Amsden 1992; Wade 1990).[4] Critiques of statism, some of it drawing from Southeast Asian cases, stress the progressive role of private business classes, state/business policy networks or growth coalitions, and non-state institutions such as business associations and sub-contracting networks (MacIntyre 1994; Doner 1992; McVey 1992; Hamilton 1991). The puzzle of what political arrangements support effective industrial policy is no less pertinent to technology policies, inasmuch as enhanced technological capabilities are essential to the maturation of infant industries and the achievement of dynamic comparative advantage. Indeed, the strongly industry- and firm-specific character of technological change makes the administrative challenges to government policy – measuring performance and ensuring accountability – particularly difficult and critical.

Malaysia presents a somewhat contradictory mixture of the political factors supporting effective industrial policy. While the Malaysian state does not approach the degree of dominance historically evident in Korea or Taiwan, many observers argue that it enjoys the highest levels of political autonomy and bureaucratic capacity in Southeast Asia, Singapore excluded (Crouch 1984; MacIntyre 1994). On the other hand, inter-ethnic redistribution has contended with national economic development for official priority, and political relations between the state and private business were not always cordial during the implementation of the New Economic Policy (NEP) from the 1970s (Jesudason 1989; Lubeck 1992). Beginning in the mid-1980s, liberal economic reforms facilitated a rapprochement between political and business elites, with the government intensifying formal consultations with private-sector representative associations (World Bank 1993: 186–7). Clientelist linkages between government and business have changed, but persist in the new liberalised environment, and closer formal policy consultation under the rubric of Malaysia, Inc. has yet to spawn the indigenous industrial entrepreneurship which might spearhead a nationalist thrust into high-technology industrialisation. At the same time, the Malaysian state seems to have preserved some autonomy from business groups if not broader distributional pressures, and remains somewhat capable of pursuing coherent and disciplined policy initiatives.

In sum, the ambitious scope of the country's technology policy effort, together with the challenges it confronts, make Malaysia a compelling case for the study of national technology development programmes in late industrialisation. Analysis of its experience in industrial technology development and the role of its technology policies and institutions promises to shed light on several critical issues in the political economy of development. First, what are the distinctly national sources of 'competitiveness', or more specifically, industrial dynamism understood in terms of capability-building, productivity growth and structural change? How do institutional mechanisms for industrial technology development emerge as industrialisation progresses towards more advanced stages? Second, what is the role of the state and private-sector actors in creating the conditions for such industrial dynamism? Can national innovation systems be self-consciously engineered to propel growth? Are optimal technology policies limited to functional investments in human capital and physical infrastructure, or are selective and strategic interventions in technology development integral to successful late industrialisation? Are the political and administrative prerequisites for effective intervention related to state autonomy, to well-organised private business sectors, or both? Finally, to what extent have attempts to govern national development been rendered obsolete by the transnational character of industrialisation, in which MNCs integrate and manage production and innovation across national borders?

Models of innovation and technological development

Evolutionary models in late industrialisation

An inquiry into national innovation systems might best begin with a conceptual understanding of the innovation process itself. Departing from Kenneth Arrow's seminal (1962) article on 'learning by doing', a growing literature in the economics of innovation has depicted technological change as a complex evolutionary process at odds with the linear, science-driven model which dominated post-war thinking about science policy (Nelson and Winter 1982; Mowery and Rosenberg 1989: 7–9). In the old model, innovation progresses in linear fashion from exogenous laboratory research breakthroughs through development, prototype and production to commercialisation in the market. By contrast, evolutionary models include three key features. First, they understand the innovation process as interactive or partly endogenous.[5] Industrial innovation reflects neither purely 'market-pull' nor 'science-' or 'research-push' forces, but rather arises as innovators blend information about market and production conditions with the changing stock of scientific and technological knowledge to make product or process improvements. This means that, while formal R&D is frequently critical, much of the activity and cost of innovation occur in less formal engineering, testing, quality control and process control activities aimed at improving performance or solving production problems. In short, technological development encompasses far more than formal R&D, which itself often begins as an outgrowth of these production-based learning activities.

Second, evolutionary models depict innovation as inherently and fundamentally uncertain, making technological change both strategic and cumulative. Decisions to invest in innovation (e.g. R&D projects, or purchasing a technology licence) confront many possible outcomes in terms of their impact on productivity, each with vague or even unknowable probabilities. They comprise strategic rather than narrowly rational optimisation problems.[6] The direction of technological change will therefore be influenced by firms' strategies as well as by the strategic biases created by surrounding institutions and histories, e.g. patent regimes, technical traditions, etc. Moreover, multiple possible outcomes at a single stage of development will, over time, yield diverging paths or 'trajectories' of technical change, along which firms and industries advance in cumulative fashion (Dosi 1982). New products and processes usually emerge out of attempts to improve upon old ones in specific ways. In this way, the possibilities for technological advance at a given stage build upon, and are limited by, the choices made and capabilities developed earlier.

Third, evolutionary models conceive of technology in broad terms as a set of linked capabilities based on different types of knowledge. These include formal knowledge embodied in blueprints, manuals, machinery or products on the one hand, and 'tacit', non-codified, experiential knowledge on the other.[7] Since technology is partly tacit, the full set of capabilities necessary for its optimal use often cannot be obtained through market transactions or imitation. Rather, the purchaser or recipient must make active efforts to assimilate and apply acquired technology in its own specific production routines. Such investments to imitate or master acquired technologies can be as costly as those required to generate entirely new innovations.[8] Moreover, improving technology over time, i.e. achieving dynamic efficiency, involves a deeper level of technological knowledge and requires capabilities distinct from those required for static efficiency (Bell and Pavitt 1993).

Although evolutionary models were developed to explain innovation at the global technological frontier (the key concern of advanced industrial countries), the non-linear, path-dependent and tacit characteristics of technological change make innovation similar in some important ways to technological catch-up, the task facing most developing country firms. Like innovators at the frontier, developing country firms must make deliberate, costly, and risky-cum-strategic investments in learning in order to assimilate acquired technologies (Fransman and King 1984). Choosing the right technologies requires firms to identify weaknesses in production and opportunities for improvement. Mastering them entails integrating newly acquired formal technical knowledge with previously accumulated capabilities and production routines, often through trial and error. The hypothesis that developing countries enjoy an inherent 'latecomer's advantage' in the availability of a global stock of easily transferred technologies tends to overlook the risks and costs of technology acquisition, which stem from the imperfect tradability of the full range of relevant capabilities (Amsden 1992). Similarly, the popular notion of technological 'leapfrogging', by which developing country firms might skip entire vintages of technology and adopt state-of-the art techniques, overlooks the necessity of path-dependent learning, or the cumulative deepening of technological capabilities, to sustain productivity growth (Soete 1985; Hobday 1995). As Amsden (1991) argues, the opportunity to acquire and apply pre-existing technology is the distinguishing characteristic of late industrialisation. However, technological acquisition and catch-up is far from automatic or costless, and firms, industries and countries display tremendous variation in technological progress.

Evolutionary models thus inform the growing body of empirical work on technological change in developing country settings. This literature depicts technology development as an evolutionary process of accumulating specific capabilities to use and improve technology. Dahlman *et al.* (1985) proposed a framework which distinguished technological capabilities related to operating *production* efficiently, those required for *investment* to create new production capacity, and those to engage in *innovation* of products and processes.[9] Reflecting the path-dependent nature of innovation, developing country firms typically (though not always) accumulate these capabilities in sequence, gradually deepening in-house capacities from production management towards more innovative design and adaptive functions.[10] Technologically dynamic firms make conscious efforts to monitor their performance and assess their technological strengths and weaknesses, search for and evaluate external sources of technological support, and use external technology sources to complement and augment internal capabilities. As firms acquire deeper capabilities, they become better able to improve productivity over time and to enhance the value added in production (Bell and Pavitt 1993).[11]

Some authors broaden the firm-level model of capability accumulation to describe the technological development of whole industries and economies. Hobday (1995) placed the accumulation of technological capabilities at the heart of the modal corporate growth strategies which propelled industrial success in the four first-generation Asian NICs. As they deepened technological capabilities, NIC firms moved from simple sub-contract assembly roles to become original-equipment manufacturers (OEM), own-design manufacturers (ODM), and in some cases own-brand manufacturers (OBM) with full international marketing capabilities (Hobday 1995: 186–95). Linsu Kim (1980), drawing on Korea's experience, proposed a model of national technological development in which newly industrialising countries progress through stages analogous to those of individual firms: *implementation* of imported technologies in production; *assimilation* of technology through efforts to diffuse and adapt it; and *improvement* of technology using local scientific and engineering capabilities.[12]

The concept of evolutionary stages should imply neither spontaneous and automatic progress, nor strict linearity. Both the mix of technological capabilities and the sequence in which they are developed can differ significantly across industries and countries, as well as individual firms. As fundamental uncertainty would suggest, important trade-offs are endemic to the technology development process (Ernst and O'Connor 1989: 34–6). For example, a central strategic decision for developing country governments and firms is what balance to strike between pursuing deeper local design capabilities on the one hand, and keeping up with global technological change through licensing or purchasing the latest foreign technologies.[13] The strategic choices made in response to this and similar dilemmas generate divergent and path-dependent technological development trajectories (Simon 1995b; Dosi 1982; Hobday 1995: 195–7). Notwithstanding these variations, however, the core features of evolutionary technology development define a general model with several critical implications for the role of national innovation systems in late industrialisation.

Implications of the evolutionary innovation approach for technology policy

What are the implications of evolutionary theories for late industrialisers? The most fundamental one is that, due to uncertainty and imperfect tradability, market failures are likely to confront individual firms' investments in technological learning. The need for cumulative, production-based learning suggests that public investments in technology cannot themselves determine the course of industrial technology development. Market failures, however, create a strong rationale for nuanced policy or institutional support for firms' efforts to acquire and deepen technological capabilities. Non-government institutions, including sub-contracting networks, business associations, venture capital sources, and specialised commercial providers of technical services, may also help to overcome market failures in technological accumulation. If such private institutions and linkages fail to emerge spontaneously, however, policy action may be warranted to promote them. Beyond static market failures, evolutionary innovation models indicate that dynamic learning economies are pervasive in late industrialisation, thereby providing a powerful rationale for selective infant-industry policies (Pack and Westphal 1986). Governments may justify protecting local industry and subsidising investments in technological learning because of the essential role of production experience in deepening technological capabilities. Of course, the general criticism of industrial policy holds – protection from imports may provide time for infant industries to move up the learning curve, but simultaneously removes a powerful incentive for them to do so. Alternative sources of pressure for performance improvement are required, whether from domestic or export market competition or from the state's administrative 'discipline'. In this context, the political economy pitfalls of selective industrial policies – the difficulty of 'picking winners', the likelihood of rent-seeking – apply in equal or greater force to the subtle task of encouraging technical change in industry. The evolutionary approach further argues that production experience alone is inadequate without deliberate efforts to deepen capabilities; thus, any infant-industry strategy must go beyond sheltering national industries to include specific investments in skills, infrastructure and technological absorption.

While pointing to the need for policy or institutional remedies for market failures, evolutionary models also stress the critical importance of firms' own production-based efforts in technological learning. This implies that national technology policies must seek to bolster industry's internal technological investments and capabilities, as much as or more than to provide sources of external technology support.[14] An emphasis on industry-centred measures reflects evolutionary models' scepticism about 'research-push' factors in innovation, but it does not follow that there is little need for assertive or strategic intervention. Given the diffuse nature of the externalities involved in technology development, not to mention constraints such as traditional management attitudes, developing country firms are often unaware of the technological dimensions of and solutions to their competitive problems. Thus, the demand for technology support is often latent and vaguely defined. National innovation systems must therefore seek to stimulate technology *demand* as much as to *supply* the industrial sector with greater quantities of R&D, skills, information, etc.[15] Measures which prompt industry to identify technological weaknesses and opportunities, thus activating technology might be as important to demand, as subsidies to overcome the market-failure constraints. In this context, standards-setting and certification of skills, product technologies and process/quality management systems can mobilise firms' awareness of and demand for technological development.[16]

For similar reasons, the scope of technology policy must expand from formal R&D to other capability-building investments, such as information gathering, quality improvement, skills development, production engineering and mastery of imported technologies. Especially in earlier stages of industrialisation and in supporting smaller firms, policies should seek to stimulate technological effort in improving production and labour processes on the shop-floor, rather than in devising entirely new products or processes. Firms engaged in more basic levels of capability-building are unlikely to utilise external sources or incentives for formal R&D. However, they might well need information services, training support, and help with selecting, mastering and optimising imported technology. Other important targets for policy should be the diffusion of improved production technologies and best-practice management techniques; provision of technological information and standards-writing; assistance with technology selection; providing specialised technical training; and consulting for technical problem-solving and trouble-shooting.[17]

Understanding innovation as driven by the interaction between 'knowledge push' and 'market demand' factors also puts the function of marketing in a new, and more important light. Firms' incentives to invest in developing technological capabilities are heightened by the need to compete for demanding customers, be they downstream producers or final consumers.[18] Competing in export markets creates tremendous pressure to constantly upgrade quality, and this provides a major incentive for technological development. Beyond incentive pressures, the marketing function may provide new technological resources. Firms' interactions with customers often convey vital information about which routes of technological change are likely to be profitable and what types of improved technologies are already available. Developing country firms are often at a major disadvantage because they operate at a remove from quality-sensitive markets and rely on foreign assemblers or trading companies for exports, and this may filter much of the 'extra' information out of export transactions. It is now understood that exporting and direct linkages with major Western retailers allowed East Asian NIC firms to capture important technological externalities. In short, whereas infant-industry arguments apply to protection of firms' production-based learning, they do not imply extended quasi-autarkic withdrawal from global markets.[19]

This analysis points to an important distinction between promoting local industrial *production* to develop technological capabilities and relying on *indigenous sources of innovation or technology*. A core lesson of comparative analyses of late industrialisation in countries like Brazil, Korea, India and others is that foreign or imported technology usually complements, rather than substitutes for, efforts to build local technological capabilities (Evans 1992; Lall 1987, 1992, 1993b; Dore 1984).[20] An important question, however, is whether the relationship between foreign and indigenous technologies changes as local industry accumulates capabilities. A general hypothesis is that developing countries will gradually substitute locally developed innovations for foreign technologies as industrial capabilities deepen. One result of this transition is a shift in the primary mode of technology acquisition from fully internalised or 'packaged' forms, such as FDI, to more externalised or 'unbundled' modes, such as technology licensing or technology-specific strategic alliances. Evidence of such a shift can be drawn from Korea and Taiwan, who welcomed foreign investors while starting up export-oriented industries (e.g. electronics), but gradually restricted FDI in favour of expanded arm's-length licensing (Mardon 1990; Dahlman and Sananikone 1990).[21] Similar arguments for greater selectivity towards FDI in Malaysia have been frequently advanced (Abdullah 1995).

In contrast to this sequence, however, Malaysia has been at the forefront of a global trend to liberalise foreign investment and technology transfer regulations over the past decade. In part, the trend reflects a growing recognition that strict and non-selective regulation of technology acquisition *per se* cannot redress uneven bargaining power in international technology transactions, and often simply discourages the volume or quality of technology inflow.[22] Second and more importantly, the core technologies necessary for international competitiveness have become increasingly proprietary as rapid innovation, compressed product cycles, and the diffusion of electronics-based processes and components have affected many industries, including segments of 'mature' industries such as textiles and foundries (Dahlman 1989; Ernst and O'Connor 1989). Developing countries are frequently unable to use licensing or other 'unpackaged' modes in their efforts to catch-up technologically, and attracting FDI has virtually become a universally assumed prerequisite for technology acquisition in most high-growth industries. The question remains open as to whether this sea-change in FDI policies bodes well for long-run technological development in host economies. If foreign technology can no longer be 'unbundled' to provide local industry alternative means to acquire technology, MNCs would control the pace of technology development in FDI-reliant economies such as Malaysia. On the other hand, in the new era of global production networks, shaping local industrial structure to complement FDI might be the *sine qua non* of continued technology access and, thus, a way of opening new opportunities for positive-sum bargaining over technology transfer.[23]

Finally, while evolutionary models caution against a linear research-push approach to fostering technology development, they do not imply a rejection of 'supply-side' investments in national technological resources. The most important of these is the creation of technical human capital, though public investments and promotion of R&D may also be important in various specific ways, as both types of investments address serious market failures. Broad functional investments in human capital formation, including the provision of high-quality basic education, strong vocational training programmes, and university training of scientists and engineers, are almost universally accepted as an appropriate government role. As industrialisation moves beyond basic capability levels, however, industry's demand for technical skills becomes more specialised, and investments in human capital formation are likely to involve more discretionary judgements. Again, a variety of institutions can emerge to meet the medium-term demand for specialised technical skills, ranging from firms' in-house training units to private- and public-sector training centres. Fostering the emergence of such institutes, and encouraging co-operative training relationships between industry, universities and other sources of technical training are a critical counterpart to broad investments in education.

The need to accumulate pre-commercial or basic knowledge locally calls for similar types of specialised investments in scientific and technological research, often in university and public-sector research. While public-sector R&D may rarely lead directly to original industrial innovations, it nonetheless can contribute to industrial technology development by building institutional and human reservoirs of relevant scientific and technological knowledge. The links between such intellectual capital resources and industrial development are often hard to measure, but the emergence of 'Silicon Valley'-type agglomerations of technologically dynamic manufacturing industries around major universities illustrates the importance of knowledge externalities. Given that many developing countries have invested scarce resources in public R&D with little effect on industrial growth, the need for selectivity and relevance to industrial needs are central issues.[24] Yet, scientific and other basic research is by nature exploratory and pre-commercial, its contribution to industrial development is indirect and anticipatory, and is realised over long time-frames through flows of human-embodied knowledge. Thus, ensuring the relevance of the public research agenda is often less a matter of enhancing the commercialisation of public R&D than of fostering diverse channels of information-sharing and personnel exchange between industry, academia and government researchers. This might be accomplished by having public and university laboratories perform non-R&D services for industry, or by using industry consultations to guide public-research funding decisions.[25]

The evolution of technology policy in Malaysia

Industrial technology development has been a central national development goal in Malaysia for over fifteen years. Malaysia's technology policy has evolved rapidly, however, in response to changing economic and political circumstances. Three phases in the evolution of technology policy making are evident: from Independence to the early 1980s, from the mid-1980s to the early 1990s, and from 1992–93 to the present. Historically, Malaysia's science and technology infrastructure reflected its economic structure, dominated as it was by rubber exports. The British colonial inheritance included world-class research institutions in rubber cultivation and processing, which the post-Independence government extended in maintaining the country's global pre-eminence in rubber. As older rubber plantations became less productive in the late 1960s, Malaysia embarked upon the commercial cultivation of oil palm for export. New education and research facilities contributed to rapid increase in agricultural yields, processing efficiency and product development. Support for small-holder agriculture, in which the politically dominant Malay population was concentrated, was a high policy priority during the early Independence decades, and the Malaysian Agricultural Research and Development Institute (MARDI) played important research and technical assistance roles. Local universities also conducted research and training useful to agricultural and other resource-based industries.

Within the framework of industrial policy, technological development was accorded a relatively low priority. The manufacturing sector's chief mode of acquiring technology was through joint ventures and direct foreign investment by multinational corporations (MNCs), first in the import-substituting sector, and during the 1970s in export-processing operations within subsidised Free Trade Zones (FTZs). One of the chief criticisms of the early import-substitution industrialisation (ISI) programme was that the government's investment incentives and tariff protection for domestic industry created an unintended bias towards capital-intensive production techniques, resulting in low employment generation (Jomo and Edwards 1993: 24). A shift in strategy to more labour-intensive export-oriented industrialisation was codified in the 1968 Investment Incentives Act, the 1971 Free Trade Zones Act, and related labour law reforms, which sought to attract export-oriented foreign investment. The government's desire to accelerate employment creation was sharpened by the election debacle and subsequent ethnic riots of 1969, and under the ensuing New Economic Policy (NEP), social restructuring through employment generation became a paramount motivation for manufacturing-sector development. The revamped incentives and facilities complemented foreign MNCs' interests in locating their labour-intensive assembly operations in off-shore locations for re-export to home or third countries. While

18

investment projects promoted under the 1968 Investment Incentives Act and the 1975 Industrial Coordination Act (ICA) were required to register technology transfer agreements with a Technology Transfer Unit in the Ministry of Trade and Industry, in practice, the regulations were quite passive, concerned more with policing restrictive contract terms than with screening and measuring the technological content of promoted projects (Anuwar 1992: 89). Studies of the electronics industry development during the 1970s and early 1980s indicate extremely limited technological development within MNCs' Malaysian operations, and noted few spill-overs to the local economy.

The national-level science and technology (S&T) policy machinery established in the 1970s served primarily to nurture R&D capabilities in the public sector and universities. The National Council for Scientific Research and Development (MPKSN) was established in 1975 to provide policy advice and to co-ordinate allocation of public S&T resources. The creation of the Ministry of Science, Technology, and Environment (MOSTE) followed in 1976. In their first decade of operation, these agencies had a low profile within the bureaucracy. MOSTE, as a minor ministry with a limited budget, lacked the political and financial resources to influence the broader range of trade and industry policies affecting the country's technological development. Moreover, the leading research institutes remained under the control of other line-ministries, with the Ministry of Trade and Industry having purview over industrial-sector policies and the then newly formed Standards and Industrial Research Institute (SIRIM). The National Science Council, though inter-ministerial in composition and chaired by the Chief Secretary to the Government, was also unable to impose a co-ordinated agenda on the various ministries, and concerned itself primarily with supporting basic research activities in the university and public sectors. Private-sector interest and input into the Council's decision making were negligible.

Mahathir's appointment as Prime Minister in 1981 heralded decisive shifts in economic policy which resulted in a greater emphasis on technology development. Initially taking the form of a second round of import-substitution through state investments in heavy industries, his new industrial programme attempted to reconcile ethnic redistributional goals of the New Economic Policy (NEP) with a much more concerted effort to deepen the industrial structure and accelerate technological development (Bowie 1988). In early 1986, the government issued the Industrial Master Plan, 1986–1995 (IMP) as an indicative guide to a programme of sectoral interventions. The IMP included a separate volume on technology development issues which identified a weak indigenous technological base as a major threat to future growth. The report recommended aggressive strategic investment and regulation to build up local capabilities, noting that 'Although a beginning has been made in the establishment of some modern industries like electronics, this has not been accompanied by corresponding build up of technological competence. . . . This is partly for the reason that these industries are largely foreign owned, partly or wholly [sic], and depend almost exclusively on external sources for technology' (MIDA/UNIDO 1986: 5).

19

From the mid-1980s, the structure and content of S&T policy-making was transformed in an attempt to mobilise technology development through central co-ordination and strategic targeting to support the ambitious industrialisation programme. In line with the heightened priority accorded S&T policy, a Science Advisor was appointed to the Prime Minister's office in 1984 as a locus of policy co-ordination and a source of new initiatives from above the ministerial bureau-cracies. Under his supervision, a national science and technology policy document was issued in 1985, followed by a separate S&T chapter in the Fifth Malaysia Plan (1986–90) and subsequent plans. Among several significant policy measures launched in the late 1980s was the extension of tax incentives for research and development (R&D), the creation of new technology institutions for specific indus-trial sectors, the establishment of centralised policy planning and funding, and intensified consultations with industry representatives. The Science Advisor was also instrumental in creating the Intensification of Research in Priority Areas (IRPA) programme in 1986, which gathered all public R&D funding under a single allocation and review process. The IRPA programme sought to provide a strategic policy instrument with which to harness public research investments to industrial development goals. Central planners hoped to use the IRPA allocation process to rapidly boost the overall national R&D investment, set strategic tech-nology priorities, and alter the incentives facing public institutions to encourage greater interaction with the industrial sector.

The emergence of a distinct technology policy framework culminated in the 1990 Action Plan for Industrial Technology Development (APITD), a document which built upon the 1986 IMP and became the primary reference for further policy action. The Action Plan diagnosed five basic structural weaknesses in Malaysian technology development, among them inadequate institutional infra-structure and low private-sector investments in technology, and offered forty-two recommendations to create a comprehensive and integrated national innovation system. Following its issuance, the existing S&T policy architecture was revamped. The major industrial technology institutes were transferred to the Ministry of Science, Technology, and Environment in an effort to elevate its co-ordinating role. The National Science Council was reformed to include more private-sector representatives and charged with exercising closer oversight of IRPA-funded pro-jects. New peak-level policy-making bodies were created outside the formal bureaucratic structure to more closely link government officials and private busi-ness leaders. These include a technology committee of the Malaysian Business Council and a special consultative body called the Malaysian Industry–Government Group for High Technology (MIGHT). Finally, the Cabinet formed a new Committee on Science and Technology chaired by the Prime Minister to authorise new technology legislation and programmes.

The reforms of the late 1980s and early 1990s produced enormous growth in public investments in S&T. Budget allocations rose from RM540.5 mill. (approxi-mately US$216 mill.) under the Fifth Malaysia Plan 1986–90 to RM1160 mill. in the Sixth Plan 1991–95, with the share of capital investments in S&T infrastructure (as opposed to current expenditure on R&D) rising from 23 per cent to 48 per cent of the total. These expenditures mainly fuelled a rapid expansion of research capacities in public technology institutes. At the same time, the Science Advisor and the National Science Council sought to implement strategic targeting of technology development, in line with the Action Plan's identification of five critical areas – automated manufacturing technology, advanced materials, biotechnology, electronics and information technology (later joined by other designated fields, including energy, environmental and aerospace technology). The Council established technical working groups with public and private representatives to develop policy recommendations in each target area. The policy makers simultaneously sought to use the IRPA R&D funding allocation process to engineer reforms within the country's system of public research institutions (PRIs). The National Science Council instructed each PRI to screen and justify research proposals in terms of their relevance to development needs, and declared a preference for projects identifying a specific industrial or commercial clientele.

This vigorous drive to build the national innovation system soon encountered a basic paradox. The principal aim of reform was to integrate S&T with industrial policies to create a Japanese-style, 'demand-driven' technology infrastructure focused on applied research and guided by specific sectoral needs, this in contrast to an 'American-style' science-push system emphasising basic R&D and driven by academic curiosity or bureaucratic priorities. Yet to implement systemic reform, technology policy became increasingly centralised and top-down in nature.[26] The incongruity stemmed from the basic political trends shaping economic policy making more broadly, as the Mahathir administration concentrated authority under the chief executive and sought to trim the bureaucracy's direct involvement in the economy, to address poor public-sector management (which it blamed for the failure of the heavy-industries programme), rent-seeking and waste; and to discipline the public sector to serve private foreign and local investors. In the realm of S&T policy, this meant using centralised funding and oversight to guide public universities and research institutions towards industrially relevant work and to target strategic technologies to support industrial development goals.

The 1990 Action Plan stressed the need for new measures to stimulate technology demand within the private sector as well as the reform of public R&D and human resource systems. However, consistent with the political priority on public-sector reform, the overwhelming focus of technology policy initiatives was on the supply side, and new technology programmes or subsidies for the private sector were minimal. Though hampered by ongoing administrative difficulties and a lack of technically qualified bureaucratic personnel, supply-side reforms eventually did make significant progress in changing the ethos and operation of the public R&D infrastructure. Yet, the policy machinery as a whole remained poorly equipped to evaluate, at a detailed sectoral level, the actual capabilities and external assistance needs of the private sector, much less to encourage the pace or direction of private-sector technology development.

At the same time, the sweeping economic liberalisation implemented in the

wake of the mid-1980s recession altered the character of Malaysia's industrial policies in ways that were increasingly at odds with an ambitious, centrally
co-ordinated technology development strategy. Among several other measures,
the government eased restrictions on foreign investment to permit 100 per cent foreign equity ownership in a broader range of export-oriented industries and
extended new duty and tax privileges to attract what soon become a flood of foreign direct investment (FDI) from Japan, Taiwan and South Korea. The embrace
of MNC-led industrialisation paid swift dividends in the form of accelerated
growth, but the foreign-dominated export industries had little need or interest in
accessing the public sector's R&D institutions, no matter how demand-oriented
they might be. While the Industrial Master Plan's sectoral growth targets were
more than fulfilled, qualitative issues involving inter-industry linkages, productivity
growth and indigenous technological development remained problematic, but
were a lower priority, at least temporarily.

At the start of the 1990s, however, the government observed that the foreign-
owned manufacturing sector was more technologically dynamic than had
previously been believed. The electronic components sub-sector, concentrated in
Penang and Kuala Lumpur, responded to intensified global competition in the late
1980s with rapid automation and process technology upgrading. Genuine technological learning within Malaysian-based subsidiaries – notably the accumulation of
process engineering capacities and technical and workforce skills – both encouraged and enabled such progress (Lim and Pang 1991). Some reports suggested that
MNCs' Malaysian subsidiaries had begun to approach the global frontier in several
aspects of manufacturing process technology. Congruent with intra-firm upgrading, some studies identified rapidly growing linkages between electronics MNCs
and local vendors of components and more technologically sophisticated machine
tools (Rasiah 1994: 285–91). Meanwhile, an influx of new Japanese and East
Asian consumer electronics producers brought about a long-hoped-for diversification of the electronics sector, partly mitigating the manufacturing sector's narrow
reliance on semiconductor assembly and export. In addition to diversification, the
IMP had targeted consumer electronics with the rationale that the sub-sector
offered much greater potential than semiconductors for the growth of technologically dynamic linkages with local suppliers of parts and components. The
appreciation of the yen and other East Asian currencies gave Japanese and
Taiwanese investors an added incentive to increase local content swiftly. In sum,
conjuncture of forces in the late 1980s made MNCs relatively more disposed to
technological development and linkage formation within the Malaysian economy.

In response to this perceived opportunity, as well as to the initial disappointments
of supply-side technology reform, a new emphasis began to characterise industrial
and technology policies after 1993, which has since become the dominant theme
in policy reforms. The new approach seems to take its cue from the growing literature on the relationship between industrial structure and international
competitiveness, in particular a focus on sub-contracting networks (Wong 1991)
and broader 'industrial clusters' (Porter 1990). In contrast to the attempt to guide

technological change through strategic supply-side investments, new policy initiatives focus on creating appropriate intra- and inter-firm networks to capture technological externalities emanating from the demands of MNCs as customers for components and inputs. Stable networks and close interaction between technology users (in Malaysia, MNC or other foreign buyers) and producers (local sub-contractors) are central to the development of competitive industrial clusters, as recent work on sub-contracting networks in Japan and the East Asian NICs highlights. More broadly, Malaysia's new industrial policy strategy echoes similar successful attempts by Singapore to capitalise on MNCs' globalisation strategies by inducing foreign companies to upgrade their locally based subsidiaries to undertake higher-technology and more locally integrated production.

In an explicit effort to emulate Japanese *keiretsu* structures, the government has launched formal vendor development programmes to address the problem of weak industry linkages by encouraging large foreign and local assembly firms to assist designated local suppliers. First, officials have made vendor development a point of negotiation with established and new foreign investors, while also enlisting state-linked corporations and selected domestic private manufacturers in the effort. At the same time, the government has given its programmes to assist small and medium-scale industries (SMIs) more prominence. During the NEP era, SMI assistance programmes proliferated as a means to assist new *Bumiputera* (mainly ethnic Malay) entrepreneurs to establish small start-up businesses, though these programmes all too often devolved into patronage and mismanagement. Recent reforms have augmented SMI-assistance programmes' social ethnic promotional mission with an emphasis on upgrading existing enterprises' basic technological capabilities and on encouraging improved quality-control and management practices. SIRIM, for example, has aggressively promoted the diffusion of the international ISO 9000 quality-control certification system. The new vendor development initiatives have encountered initial difficulties, but it is still too early to evaluate their actual impact.

In the meantime, foreign companies have significantly increased local procurement and sourcing, and new geographic and sectoral clustering appears to be taking place, as in Penang, where many disk-drive producers and their suppliers have relocated from Singapore. Most of this activity has involved linkages between MNC assemblers and other foreign supplier firms who have followed them to their Malaysian production sites. A small but growing number of local firms have also begun to serve as sub-contract assemblers to the major electronics MNCs. Several MNCs have also established formal R&D centres in their Malaysian complexes for their own reasons (e.g. cosmetic production modifications or other design functions), but also in line with government exhortations. Finally, both the federal and some state governments have sought to provide new high-technology infrastructure for local and foreign companies in the form of several technology parks.

Reform of the public technology infrastructure has continued in the 1990s, particularly in the areas of the legal status and management practices of research institutions (RIs). Again, reforms have reflected broader political trends shaping the

23

state's role in the economy. In the past decade, an increasing number of governance institutions and functions have been 'debureaucratised' – i.e. removed from the formal civil service structure through a process of corporatisation and privatisation, while policy initiative and co-ordination have been lodged in policy networks directly linking political and business elites (Leigh 1992). The government established the Malaysian Technology Development Corporation (MTDC) as a joint public–private technology venture capital company in 1992 to facilitate the commercialisation of public research findings. The peak-level public–private MIGHT forum, mentioned above, is another example of the state elite's effort to mobilise private-sector technology investments through direct, extra-bureaucratic policy networks. MIGHT organises sector- and technology-specific interest groups to study technology trends and identify business opportunities.

Meanwhile, the system of public research institutions has been moved towards a contract research system, and individual institutes have been prepared for corporatisation as independent government-held companies. Universities have similarly been pressured to develop industry linkages through designated contract research and consultancy units. In the industrial policy realm, the government has also sought to achieve technology development goals through quasi-private instruments. The leading privatised utilities and government-related companies have been directed to participate in vendor-development programmes and to establish their own technical training institutes. A successful industry-run skills training centre in Penang has been adopted as a model for replication in other states, and new technical training institutes have been set up on a bilateral basis with German, Japanese and French government agencies.

The focus on industrial clustering as a path to technological upgrading was fully articulated in 1996 in the *Seventh Malaysia Plan, 1996–2000* and the *Second Industrial Master Plan, 1996–2005* as the key principle guiding industrial policy. The strategy envisions a more selective industrial policy driven by private-sector patterns of specialisation rather than state plans. At the same time, state officials appear committed to continued intervention in the economy to achieve several objectives, including promoting *Bumiputera* enterprise and other favoured corporate interests, and revamping the educational and training system to meet the requirements of a rapidly evolving industrial structure. In sum, though industrial and technology policies have gradually shifted from expansive aspirations to strategically direct structural change to a model more focused on private-sector dynamics and institutions, the Malaysian state retains its activist stance in fostering technological upgrading. It continues to emphasise strategic intervention, if increasingly in a supportive and facilitating role.

In 1996, Malaysian Prime Minister Mahathir announced his latest and most ambitious industrial technology policy initiative thus far – the establishment of a Multimedia Super Corridor (MSC). The MSC has been defined to be a special development zone located in a swathe of land fifteen by fifty kilometres, south of the federal capital of Kuala Lumpur, and will include the new federal administrative centre at Putrajaya, the new Kuala Lumpur International Airport (KLIA) at

Sepang and a new 'hi-tech' city called Cyberjaya. The MSC initiative seeks to attract investments in multimedia software development, primarily from the leading transnational companies that currently dominate the industry. To win MSC status, IT companies must indicate plans to undertake new development activities. In turn, the Malaysian Government has promised to generously invest, to the tune of more than a billion ringgit annually, in the physical infrastructure as well as other support desired by IT companies. Other special incentives for MSC investors include generous tax breaks and exemptions from various laws such as those restricting the number of foreign personnel a company can hire to no more than five.

In addition, the government plans to spur new development activities by offering lucrative procurement contracts for seven 'flagship' IT applications, including telemedicine, smart schools, electronic government operations, smart cards, international manufacturing co-ordination, electronic marketing and R&D.

Since launching the project, the Malaysian government has gone out of its way to impress potential investors with its commitment to creating the physical and legal conditions they desire. For example, to the surprise of many, Malaysia reversed its previous opposition to the US-sponsored Information Technology Agreement (ITA) under the auspices of the World Trade Organisation, presumably to reassure the mainly US-based companies it hopes to attract to the MSC. Similarly, in 1997, the government promulgated new laws elaborating IT-related intellectual property rights, and has begun to enforce existing intellectual property rights laws with a new-found zeal.

Although the envisaged government investments in the MSC should have a crowding-in rather than crowding-out effect, many concerns have been raised with regard to the scheme. An open question is whether any government can adequately plan for future developments in this extremely fluid and unpredictable industry. Without tremendously detailed information at its disposal, along with the ability to quickly shift planning and policies in light of rapidly changing market trends, the relevant authorities will find it impossible to target public investments to effectively play a supportive role, let alone a leading one. For the same reasons, it will be extremely difficult to monitor the activities of firms receiving MSC incentives and contracts to ensure the growth of genuine innovation activity and skills transfer. Without such careful analysis, however, there is a real danger that heavy public investments in IT will result in little more than a public subsidy of multinational and favoured local businesses, while distracting or deterring the growth of non-MSC firms that might discover unanticipated high-growth niches. While the government has made progress in reforming public technology institutions and policies, it is precisely the sparseness of such capacity for continuous, detailed, sector-specific assessment of market and industry trends which is the greatest constraint on effective policy implementation. Ultimately, of course, the MSC initiative will have to be judged on its own merits, more specifically by whether the net benefits outweigh its costs – taking externalities into consideration as well – when evaluated from a long-term dynamic perspective.

Overview

Malaysia's transition to technology-based industrialisation remains in flux, and diverging interpretations of its nature and prospects are inevitable. The evolution of Malaysia's technology policies demonstrates an ability to adjust policy making (at least its principles and goals, if not fully its implementation and practice) in response to new economic circumstances and conceptual understandings of the sources of technological development and industrial competitiveness. What is less clear is whether the efforts to elaborate and reform technology policies and institutions, and thus build a national innovation system, have had significant impact on the course of industrialisation thus far, and whether they are likely to do so in the future. Those sceptical of statist political economy claims are likely to view the technology policy framework as having been largely inconsequential, and, like most nations, Malaysia offers much evidence of policy failure or ineffectiveness. On the other hand, measuring the effects of state interventions against their own ambitious strategic goals may obscure the importance of infrastructural, indirect or even unintended policy impacts. Adaptive and supportive policies (e.g. physical infrastructure, investment incentives) are likely, at the very least, to have facilitated the technical upgrading observed within industry thus far. Whether conceived as leading or following market-driven changes, the need for supporting policies and institutions presumably will grow as technology levels rise in the economy.

The chapters in this book by Jörg Meyer-Stamer and Wong Poh Kam offer theoretical and comparative perspectives respectively, from which to consider the role of technology policy in Malaysia. The theoretical chapter by Meyer-Stamer identifies the administrative problematique underlying the question of national technology systems and policies. It asks whether and how the state can guide technology development through goal-oriented economic 'governance', particularly in an era of growing industrial complexity when private technical competencies often surpass those of state agencies. Instead of hierarchical state leadership through instruments like public R&D expenditures and subsidies, Meyer-Stamer points to the growing importance of 'heterarchical' policy networks, in which the state oversees a process of negotiated co-operation between business actors to advance technological change in agreed-upon directions. He suggests, however, that policy networks will only be effective when a 'development-oriented consensus between state and important social actors [is achieved]', a circumstance likely when incremental technological change calls only for an infrastructural government role, or when economic crisis weakens conservative societal forces resisting adaptation to radical technological changes.

Wong Poh Kam reviews the experience of the first-generation East Asian NICs through a description of the strategies they employed to overcome late-comer disadvantages in technological development. Wong stresses the variety of firm-level strategies for accumulating technological capabilities, ranging from a 'reverse product life-cycle' strategy, which ultimately leads to own-brand exports, to 'process capability specialisation', in which an NIC firm serves as a sub-contract assembler or specialised components producer for global high-tech industries. The chapter makes the important point that, while strategic state intervention made vital contributions to the industrial technology development process in each of the NICs, the specific state roles and policies varied according to the modal strategies of leading industrial actors.

Kit Machado examines relations between Japan and Southeast Asia in terms of the technological dominance of Japanese industrial firms in the ASEAN countries, including Malaysia. He highlights the changing nature and increasing complexity of East Asian industrial investments from Japan, 'first-generation' East Asian newly industrialising economies as well as 'second-generation' Southeast Asian newly industrialising countries (Jomo *et al.* 1997). Machado emphasises the emergence of regional production networks, especially those organised by Japanese firms, suggesting that there is little evidence of greater pluralisation (as suggested by a superficial survey of foreign investment trends) and less hierarchy in the regional division of labour. He attributes this to the essentially proxy or dependent nature of much of the investment from the first-generation NIEs and the second-generation NICs which tends to consolidate if not extend the hierarchical Japan-centred regional division of labour rather than to pluralise it. These trends, in turn, affect the impact of the transnationalisation or regionalisation of manufacturing on national efforts to promote industrial technology development.

The chapters by Greg Felker, Sanjaya Lall and Rajah Rasiah analyse Malaysia's national technology policies and institutions at the systemic level, evaluating its structure and contribution to economic development. Echoing Meyer-Stamer, Felker considers the political factors shaping consensus and co-operation between the state, domestic business and MNCs in various parts of Malaysia's innovation system. He argues that the Malaysian state's concerted efforts have yielded progress in creating a technology infrastructure, but that conflicting interests, including a legacy of mistrust between government and domestic business as well as MNC resistance to regulatory governance, have frustrated closer co-operation between the relevant actors. The result has been a significant gap between ambitious policy goals and actual outcomes.

Lall offers a rich analysis of the economic factors underpinning Malaysia's international competitiveness, and argues that 'the progress of the Malaysian industrial sector and exports has "outrun" the development of domestic industrial capabilities'. He suggests that continued success will probably require more effective policy interventions to build the domestic base of skills, R&D and supplier industries; this is true of, and indeed integral to, an MNC-led strategy. Moreover, Lall contends that discretionary industrial policies have made a more positive contribution to Malaysia's current success than is usually portrayed, and that recent reforms bode well for increased effectiveness.

Rasiah provides a broad overview of the state and non-state industrial institutions which make up Malaysia's innovation system, including financial and human resource institutions. He points to institutional weaknesses in skills formation, technology transfer and development, much of which stem from limited government capacities to monitor outcomes in order to effectively link incentives and policies to a domestic firm's technology development performance.

Trained as an engineer and with considerable experience in Japan's technology policy-making agencies as well as the World Bank, Kondo offers a critical perspective of technology policy in Malaysia. He acknowledges considerable official commitment, reflected in various policy initiatives and measures to enhance value-added and raise technological levels. However, he argues that the policies are overly oriented towards the public sector and not sufficiently sensitive to private firms' concerns; hence, for example, some policies are not attractive to private companies concerned with retaining trade secrets, including technological confidentiality. He also hints that some policies and the accompanying rhetoric, implementation and enforcement are reflective of poor understanding by key policy makers of the major technological problems and challenges faced by private firms and the national economy – which are not the same. He favourably reviews several policy and institutional initiatives, including the Vendor Development Programme, the role of the Standards and Industrial Research Institute of Malaysia (SIRIM) and the Penang Skills Development Centre. Among other things, he recommends greater official attention to production technology problems generally, rather than the current hi-tech fetish, and also urges greater involvement of and greater orientation to private industry in technology policy formulation.

K. Thiruchelvam also examines the innovation system at the micro-level, comparing research management practices in the public system with those of private industry. He finds that slow adoption of best-practice research management within public-sector institutes has undermined the goals of broader system-wide reform. Improving the public research system's performance will require committed and deliberate action to increase management discipline, to adopt a holistic view of the research mission from pre-technical studies to utilisation measures, and to forge industry partnerships in R&D. He argues that further policy-level reforms, such as strengthening the IRPA process, making public research institutions more autonomous, and implementing genuinely competitive bidding for public research funds, can alter incentives to encourage the necessary change in the culture and practice of public research management.

Chris Edwards considers the crucial human resource dimension of Malaysia's technological transition, analysing the implications of labour market trends and government policies for the creation of a more highly skilled labour force. Though weaknesses in the country's stock of skilled labour pose a vital threat to continued industrial upgrading, Edwards finds that recent policy changes from a 'supply-side' to a 'demand-driven' approach to human resource planning and technical training bode well for the future. On the other hand, Malaysia's rapidly growing reliance on unskilled foreign immigrant labour has serious negative effects on income distribution and upgrading technology in the economy, delaying some sectors' investments in modernising equipment and diverting new investment from high-skill to low-skill activities. He suggests that temporarily slowing the rate of economic growth might allow skills formation to catch up with industrial expansion and place the economy on a higher long-run trajectory.

This collection of studies reveals the complexity and dynamism of the industrial technology development policy process associated with Malaysia's rapid industrialisation. Weighing both structural features and emerging trends, the studies differ in their assessments of the strength and effectiveness of Malaysia's national innovation system. In considering the state's deliberate attempts to construct an integrated institutional system, they reveal problems of design and implementation, though few of the authors maintain that appropriate technology policies are irrelevant and unimportant to the success of technological upgrading. Indeed, most assert the need for a more focused, supportive and effective public role.

In problematising the institutional and strategic dimensions of industrial technology development, all the studies seek to move beyond facile understandings of technology development as a simple function of market-driven processes. It should be noted that, whereas technological change is central to long-run economic growth, the relationship between the two is complex and indirect. The recent debate about the contribution of productivity growth to East Asian economic success underscores this point (Krugman 1994). If current trends indeed represent a successful transition to self-sustaining, technologically progressive industrialisation, it will not be the exclusive product of state leadership, or the 'natural' maturation of local firms, or even benign MNC-led globalisation. Rather, it would be an expression of the creation of new types of industrial governance appropriate to an era of globally integrated production – a particular intersection of strategies and governance roles played by the state, domestic businesses, MNC subsidiaries and MNC parent companies. For example, Singapore's successful MNC-led model involved a high degree of strategic intervention through a range of non-trade policy instruments, combined with specific changes in MNCs' strategies and network structures.

Further, the positive examples of technological development within Malaysian industry remain much smaller in scale than earlier patterns in the first-generation NICs, the only developing countries to succeed in ascending into the ranks of industrialised economies during the post-war era. From this standpoint, the effort to build a national innovation system remains a critical task, notwithstanding the constraints on state policies posed by globalisation. Malaysia has been exceptionally fortunate in enjoying the beneficial influences, such as technology diffusion, which the international economy has afforded during the last decade. The policy and institutional framework has been notably successful in the permissive sense of attracting and not discouraging foreign investment and technology. The current economic turmoil in Asia, however, reminds us that firms, industries and national economies which do not move ahead may indeed fall behind. The still urgent mission of Malaysia's national innovation system is to convert the economy's global fortunes into a strengthened local impetus for industrial progress and technological change.

29

Notes

1 The share of manufacturing in GDP has risen to 30 per cent in 1995, while the primary sector has declined to 24 per cent.

2 Figures are from the World Bank's *World Development Report 1997*, Table 11, p. 234 and Table 15, p. 242, except for the 1995 manufactures share in exports, which is taken from MITI (1995/96: 38). Export growth figure is for export volume rather than value.

3 Indeed, the East Asian success stories (particularly Japan and South Korea, less so Taiwan) featured a progressive expansion of the role of local industry over foreign capital in spearheading industrialisation, even in high-technology industries. The two city-states of Hong Kong and Singapore provide counter-examples, whose relevance to the Malaysian case should be an important point of debate. In the case of Hong Kong, local industrialists (including leading figures from Shanghai's textiles industry fleeing the revolutionary PRC) were well-established prior to the take-off of foreign direct investment. Local industry subsequently played a major role in industrialisation despite the absence of FDI controls. In Singapore, by contrast, development policies have explicitly sought to maximise foreign investment in manufacturing, and MNCs remain dominant in most industrial branches. While Singapore might arguably provide a positive argument for the viability of Malaysia's FDI-led development strategy, one of the stated goals of Malaysian industrial and technology policies is to mitigate the risks of FDI-reliance by strengthening capabilities within local industry.

4 A highly controversial issue is the linkage between authoritarianism and effective industrial policy making. Haggard (1990) and others have argued that authoritarian regimes are neither necessary nor sufficient for effective intervention, but that there is an 'elective affinity' between certain authoritarian corporatist political structures and developmentally rational economic policies (Wade 1990: 24–9). Many authoritarian regimes are actually penetrated by powerful political constituencies, and are therefore incapable of 'disciplining' rent-seeking coalitions or shielding economic policy from distributional demands. However, pluralist democratic regimes are, by design, subject to the pull of competing social claims, and so find it difficult both to extract and transfer surplus to capitalist elites and to hold subsidy recipients accountable to performance goals. Malaysian politics is formally democratic, though the political hegemony of the ruling coalition suggests the system is at most 'quasi-democratic' (Case 1993). Leong (1991) argues that Malaysia represents a case of a democratic regime successfully insulating economic policy making from distributional pressures. Bowie (1994) identifies an inter-penetration of business and political elites associated with a rising authoritarian trend.

5 Detailed innovation studies show that information generated in the use of technology, whether in production (process technologies) or final marketing and consumption (of products), is frequently decisive in stimulating technological change. Histories of specific technologies reveal a similar macro-level pattern, wherein technological innovation, or discovery of a certain technology's functional properties, has often preceded scientific understanding of its causes and stimulated basic research to uncover them. In this way, technological changes in industry have often driven scientific research agendas (Rosenberg 1982). Freeman (1987) and others have shown, nonetheless, that science has become progressively more critical to innovation in a number of industries over the twentieth century, a trend evidenced in the growth of industrial R&D facilities and the linkages between industry and universities. At the same time, changing production and market conditions, such as consumer preferences or factor costs, alone do not provide information fully sufficient to determine a unique optimal path of technological change (Mowery and Rosenberg 1989). Explanations of technical and institutional change as optimising responses to changing market conditions, or 'market-pull' models, are found in Schmookler (1966) and Binswanger and Ruttan (1978), *passim*.

6 Lundvall (1992: 47) goes even farther, to claim that 'Not only does innovation imply uncertainty and thus bounded and differentiated rationality . . . it points towards a break with an instrumental and strategic rationality'.

7 Technology, in its codified form, has public-goods characteristics that make it significantly non-proprietary, subject to diffusion, and dependent upon intellectual property rights or other institutional means to control its appropriation. However, the tacit elements of technology, acquired through accumulated experience and embedded in the organisational routines of individuals, firms and institutions, make technology imperfectly tradable.

8 Assimilating technology usually entails adjusting or improving products or processes to better fit the conditions particular to a firm or country, and so involves learning-by-using, often in pilot production, prototyping or reverse engineering products. However, it may also involve formal R&D designed to develop a deeper understanding of a technology's properties. Indeed, perhaps the greater part of industrial R&D is undertaken by firms in order to gain a deeper understanding of externally acquired technologies, rather than generating new breakthroughs (Cohen and Levinthal 1990).

9 Production capabilities include: production management, production engineering, control systems for raw materials, production scheduling, quality-control and trouble-shooting, repair and maintenance, and basic marketing. Investment capabilities include: search and selection of technology; project management; project engineering; procurement and contracts; skills training and acquisition. Innovation capabilities range from minor adaptations to major transformations of production tools, processes or final products.

10 Lall (1992) proposes a slightly more complex matrix framework of capabilities, in which three macro-categories of technological capability (investment, production and linkage-management) may be developed to varying depth (basic: routine and experience-based, intermediate: adaptive and duplicative, or search-based, and advanced: innovative, risky and research-based). Many other typologies of technological capabilities have emerged with particular variations on the ones proposed by Dahlman, Westphal *et al.*

11 It is important to note that seeking the fastest route to self-reliance in deeper capabilities is not necessarily an optimal strategy, particularly if rapidly evolving product cycles threaten existing technologies with obsolescence. For example, deepening from production to innovative capabilities in electro-mechanical machine tools might provide a less sound basis for long-run growth than moving horizontally to manufacture computer numerically controlled (CNC) machines under licence, even at the cost of delaying the development of in-house design capabilities. *Ceteris paribus*, however, capability-deepening better equips firms to adapt to changing technology and market conditions.

12 While firm-level investments are the primary mechanism of progress, he argues, government policies are essential in stimulating and supporting the transition to more advanced stages. Public investments in technology creation anticipate the development of industrial capabilities, such that the balance of initiative, for example as measured in R&D expenditures, gradually shifts from the public to the private sector as development proceeds.

13 Another important strategic trade-off faced by rapidly developing economies lies between promoting large-scale industry to capture scale economies in production and innovation, versus encouraging small- and medium-scale enterprises to preserve domestic competition and achieve greater flexibility (Mody 1989).

14 To elaborate, technology policy must encourage and make use of any institutions that can access and integrate information on production-driven capabilities and needs with an awareness of available technological solutions. Quite often, this means enhancing firms' incentives and capabilities to invest in technological accumulation by providing direct subsidies. Another important possibility is to promote the technology-related activities of business and non-governmental organisations, such as sub-contracting

networks, formal industry associations, etc. whenever they prove effective in bringing together detailed production-based technology demands with 'supply-side' information on various technologies and areas of expertise.

15 Reform efforts in Malaysia and elsewhere have thus far concentrated on making the public institutions which create these assets more responsive to the needs of industry. As mentioned above, however, firms are quite often unclear or even complacent about their need to invest in technological improvement. Even when motivated, firms are frequently financially constrained, and so do not manifest effective demand for external technology support programmes and services.

16 Programmes like the ISO 9000 that certify quality control systems can be important tools for prompting industry to undertake greater self-assessment of production capabilities, identify needs and seek resources for improvement. By linking firms' immediate desire for credibility in the market to quality-improvement protocols, this programme both activates demand for technical improvement and points firms towards resources to achieve it.

17 A general difficulty in subsidising non-R&D investments is measuring their impact and the actual progress towards improved capabilities. Whereas formal R&D projects are somewhat easier to identify and monitor, many other production-related improvements are fairly routine, making promotional programmes subject to waste or abuse. Nonetheless, difficulties in measurement do not diminish their importance, and efforts to improve the administration of policies focusing on training, quality improvement, etc. are likely to yield a high pay-off.

18 Porter (1990) emphasises the role of quality-sensitive home markets and intense domestic market competition in fostering globally competitive industries.

19 A contradiction is apparent, since infant-industry promotion usually involves restricting foreign investment, and allowing local firms to undertake technological learning while producing for a protected domestic market. While infant industries are in the initial learning stages, therefore, they must have alternative means of keeping up with international market and technology trends. Meanwhile, opportunities for exports should be pursued at the earliest possible point in an industry's development. It is this mix of selective import-protection for targeted industries and export-promotion which characterises accounts of successful infant-industry policies in Korea and Taiwan (Pack and Westphal 1986; Wade 1993).

20 As Lall (1993b: 102) observes, the relationship between technology import and indigenous capabilities is more complex than the substitute/complement dichotomy allows. In the absence of indigenous efforts to learn, a passive reliance on imported technology can become habitual and lead to production inefficiencies and recurrent direct costs. Such concerns are often voiced in Malaysia, where payments on technology licences are a significant component of structural deficits in the invisibles account of the balance of payments.

21 One important application of this analysis is the question of whether and when to promote a local capital goods industry. The machinery sector plays a central role in industrial technology development by embodying process technology innovation in equipment and diffusing it through sales to a range of industries (Fransman 1986). Imported capital goods are a vital source of improved manufacturing technology, but the absence of a local machine-tool industry frustrates the type of user–producer interaction which drives process innovation in various engineering industries (Lundvall 1988). Promotion of local capital goods production might thus be desirable, but also risks damaging the competitiveness of downstream exporters if the technological learning process in machinery is prolonged and quality lags behind internationally available equipment. The importance of supporting industries more generally has been heightened by the rise of flexible production systems and increased out-sourcing in many industries. The technical competence of a country's base of ancillary industries and components suppliers is

vital to attracting high-quality manufacturing FDI and capturing the potential technological spill-overs it offers. In turn, participation in multinational corporations' supplier networks helps local industry acquire new technological capabilities. As noted above, however, technologically self-reinforcing linkages may not form spontaneously, and independent efforts to boost supplier firms' technical capabilities and to induce linkage relationships are likely to be critical (Meyanathan 1994).

22 As Lall (1993a: 92) observes,

> many developing country governments have intervened extensively in the import of technology in order to lower its costs and improve the capabilities of local enterprises. The results have, however, generally been counterproductive. Rigid and cumbersome regulations on the content and terms of technology transfer have tended to reduce the quantity and quality of inflows, to the detriment of the buying country. The growth of local TCs [technological capabilities] has been hampered rather than helped by over-enthusiastic regulations. The desire to legislate and regulate have often ignored market realities, which reflected the costs and risks of innovation and the costs implicit in transferring technology to enterprises that lacked many of the capabilities needed to absorb it.

23 Singapore's FDI-based industrial strategy might well be the critical test-case for this argument. The Singaporean government has enjoyed considerable success in fostering a transition to high-technology industry by making targeted investments in its workforce skills and supplier base to provide MNCs with vital complementary assets to engineering-intensive production and design activities. Malaysia has implemented similar policies vis-à-vis foreign investors. The number of MNCs establishing formal design units has increased significantly, but the ultimate impact on local technological capabilities is an important question for study.

24 Creating excellent graduate research and education programmes is expensive, moreover public basic R&D often fails to contribute significantly to industrial development. The late emergence of basic research capacities and graduate degree programmes in science and engineering in Japan, South Korea and other countries illustrates that technology development may progress for long periods without them. Yet, ready access to advanced scientific and technological knowledge does become increasingly important as local industry approaches deeper levels of technological capability, and creating high-quality research institutions requires significant lead time.

25 At the same time, over-specific efforts to guide research towards industry applications may interfere with the primary scientific and educational missions of universities and other research institutions. The high costs of basic research capabilities derive in part from the essential role of creative freedom in maintaining standards of excellence.

26 Interestingly, this contradiction echoed that seen in the similar efforts of the Latin American newly industrialising countries (NICs) in the 1970s to construct technology support systems. See Bastos and Cooper (1995: 16–18) and other essays in the same volume.

References

Abdullah Mohamed Tahir (1995) 'Industrial policy and industrial development: issues and policy directions'. In *Managing Industrial Transition in Malaysia*, ed. V. Kanapathy. Kuala Lumpur: ISIS.

Amsden, A.H. (1989) *Asia's Next Giant: South Korea and Late Industrialization*. New York: Oxford University Press.

Amsden, A.H. (1991) 'The Diffusion of Development: The Late Industrializing Model and Greater East Asia'. *American Economic Review*, May 81(2): 282–86.

Amsden, A.H. (1992). 'A Theory of Government Intervention in Late Industrialization.' In *State and the Market in Development: Synergy or Rivalry?*, ed. L. Putterman and D. Rueschemeyer. Boulder, CO: Lynne Rienner.

Anuwar Ali (1992) *Malaysia's Industrialization: The Quest for Technology*. Singapore: Oxford University Press.

Ariff, M. (1991) *The Malaysian Economy: Pacific Connections*. Singapore: Oxford University Press.

Arrow, K. (1962) 'The Implications of Learning by Doing'. *Review of Economic Studies* 29, June (3): 155–73.

Bastos, M.I. and C. Cooper (1995) 'A Political Approach to Science and Technology Policy in Latin America'. In *Politics of Technology in Latin America*, ed. M.I. Bastos and C. Cooper. London: Routledge: 1–27.

Bell, M. and K. Pavitt (1993) 'Technological Accumulation and Industrial Growth: Contrasts Between Developed and Developing Countries'. *Industrial and Corporate Change* 2(2): 157–210.

Binswanger, H. and V.W. Ruttan (eds) (1978) *Induced Innovation*. Baltimore: Johns Hopkins University Press.

Bowie, A. (1994) 'Dynamics of Business–Government Relations in Industrializing Malaysia'. In *Business–Government Relations in Industrializing East Asia*, ed. A. MacIntyre. Sydney: Allen and Unwin.

Case, W. (1993) 'Semi-Democracy in Malaysia: Withstanding the Pressures for Regime Change'. *Pacific Affairs* 66 (2): 183–205.

Cohen, W. and D. Levinthal (1990) 'Innovation and Learning: The Two Faces of R&D'. *Economic Journal*, No. 99, September.

Crouch, H. (1984) *Domestic Political Structures and Regional Economic Cooperation*. Singapore: Institute of Southeast Asian Studies (ISEAS).

Dahlman, C.J. (1989) *Impact of Technological Change on Industrial Prospects for the LDCs*. Washington, DC: World Bank.

Dahlman, C.J. (1994) 'Technology Strategy in East Asian Developing Economies'. *Journal of Asian Economies* 5(4): 541–72.

Dahlman, C.J. and O. Sananikone (1990) 'Technology Strategy in the Economy of Taiwan: Exploiting Foreign Linkages and Investing in Local Capabilities', unpublished ms. Washington, DC: The World Bank, December.

Dahlman, C.J., B. Ross-Larson and L.E. Westphal (1985) *Managing Technological Development: Lessons from the Newly Industrializing Countries*. Washington, DC: The World Bank.

Doner, R.F. (1992) 'The Limits of State Strength: Towards an Institutionalist View of Economic Development'. *World Politics* 44, April: 398–431.

Dore, R. (1984) 'Technological Self-Reliance: Sturdy Ideal or Self-Serving Rhetoric'. In *Technological Capability in the Third World*, ed. M. Fransman and K. King. New York: St. Martin's Press: 65–80.

Dosi, G. (1982) 'Technological Paradigms and Technological Trajectories: A Suggested Interpretation of the Determinants and Directions of Technical Change'. *Research Policy* 11(3): 147–162.

Dosi, G., C. Freeman, R. Nelson, G. Silverberg and L. Soete (eds) (1988) *Technical Change and Economic Theory*. London: Pinter.

Enos, J. and W.H. Park (1987) *The Adaptation and Diffusion of Imported Technologies in the Case of Korea*. London: Croom Helm.

34

Ernst, D. and D. O'Connor (1989) *Technology and Global Competition*. Paris: OECD Development Centre.

Evans, P. (1992) 'Greenhouses and Strategic Nationalism: A Comparative Analysis of Brazil's Informatics Policy'. In *High Technology and Third World Industrialization: Brazilian Computer Policy in Comparative Perspective*, ed. P. Evans, C. Frischtak and P. Tigre, International and Area Studies – Research Series Number 85, University of California, Berkeley: 1–37.

Fransman, M. (ed.) (1986) *Machinery and Economic Development*. London: Macmillan.

Fransman, M. and K. King (eds) (1984) *Technological Capability in the Third World*. New York: St. Martin's Press.

Freeman, C. (1987) *Technology Policy and Economic Performance*. London: Pinter.

Haggard, S. (1990) *Pathways from the Periphery*. Princeton, NJ: Princeton University Press.

Hamilton, G. (ed.) (1991) *Business Networks and Economic Development in East and Southeast Asia*. Hong Kong: Centre of Asian Studies, University of Hong Kong.

Heng Pek Koon (1992) 'The Chinese Business Elite of Malaysia'. In *Southeast Asian Capitalists*, ed. Ruth McVey. Ithaca, NY: Cornell Southeast Asia Program.

Hobday, M. (1995) *Innovation in East Asia: The Challenge to Japan*. Aldershot, UK: Edward Elgar.

Ismail Muhamed Salleh (1990) *Small and Medium Scale Industrialisation: Problems and Perspectives*. Kuala Lumpur: ISIS Malaysia.

Jesudason, J.V. (1989) *Ethnicity and the Economy: The State, Chinese Business, and Multinationals in Malaysia*. Singapore: Oxford University Press.

Johnson, C. (1987) 'Political Institutions and Economic Performance: The Government–Business Relationship in Japan, South Korea, and Taiwan'. In *The Political Economy of the New Asian Industrialism*, ed. F. Deyo. Ithaca, NY: Cornell University Press.

Jomo K.S. and C. Edwards (1993) 'Malaysian Industrialisation in Historical Perspective' in *Industrialising Malaysia: Policy, Performance, Prospects*, ed. Jomo K.S. London: Routledge.

Kim, L. (1980) 'Stages of Development of Industrial Technology in a Development Country: A Model'. *Research Policy* 9: 254–77.

Krugman, P. (1994) 'The myth of Asia's miracle'. *Foreign Affairs* 73(6): 62–78.

Lall, S. (1987) *Learning to Industrialize: The Acquisition of Technological Capability by India*. Basingstoke: Macmillan.

Lall, S. (1992) 'Technological Capabilities and Industrialization'. *World Development* 20(2): 165–86, February.

Lall, S. (1993a) 'Policies for Building Technological Capabilities: Lessons from Asian Experience'. *Asian Development Review* 11(2): 72–103.

Lall, S. (1993b) 'Promoting Technology Development: The Role of Technology Transfer and Indigenous Effort'. *Third World Quarterly* 14(1): 95–108.

Lall, S. (1995) 'Malaysia: Industrial Success and the Role of Government'. *Journal of International Development* 7(5): 759–73.

Lall, S. (1996) *Learning from the Asian Tigers*. London: Macmillan.

Lall, S., R. Boumphrey and B.J. Hitchcock (1994) 'Malaysia's Export Performance and its Sustainability', unpublished. Manila: Asian Development Bank.

Lee Kiong Hock (1996) 'Labour Market Issues: Skills Training and Labour Productivity'. Paper presented at the 'National Convention on Seventh Malaysia Plan', Kuala Lumpur, 5–7 August.

Leigh, M. (1992) 'Politics, Bureaucracy, and Business in Malaysia: Realigning the Eternal

Triangle'. In *The Dynamics of Economic Policy Reform in South-East Asia and the South-West Pacific*, ed. A.J. MacIntyre and K. Jayasuriya. Singapore: Oxford University Press: 115–23.

Leong C.H. 1991 'Late industrialization along with democratic politics in Malaysia'. Ph.D. dissertation, Harvard University.

Lim, L.Y.C. and E.F. Pang (1991) *Foreign Direct Investment and Industrialization in Malaysia, Singapore, Taiwan, and Thailand*. Paris: OECD Development Centre.

Lim Mah Hui (1981) *Ownership and Control of the One Hundred Largest Corporations in Malaysia*. Singapore: Oxford University Press.

Lubeck, P. (1992) 'Malaysian Industrialization, Ethnic Divisions, and the NIC Model: The Limits to Replication'. In *States and Development in the Asian Pacific Rim*, ed. R.P. Appelbaum and J.W. Henderson. Newbury Park, CA: Sage.

Lundvall, B. (1988) 'Innovation as an Interactive Process – From User–Producer Interaction to the National System of Innovation'. In *Technical Change and Economic Theory*, ed. G. Dosi and R. Nelson. London: Pinter.

Lundvall, B. (ed.) (1992) *National Systems of Innovation: Towards a Theory of Innovation and Interactive Learning*. London: Pinter.

MacIntyre, A.J. (ed.) (1994) *Business and Government in Industrializing Asia*. Ithaca, NY: Cornell University Press.

McVey, R. (1992) *The Materialization of the Southeast Asian Entrepreneur*. Ithaca, NY: Cornell Southeast Asian Program.

Mardon, R. (1990) 'The State and Effective Control of Foreign Capital: The Case of South Korea'. *World Politics* 43: 111–38.

Meyanathan, S. (ed.) (1994) *Industrial Structures and the Development of Small and Medium Enterprise Linkages: Examples from Asia*. Washington, DC: The World Bank.

MIDA/UNIDO (1986) *Medium and Long Term Industrial Master Plan: Malaysia, 1986–1995*, Vol. III, Part 6, R&D and Technology Policies. Kuala Lumpur: Malaysian Industrial Development Authority.

Mody, A. (1989) *Institutions and Dynamic Comparative Advantage: Electronics Industry in South Korea and Taiwan*. Industry Series Paper No. 9. Washington, DC: The World Bank.

Mowery, D.C. and N. Rosenberg (1989) *Technology and the Pursuit of Economic Growth*. Cambridge: Cambridge University Press.

Nelson, R.R. (ed.) (1993) *National Innovation Systems: A Comparative Analysis*. New York: Oxford University Press.

Nelson, R.R. and N. Rosenberg (1993) 'Technical Innovation and National Systems'. In *National Innovation Systems: A Comparative Analysis*, ed. R.R. Nelson. New York: Oxford University Press: 3–21.

Nelson, R.R. and S.G. Winter (1982) *An Evolutionary Theory of Economic Change*. Cambridge, MA: Belknap Press.

Ng, C.Y., R. Hirono and R.Y. Siy (eds) (1986) *Effective Mechanisms for the Enhancement of Technology and Skills in ASEAN: An Overview*. Singapore: Institute of Southeast Asian Studies (ISEAS).

OECD (1992) *Technology and the Economy: The Key Relationships*. Paris: OECD.

Ohmae, K. (1995) *The End of the Nation State: The Rise of Regional Economies*. New York: The Free Press.

Onis, Z. (1991) 'The Logic of the Developmental State'. *Comparative Politics* 24(1): 109–26.

Osman-Rani, H., K.W. Toh and Anuwar Ali (1986) *Effective Mechanisms for the Enhancement of Technology and Skills in Malaysia*. Singapore: Institute of Southeast Asian Studies (ISEAS).

Pack, H. and L. Westphal (1986) 'Industrial Strategy and Technological Change: Theory vs. Reality'. *Journal of Development Economics* 22: 87–128.

Porter, M. (1990) *The Competitive Advantage of Nations*. New York: The Free Press.

Rasiah, Rajah (1994) 'Flexible Production Systems and Local Machine-tool Subcontracting: Electronics Components Transnationals in Malaysia'. *Cambridge Journal of Economics* 18: 279–98.

Rasiah, Rajah (1995) *Foreign Capital and Industrialization in Malaysia*. New York: St. Martin's Press.

Rosenberg, Nathan (1982) *Inside the Black Box*. Cambridge: Cambridge University Press.

Samuels, R. (1994) *'Rich Nation, Strong Army': National Security and the Technological Transformation of Japan*. Ithaca, NY: Cornell University Press.

Schmookler, J. (1996) *Invention and Economic Growth*. Cambridge, MA: Harvard University Press.

Simon, D.F. (ed.) (1995a) *Corporate Strategies in the Pacific Rim: Global versus Regional Trends*. New York: Routledge.

Simon, D.F. (ed.) (1995b) *The Emerging Technological Trajectory of the Pacific Rim*. Armonk, NY: M.E. Sharpe.

Soete, L. (1985) 'International Diffusion of Technology, Industrial Development and Technological Leapfrogging'. *World Development* 13(3): 409–22.

Storper, M. and A.J. Scott (eds) (1992) *Pathways to Industrialization and Regional Development*. London: Routledge.

Wade, R. (1990) *Governing the Market*. Princeton, NJ: Princeton University Press.

Wade, R. (1993) 'Managing Trade: Taiwan and South Korea as Challenges to Economics and Political Science', *Comparative Politics* 25(2): 147–67.

Wong Poh Kam (1991) *Technological Development through Subcontracting Linkages*. Tokyo: Asian Productivity Organization.

World Bank (1993) *The East Asian Miracle: Economic Growth and Public Policy*. New York: Oxford University Press.

World Bank (1997) *Enterprise Training, Technology, and Productivity*. Washington DC: The World Bank.

World Bank (1997) *World Development Report*.

Yoshihara, K. (1988) *The Rise of Ersatz Capitalism in Southeast Asia*. Singapore: Oxford University Press.

2

TECHNOLOGY, COMPETITIVENESS AND GOVERNANCE

Jörg Meyer-Stamer

In this chapter, I will argue that the discussion on technology policy and competitiveness should not only focus on the question of which policy measures are necessary, but also and especially on the question of how to formulate and implement policy. Drawing on the experience of advanced industrialised countries and using arguments from sociological, political science and neo-Schumpeterian discussions, I will argue that hierarchical patterns of governance are increasingly unlikely to succeed in guiding technological development as societies, economies and industries become increasingly differentiated. In order to govern technological change, it becomes increasingly important to rely on policy networks which involve the state and key societal actors. The governance of technological change, the argument goes on, is particularly important in situations of radical change in order to create stable expectations and to avoid socially undesirable directions of change. In a situation of incremental technological change, governance will mean creating a fostering environment, rather than trying to steer the direction of change. A rough typology is introduced to show that the prospects for success vary depending on given conditions. These arguments are valid not only for advanced industrialised countries, but also for rapidly growing newly-industrialising countries (NICs). Therefore, experiences in advanced countries with new patterns of governance, especially policy networks, are relevant for the NICs as well.

Who governs technological change?

A central theme of the sociological study of innovation is the potential for intentional governance of technological development. This question is usually discussed at two levels. Is it possible to govern technology at all? And if so, what instruments should technology policy make use of, and at what levels?

The sociological discussion on innovation reveals conflicting views on whether it is possible to govern the process of technological change. The theoretical–conceptual discussion has moved back and forth from a position of governance pessimism to a position of governance optimism. The original governance pessimism resulted from the 'science-push' view that technological change is driven by pioneering scientific innovations, which can only be harnessed economically after they have matured and potential commercial applications have become apparent. In this view, inventions cannot be planned, and basic scientific research cannot simply be governed. The 'science-push' thesis was later superseded by the 'demand-pull' thesis, according to which social, though often also business-related, needs trigger specifically targeted research efforts (Rammert 1992).

The more recent discussion has proceeded on the assumption that neither of these two theses – each of which assumes a clear-cut sequence from basic research to the finished product – adequately describes the process which links science, research, development and the market. There is, rather, a complex interaction among actors located at various points along the innovation chain. The discussion on the governance of technology centres on the question to what extent it is possible, in the context of this interaction, to influence this process in an active and purposive way. This discussion is strongly influenced by the more extensive controversy on the possibilities of political governance of social relations, including the economy (Martinsen 1992). This larger debate focuses on the evaluation of 'socio-technological' governance patterns of the type pursued in the 1960s and 1970s. There is not much doubt that the policies to shape social contexts pursued in this period were not particularly successful; this is one of the findings of the comprehensive research on the problems involved in implementing political programmes. The reasons can be found in two factors: the growing complexity of modern industrial societies and reversal of the competence differential between state and social actors.

Growing social complexity creates a situation in which the consequences of individual policies, as well as the interactions among them, are difficult to grasp. Political initiatives get stuck in the 'policy entanglement trap'; 'instead of the premises of utter sovereignty and internal hierarchy germane to early modern thinking on the state, government policy is today tied into an increasingly ramified and dense nexus of transactions and inherently social dependencies and negotiation-based relationships' (Scharpf 1991). Governance pessimists thus conclude that governance can at best be the result of self-organisation within social subsystems, whereas attempts at governance at the level of society as a whole are doomed to failure (Luhmann 1989). To underpin their argument, the governance pessimists point both to negative experiences in the field of technology governance and to examples in which the state consciously refrains from any attempts at governance. One example is the Europe-wide EUREKA R&D promotion programme, which is geared to stimulating cooperation between firms from different countries, but which pointedly avoids efforts of the governments involved to determine the content and direction of the cooperative research agenda (Willke 1988).

The reversal of the competence differential finds expression in the fact that the state is increasingly forced to rely on the technical competence of social actors to regulate given social activities. It is inconceivable, for instance, that the state itself could set technical standards in all areas of industry. The expense of developing the necessary technical competence within the bureaucracy would exceed the state's resources and would in any case be inefficient since the required know-how is already available in society. (Moreover, since the requisite technical knowledge is widely dispersed in society, no single group holds an information monopoly that would allow it to manipulate standards-writing to its private advantage.) This example supports the supposition that the state's potential role in social governance is much more limited than often assumed.

However, governance optimists can point to instances of successful goal-oriented technology policies, for example, in complex sectors such as telecommunications (Schneider and Werle 1991). They hold the view that the solution to the compe-tence problem, as well as in part the solution to the complexity problem, is to transpose to society the process of deciding on rules with defined policy fields. Germany's DIN Commissions, which define technical standards, are an example of this. In this case, the state assumes a function as organiser and supervisor, rather than sole executor, of the decision-making process. Though not monopolising rule-making functions, that state plays several vital roles:

- it ensures that certain procedural rules are observed;
- it ensures, as the case may be, that the important actors are involved (in the DIN Commissions, for instance, a consumer council and an environmental coordination unit have been set up) (Voelzkow 1993: 116);
- it can threaten to issue regulations on its own, which, for the actors involved, would most probably be suboptimal so that there is an incentive for a con-structive discussion process (Scharpf 1991: 629).

Features of policy networks

This kind of governance pattern, in which the state superintends a process of negotiated rule-setting among societal actors, may be described with the familiar concept of 'policy networks'. Policy networks gain in significance as decisions which clearly go beyond merely technical decision-making, and which were for-merly the province of the state alone, are negotiated in networks which involve a number of actors. Policy networks – with state participation, though not necessar-ily under state leadership – are emerging in various areas in which political initiatives are negotiated. According to researchers who have examined such expe-riences in a systematic way, the concept of policy networks constitutes

> not only . . . a new analytical view of an unchanged reality. The concept of policy networks signals instead, for the understanding prevalent today, an actual change in the structures of political decision-making. Instead of being created by a central authority, be it executive or legislative, policy today often emerges in a process in which a great number of both public and private organisations are involved
>
> (Mayntz 1993: 40)

The danger of policy formulation in policy networks is that individual actors represent only parochial interests and that, moreover, the costs of negotiated policies will be shifted, or 'externalised', to broader communities or to society as a whole. Two points argue against this objection, however:

- Experience has shown that, in traditional political structures, it is very difficult to implement specific policies against articulated interests, even when they represent the broader public interest. This is particularly true of specific sectoral policies: industrial policy or technology policy will, for the most part, aim to stimulate or direct certain types of behaviour on the part of social actors (especially firms). If these actors flatly refuse to cooperate, and the state's sanction potential is limited (which can be typical of technology policy, for what sense would it make to penalise a firm for not availing itself of R&D subsidies?), any such policy is doomed to failure. It is therefore essential to include the relevant interests in the process of policy formulation. It may be noted that formally recognising that key social groups have a *de facto* influence over successful implementation does not jeopardise larger public interests.
- Moreover, the border between the representation of particular interests and objectively necessary information-gathering is a fluid one. In classical pluralist systems, relations between the state and social actors were hierarchical and radial, and direct interaction between societal actors was limited. It was the state's responsibility to gather the information required to formulate policy, to synthesise policy proposals, and to discuss them with individual interest groups. In network-like negotiation systems, societal actors interact directly with one another.

The success or failure of negotiation systems depends on both the form and character of the interaction among actors. Each actor must have a considerable degree of internal coherence, e.g. to be able to tackle internal conflicts (without calling upon external arbitrators such as, in corporatist systems, the government or the judiciary). The success of the interaction rests on various factors:

- the basis of trust between the actors concerned;
- the willingness to disclose relevant information;
- commitment to a fair exchange, reciprocity, or a just distribution of costs and benefits;
- orientation towards solving collective problems or achieving collective gains, i.e. an approach which aims at more than a minimum consensus. This point is crucial if governance decisions, in the specific sense of the term, are in fact made within a policy network.

The rules of interaction fundamentally require

that each participant restrict his scopes of action by considering the possible divergent interests of other participants and the effects that one party's actions may have on them – not only in order to anticipate and avoid possible sanctions, but also because each actor is conceded his own legitimate claim to such respect of his interests

(Mayntz 1993: 49)

Policy networks frequently emerge on their own. Sometimes, however, they are stimulated from outside; one example is the regional industrial policy or structural policy in Germany (Jürgens and Krumbein 1991). The organisation, moderation and prevention of any externalisation of costs frequently require – even though this may at first seem paradoxical – state intervention. Yet, the paradox is resolved when considering the fact that networks are often sectorally or spatially limited, i.e. there is still some 'superordinate' authority; in the case of regional structural policy, for instance, this is the government of the state concerned. The state can ensure that external moderators are installed who are – perceptibly for the local actors – neutral and in a position to advance confidence-building among the local actors. It can also – like the German government in the case of DIN – influence the composition of networks, i.e. ensure, in particular, that those actors are included who might otherwise have to bear the externalised costs. Even when it does prove possible to extend a network substantially, it is quite likely that this will not only create, but at the same time restrict, scopes of action. 'The creation of policy networks narrows the range of ideas likely to receive a hearing as it establishes authoritative voices and modes of discourse' (Weir 1992: 210).

It is thus important to recognise that hierarchical governance forms and pluralistic structures for interest representation will never be entirely replaced by 'heterarchical' policy networks. Hierarchy and heterarchy simultaneously complement and obstruct each other: heterarchical organisational patterns make governance possible in many areas; but they are in need of hierarchical governance. Hierarchical authority, expressed in the state's role, will often take the form of procedural governance to ensure a sufficient degree of transparency in the composition of networks and the way decisions are reached within them; this prevents them from developing in the direction of secret societies. Furthermore, policy networks need a source of innovation equivalent to the entry of new firms to the market when industries are in a phase of radical change. This function is assumed in the political sphere, for instance, by social movements. It must be possible to expand a policy network to include such actors as they emerge in order to introduce new views and identify new problems. For instance, the German energy policy network clearly suffers from the fact that its composition has not significantly changed since the 1960s; thus, its capacity to learn and to adapt is severely limited.

Governance of technological change

The foregoing was meant to be a general outline of possible modes of governance and introduces the analytical distinction between hierarchic and heterarchic

governance. When discussing the possibilities for governing technological development and the possible aims of technology policy, it is helpful to introduce a second
distinction, namely that between different types of technological change. Many
authors implicitly refer to radical technological change when they talk about possible governance patterns for technological development (when, for instance, they
analyse the development of nuclear technology or telecommunication systems).
However, the growing interest in industrial standardisation processes stems from the
realisation that incremental change is also a critical aspect of technological development. The same is true of the discussion on legal instruments of governance, in
particular the fuzzy legal construct of 'state of the art' which the German legislators
have included in technology-related legislation to ensure that regulations remain
valid in a dynamic context – i.e. gearing legal language to the process of incremental
innovation (Rossnagel 1993). Indeed, the discussion of technology governance gains
clarity when a distinction is made between technology policy with reference to
incremental technological change and technology policy for radical change or
changes of 'technology system'. Incremental innovations

> occur more or less continuously in any industry or service activity
> although at differing rates in different industries, depending upon a com-
> bination of demand pressures and technological opportunities. . . .
> Radical innovations are discontinuous events and in recent times are usu-
> ally the result of a deliberate research and development activity in
> enterprises and/or in university and government laboratories. . . .
> Changes of 'technology system' . . . are far reaching changes in technol-
> ogy affecting one or several sectors of the economy, as well as giving rise
> to entirely new sectors.
>
> (Freeman 1987: 61ff)

Technology governance in the face of radical change

One feature of radical technological change is that it challenges established development corridors – trajectories in Dosi's (1982) sense – and paves the way for the
definition of new paths. The search for a new corridor can, in principle, proceed in
two different ways. The first variant, recommended by neoliberals, is the
ungoverned search process: the process of adjustment is left to market forces, i.e.
each firm searches for a new organisational pattern of its own, a new strategy, a new
line of core products. Some firms may join forces to seek and define a new technological corridor through joint efforts. There are two types of incentive for a firm
seeking to define a new corridor through its own ideas and efforts. The first incentive is that a first-mover in the new corridor will enjoy major innovation rents. The
second incentive results from the opportunity to define or modify a standard within
a given framework; this establishes a competitive advantage *vis-à-vis* competitors.

Since, however, the participants in this type of search for a new corridor move
in many different directions, the social costs of the search are high. Since it is, *a*

priori, unlikely that the majority of firms will, by chance, explore in the direction that proves right in the end, it is highly probable that a large share of the search costs will have to be written off as losses. Apologists of the market are not impressed by this objection: 'In a western-style market economy system it is a simple fact of life that companies are faced with the need to find future markets on a trial-and-error basis. This is something that cannot be replaced by "collective reasoning", no matter what kind of corporate group is involved' (Glos 1992: 109).

The other variant is a search process governed by all important actors. This was a core element of the Japanese success model, and MITI's famous formulation of 'visions' was nothing other than a search process shared by MITI bureaucrats and representatives of the most important firms involved in defining development corridors. This should not be confused with one-sided governance decisions at the central level which the state then seeks to implement by providing targeted research funds or by establishing norms and standards (Hilpert 1993). As soon as a joint search direction, i.e. a corridor, has been found, a critical mass of investments in R&D and production capacities is certain to follow without delay, and this in turn gives rise to cumulative learning processes. To this extent, a policy focus on state technology subsidies, (which have, for the most part, been low in Japan), is misguided, since an incorrect direction of technology search encouraged by subsidies can generate even higher search losses than free-market competition. The advantage of defining technological corridors for firms lies in the possibility of avoiding undesirable developments and thus wasting resources, not in any substitution of subsidies for internal funds.

The Japanese governance model was comparatively successful: in the early 1970s, the Japanese identified microelectronics as a future key technology when Germany was still struggling to attract steel works and oil refineries (Koshiro 1986). Another example is the development of the gallium arsenide chip: although the US invested far more resources in its development, Japan was several years ahead of the US in the mid-1980s, for MITI-coordinated mechanisms were used to define a joint development corridor (Van de Ven 1993: 351f). The argument that it was in Japan that important industries such as consumer electronics emerged without any industrial policy (or even against the tide of industrial policy) can also be turned around: the inability of the consumer electronics industry to organise a joint search process for radical innovations raises the costs for individual firms, retards development, and explains the absence of really new products that, in the early 1990s, would have been able to help industry out of its crisis.

Technology governance in the face of incremental technological change

In a phase of incremental technological change, it is more difficult to justify active state governance of technological development, since as soon as a corridor has been defined, market-mediated, decentralised company-level governance is likely to prove to be the superior model. Here, there is a need for active governance,

above all when negative externalities (e.g. environmental damage or safety problems) emerge. This is a classical field for state governance of technological issues,
although it is also a field in which shifts in relative technical competence have
increasingly removed decision-making from the public sector and turned it over to
panels established by industry. In this case, the state supervises compliance with
given procedural rules, i.e. engages in contextual governance.

While active governance is less relevant, a more passive form of governance may
still be important. This is always the case when discretionary technology-related
policies are implemented that are in themselves not necessarily controversial. The
establishment of a technology institute at a given location for a given industry, for
instance, is discretionary governance in the sense that it is also a decision against
establishing an open number of technology institutes for all other conceivable
industries. This example points to the main function of technology policy in the
context of incremental technological change: the shaping of the business environment, i.e. the development of technology institutes, advisory services, specialised
training institutions, and so on, which are designed to support firms in their
technology-related search and learning processes. Here, the main task of technology policy is to shape the mesospace, rather than the detailed governance of
individual lines of technical development.

Technology governance between hierarchy and heterarchy

In the field of technical development, the state is frequently the only actor in a position to internalise externalities, take general interests into account, and introduce
longer-term considerations. In so doing, however, it faces difficulties in that its
technical competence is limited and the decisions it takes entail a high risk of failure. This 'competence bottleneck' makes hierarchical governance difficult and
forces the state to involve the social actors that possess the necessary know-how. But
these actors will often have established interests of their own. In a situation of radical change, this can mean that their actual interest is to prevent, delay, or shape in
a specifically distorted manner, the definition of a new corridor that would depre-
ciate part of their knowledge. Yet, in a situation of incremental change, firms will
also offer resistance to any state-level regulatory interventions opposed to their
immediate interests.

It can thus be assumed that a 'heterarchical' model of technology governance is
not a panacea, and that any such model will entail sizeable problems and constraints. Success is most likely in situations with two specific 'constellations' of
conditions:

- Technological change is incremental, development corridors and joint views
  are well-defined. An example is a regional technology policy involving various local actors who reach agreement on measures designed to strengthen an
  industrial location, or the policy pattern in industrial districts. Another example is the greater part of standardisation activities which do not require the

45

definition of a new corridor, which involve a relatively low number of relevant actors (e.g. where the concern is not to define a standard that affects a number of different industries) (Kubicek 1993), and in which the standards concerned do not affect the core of the competitive advantage of the firms involved.

• An acute crisis in which the conservative interests geared to perpetuating a corridor are weak while no obvious corridor has as yet been clearly defined, so that the benefits of defining a corridor in time are evident to those concerned.

Governance is complicated in two other constellations:

• An early phase of radical change in which the reward for anticipatory policy would be substantial (i.e. no deep structural crisis is driving change), while the interests geared to the preservation of structures are still strong. Any such constellation is further complicated when the process of radical technological change is linked with the market entry of new firms – they will find it difficult to join existing networks between established firms and other actors, while these networks, at the same time, become dysfunctional due to the exclusion of important actors.

• A constellation of political confrontation in which – owing to past conflicts and the mistrust stemming from them or because of far-reaching ideological differences – it proves impossible to bring about a shared vision of the actors involved.

The notion of a uniform technology policy controlled centrally by the state is obsolete. More recent thinking on the governance of technological development accepts the diversity of actors, levels of intervention, levels of negotiation, and policy instruments. The classical instruments of technology policy – financial support of institutions engaged in research and technology transfer and in-house R&D – are supplemented by instruments designed to promote soft factors: diffusion of information on new organisational concepts, network-building (Callon *et al.* 1992). Technology-related measures are formulated at different levels within policy networks in which the state often plays a subordinate role.

Technology policy cannot be grasped adequately if it is seen as an activity restricted to given sectors, one that only concerns scientists in research institutes and universities, R&D people in firms, and their promoters in government administration. Technology policy is interwoven with the polity in two ways. On the one hand, governance patterns of technology policy are not independent of the evolution of governance patterns as such; in a society marked by a low level of strategic capacity and confrontations between social actors, it will hardly be possible to establish a network of actors to formulate a long-term strategic technology policy. Moreover, macropolicy (general economic framework, legal system, etc.) and other sectoral policies have important implications for technology policy. On the other hand, the results of technology governance can entail far-reaching structure-modifying impacts on the polity; as soon as this becomes evident, actors normally not included in the nexus of actors concerned with technology policy will seek to gain influence on the formulation of technology policy.

Implications for developing countries

At least three reasons suggest that it is time to abandon the notion of an industry-oriented technology policy *sui generis* in advanced developing countries:

- The relationship between state and firms is no longer clearly hierarchical, even in advanced developing countries. Even in countries like South Korea, where the state played a key role in managing the industrialisation process, the state's superiority in competence has been erased after a long period of capacity-building at the firm level within industry (Messner 1992). In formerly inward-looking countries, the state has lost both legitimacy and competence in the crisis of import-substitution industrialisation. In both types of countries, there are firms in various sectors that better understand the techno-organisational logic pursued by their industry than do state actors. They know their competitors, and they observe the worldwide trends in their field. They are thus no longer in need of state guidance or supervision in defining their business strategy and in reaching decisions on acquiring technology abroad for example.
- The notion that technology policy in developing countries, as opposed to industrialised countries, is generally characterised by a catch-up situation is incorrect to the extent that this situation is often encountered in industrialised countries as well. A real or supposed lag *vis-à-vis* other industrialised countries is typically the reason why such countries formulate a specific technology policy. At the same time, after several decades of industrialisation, the predominant question in many developing countries is no longer how to protect infant industries. The dominant industries have built up a certain measure of technological competence, though they may, after a long phase of protection from competitive pressure, be forced to undertake major efforts to increase their competitiveness at short notice.
- In both industrialised and advanced developing countries, the concern is to implement different types of technology policy instruments for different types of industries (see Pavitt 1984 for a typology of technological patterns in industry). The difference between technology policy measures for a supplier-dominated industry and for a science-based industry in one and the same country is probably greater than that between technology policy measures for one of these industries in an industrialised country and in an advanced developing country or NIC.

One qualification is nevertheless necessary, in that the basic orientation of technology policy will differ between three groups of developing countries:

- In the first-generation East Asian NICs, the dominant patterns of technology policy correspond to those encountered in industrialised countries. Since the end of the 1970s, these countries have made major efforts to develop a comprehensive, differentiated and specialised network of technology institutions that work closely with firms. The firms themselves have clearly stepped up their R&D spending. The technology policy of these countries aims both to shape the process of radical technological change and to influence the further development of the techno-institutional landscape.

- The industrial structure of poor countries is, for the most part, rudimentary. The dominant firms are small businesses, frequently in the informal sector, which exhibit technological learning processes that may be flanked by supporting institutions – e.g. technology extension. But the goal here is not so much to increase competitiveness in the sense of closing the gap with the best practice, but to impart elementary qualifications in dealing economically with means of production and inputs, in reducing quality fluctuations, or in the fields of book-keeping and marketing. There also exist isolated larger firms, often state-owned and built up with development cooperation funds, that are frequently concerned with no more than securing operations or achieving a somewhat satisfactory utilisation of their capacities. These firms need – aside from an incentive structure that stimulates efficiency gains–qualified workers, technicians, engineers and managers above all; but in poor countries, the number of such persons is usually low, and it thus proves difficult to create personnel stability – qualified employees are enticed away by other firms, the state or development cooperation projects.

- The large group of semi-industrialised middle-income countries make up the middle ground between these two groups. Three patterns of technology policy can be observed here. The first is a continuation of traditional policy with a clear focus on prestige projects. There is not much connection between such projects – for example, in aeronautics and space or nuclear technology – and civilian industrial development; they, for the most part, provide no contribution to the development of industrial competitiveness, and instead absorb resources that could be harnessed for this purpose. The second pattern entails getting along largely without any technology policy; it can be observed in several countries that are consistently pursuing the orthodox structural adjustment recommendation and have reduced state activities to a minimum. Technology policy is here limited to selective interventions in areas in which the pressure stemming from acute problems is matched by political clout on the part of the industries concerned. The third pattern is a technology policy that supports, in existing industries, modernisation processes and efforts aimed at improving competitiveness, and that, to a limited extent, try to encourage and support the creation of new industries.

The following considerations will focus on the implementation of the last-named pattern, which is a crucial precondition for stimulating growth in middle-income countries. Without any doubt, this pattern poses considerable demands on the competence of the state. A constellation comparable to that in the East Asian NICs in the past (where a competent bureaucracy, endowed with a large measure of autonomy, was able to address the problem of institution building selectively and strategically; see Cumings 1984) is the exception. The rule is (following several waves of layoffs in which many competent employees have drifted off to the private sector, which offers higher salaries) a moderately competent, often demotivated, administration that sees itself confronted by remnants of redistribution-oriented social groups. The transformation of this constellation into one marked by a situation of state autonomy and close interaction between state and social actors geared to problem-solving is a complicated and protracted process (Evans 1992: 179). In terms of technology policy, these are the two constellations where governance is complicated or even impossible.

The central condition required to catalyse technological change in such an environment is the ability to achieve a development-oriented consensus between the state and important social actors, i.e. an understanding that, first, development *per se* (and not maximisation of development aid or the private welfare of the upper class) is the primary goal, and, second, that it is necessary to aim at a specific technology corridor in order to develop a national specialisation profile. A basic consensus of this sort is the *sine qua non* for the social project of pro-actively developing competitive advantages.

The first task of central government is to secure stable, predictable framework conditions that encourage private initiative. Beyond this, state and social actors have to share the burdens for continuous investments in education and training, science and technology (which can often be built on the basis of an existing institutional infrastructure, even if it requires substantial rehabilitation); this is the precondition for developing the national base of dynamic comparative advantages, above all in existing industries which display competitive potential, but need a supporting environment. Here, the relevance of policy networks is obvious as only the early involvement of the addressees of competitiveness-enhancing policies will lead to an adequate problem definition, and a corresponding formulation of policy measures. Moreover, involving organisations like business associations in the execution of technology extension, quality awareness building, or management upgrading programmes may significantly enhance their impact.

At the same time, the state may consider using selective, performance-related protection and targeted support to stimulate the development of given branches of industry. This, however, will prove successful only if the state gains a sufficient degree of autonomy *vis-à-vis* particular interests to enforce performance criteria. In this way, it is possible both to develop an efficient national industry – a *sine qua non* for international competitiveness – and to attract foreign investors who contribute value-added and technology to the national economy.

This process often cannot proceed on a nationwide basis, particularly in large developing countries. In fact, the study of regional policy has abandoned the notion that it is desirable to aim for a uniform geographical dispersal of industrial activities (Hansen *et al.* 1990). The growing discussion on industrial districts and other approaches to define innovation and competitiveness point to the great significance of spatial concentration for the accumulation of external effects and learning processes. This opens up new political possibilities for the development of competitiveness: even if it should prove impossible to reach a tenable consensus at the central government level, this may prove possible within a local or regional framework. This, of course, presupposes a sufficient degree of competence and governance autonomy at the local or regional level. Local or regional technology policy initiatives will develop, particularly when it is clear that central government measures will not displace local efforts.

These considerations result in an institutional profile of technology policy that differs fundamentally from the traditional policy framework. In the past, technology policy was, in many countries, an activity that was organised by an isolated unit – for instance, a technology ministry that operated in competition with the planning ministry and the industry ministry. Moreover, a constellation of the type existing in Brazil, with a number of largely independent sectoral agencies, was not uncommon. The resulting governance pattern was hierarchical, centralised and uncoordinated. A governance pattern of this type can, in no case, meet the new demands for policies to support the development of industrial competitiveness. For this reason, there is a need for a new institutional pattern and a new governance pattern. If the important political actors share the view that technological competence is the key to successful economic development, technology policy will cease to be a niche matter, and begin to move into the centre of economic and industrial policy. Institutionally, this can imply questioning the existence of technology ministries or similar institutions. At the same time, technology will take on a new character at the central government level: the concern will no longer be to formulate detailed initiatives for individual (sub)sectors, but to modify the framework conditions that block dynamic technological development. The detailed initiatives should – in a way analogous to experience in the industrialised countries – be formulated by the state and social actors at the regional or local level. The matter at hand is not to establish state or provincial technology ministries or municipal technology offices, but to create the conditions that make it possible for government-level actors and representatives of industrially relevant groups to jointly formulate initiatives aimed at improving conditions for technology development in specific localities.

A network-like governance pattern of this type presupposes a high degree of readiness to learn and to change among all those concerned. Only those societies politically capable of creating governance patterns that stimulate joint learning and exchange between different groups within society will be able to close the gap with the developed industrial nations. It is thus 'soft' factors, such as organisation and learning capacity, which become central determinants of the success of industry-oriented development models, at the level of both individual companies and national economies.

References

Callon, M., P. Laredo and V. Rabeharisoa (1992) 'The Management and Evaluation of Technological Programs and the Dynamics of Techno-economic Networks: The Case of the AFME', *Research Policy* 21(3): 215–37.

Cumings, B. (1984) 'The Origins and Development of the Northeast Asian Political Economy: Sectors, Product Cycles, and Political Consequences', *International Organization* 38(1): 1–40.

Dosi, G. (1982) 'Technological Paradigms and Technological Trajectories: A Suggested Interpretation of the Determinants and Directions of Technical Change', *Research Policy* 11(3): 147–62.

Evans, P.B. (1992) 'The State as Problem and Solution: Predation, Embedded Autonomy, and Structural Change', in S. Haggard and R. R. Kaufman (eds), *The Politics of Economic Adjustment*, Princeton, NJ: Princeton University Press, pp. 139–81.

Freeman, C. (1987) *Technology Policy and Economic Performance: Lessons from Japan*, London: Pinter.

Glos, M. (1992) 'Do We Need a Strategic Industrial Policy à la MITI?', *Intereconomics* 27(3): 107–11.

Hansen, N., B. Higgins and D. Savoie (1990) *Regional Policy in a Changing World,*. New York: Plenum Press.

Hilpert, H.G. (1993) 'Japanische Industriepolitik – Grundlage, Träger, Mechanismen', *Ifo Schelldienst* 46(17–18).

Jürgens, U. and W. Krumbein (eds) (1991) *Industriepolitische Strategien: Bundesländer im Vergleich*, Berlin: Edition Sigma.

Koshiro, K. (1986) 'Japan's Industrial Policy for New Technologies', *Zeitschrift für die gesamte Staatswissenschaft* 142(1): 163–77.

Kubicek, H. (1993) 'Organisatorische Voraussetzungen des branchenübergreifenden elektronischen Datenaustausches – Neue Aufgaben für die Wirtschaftsverbände?', in H. Kubicek and P. Seeger (eds), *Perspektive Techniksteuerung*, Berlin: Edition Sigma, pp. 143–68.

Luhmann, N. (1989) 'Steuerbarkeit – Streitgespräch mit Fritz W. Scharpf', in H.-H. Hartwich (ed.), *Macht und Ohnmacht politischer Institutionen*, Opladen: Westdeutscher Verlag, pp. 83–9.

Martinsen, R. (1992) 'Theorien politischer Steuerung – Auf der Suche nach dem Dritten Weg', in K. Grimmer *et al.* (eds), *Politische Techniksteuerung*, Opladen: Leske und Budrich, pp. 51–74.

Mayntz, R. (1993) 'Policy-Netzwerke und die Logik von Verhandlungssystemen', in A. Heritier (ed.), *Politische Vierteljahresschrift, Sonderheft 24, Policy-Analyse. Kritik und Neuorientierung*, Opladen: Westdeutscher Verlag, pp. 39–56.

Messner, D. (1992) 'Die südkoreanische Erfolgsstory und der Staat: Von der Allmacht des Entwicklungsstaates zur Krise des "hierarchischen Steuerungsmodells"', *Vierteljahresberichte* 130: 401–18.

Pavitt, K. (1984) 'Sectoral Patterns of Technical Change: Towards a Taxonomy and a Theory', *Research Policy* 13: 343–73.

Rammert, W. (1992) 'Wer oder was steuert den technischen Fortschritt? Technischer Wandel zwischen Steuerung und Evolution', *Soziale Welt* (1):7–25.

Rossnagel, A. (1993) 'Rechtpolitische Anforderungen an die verbandliche Techniksteuerung', in H. Kubicek and P. Seeger (eds), *Perspektive Techniksteuerung*, Berlin: Ed. Sigma, pp. 169–80.

Scharpf, F. W. (1991) 'Die Handlungsfähigkeit des Staates am Ende des zwanzigsten Jahrhunderts', *Politische Vierteljahresschrift* 32(4): 213–34.

Schneider, V. and R. Werle (1991) 'Policy Networks in the German Telecommunications Domain', in B. Marin and R. Mayntz (eds), *Policy Networks: Empirical Evidence and Theoretical Considerations*, Frankfurt: Campus, pp. 97–137.

Van de Ven, A. H. (1993) 'The Emergence of an Industrial Infrastructure for Technological Innovation', *Journal of Comparative Economics* 17: 338–65.

Voelzkow, H. (1993) 'Staatliche Regulierung der verbandlichen Selbstregulierung – Schlüssel für eine gesellschaftliche Techniksteuerung?', in H. Kubicek and P. Seeger (eds), *Perspektive Techniksteuerung*, Berlin: Edition Sigma, pp. 105–28.

Weir, M. (1992) 'Ideas and the Politics of Bounded Innovation', in S. Steinmo *et al.* (eds), *Structuring Politics. Historical Institutionalism in Comparative Analysis*, Cambridge: Cambridge University Press, pp. 188–216.

Willke, H. (1988) 'Staatliche Intervention als Kontextsteuerung', *Kritische Vierteljahresschrift für Kriminologie und Gesetzgebung*, pp. 214–28.

3

TECHNOLOGICAL CAPABILITY DEVELOPMENT BY FIRMS FROM EAST ASIAN NIES

Possible lessons for Malaysia

Wong Poh Kam

Historically, the East Asian newly industrialising economies (NIEs) shared common characteristics with many other developing countries in that they were all late-industrialising countries in the global economy (Hikino and Amsden 1994). These countries face two common problems in terms of developing high-tech industrial capability: first, they were typically distant from the leading user markets in North America, Europe and Japan; secondly, they were also far away and disconnected from the leading sources of innovation in advanced countries. Despite these dis-advantages, however, the East Asian NIEs have managed to achieve significantly faster high-tech industrial growth over the last three decades than other developing countries. By the mid-1990s, many indigenous firms from these countries had achieved remarkable technological 'catch-up', and, in some cases, had even pulled ahead of market leaders from the advanced Organization for Economic Cooperation and Development (OECD) countries. How did these firms from the East Asian NIEs manage to become competitive in a wide range of high-tech industries?

There has been a large literature in recent years on the common factors con-tributing to the rapid industrialisation of the four East Asian NIEs (South Korea, Taiwan, Hong Kong and Singapore). The most influential of these books, *The East Asian Miracle* by the World Bank (1993), put much emphasis on common factors such as political stability, prudent macroeconomic policies, export-orientation, and public policies leading to high savings rate and heavy investment in human resource development. However, this largely neoclassical explanation, stressing 'market-friendly' interventions and 'getting prices right', has been rightly criti-cised as ignoring the substantial state intervention in these countries (see e.g. Amsden 1989; Wade *et al.* 1994). Moreover, recent research findings show that the East Asian NIEs, in fact, had quite different strategic approaches to industrial

53

technological capability development (e.g. see Hobday 1995; Mathews 1995; Kim 1993; Hou and Gee 1993; Wong 1995a). In effect, from the perspective of technology development, there is not one East Asian NIE miracle, but four different ones. The aim of this paper is to briefly summarise the key technological capability development strategies pursued by successful high-tech firms in the three East Asian NIEs of Korea, Taiwan and Singapore, especially in recent years, and to highlight a number of implications for future industrial development strategy in Malaysia.

Technological capability development in late-industrialising countries

Key dimensions of technological capabilities

Technological capabilities have traditionally been conceptualised as embodying a range of functional competencies from pre-investment search/evaluation and project execution to process and product engineering, with the level of capabilities required ranging from routine operation to adaptive improvement and major innovation (see e.g. Dahlman *et al.* 1987; Lall 1992). For the purpose of this paper, I propose a four-dimensional measure of the capabilities of high-tech firms (see Fig. 3.1).

Technology application/operation capabilities: this refers to the ability of a firm to apply or operate an available technology to make products or to deliver services at competitive quality and cost.

Process-technology innovation capabilities: this refers to the ability of a firm to improve the process of delivering products or services, resulting in superior quality or lower cost *vis-à-vis* its leading competitors. The capabilities may involve applying available technologies in new, innovative ways.

Product-technology innovation capabilities: this refers to the ability of a firm to innovate products embodying new or improved technological components or designs.

Technology marketing capabilities: this refers to the ability of a firm to develop the appropriate product branding, competitive positioning, distribution/marketing channels and intellectual property right (IPR) protection mechanisms to capture viable market shares.

Figure 3.1 Four key dimensions of technological capabilities

Basically, the first two dimensions of capabilities cover process capabilities (abilities to make given products), while the last two dimensions cover product capabilities (abilities to design or create products). Our definition departs from traditional approaches (e.g. Lall 1992) in that we explicitly incorporate the capabilities to market and position products as a dimension of technological capabilities. This is in recognition of the recent technology management literature highlighting the increasing importance of marketing capabilities once a technology develops beyond the emerging stage. Other dimensions of technological capabilities highlighted by other writers, e.g. the ability to identify, evaluate and procure technology, can be subsumed under technology use/operation capabilities.

Technology capability development mechanisms

The mechanisms for developing technological capabilities are well documented in the literature and basically boil down to the various processes by which technological know-how can be learned or acquired (see Fig. 3.2). These mechanisms are generic and applicable to firms from both advanced and late-industrialising countries. Most firms would need to pursue more than one of these mechanisms at any one time, and often need to change the mix of mechanisms over time as the firms progress technologically.

---

learning by working in companies possessing the technology

imitation/reverse engineering

subcontracting (and learning associated with the process)

licensing

technology transfer agreements

recruitment of experienced/trained personnel

use of consultants/contract R&D firms

purchase of technology

acquisition of technology sources

own R&D

joint R&D with others

technology swapping (cross-licensing)

Figure 3.2 Generic technology capability development mechanisms

From the perspective of firms from the three East Asian NIEs of Korea, Taiwan and Singapore, what is significant to note is that the state has played vitally important roles in facilitating one or more of these mechanisms (Kim 1993; Hou and Gee 1993; Wong 1994). Moreover, state roles have been different in the three East Asian NIEs at different stages of their development. State intervention has also varied for different high-tech industries (e.g. semiconductors, the automotive industry, computers, machine tools). The impacts of these interventions have also varied, with examples of outstanding success as well as cases of mixed performance and significant failure. While the diversity of approaches and experiences thus defy simple generalisations, for the purpose of this paper we will highlight some of the more successful state interventions in facilitating the growth of indigenous high-tech firms in the three East Asian NIEs.

Generic technology capability development routes of East Asian NIE firms

Based on the experiences of successful high-tech firms from the three East Asian NIEs, we can identify the following five generic routes of indigenous firms in late-industrialising countries to develop their technological capabilities.

'Reverse product life-cycle' learning strategy (from OEM to ODM to OBM)

In this generic approach, the indigenous firms start by first entering simple component subcontracting or contract assembly operations, typically on an OEM (original equipment manufacturing) basis, then moving upstream into doing product design and original design manufacturing (ODM) for end-buyers, and finally developing their own products and selling under their own brand names, i.e. own-brand manufacturing (OBM). With reference to Figure 3.1, this involves starting first with developing process capabilities, and following that by extension into product capabilities.

This approach has been typical of many Taiwanese information technology (IT) companies that started by making personal computer (PC) clones or manufacturing key components of IT systems. The key emphasis in this strategy is to use the experience of supplying to sophisticated customers as a means of learning about the product technology as well as related business further downstream. The move from manufacturing to design is often first effected through feedback provided by the suppliers of their manufacturing know-how to the buyers to help ensure that the product design can be manufactured.

The viability of this 'reverse product life-cycle' learning strategy depends initially on the availability and willingness of buyers to outsource manufacturing by licensing their design. For example, the successful entry of Korean firms into semiconductor wafer fabrication in the early 1980s was partly due to the presence, at that time, of a number of small, financially distressed US 'fabless' chip designers – i.e. companies that produce integrated circuit (IC) chip designs but do not own wafer fabrication plants and have to rely on third-party wafer fabrication companies to fabricate the IC chips for them (e.g. Micron, Vitelic, Zymos) – willing to license their designs. The success of the Koreans subsequently made chip designers reluctant to further license technologies, but, by then, the Koreans had

56

learnt enough to develop their own designs (e.g. the breakthrough of the 4 megabyte DRAM – direct random-access memory).

'Late-follower' to 'fast-follower' strategy

An important variant of the above 'reverse product life-cycle' strategy is for the indigenous firms to become fast-followers in product markets. The firms start by producing relatively mature products, either under technology licence from companies in the advanced nations, or through imitative learning if the technologies involved are not proprietary. The initial products tend to be based on technologies several generations away from the latest leading edge and usually targeted at low-price market segments. This entry strategy allows the firms to leverage initial lower-cost advantage to take over low-end products from the market leaders. By mastering the mature product and process technologies quickly, the firms seek to shift to making products of higher sophistication involving technologies closer to the leading edge. Over time, by investing heavily in learning and by following the direction of the technological leaders through imitative R&D and product development, the firms seek to close the technological gaps between themselves and the technological leaders, in effect becoming fast-followers.

In contrast to the OEM–ODM–OBM route, firms pursuing this imitative learning strategy compete directly in the end-user markets, albeit starting at the low-price end. The execution of this strategy thus needs to be complemented by concomitant investment in marketing and brand development. In particular, the firms need to be able to transform their image as low-end, low-tech producers into one of sophisticated, high-quality and high-technology manufacturers over time, which is often a difficult task, especially for mass consumer products. As they move closer to the leading-edge products, they will be increasingly perceived as competitive threats by the major market leaders, and, hence, technology licensing will increasingly become unavailable, forcing these firms to invest substantially more in their own product and process R&D.

Process capability specialist strategy

Rather than seeking to move into OBM product innovation, with the attendant higher risks of productisation (i.e. the process of translating technologies and marketing concepts into specific product specification and development plans) and developing their own marketing capabilities, some firms have chosen to focus their energies and resources on becoming specialists in manufacturing for others. This can take the form of becoming a specialist contract assembler, with core competence in process operations and process innovation (the first two dimensions in Figure 3.1), which enables the firm to move up the process sophistication ladder, and to always stay at the lowest-cost or highest process-quality frontier. Another variant is for the firm to concentrate on supplying specialised niche components or undertaking certain process steps. Many firms from Singapore, that initially started as subcontractors and contract manufacturers for world-class MNCs, have adopted this strategy (e.g. Ventures, Flextronix), while Korea's Anam is another example.

To pursue this strategy, the firms need to focus their resources on constantly improving their operational efficiency, either through process R&D, or by acquiring the latest technologies and incorporating them into production as soon as possible to reap first-mover advantage in learning economies. Besides keeping in close contact with leading technology suppliers, the firms also need to keep in close touch with customers to anticipate future process requirements. Eventually, the firms will need to invest increasing amounts in process R&D to move with the technology frontier.

Technology pioneering / product innovation strategy

A few firms from the East Asian NIEs have opted for the much more difficult strategy of becoming technology pioneers or product innovators in the global market. This strategy is more difficult for firms from the East Asian NIEs because, as pointed out earlier, they need to overcome two inherent disadvantages compared to firms from the advanced countries: first, they are more distant from the leading-user markets, which tend to be located in the most advanced countries; and second, they are also distant from the main sources of advanced science and technological knowledge, which also tend to be located in advanced countries.

To overcome their disadvantages, firms from the East Asian NIEs that have succeeded in becoming technological pioneers appear to have adopted one of the following four approaches:

- One is to establish a strong presence, despite great cost, in the leading-user market to pursue product technology or market distribution channel development, while tapping supporting resources in the home base. This was done by Creative Technologies of Singapore, Acer of Taiwan and the Korean *chaebols*. This calls for either extraordinary entrepreneurship or the backing of financially strong corporate groups with long-term vision and deep pockets. A key part of this strategy is heavy investment in brand-name development through advertising and marketing channel development, which typically take a long time to pay off.
- The second approach is to invest in, or acquire outright, promising high-tech start-ups in the advanced countries. This tends to be risky as firms from East Asian NIEs typically lack the ability to evaluate such investments, given that much of the assets of such companies are actually intangible and embodied in the founders and could easily be lost through mobility of key personnel. Managing across cultures may represent another problem. Nonetheless, windows of opportunity to acquire new small high-tech start-ups or relatively established, but financially distressed, firms do occur from time to time.
- The third approach is to lure highly qualified personnel who embody advanced technological know-how to relocate in the East Asian NIE

concerned, through venture capital funding, subsidies to start up operations, or appointment to leadership position in local research institutions. Taiwanese and Korean firms, in particular, have targeted highly trained and experienced nationals working in the US, while Singaporean firms are trying to exploit the ethnic Chinese and Indian diasporas.

- The last, but not the least, approach is for firms to engage in substantial R&D, either on their own or in collaboration with others, such as local universities, other local firms or foreign firms, with the hope of achieving technological leadership over competitor firms in advanced countries. To offset the advantages that firms from advanced countries may have, the local firms must believe that they have access to compensating factors. These could include cheaper R&D manpower, special regional advantage (e.g. Chinese pharmaceuticals), special government support (e.g. government R&D subsidies or low-interest capital, technology transfer from public research institutes, potential protection of the domestic market, government procurement, at least initially), some earlier technological breakthrough conferring a leadership opportunity, or special insight into a niche area overlooked by firms from more advanced countries.

A variant of this strategy is to locate R&D in countries in the region that have abundant R&D manpower, but lack product commercialisation infrastructure (e.g. China, India and Russia). The comparative advantage of the East Asian NIE firm in this case may be due to geographic/cultural proximity or prior business network contacts established.

Some of the more successful companies from East Asian NIEs have adopted more than one of the above approaches, either simultaneously or at different stages of growth. For firms that have already achieved at least some innovation capabilities of their own, strategic alliances with advanced firms will become an increasingly important option as well, but this option is typically not available to firms that have little technology to offer.

Applications pioneering strategy

This strategy entails an East Asian NIE organisation becoming an innovator, not of new product technologies, but in the application of existing technologies in innovative new ways, typically in an area where the organisation has considerable complementary skills. Three examples from Singapore are instructive: (i) the Port of Singapore Authority (PSA) has pioneered the application of relatively proven technologies, such as neural networks and fuzzy logic, in automating container handling; (ii) Eutech Cybernetics has pioneered the use of well-established digital signal processing technologies in improving instrumentation portability; (iii) SNS has used established electronic data interchange (EDI) technology to develop TradeNet, which has considerably improved the efficiency of the export/import trade transaction process.

The success of this strategy hinges on the company being an innovative adapter of available new technologies, rather than a creator of radically new technologies. The company must also have good knowledge of the business it is competing in, so that the new technologies can be adapted to best improve the competitiveness of the company in its chosen business. This 'fusion' of business and technology know-how in effect involves the creation of more advanced capabilities.

These five strategic routes to technological capability development are not mutually exclusive, but appear to represent the key strategic directions of competitive capability development of firms from the East Asian NIEs over the last 20 years. On the whole, firms from Singapore appear to emphasise process specialisation and applications pioneering, although the other routes are also becoming important. With the growth of the big *chaebols*, Korea emphasised reverse product life-cycle and fast-follower strategies, focusing particularly on sectors where large-scale economies were important. More recently, product technology pioneering has begun to be pursued by the leading Korean *chaebols*. Taiwan, with its large number of small and medium enterprises (SMEs), mainly pursued the reverse product life-cycle learning and fast-follower routes, focusing in particular on design-intensive sectors like personal computers (PCs) and peripherals, machine tools, and precision engineering products. In recent years, product technology pioneering and process specialist strategies have also become important.

Facilitating roles of the state

It is interesting to note that the governments have played important roles in facilitating each of the above generic routes to technology capability development in Korea, Taiwan and Singapore. We highlight below three such specific roles that have contributed significantly to the successful technology capability development strategies of particular East Asian NIE firms.

Government facilitation of DFI-induced technological learning

Through the Economic Development Board (EDB), the Singapore government has encouraged MNCs to bring in successive waves of new technologies to their subsidiaries' operations in Singapore. Although some have criticised this MNC-led approach as stunting the growth of local firms, these MNC operations have spawned considerable supporting industries in Singapore and induced substantial technological capability development among many local subcontracting and contract assembly firms (Wong 1995b, 1996). Moreover, innovative public-assistance programmes, such as the Local Industry Upgrading Programme (LIUP) to promote the adoption of new information and automation technology by SMEs, advanced technical manpower training programmes like INTECH, and the early promotion of the ISO 9000 certification infrastructure have facilitated the technological and management learning processes of these supporting industries. Many of these local supporting firms have pursued the process specialist route, and most have since internationalised their operations to the near-NIEs like Malaysia and China, not only following the relocation of their customers to these countries, but also diversifying into new markets as well. Regionalisation incentives provided by the host governments have encouraged and facilitated these overseas ventures. Moreover, new innovative R&D incentives, like the Research Incentives Scheme for Companies (RISC), have been introduced by the government to fund integrative process-technology capability development efforts in these companies, even though such efforts cannot be neatly packaged into specific R&D projects. A smaller, but increasing, number of companies have also pursued the reverse product life-cycle strategy, moving into new product R&D while building upon their traditional strengths in low-cost, high-quality manufacturing.

Technology assimilation / transfer and cooperative R&D promotion through public research institutes (PRIs)

Taiwan has been most successful in using public research institutes (PRIs) to promote the diffusion of industrially relevant technologies. For example, the Industrial Technology Research Institute (ITRI) has been widely credited with helping to create an advanced semiconductor industry cluster in Taiwan through a well-thought-out and well-executed strategy of assimilating foreign technology and transferring it to local enterprises through spin-offs (see e.g. Mathews 1995; Lin 1994; NRI 1995). The successful execution of this strategy depended on a number of factors, including careful long-term technology development planning and vision at the top (e.g. the Electronics Industry Development Project (EIDP)), competent leadership at the helm of ITRI (Dr Morris Chang), an abundant supply of well-trained engineers, and the significant presence of, and strong linkages with, competitive local electronics industries which provide significant markets and customer feedback.

Besides successful spin-offs from PRIs such as UMC and TSMC, there are also many examples of PRI-orchestrated R&D consortia in Taiwan. These have been promoted in the belief that the many small and medium enterprises in Taiwan would under-invest in new technology development if left on their own. Over the last 15 years, it has been estimated that over 60 such R&D consortia have been established in various industrial sectors in Taiwan. Although the records of these R&D consortia are mixed in terms of eventual market commercialisation, it is undeniable that there has been much faster diffusion of product technological capabilities among the participating firms as a result of these consortium programmes. In particular, the significant inroads that Taiwanese firms have made into ODM in recent years have partly been facilitated by these R&D consortia.

Although on a smaller scale, the Korean government also actively supported the development of indigenous capabilities in the semiconductor industry through public research institutes like KIET (which was later merged into ETRI), particularly in the early stages (Mathews 1995). The considerably larger resources of the big *chaebols* have meant that further direct government involvement in technology transfer was deemed unnecessary once the basic 4M (megabyte) DRAM technology was diffused among Samsung, LG and Hyundai.

More recently, the Singapore government has also started to promote R&D consortia as a means to hasten the technological capability development of local firms. Involvement with foreign firms or R&D institutions is particularly emphasised to facilitate technology transfer from advanced sources. Examples include the Digital Media Consortium (involving three local firms, three PRIs, and MIT's Media Lab) and cooperative R&D programmes in aerospace and marine technologies.

Promoting the growth of sufficiently large-scale high-tech enterprises

In the early stage of development of 'strategic' industries in Korea, the Korean government encouraged the growth of large-scale *chaebols* to bring about economies of scale in capital-intensive industries deemed 'strategic'. A variety of policy tools were used (see e.g. Kim 1993), including subsidised financing, protection of the domestic market, incentives for technological learning through capital goods imports or turnkey projects (as opposed to direct foreign investment), and turning over failing state enterprises to the *chaebols*. Although there were notable failures in this heavy-industry strategy, several big *chaebols*, like Samsung, LG (formerly Lucky-Goldstar), Hyundai and Daewoo, did develop significant technological capabilities in a wide range of export-oriented, capital-intensive industries as a result. Where Korea differs from other developing countries in promoting big businesses is that the state effectively exercised discipline over these *chaebols* by penalising poor performances and only rewarding good ones. This 'contest-based' approach (Amsden 1989) enabled a number of high-performing *chaebols* to quickly establish large-scale production, marketing/distribution or R&D economies to compete successfully in several global industries like shipbuilding, automobiles, consumer electronics, telecommunications equipment and semiconductors. The large size of these *chaebols* enabled them to build global brand names and distribution channels, and, hence, move quickly into OBM in a wide range of consumer products. Deep pockets have also enabled the *chaebols* to acquire technology capabilities quickly by buying up established companies (recent examples include Maxtor, NCR microelectronics, AST). However, the large size of the *chaebols* appears to be a source of disadvantage when it comes to competing in technologically dynamic industries like PCs, software, biotechnology and speciality chemicals where scale economies are not important or less critical. Furthermore, political democratisation in recent years has led to increasing calls for the *chaebols* to be controlled, broken up or subject to fewer privileges and more competition domestically.

Although the development of big businesses in Korea had become excessive, the basic idea of 'contest-based' resource allocation and the need to achieve sufficient scale economies, particularly in technology-intensive businesses, remain valid concerns. The Singapore government has stressed the need to develop high-tech firms of sufficient scale by setting up a government-controlled group, the Singapore Technology Group, to spearhead entry into various high-tech industries (e.g. semiconductor wafer fabrication, chip design, aerospace repair and maintenance, systems software) where local entrepreneurs had been found wanting. A number of large-sized Taiwanese firms have also emerged in recent years that have been beneficiaries of the government's high-tech promotion policies (e.g. ACER, Tatung, NanYa Plastics, TSMC).

The three examples above of facilitating government roles serve to illustrate some key distinguishing features of the Singaporean, Taiwanese and Korean government strategies to promote indigenous technological capability development. It should be recognised, of course, that the various common state facilitating roles emphasised by *The East Asian Miracle* (World Bank 1993), such as high investment in education (especially technical education) and infrastructure, export orientation, and macroeconomic stability, etc., have also been of great importance, and, in some sense, represent preconditions for the success of the above policies.

Implications for Malaysia

As Malaysia enters a new phase of industrialisation, with increasing stress on high technology, the specific strategic routes that firms can take to advance their technological capabilities need to be analysed. Government policies to facilitate the development of these firms should take into account the likely strategic routes desired or achievable.

The experience of the three East Asian NIEs suggests that, besides the broad policy prescriptions of *The East Asian Miracle* to get economic fundamentals right, pro-active state interventions have facilitated the development of indigenous technological capabilities. However, the appropriate choice of specific forms of intervention depends on the specific context and conditions in the individual countries. There is no single route to technological competitiveness. All the three East Asian NIE state intervention roles highlighted earlier represent possible options for Malaysia to consider.

References

Amsden, A. (1989) *Asia's Next Giant: South Korea and Late Industrialization*, New York: Oxford University Press.

Dahlman, C.J. and L.S. Kim (1992) 'Technology Policy for Industrialization: An Integrative Framework and Korea's Experience', *Research Policy*, 21, pp. 437–52.

Dahlman, C.J., B. Ross-Larson and L.E. Westphal (1987) 'Managing Technological Development: Lessons from the Newly Industrializing Countries', *World Development* 15(6), pp. 759–75.

Fishlow, A. *et al.* (eds) (1994) *Miracle or Design? Lessons from the East Asian Experience*, Washington DC: Overseas Development Council.

Hikino, T. and A.H. Amsden (1994) 'Staying Behind, Stumbling Back, Sneaking Up, Soaring Ahead: Late Industrialization in Historical Perspective', in W.J. Baumol, R.R.

Nelson and E.N. Wolff (eds), *Convergence of Productivity: Cross National Studies and Historical Evidence*, New York: Oxford University Press.

Hobday, M. (1995) *Innovation in East Asia: The Challenge to Japan*, London: Edward Elgar.

Hou, C.M. and S. Gee (1993) 'National Systems Supporting Technical Advance in Industry: The Case of Taiwan', in R.R. Nelson (ed.), *National Innovation Systems: A Comparative Analysis*, New York: Oxford University Press, pp. 384–413.

Kim, L.S. (1993) 'National System of Industrial Innovation: Dynamics of Capability Building in Korea', in R.R. Nelson (ed.), *National Innovation Systems: A Comparative Analysis*, New York: Oxford University Press, pp. 357–83.

Lall, S. (1992) 'Technological Capabilities and Industrialization', *World Development*, 20(2), pp. 165–86.

Lin, O.C.C. (1994) 'Development and Transfer of Industrial Technology in Taiwan, R.O.C.', in O.C.C. Lin *et al.* (eds), *Development and Transfer of Industrial Technology*, Amsterdam: Elsevier, pp. 1–30.

Mathews, J.A. (1995) *High Technology Industrialization in East Asia: The Case of the Semiconductor Industry in Taiwan and Korea*, Taipei: Chung-Hua Institution for Economic Research.

Nelson, R.R. (ed.) (1993) *National Innovation Systems: A Comparative Analysis*, New York: Oxford University Press.

NRI (1995) 'Rapid Growth of Taiwan's IC Industry through Joint Public–Private Sector Efforts', *Nomura Asia Focus*, Dec. 1995/Jan. 1996, pp. 21–7.

Wong P.K. (1994) 'Singapore's Technology Strategy', in F.F. Simon (ed.), *The Emerging Technological Trajectory of the Pacific Rim*, New York: M.E. Sharpe, pp. 103–31.

Wong P.K. (1995a) 'Competing in the Global Electronics Industry: A Comparative Study of the Innovation Networks of Singapore and Taiwan', *Journal of Industry Studies*, 2(2), pp. 35–61.

Wong P.K. (1995b) 'Technology Transfer and Development Inducement by Foreign MNCs: The Experience of Singapore', in K.Y. Jeong and M.H. Kwack (eds), *Industrial Strategy for Global Competitiveness of Korean Industries*, Seoul: Korea Economic Research Institute, pp. 130–59.

Wong P.K. (1997) 'Supply Infrastructure for Flexible Production: The Case of Hard Disk Drive Industry in Singapore', *Industry and Innovation*, 4(2).

World Bank (1993), *The East Asian Miracle*, New York: Oxford University Press.

4

COMPLEXITY AND HIERARCHY IN THE EAST ASIAN DIVISION OF LABOUR

Japanese technological superiority and ASEAN industrial development

Kit G. Machado

Current trends in the international political economy are simultaneously restructuring global and regional divisions of labour and affecting the power and well-being of states, corporations, financial institutions, classes, groups and individuals. Central among these trends is acceleration of a transition that has been under way since mid-century between an 'international economy' of classic arm's-length trading relationships and a 'world economy' comprised of transnational production networks. The distinction comes from Cox (1987), which is one of the fullest and most interesting theoretical expositions of this trend, but there are many current analyses that elaborate the same theme (Bonacich *et al.* 1994; Doherty 1995; Gereffi and Korzeniewicz 1994; Harrison 1994). These networks centre on transnational corporations (TNCs) that manage the activities of production sites in many countries. The stages of manufacture of their products in this new international division of labour are carried out or the parts and components of their products are made in states at different levels of industrial development. The resultant intermediate goods are traded, frequently on an intra-firm basis, for eventual incorporation into finished products. The latter are then sold internationally and/or locally. This activity is organised both globally and regionally. Local producers may be owned or directly controlled by TNCs or they may simply be licensees or subcontractors. Development of transnational production networks is fuelled by TNC foreign direct investment (FDI) and facilitated by the public policies of the states whose economies this activity serves to integrate. TNC predominance in these networks is based primarily on their control over technology, capital and marketing mechanisms. These are world-wide processes, but no region has been more affected by them than East Asia.

This chapter examines the growing complexity of intra-East Asian investment patterns and of regional production networks and their implications for industrial development in the ASEAN states, with focus particularly on the Malaysian case. I have shown elsewhere (Machado 1995) that Japanese TNCs in concert with Japanese financial institutions and key ministries and agencies of the Japanese government have systematically promoted expansion and integration of production in East Asia on a sector-by-sector basis. The result has been extension throughout the region of a vertically integrated, hierarchical, Japan-centred regional division of labour that forms the boundaries within which national industrial development efforts of other regional states, to greatly varying degrees, take place. These boundaries are maintained, most importantly, by Japan's technological superiority over its neighbours. Patterns of FDI and the division of labour in East Asia have become increasingly complex since the late 1980s, however, as firms based in the Asian Newly Industrialising Countries (ANICs) (Korea, Taiwan, Hong Kong and Singapore) and, to a lesser extent, in some ASEAN-4 (Indonesia, Malaysia, Thailand, the Philippines) countries have become international and regional investors. Indeed, in some recent years, aggregate ANIC investment has matched or exceeded (in some cases, substantially exceeded) Japanese FDI in some other regional countries.

What follows begins with an analysis of the expansion of Japanese production networks in East Asia and the growth of ANIC and ASEAN-4 FDI. The reflection of these trends in Malaysia is then briefly examined. The primary concern of this chapter, the extent to which growing complexity is increasing pluralisation and decreasing hierarchy in the regional division of labour and improving prospects for industrial development in ASEAN states, is considered next. I conclude that increasing complexity does not translate into pluralisation to the degree that an uncritical examination of FDI data would suggest. This is because in many cases, ANIC and ASEAN-4 manufacturing investment is found not to be autonomous, but rather a direct proxy for or in some degree dependent (particularly, technologically dependent) on firms based primarily in Japan, but also in other industrially advanced countries. I further conclude that such Japanese proxy or dependent investment tends to extend and consolidate the hierarchical, Japan-centred regional division of labour, not to make it more pluralistic. These conclusions bear on one of the critical issues in the political economy of development with which this volume is concerned, the impact of the transnationalisation of industry on national efforts to promote industrial technology development.

I have argued elsewhere that ASEAN states have derived some significant economic benefits, including technological advancement, from the spread of industry and the high rates of growth that have accompanied integration into Japan-centred regional production networks. In some cases, interested parties in these states have, to their advantage, successfully extended or even occasionally broken through the boundaries tended by Japanese interests, and in others, the latter have, on their own initiative, adjusted them. The Malaysian experience is a case in point. Generally, however, the costs of incorporation in production networks have been diminished autonomy and acceptance of benefits that are largely concessions granted on Japanese terms or, less frequently, extracted only after hard bargaining, rather than gains anchored in national industrial strength (Machado 1994). Given the enormous asymmetries of economic power and technological capacity between Japan and the ASEAN states reflected in the hierarchical regional division of labour, the likelihood that the latter states will make secure and self-sustaining (as distinct from dependent) industrial advance appears to be a very long-term prospect. I conclude that the recent growth of ANIC and ASEAN-4 investment and the growing complexity of the regional division of labour that follows from this, at best, promises to modify this picture in small ways, not to alter it fundamentally.

Foreign direct investment, production networks and the growing complexity of the East Asian regional division of labour

Japanese FDI and expanding production networks

Japanese post-war overseas investment only began on a significant scale in the late 1960s.[1] Between 1969 and 1990, there were three 'waves' of FDI characterised by accelerating rates of year-on-year growth, a crest, and then either slower growth or decline (*Nihon boeki shinkokai*, 1993: 63–4). Japan's world-wide cumulative FDI stood at US$2.0 billion in 1968, but by the end of the third wave in 1990 it had reached US$310.8 billion. Some perceived a 'new wave' starting to rise in 1993 (NRI and ISEAS 1995). As Table 4.1 shows, the cumulative total reached US$514.3 billion by the end of FY 1995 (31 March 1996). Japanese FDI was concentrated in third-world natural resources until the mid-1970s, but it was relatively evenly distributed across the major regions of the world up to that time. After that, it began to increase in manufacturing in North America and in both industry and additional natural-resource development in Asia (overwhelmingly East Asia) while lagging in Europe. Then, from 1984 through 1990, FDI increased very substantially in both North America and Europe while lagging in Asia.

Overseas manufacturing investment initially represented an effort to cut costs in the face of rising wages and land prices in Japan and to solve market access problems by jumping over other countries' protective barriers. After the advent of flexible exchange rates in 1971, periodic episodes of yen appreciation had adverse consequences for the price competitiveness of Japanese exports and was thus also a stimulus to new 'efficiency-seeking' overseas investment, which included relocation of many established Japanese firms in lower-wage countries. The sharp continuing rise in the value of the yen after the 1985 Plaza Accord and increasing market access problems were major motivations for the big increases in investment in North America and Europe and in third-world export platforms during the third wave of Japanese FDI. In 1995, as Table 4.1 shows, by far the largest cumulated amount of Japanese FDI, US$225.5 billion (44 per cent), was in North America, and the amount in Europe, US$98.3 billion (19 per cent), exceeded the amount in Asia, US$88.5 billion (17 per cent). The primary feature of the 'new

KIT G. MACHADO

Table 4.1 Amounts of Japanese cumulative FDI and numbers of overseas companies

| FDI in | Amount (US$ bn) | | No. of companies | | | |
| | | | All sectors | | % of world manuf. | Manuf./ total Japanese (%) |
	1985	1995	1985	1996	1996	1996
Asia	19.5 (23%)	88.5 (17%)	2,333 (39%)	10,099 (45%)	5,615 (63%)	(56%)
North America	27.0 (32%)	225.5 (44%)	1,524 (25%)	5,463 (24%)	1,715 (19%)	(31%)
Europe	11.0 (13%)	98.3 (19%)	1,172 (19%)	4,156 (19%)	876 (10%)	(21%)
Other	26.2 (31%)	102.0 (20%)	994 (17%)	2,683 (12%)	669 (8%)	(25%)
Total	83.7 (100%)	514.3 (100%)	6,023 (100%)	22,401 (100%)	8,875 (100%)	(37%)

Sources: Amounts: * 1985 – Dobashi 1988: 13.
1995 – *Nihon boeki shinkokai* 1997: 517–18.
Companies: *Toyo Keizai* 1997: 54–69.
Note: * These Japanese Ministry of Finance figures for FDI represent the sums of equity investment, cash loans, establishment of overseas branches and, through 1981, acquisition of real estate. By the end of 1990, 58 per cent of cumulated FDI was in equity and 40 per cent in loans (*Toyo Keizai* 1992: 1027).

wave', has not been a big increase in overall FDI but an upturn from 1993 in the total amount and a substantial increase in the proportion of Japan's manufacturing FDI going to Asia, particularly ASEAN countries and China. Total FDI outflow increased 20 per cent in 1994 and 15 per cent in 1995, though it still remains far below peak-year (1989–90) levels (UNCTAD/DTCI 1996: 46). The portion of manufacturing FDI in Asia climbed from 20 per cent in third-wave peak year 1989 to 33 per cent in 1993, while the portion going to North America declined from 59 per cent to 37 per cent in the same years (NRI and ISEAS 1995: 4). Manufacturing FDI going to Asia exceeded that going to North America for the first time in 1994 and did so again in 1995 (UNCTAD/DTCI 1996: 47).

The more than US$69 billion of Japanese FDI in East Asia (particularly the US$30.5 billion in manufacturing) cumulated since 1985 has been the primary force behind the rapid expansion of the regional division of labour. As Table 4.1 shows, the total number of individual Japanese companies increased almost three and three-quarters times between 1985 and 1996. While amounts of FDI were lower in Asia than elsewhere until 1993, the largest number of individual companies has consistently been in Asia. There were 2333 companies (39 per cent of the total) in 1985 and 10,099 (45 per cent) by 1996. Clearly, there are larger numbers of smaller Japanese investments in Asia than elsewhere. While Japanese TNCs have an extensive presence and take the leading role in Asia, there is a

68

disproportionate amount of activity by small and medium industries (SMIs) in the region. Many SMIs are manufacturing firms, and a number are suppliers to locally based TNCs (Takeuchi 1993). A much larger portion of Japanese companies in Asia are in manufacturing (56 per cent) than in any other region, and by far the largest number of Japanese overseas manufacturing companies, 5615 (63 per cent), are in Asia. These facts are of particular importance because manufacturing companies are the key components of expanding production networks.

Central to the promotion of a regional division of labour is the effort by Japanese government and corporate interests to promote what they euphemistically call in English 'complex international work sharing' (MITI Japan 1992: 101–18) in manufacturing based on 'agreed specialisation' between the firms in Japanese regional production networks. The aim is to optimise complementarity within specific transnational industrial sectors (Aoki 1986; Dobashi 1988). 'Work sharing' means that the stages of manufacture of a product are carried out or the parts and components of a product are made in different countries, depending primarily on the cost efficiencies they offer, and that the resultant intermediate goods (semi-finished goods and parts) are traded between them for eventual incorporation into finished products. 'Agreed specialisation' means that corporate leaders determine which local firms are to produce what, where. At its simplest, 'work sharing' is what takes place in the manufacture of semiconductors when 'the first half of [the] . . . process (e.g., chemical and exposure treatment) – which requires high technology – take[s] place in Japan, while the labour intensive second stage of assembly, testing and the like occurs in Southeast Asia' (MITI Japan 1992: 103). In its more complex forms, it takes place within 'reciprocal networks for interchanging spare parts, components, and finished items' (RIM Studies Group 1988: 9). Such processes are particularly advanced in the electronics and motor vehicles industries. For example, East Asian motor vehicle assemblers and parts and component makers affiliated with each of the major Japanese firms are increasingly integrated into regional production networks, which are in turn tied into their global networks. These are 'complementation' systems involving the exchange of parts and components made in one country for use in several other countries. Japanese TNCs favour this approach partly because it permits taking advantage of an economy of scale in part and component making, something it is impossible to do in the many countries with small domestic markets.

The character of Japanese corporate organisation and practice extended overseas is made much clearer in the unsentimental analyses of Japanese management specialists and economists than it is by MITI and corporate officials. A professor of business explains that vertical integration is common in Japanese corporations. This means that the 'market mechanism is replaced by internal transactions' and that 'the stages of production and distribution are included in one hierarchical system'. Such integration 'serves to unify the decision-making on and operation of several processes for a common purpose . . . [and to accomplish it] . . . some kind of power is necessary. . . . It [need not] come from ownership, but [can come] from unequal transactions between the [core corporation] and the integrated

69

companies' (Kono 1984: 118–20). Tokunaga (1992a) explains that the reason Japan counts loans as FDI is that the 'essence of FDI . . . is . . . not necessarily to acquir[e] "ownership" but to exercis[e] effective influence on the management of a foreign-located firm'. He also stresses that if such a firm is important to 'the main company's business activities, and further, if it has strong bargaining power in the area of technology or other matters . . . management control must be sought by the Japanese firm' (Tokunaga 1992a: 14–15). If substantial technology is being transferred, he says, 'Japanese firms aggressively pursue the acquisition of majority ownership of their overseas . . . production facilities . . . a crucial strategy . . . to keep local firms from becoming competitive on their home ground' (Tokunaga 1992a: 43).

In extending production networks, many Japanese corporations have also structured them in an increasingly 'multi-layered' way. This is associated with their strategy of decentralising global operations and giving them greater regional focus. The aim has been to hasten and improve decision-making about activities in the proximate market. This has led to the development of more integrated and 'multi-layered' management and production networks within major world regions. By 1993, one out of every 20 overseas Japanese-affiliated firms was a regional headquarters (UNCTAD/DTCI 1996: 47). 'Multi-layering' has been particularly pronounced in East Asia. Many Japanese TNCs have established regional management systems in sub-regions of Asia. Singapore has become the chief regional centre for Southeast Asia, as that country's Operational Headquarters (OHQ) scheme (Rodan 1993) has proved attractive to Japanese TNCs. OHQs perform administrative, technical and managerial functions, do R&D and design work, and manage finances for regional affiliates of TNCs. Affiliates of Japanese TNCs in some countries have also been used to establish their own affiliates in third countries. According to JETRO, by 1993, 47 per cent of Japanese-affiliated firms in Hong Kong and 43 per cent in Singapore had established foreign affiliate networks in the region. While only 4 per cent of Japanese-affiliated firms in Malaysia and Thailand had established affiliates in other Asian countries, 35 per cent of those in Thailand and 28 per cent in Malaysia planned to do so by the year 2000 (cited in UNCTAD/DTCI 1996: 47). As will be seen in another context, implementation of this Japanese corporate strategy is reflected in FDI statistics as an increase in Hong Kong and Singapore regional investment.

Japanese corporate ties with and co-ordination of the activities of their regional subsidiaries are central to the production networks under construction in East Asia, but understanding the real complexity of these networks requires looking at a broader set of relationships. A recent survey found that in the ANICs and ASEAN states together, 30 per cent of Japanese affiliates used at least 20 local companies as subcontractors, and another 21 per cent used between 5 and 19 (MITI Japan 1992: 141). Some firms that act as subcontractors to Japanese corporations in Japan have followed them to regional production sites, set themselves up as local firms, and continued to supply these corporations' affiliates there. Larger Japanese companies may, but do not necessarily, hold a stake in such firms. Wholly locally owned firms may also act as subcontractors. Tokunaga (1992b: 14–16) argues convincingly that if local firms, Japanese-affiliated or not, are incorporated 'in a Japanese corporation's intra-company production network . . . [they are] . . . overseas production facilities of Japanese corporations'. He stresses that Japanese corporations may incorporate local firms in their networks by furnishing directors, technology, raw materials, parts, or semi-finished products, and through such practices as production sharing and renting or lending capital equipment and buying products back.

Japanese financial and transportation services extend regional networks beyond simple production and trade relationships. Japanese banks have branch offices throughout East Asia, and other Japanese financial institutions have established ties for joint lending with local finance companies and merchant banks. Some Japanese joint ventures in the region have also listed on local stock markets to boost local fund-raising, and Japanese securities houses have established a regional presence to facilitate this. International and domestic integrated inter-modal transportation systems, which co-ordinate all elements required for door-to-door physical distribution on a world-wide basis, have also been organised both by Japanese transportation firms and on an intra-company basis (Tokunaga, 1992b: 25–30). All of the foregoing support expansion of regional production networks and advance ties between the regional and global divisions of labour.

The integrative power of expanding regional production networks has been augmented by an accompanying increase in intra-firm trade. The portion of intra-firm trade is a good indicator of the extent of an 'intra-industry international division of labour' (Kobayashi and Hayashi 1993: 39–40). Table 4.2 shows the extent to which Japanese overseas manufacturing firms purchased their inputs from and sold their products in Japan, in third countries and locally in 1989 and 1992. It also shows what portion of those transactions were on an intra-firm basis. The 1992 figures show that firms in East Asia buy mainly in Japan (38 per cent) and locally (48 per cent) and sell mainly locally (66 per cent). They also show that a big proportion of their purchases from Japan (78 per cent) and of their relatively small sales there (84 per cent) and a significant portion of their purchases (43 per cent) and sales (43 per cent) in third countries were intra-firm, while only a small portion of local purchases or sales were on that basis. Table 4.2 also shows significant to very large increases between 1989 and 1992 in the proportion of intra-firm transactions between Japanese overseas affiliates in East Asia and both Japan and, in most cases, third countries. Combined transactions in Toyota's 'complementation' system for exchanging motor vehicle parts and components among its ASEAN affiliates provides a good example of the developments reflected in such figures. They were US$25 million in 1993 (EIU 1993: 37), but they had risen to US$160 million on the basis of trade in 12 parts and components by the end of 1994. They were set to grow to US$1.3 billion on the basis of trade in about 100 parts by 1998 (*The Nikkei Weekly* 1995a). Most of this would be intra-firm trade. Such increases clearly under gird expanding production networks and East Asian economic integration.

71

Table 4.2 Intra-industry international division of labour: intra-firm purchases and sales of Japanese overseas affiliates in manufacturing, 1989 and 1992*

	Year	Purchases				Sales			
		Amount (bn. yen)	Sources (% / % intra-firm)			Amount (bn. yen)	Destination (% / % intra-firm)		
			Japan	3rd Country	Local		Japan	3rd Country	Local
World Manuf.	1989	15,410	46 / 83	9 / 38	46 / 5	22,267	8 / 62	12 / 44	80 / 8
	1992	9,929	41 / 84	13/ 57	47 / 9	25,114	6 / 78	17 / 38	77 / 17
Asia Manuf.	1989	3,411	39 / 63	11 / 24	50 / 4	5,095	16 / 59	20 / 37	64 / 7
	1992	3,413	38 / 78	14 / 43	48 / 4	7,943	16 / 84	18 / 43	66 / 6
NICs Manuf.	1989	1,289	37 / 71	10 / 27	53 / 5	3,238	20 / 56	23 / 36	57 / 5
	1992	1,534	40 / 77	13 / 62	47 / 6	4,280	15 / 89	19 / 23	66 / 5
ASEAN Manuf.	1989	1,222	41 / 53	14 / 21	46 / 3	1,744	10 / 68	16 / 40	73 / 9
	1992	1,730	36 / 81	15 / 28	50 / 3	3,296	16 / 82	19 / 62	65 / 8

Sources: *Tsushosangyosho* 1991: 200–35, 1994: 188–223.

Note: * Data on purchase sources and sales destinations are from MITI surveys of overseas firms. The rate of survey return for manufacturing firms was 75 per cent in 1989 and 78 per cent in 1992. Sales and purchase amounts are overall figures.

The expansion of Japanese production networks in Asia after 1985 reflected two corporate strategic responses to immediate problems. The first was to increase 'outsourcing' from overseas affiliates to cut production costs. The other was to try to dampen trade friction with North America and Europe by increasing exports to those markets from production facilities in third countries rather than from Japan (as well as expanding production facilities in those regions). More generally, however, Japanese corporations have long regarded the fragmentation of the East Asian market as an obstacle to expanding and operating profitability in the region. With the help of the Japanese government and of supportive domestic interests in the region, they have been attempting to reduce this fragmentation. To this end, they have, for some years, been promoting an expanded regional division of labour and have stressed that the best way for East Asian countries to develop is to follow the leadership of Japan. In the context of growing pressures on the Japanese economy and widespread adoption of export-oriented industrial strategies and more open economic policies in other East Asian countries, such Japanese efforts have in recent years become more assertive.

American economist Leon Hollerman (1988: 8–11) offers a most convincing explanation of the foregoing trends, arguing that Japan's 'domestic industrial policy . . . has evolved into [a] geopolitical strategy [which] co-ordinate[s] Japan's external relations with the transformation of its indigenous industrial structure, . . . [including] calculated disaggregation . . . of the production process, with some stages being assigned abroad and some retained at home'. In this process, 'Japan retains for itself the higher value added operations that yield the best rates of return'. At the same time, 'export of plants and equipment [establishes a] dependency relationship [in terms of financing, maintenance, management and distribution of output] . . . between Japan and its clients' (Hollerman 1988: 11). He further contends that Japan aims to become a 'headquarters country' able to 'impose central management on a world network of joint ventures, subsidiaries, and affiliates . . . [and to] . . . co-ordinate the relations of its foreign clients with each other as well as with itself' (Hollerman 1988: xi). Both Japanese government and corporate interests have actively promoted the foregoing trends in a variety of ways.

While Japan is currently the predominant economic power in East Asia, Japanese TNCs do not have the region entirely to themselves. American trade with East Asia continues to be highly important on both sides of the Pacific. Figures on intra-firm trade and of FDI-associated foreign affiliate sales, however, make it clear that East Asia is generally, though unevenly, more linked commercially with Japan than it is with the US (UNCTAD/DTCI 1996: 45). Moreover, the stock of Japanese investment in East Asia exceeds that of the United States generally, and it exceeds it in every regional country except China (where it is about the same), the Philippines and Singapore (UNCTAD/DTCI 1995: 49–50/Table II.1). Ethnic Chinese or Sino-capitalist business networks also play a notable role in the East Asian regional economy. Their power and importance is, however, frequently exaggerated (e.g. Weidenbaum and Hughes 1996) by analysts who pay more attention to the amount of money flowing through these networks than to how that money is invested or who it is invested with. The latter issues are of major importance in assessing the structure of regional production. Sino-capitalist firms and the networks that they form are not primarily engaged in manufacturing, and to the extent that they are, these firms are in many cases either dependent on ties to Japanese or other TNCs or engaged in relatively low-technology activities. US-based and ethnic Chinese companies diversify the division of labour in East Asia, but they do not begin to match the integrative force of Japanese firms in the regional economy. This leaves ANIC and ASEAN-4 FDI (which includes virtually all of the ethnic Chinese overseas investment) for more detailed consideration.

ANIC and ASEAN-4 FDI

There has been an increasing world-wide incidence of investment abroad by firms from developing countries. Much of this investment is within their own regions (UNCTAD/DTCI 1995: 26–36). This trend has been clearly manifest in East Asia since the 1980s. ANIC FDI has played a large role and Malaysian and Thai FDI has played a modest role in the growing complexity of the regional division of labour. Table 4.3 compares the total world-wide stock of outgoing FDI for Japan and the other regional countries from 1980 to 1995.[2] This shows that the total stock of Japanese FDI was almost twelve times that of the ANICs and ASEAN-4 in 1980 but only about twice that of the latter groups by 1995. It also shows that while the total stock of Japanese FDI increased only 1.5 times between 1990 and 1995, that of the other countries increased between 1.9 and 6.5 times during the same years.

Table 4.3 Total outward FDI stock: Japan, Asian NICs and ASEAN-4 (US$ billion)

Outward stock of	1980	1985	1990	1995	'95/'90
Japan	18.8	44.3	204.7	305.5	1.5
ANICs					
Hong Kong	0.1	2.3	13.2	85.2	6.5
Taiwan	0.1	0.2	12.9	24.3	1.9
Singapore	0.7	1.3	4.7	13.8	2.9
South Korea	0.1	0.5	2.1	11.1	5.3
ASEAN-4					
Malaysia	0.4	0.7	2.3	8.9	3.9
Thailand	–	–	0.4	2.3	5.8
Philippines	0.2	0.2	0.2	0.2	–
Indonesia	–	–	–	0.1	–
Total ANICs & ASEAN-4	1.6	5.2	35.8	145.9	4.1
Japan/Total ANICs & ASEAN-4	11.8	8.5	5.7	2.1	

Source: UNCTAD/DTCI 1996: Annex Table 4. Definitions and sources of data for tables are given on pp. 219–26.

In each case, much or most of the ANIC and ASEAN-4 investment, particularly in manufacturing, is elsewhere in East Asia. Table 4.4 gives a partial picture of the increased complexity of the pattern of intra-regional investment by showing ANIC, ASEAN-4, Japanese and US FDI flows in the ASEAN-4 states and Vietnam during a recent three-year period. In 1991–93, ANIC investment outpaced Japanese FDI in Indonesia (21 per cent to 12 per cent), Malaysia (27 per cent to 20 per cent), and Vietnam (48 per cent to 10 per cent). While ANIC investment was only a bit less than half Japanese FDI in Thailand (16 per cent to 33 per cent) and the Philippines (14 per cent to 25 per cent), it was about the same as US investment. While still small, ASEAN-4 FDI contributed 5 per cent of the total in Malaysia, 7 per cent in Thailand, and 10 per cent in Vietnam. Two points need to be borne in mind in considering this data. First, as the brief discussion of Japanese TNCs' use of Hong Kong and Singapore affiliates in their 'multi-layering' strategies makes clear, counting all capital outflow from these countries as nationally based is misleading. Moreover, recalling Tokunaga's (1992a: 14) previously cited point, to the extent that non-Japanese-affiliated ANIC or ASEAN-4 firms are technologically dependent on and/or largely suppliers to Japanese firms, they are effectively 'overseas production facilities of Japanese corporations'.

Two important regional factors and several factors common to most or all of the NICs and leading ASEAN-4 investors account for their increasing FDI in East Asia. On the pull-side, the facts that the ASEAN-4 states, China and Vietnam have all in recent years liberalised their policies on inward investment and that most of them have been experiencing very high rates of growth have made them

74

Table 4.4 Origins of FDI in ASEAN-4 (1991–93), Vietnam (1988–95) (US$ billion/%)

Destination/ Origin	Indonesia	Malaysia	Thailand	Philippines	Vietnam
ANICs	5.754 (21)	4.200 (27)	3.119 (16)	0.245 (14)	7.210 (48)
Taiwan	0.718	2.316	1.071	0.028	2.590
Singapore	2.272	0.795	1.336	0.050	1.420
Hong Kong	1.456	0.300	0.603	0.031	1.890
Korea	1.308	0.789	0.109	0.136	1.310
ASEAN-4	0.150 (–)	0.756 (5)	1.241 (7)	0.012 (1)	1.439 (10)
Indonesia	–	0.738	0.347	0.001	0.288
Malaysia	0.082	–	0.592	0.009	0.842
Thailand	0.060	0.009	–	0.002	0.181
Philippines	0.008	0.009	0.302	–	0.128
Japan	3.276 (12)	3.054 (20)	6.407 (33)	0.425 (25)	1.480 (10)
US	1.640 (6)	2.603 (17)	2.787 (14)	0.253 (15)	0.270 (2)
Other	16.415 (60)	5.075 (32)	5.683 (30)	0.785 (46)	4.501 (30)
Total	27.235 (100)	15.688 (100)	19.237 (100)	1.720 (100)	14.900 (100)

Sources: ASEAN-4, 1991–93 – MITI Malaysia, 1994: 324–7.
Vietnam, 1988–95 (to Jul) – NICs, Japan, US: SCCI, in *Agence France Presse*, 9 Jul. 1995.
Vietnam, 1988–95 (to Nov) – ASEAN-4: SCCI, in *Business Times* (Malaysia), 22 Dec. 1995.
Figures for approvals all come from official institutions in the host countries.

particularly attractive to investors. Hong Kong and Singapore investors were free to respond to these trends from the outset, while the governments of Taiwan and South Korea only began relaxing restriction on capital outflows in 1986. On the push-side, increased FDI reflects increasing wages and other costs of manufacturing in all of these countries that drive them to seek cheaper labour. In most of them, currency appreciation was also a problem for competitiveness. In the case of the NICs, it also reflects their mounting capital surpluses. To sort out some of the country-specific investment patterns and factors driving increasing FDI, a brief survey of the individual countries is in order. Of the ASEAN-4 countries, only the largest overseas investor, Malaysia, will be considered here.

Singapore firms have long been investing elsewhere in East Asia. About 70 per cent of Singapore FDI went just to Malaysia and Hong Kong until 1984. As the first upsurge progressed later in the decade, its overseas investment became more diversified, and, by 1990, only about half of it was going to other East Asian countries. Of Singapore's total stock of outgoing FDI in 1994, 53 per cent was in the financial sector, mostly in investment holding companies, while only 20 per cent was in manufacturing. Of the stock of manufacturing investment, however, 91 per cent was in Asia. Malaysia accounted for about 49 per cent, followed by China with 11 per cent and Indonesia, Thailand and Hong Kong, with 8 per cent each (Singapore, DoS/MTI 1996: Annex Table 3). Although electrical and electronics firms have been particularly visible in this movement, firms across the industrial spectrum are represented. Singaporean private and state enterprises have also been active in construction and industrial park development throughout the region. The Singapore government is strongly committed to growing an 'external wing', and national policy now actively encourages and supports overseas investment and 'regionalisation' of the economy (Singapore MoF 1993a, b). This meshes very well with Japanese corporate 'multi-layering' strategy. A notable portion of Singapore's FDI, particularly the higher-technology investments in ASEAN-4 states, originates with Japanese and other foreign TNCs based there. Fifty-one per cent of the outgoing stock of FDI and 27 per cent of the firms that have gone abroad are wholly or majority foreign-owned (Singapore DoS/MTI 1995: 44–7). These investments can only be understood as part of Japanese and other TNCs' strategies.

Hong Kong overseas investment began in the early 1960s, but it only started growing significantly in the late 1970s. Initially most of this investment went to the ASEAN countries and Taiwan, but in the mid-1980s, FDI in China began to accelerate rapidly. Hong Kong began to relocate manufacturing facilities, particularly in textiles and garment making and other light industries, in China. Well over half of all FDI and an even bigger share of investment in manufacturing in China appears in the records as Hong Kong investment. Hong Kong-based companies in such sectors as electronics, textiles and food production have also moved to the ASEAN countries. As in the case of Singapore, however, these figures are misleading. About 30 per cent of Hong Kong outgoing FDI originates with foreign firms based there (UNCTAD/DTCI 1996: 69). Taiwanese and Southeast Asian Chinese firms have established subsidiaries there to act as conduits for their investment in China. Hong Kong firms are also used for 'round-tripping' (channelling capital through an overseas firm back into its country of origin as FDI in order to take advantage of investment incentives – e.g. tax holidays) by both overseas Chinese and People's Republic of China firms. Much of the manufacturing investment, particularly in adjacent Guangdong, results in so called 'front shop, back factory' arrangements. That is, management, design and marketing functions remain in Hong Kong; capital, machinery and technology come from Hong Kong; manufacturing or assembly is carried out in China. Hong Kong affiliates of Japanese and other TNCs also invest throughout the region, but particularly in China (Taylor 1995). Again, these cases have to be understood in terms of the TNCs' strategies.

Taiwan investment went predominantly to the US through the 1980s, but, from 1990, investment in Southeast Asia and China accelerated rapidly. Larger firms (particularly in electronics) invest in the US primarily for market access reasons and to acquire new technologies. Labour-intensive, lower-technology SMIs (e.g. textiles, apparel and footwear, plastics, electrical equipment) going first to Thailand and Malaysia and then China and Vietnam were responsible for much of the late 1980s and early 1990s investment upsurge. Taiwan's FDI figures greatly underestimate their actual amounts. Many firms failed to report their investments to avoid double taxation, as Taiwan had few tax treaties with Southeast Asian countries until quite recently. Much Taiwanese investment in China appears as Hong Kong investment for political reasons. Of Taiwan's estimated US$25 billion FDI flow in 1987–92, US$12 billion is estimated to have gone to Southeast Asia and US$6 billion to China (*FEER* 1993: 44). This is over 70 per cent of the estimated total for those years. Taiwan has become home to a few large TNCs with widespread production networks (e.g. Acer Computer), and, recently, Taiwan has invested in more capital-intensive and higher-technology industries (e.g. steel, petrochemicals, computer components and peripherals, electronics) in Malaysia and Thailand. Several government- and Kuomintang-owned enterprises have also undertaken or planned sizeable investment in Southeast Asia in such areas as sugar refining, petroleum refining and industrial estate development (*Business Taiwan* 1995). Nonetheless, the bulk of Taiwanese FDI continues to be a product of SMI investment. Taiwan's 'Southward Policy', which aims to expand its economic ties with Southeast Asia, is also politically inspired. It hopes to improve its position relative to China by becoming a political participant in regional organisations and activities (Ku 1995).

South Korea began investing overseas in 1968, but as recently as 1987 more than half its FDI was still in the forestry and fishing industries. In the early 1980s, Korean firms began investing in manufacturing facilities in the US to circumvent trade barriers. Starting in the late 1980s, however, high-technology firms began investing in research facilities and buying existing companies in the US (e.g. electronics, steel, semiconductors, machinery, high-definition television and multimedia) in order to acquire expertise and technology needed to support production in Korea. These investment activities have been actively supported by the Korean government. At the same time, Korean firms began relocating and setting up elsewhere in Asia to take advantage of cheaper labour and land. Both lower- and higher-technology industries (e.g. textiles, plastics, automobile parts, television picture tubes, computer chips and colour monitors, washing machines, and microwave ovens) have been located in ASEAN. Lower-technology labour-intensive industries (e.g. textiles, apparel and footwear, toys, plastics) have been set up in Vietnam and China. By the end of 1995, 44 per cent of aggregate Korean FDI was in Asia and 34 per cent in North America (*Korea Economic Daily* 1996). By far the largest share in Asia was in China, followed by Indonesia, Malaysia and Vietnam. About three-quarters of the investment in Asia was in manufacturing, and a very large portion of this was devoted to export production.

The largest of the Korean TNCs have, like their Japanese counterparts, been creating global and regional networks as they extend abroad. Samsung, Korea's leading *chaebol*, has an overseas network of 314 facilities (35 are production facilities and 11 are R&D centres) in 65 countries. Of these, 142 are in the Asia/Pacific region, including 32 in Japan, 48 in ASEAN countries, and 44 in China (Samsung 1996). Its electronics network is the most comprehensive. Samsung Electronics has 15 overseas facilities and is building 5 large-scale electronics complexes around the world. Overseas production of Samsung Electronics along with that of Goldstar and Daewoo Electronics, currently constitutes 10 per cent of their combined overall production, but this is set to reach 30 per cent by 2000. Daewoo and

77

Kia Motors are both extending production facilities all over the world, and it is expected that by early in the 21st century, about 40 per cent of the total production of Korean auto-makers will take place outside the country (Sohn 1994: 30–2). A comparison of Korean firms' procurement sources and sales destinations shows that they have yet to develop the extensive network of local suppliers that Japanese firms have, and thus they import a larger share of their capital equipment and raw materials from Korea than the latter do from Japan. They also sell less locally and export more to third countries than do Japanese firms (Lee 1995: 42–3).

Malaysia began promoting what it calls 'reverse investment' in 1990. Like the NICs, Malaysia was feeling the pressure of rising domestic labour costs and competition from its lower-wage neighbours, China and Vietnam. 'Reverse investment' is also seen as a way to overcome the limitations of its small domestic market and accelerate economic growth. Malaysia expects such FDI to assist the country in securing technology as well as technical, financial, managerial and marketing skills. It has accordingly dropped a long-standing requirement that each investment be approved by the Ministry of International Trade and Industry and put policies in place actively to encourage outgoing FDI. During the first half of the 1980s, 77 per cent of Malaysian FDI was in Singapore, Hong Kong, Australia and the UK. While it remained concentrated in those countries during the first four years of the 1990s, the proportion dropped to 65 per cent, while it increased in China, the Philippines, Thailand, Vietnam and India (*Business Times* 1995). A sizeable portion of Malaysia's earlier overseas investment was in real estate, but a much larger share of its more recent FDI, particularly in Asia, has been in manufacturing and construction. Both locally owned and joint-venture Malaysian firms are active in a number of industries (e.g. textiles, mattress making, motor vehicle – bus, car and motorcycle – assembly, telecommunications) as well as road and industrial estate building, power generation and banking. Malaysia is now clearly a participant in the extension of regional production networks beyond its borders.

East Asian investment in Malaysia

Examination of the changing pattern of East Asian FDI in Malaysia provides an illustration of the trends outlined above. Table 4.5 shows sources of the stock of investment (equity plus fixed assets) in Malaysian manufacturing companies in 1986 and 1993 and sources of flows of investment (approved equity plus loans) from 1987 to 1995. Between 1987 and 1993, the aggregate investment approvals from ANIC firms very substantially exceeded those from Japanese firms (34 per cent of total approvals versus 23 per cent), and they exceeded them even more in 1994–95 (41 per cent versus 19 per cent). Aggregate ANIC investment exceeded Japanese investment in six of the nine years between 1987 and 1995, and was very close to it in one of the others. The biggest share of ANIC investment during these years came from Taiwan. Indeed, Taiwanese investment alone exceeded Japanese investment in two of those years and nearly matched it in a third. Because loans typically constitute close to two-thirds of amounts of approved investment, this flow has not translated into such a sharp increase in the stock of ANIC investment. Between 1986 and 1993, the stock of East Asian investment increased from 55 per cent to 65 per cent. This increase was matched by a corresponding decline in European investment (29 per cent to 18 per cent), while the portion of aggregate investment from the ANICs increased only slightly. The composition of ANIC investment, however, shifted, as Taiwanese and Korean shares of stock went up and Singapore and Hong Kong stock went down. As will be seen, this in turn translates into more ANIC investment in wholly or majority owned firms at higher levels of technology.

Table 4.5 Foreign investment (equity plus fixed assets) in Malaysian companies in production at end of 1986 and 1993 and in approved projects, 1987–93 and 1994–95 (RM mill./%)

Region/Country	Equity plus fixed assets				Approvals			
	1993		1986		1994–95		1987–93	
East Asia	24,930	(65)	6,257	(55)	n.a.		45,732	(62)
Japan	12,632	(33)	2,680	(23)	3,861	(19)	16,892	(23)
ANICs	11,947	(31)	3,258	(28)	8,451	(41)	24,940	(34)
Singapore	6,610	(17)	2,509	(22)	2,072	(10)	4,567	(6)
Taiwan	3,125	(8)	54	–	4,316	(21)	15,572	(21)
Hong Kong	1,790	(5)	687	(6)	1,049	(5)	1,887	(2)
S. Korea	422	(1)	8	–	1,013	(5)	2,914	(4)
ASEAN-4	337	(1)	319	(3)	n.a.		3,346	(4)
China	14	–	–	–	n.a.		554	(1)
Europe	7,135	(18)	3,293	(29)	n.a.		12,522	(17)
North America	3,514	(9)	1,139	(10)	3,063	(15)	8,685	(12)
Other	2,937	(8)	746	(7)	n.a.		7,395	(10)
Total	38,516	(100)	11,435	(100)	20,483	(100)	74,334	(100)

Sources: 1986–94: Malaysian Industrial Development Authority, *Statistics on the Manufacturing Sector*, selected years.
1995: Malaysia, Ministry of Finance, *Economic Report, 1996/97*, 1996.
Notes: – negligible.
n.a. not available.

Tables 4.6–8 portray the current pattern of this investment in Malaysian manufacturing.[3] The first shows numbers of cases of investment by interests from other East Asian countries by ownership share. The second shows numbers of cases and equity plus fixed assets by level of technology. Multiple cases of investment are found in 18 per cent of the Malaysian companies in the survey, so the number of cases (1,950) is larger than the number of companies (1,591) in which the investments have been made. Table 4.6 shows sharp differences with respect to ownership shares between Japanese, Taiwanese and Korean interests on the one hand and Singapore, Hong Kong, ASEAN-4 and the very few Chinese interests on the other. Between 53 per cent and 61 per cent of the former group have invested in wholly- or majority-owned companies. These investors are presumably all firms based in those countries. A much smaller portion of the latter group (12 per cent to 28 per cent) have majority shares. Particularly notable is the large portion of interests in the latter group that hold shares of less than 10 per cent. This is the case for over a third of Singapore interests and well over half of Hong Kong and ASEAN-4 interests, and in the latter cases, a very big portion hold shares of 1 per cent or less. In some instances, these small shares appear to be held by firms tied to firms from other countries also investing in the Malaysian company. In others, they appear to be individual and institutional portfolio investors. Hence, some cases, albeit representing a very small portion of equity, are not FDI at all.

Table 4.6 Ownership shares by interests from other East Asian countries in Malaysian manufacturing companies, 1995

Country	No.	% wholly/ majority owned	% equity (no./%)					
			100.00	99.99 – 50.01	50.00 – 30.01	30.00 – 10.01	10.00 – 1.01	1.00 or less
Japan	477	(61)	185 (39)	106 (22)	65 (14)	68 (14)	37 (8)	16 (3)
Taiwan	316	(61)	119 (38)	72 (23)	43 (14)	53 (17)	17 (5)	12 (4)
Korea	32	(53)	10 (31)	7 (22)	7 (22)	8 (25)	–	–
Singapore	794	(28)	115 (14)	115 (14)	114 (14)	186 (23)	219 (28)	45 (6)
Hong Kong	252	(21)	29 (12)	23 (9)	29 (12)	36 (14)	58 (23)	77 (31)
Indonesia	35	(15)	2 (6)	3 (9)	3 (9)	7 (20)	3 (9)	17 (49)
Thailand	32	–	–	–	6 (19)	7 (22)	3 (9)	16 (50)
Philippines	4	–	–	–	–	–	2 (50)	2 (50)
China	8	(12)	–	1 (12)	3 (37)	2 (25)	2 (25)	–

Source: Malaysian Industrial Development Authority, *Survey of Companies in Production as at 31 December 1994.*

Table 4.7 gives a rough approximation of the levels of technology (see note* to table) of the Malaysian companies in which the other East Asian interests have invested. Japanese and Taiwanese investments are most numerous (43 per cent and 42 per cent of cases) and the largest (60 per cent and 58 per cent of equity plus fixed assets) in high- and medium–high-technology companies in Malaysia. South Korean investments are also numerous (47 per cent) but smaller (19 per cent) in such companies. Not surprisingly, these are the same countries whose firms have the largest portion of controlling shares. Investing firms are most intent on having control of higher-technology companies. Level of technology is also one of the factors considered by the Malaysian government in determining the permissible ownership shares of foreign investors. In any case, it also has to be noted that Japanese and Taiwanese firms have a greater propensity to establish wholly- or majority-owned companies (61 per cent each) than they do to establish high- and medium–high-technology companies (43 per cent and 42 per cent respectively). By contrast, the overwhelming majority of cases of Singapore, Hong Kong, ASEAN-4 and Chinese investment are in medium–low- and low-technology companies.

With the exception of ASEAN-4, this is consistent with the respective portions of their investments in the same sectors. The apparently large discrepancy in ASEAN-4 investments (only 23 per cent of cases but 76 per cent of investment in high- and medium–high-technology sectors) is accounted for by a few relatively large investments in chemicals.

Table 4.7 Interests from other East Asian countries in Malaysian manufacturing companies by levels of technology, 1994

Technology Level*	Total	Cases (number / %)			Equity + Fixed Assets (RM bn / %)		
		Hi / Med – Hi	Med–Lo	Lo	Hi / Med – Hi	Med – Lo	Lo
Japan	477	207 / 43	107 / 22	163 / 34	7.603 / 60	1.908 / 15	3.125 / 25
South Korea	32	15 / 47	7 / 22	10 / 31	0.081 / 19	0.256 / 61	0.085 / 20
Taiwan	316	132 / 42	52 / 16	132 / 42	1.829 / 58	0.154 / 5	1.141 / 37
Singapore	794	197 / 25	172 / 22	425 / 54	2.035 / 31	1.346 / 20	3.229 / 49
Hong Kong	252	61 / 24	53 / 21	138 / 55	0.717 / 40	0.084 / 5	0.989 / 55
ASEAN-3	71	16 / 23	19 / 27	36 / 51	0.255 / 76	0.007 / 2	0.075 / 22
China	8	1 / 12	5 / 62	2 / 25	–	0.013 / 87	0.002 / 13
Total	1950	629 / 32	415 / 21	906 / 46	12.520 / 50	3.768 / 15	8.646 / 35

Sources: Cases: Malaysian Industrial Development Authority, *Survey of Companies in Production as at 31 December 1994.*

Equity + Fixed Assets: *Malaysian Industrial Development Authority, Statistics on the Manufacturing Sector, 1990–1994*: 18–20. These figures are as at 31 December 1993.

Notes: * Hi and Medium–Hi: Electrical/Electronic, Transport Equipment, Chemicals/Petroleum; Medium–Lo: Machinery, Non-metal Minerals, Rubber/Plastic; Lo: Basic Metals, Fabricated Metals, Food/Beverages, Paper/Printing; Textiles/Garments; Wood/Furniture.

This is a very rough classification. Greater refinement could be achieved by basing the classification on sub-sectors. Data is available to do this for cases but not equity + fixed assets, so for the sake of comparability, the rougher classification has been used for both. This classification tends to overestimate investments in the Hi/Medium–Hi category and underestimate the rest. It is, however, adequate for roughly showing the differences among the East Asian countries.

Table 4.8 shows investments in firms in three categories: first, firms wholly owned by companies from other East Asian countries; second, firms that are joint ventures between interests in other East Asian countries (mostly companies, but in some cases, individuals) and Malaysian interests (companies, government bodies, nominees, individuals); and third, firms that are joint ventures between other East Asian interests (in some cases wholly owned; in others, including Malaysian interests as well). Several things stand out in this table. First, the electrical and electronic sector is unique in two notable regards. About two-thirds of all of the firms in that sector have investment from interests in other East Asian countries, while the comparable figures for other sectors range from around one-third to one-half. Over half of the electrical and electronic firms with East Asian investment are also shown to be wholly owned by the foreign companies. As will be seen in another context,

Table 4.8 Investment by interests from other East Asian countries in Malaysian manufacturing firms by industrial sector, 1995

	Total	Electrical/ electronic	Transport equipment	Chemicals/ petroleum	Machinery	Non-metal/ minerals	Rubber/ plastic	Basic metal	Fabricated metal	Food/ beverages	Paper/ printing	Textiles/ garments	Wood furniture	Other
Firms wholly owned by companies from:														
Japan	185	83	5	11	12	7	14	9	9	3	4	11	7	10
Taiwan	120	54	1	2	4	1	4	2	13	–	1	12	23	3
Singapore	115	34	1	4	7	–	9	4	9	12	5	17	5	8
Hong Kong	29	7	–	2	3	–	5	–	–	1	1	7	2	1
South Korea	10	5	–	–	1	1	–	–	–	–	–	–	3	–
ASEAN-3	2	–	–	–	–	–	–	–	–	1	–	–	–	1
Subtotal	461	183	7	19	27	9	32	15	31	17	11	47	40	23
Joint ventures between Malaysian companies and interests from:														
Singapore	442	41	12	38	8	35	59	8	51	77	22	44	38	9
Japan	172	32	11	14	13	12	22	15	20	13	1	5	8	6
Taiwan	125	34	4	6	4	5	22	4	10	4	4	9	16	4
Hong Kong	67	6	2	5	1	–	7	2	4	8	4	18	8	2
ASEAN-3	20	1	2	1	2	3	2	1	2	3	–	2	–	–
South Korea	17	3	–	5	–	2	1	–	1	–	1	1	3	–
China	4	1	–	–	1	–	1	–	–	1	–	–	–	–
Subtotal	847	118	31	69	29	57	114	30	88	106	32	79	73	21
Joint ventures between interests from (and in some but not all cases Malaysian companies):														
Jap-Tai	13	8	–	–	–	2	–	1	2	–	–	–	–	–
Jap-HK	12	1	1	4	–	2	1	–	1	–	–	–	2	–
Jap-Kor	3	1	–	1	–	–	–	–	–	–	1	–	–	–
Jap-Sin +	64	15	4	6	4	5	5	8	5	3	–	2	5	2
Jap-Sin-HK +	28	6	1	3	1	5	2	2	–	3	2	2	1	–
Sin-HK +	93	4	5	7	2	10	8	4	9	17	2	11	11	3
Sin-Tai +	27	8	2	1	1	3	1	–	2	–	1	2	4	2
Sin-HK-Tai +	7	–	1	1	–	2	1	1	–	–	1	–	–	–
Sin-ASE +	16	1	–	2	–	1	1	2	1	3	1	1	3	–
Sin-Kor	2	–	–	–	–	–	2	–	–	–	–	–	–	–
Tai-HK +	14	3	–	2	–	1	–	–	–	–	2	4	2	–
Tai or HK +	4	–	–	–	–	–	2	–	–	–	–	1	–	1
Subtotal	283	47	14	27	8	31	23	18	20	26	10	23	28	8
Total East Asia	1591	348	52	115	64	97	169	63	139	149	53	149	141	52
All Firms	3671	511	146	247	140	222	426	116	284	468	164	335	501	111
% East Asia	43	68	36	47	46	44	40	54	49	32	32	44	28	47

Source: Malaysian Industrial Development Authority, *Survey of Companies in Production as at 31 December 1994.*

Notes: + May also include investment from other East Asian countries.

▓ Hi / Medium Hi Tech
▒ Medium Lo Tech
☐ Lo Tech

however, the portion is actually higher than indicated owing to a number of joint ventures that are wholly owned by Japanese companies and their regional affiliates. In any case, wholly owned companies do not constitute anywhere near this large a share in any other sector. Again, this reflects the relationship between technology level and the imperative for control. A number of the joint ventures between Japanese companies and ANICs, especially Singapore, and some joint ventures between ANICs reflect Japanese TNCs' 'multi-layering' strategy. Some joint ventures that bring together combinations of Singapore, Hong Kong, Taiwan and/or ASEAN-4 interests also undoubtedly involve Chinese business networks.

Table 4.9 Malaysian technology agreements by source, 1975 to July 1996

Country	1975–79		1980–84		1985–89		1990–94		1995–7/96	
	No.	%	No.	%	No.	%	No.	%	No.	%
East Asia	124	(40)	247	(42)	305	(45)	495	(60)	123	(69)
Japan	103	(33)	185	(31)	249	(37)	403	(49)	97	(55)
ANICs	21	(7)	62	(11)	56	(8)	88	(11)	24	(13)
South Korea	2	(1)	12	(2)	8	(1)	31	(4)	11	(6)
Taiwan*	n.a.	n.a.	n.a.	n.a.	n.a.	n.a.	21	(3)	3	(2)
Singapore	10	(3)	27	(5)	16	(2)	20	(2)	6	(3)
Hong Kong	9	(3)	23	(4)	32	(5)	16	(2)	4	(2)
ASEAN-3*	n.a.	n.a.	n.a.	n.a.	n.a.	n.a.	4	–	2	(1)
Europe	82	(26)	135	(23)	147	(22)	162	(20)	29	(16)
US	28	(9)	65	(11)	82	(12)	100	(12)	21	(12)
Other	79	(25)	142	(24)	143	(21)	61	(7)	5	(3)
Total	313	(100)	589	(100)	677	(100)	818	(100)	178	(100)

Sources: 1975–89: Ministry of International Trade and Industry, Malaysia, cited in Anuwar (1992: 85).
1990–96: Malaysian Industrial Development Authority.
Note: * Figures for Taiwan and ASEAN-3 (Thailand, Indonesia, Philippines) not available for 1975–89, and any agreements with either during those years would be included in Other.

As ANIC firms have become larger investors in Malaysia, they have entered into relatively more formal technology transfer agreements in the country. Table 4.9 shows technology agreements by source from 1975 through July 1996, and it can be seen that those involving ANIC firms have increased since 1990. Since that time, the number of ANIC and ASEAN-3 agreements have exceeded those entered into by US-based firms and have been catching up with those by European firms. Their number is, however, only about a quarter of the number by Japanese firms. To some extent these proportions reflect relative propensity to enter into joint ventures (that of the US being lower than that of Japan or the ANICs). In any case, referring back to Table 4.5, it is clear that the proportion of Japanese agreements in the most recent period well exceeds the proportion of Japanese investment stock (55 per cent and 33 per cent respectively), and that the reverse is true for the ANIC plus ASEAN-3 agreements (14 per cent and 31 per cent). The foregoing difference between Japanese and ANIC firms reflects several things. One is the already noted proportionally larger number of Japanese firms in higher-technology sectors, where such agreements are more prevalent. Another is the generally lower level of technology of many ANIC firms relative to Japanese firms even in the latter sectors. Still another is the difference in the extent to which Japanese and ANIC firms are central to expanding production networks, because technology agreements are very much part of such networking. A great many agreements are actually between TNCs and their local affiliates rather than with Malaysian companies, though the portion varies greatly from sector to sector, from about 10 per cent in motor vehicles to about 90 per cent in electronics (Interviews, MIDA officials, January 1997). And, as noted, licensing technology is one of the ways in which otherwise independent local firms are integrated into production networks. As many as 50 per cent of the technology agreements in the motor vehicle sector are, for example, between foreign and wholly-owned Malaysian companies supplying the sector (the remaining 40 per cent are in joint ventures between foreign and Malaysian companies). The small but still notable difference between the number of agreements entered into by Korean and the other ANIC firms also probably reflects some of the same kinds of differences.

Complexity and hierarchy in the regional division of labour

The foregoing developments raise many questions. Are the advent of ANIC- and ASEAN-4-based FDI and the increasing numbers of local suppliers being incorporated into regional production networks creating a less hierarchical and more diverse and decentralised regional division of labour? Do the trends described tend to cut across the hierarchical relationships in existing production networks and/or to create more competition between proliferating production networks? If so, will a more pluralistic, balanced and competitive environment improve the industrialisation prospects of some or all of the ASEAN states? Will it, for example, feature conditions more favourable to the improvement of technological capacities by local firms? Will a more diverse and more competitive region offer more alternative sources of capital and technology and more channels of access to markets – conditions that could improve the bargaining leverage of regional firms and states? Will ANIC-based TNCs be any more likely than Japanese TNCs willingly to facilitate the industrial advance of firms and states in the tier behind them or will they form an additional line of resistance, and, if so, will the latter firms and states have greater bargaining leverage with them?

These questions cannot all be answered here, but the place to begin an inquiry into them is with the question of the extent to which the regional division of labour is in fact becoming more pluralistic and less hierarchical as it becomes more complex. The FDI figures do not give an accurate picture, because while some investment is autonomous, much is proxy for or dependent on investment by a firm based in a third, more advanced, country. Of concern here is Japan proxy or dependent investment. These distinctions rest on the origins of investment decisions and on various types of dependence (e.g. technological, capital, market). The three types of FDI are distinguished as follows: first, *autonomous* – an independent firm takes the decision to invest; second, *proxy* – a dependent firm invests on the basis of a decision made by the firm(s) on which it is dependent; and third, *dependent* – a dependent firm takes the decision to invest. It is clearly misleading to count proxy investment and much dependent investment as FDI of the country where the investing firm is based (Bernard and Ravenhill 1995: 185–7). To the extent that FDI is in the last two categories, it tends to extend hierarchy in the Japan-centred regional division of labour rather than to diminish it.

What types of ANIC and ASEAN-4 manufacturing FDI are most likely to fall into each of these categories? The foregoing survey shows this investment to be of three basic types: first, large, more technologically advanced TNCs investing in the US, Japan and/or Europe for market access and/or technology acquisition; second, larger and medium-sized, more technologically advanced firms investing in other ANICs and ASEAN-4 states to gain cost advantages, export platforms and/or market access; and third, lower-technology, more labour-intensive SMIs investing in the ASEAN-4, but increasingly relocating to China or Vietnam for the same reasons as the latter. Mid- and low-technology SMIs are the most likely to be capital- and/or technology-independent and thus to make autonomous investments. TNCs or mid-sized firms that have 'strategic alliances' with Japanese TNCs or mid-sized firms are the most likely to make proxy or dependent investments. By definition, FDI originating with wholly- or majority-owned, locally based firms are proxy investments. Among dependent firms, those most likely to make proxy investments are either suppliers to the firms on which they are dependent or have special characteristics that in some way improve access to host countries for the firms on which they are dependent.

Proxy investment: some examples

Owing to the long-standing openness of Singapore's economy and its attractiveness as a location to many TNCs, a significant portion of Singapore FDI originates with foreign-owned firms. In 1993, 51 per cent of the stock of outgoing FDI and 27 per cent of the firms that have gone abroad are wholly or majority foreign-owned (Singapore DoS, MTI 1995: 44–7). Hence, at least half of the value and over a quarter of the cases of Singapore FDI at that time were, by definition, proxy investment. A significant portion of Hong Kong investment is in the same category. For example:[4] first, Asia Chinon Precision Sdn Bhd (floppy disk drives and printers) in Johor is wholly owned by Chinon Asia Pte Ltd of Singapore, which is in turn wholly owned by Chinon Industrial Co. Ltd of Japan; second, Omron (M) Sdn Bhd (electro-magnetic relays) in Shah Alam is 10 per cent owned by Omron Corporation of Japan and 90 per cent by Omron Management Centre Asia Pacific Pte Ltd (the firm's regional OHQ) of Singapore, which is in turn wholly owned by Omron Corporation of Japan; third, Maxell Electronics (M) Sdn Bhd. (video tapes and floppy disks) in Melaka was, until recently repatriated to Japan, 72.2 per cent owned by Hitachi Maxell Co. Ltd of Japan and 27.3 per cent by Maxell Asia of Hong Kong, which is in turn wholly owned by Hitachi Maxell Co. Ltd. of Japan. Note that however little or much Japanese equity there is in these three companies, they are (or were), with Singapore or Hong Kong proxy investment, wholly Japanese-owned firms. These are only a few of numerous examples that could be given. Japanese TNCs structure their Singapore-linked operations in this way to take advantage of Singapore's excellent location for their 'regional focus' strategy in Southeast Asia; the incentives its government offers for locating OHQ there; and of access to ethnic Chinese regional networks with local nodes. Japanese TNCs are, of course, not the only ones that organise their operations in this manner. Motorola Malaysia Sdn Bhd (semiconductor components) and Motorola (M) Sdn Bhd (semi-conductors) appear on the record as 100 per cent Hong Kong rather than American owned. Clearly, this kind of investment has to be understood in terms of TNC strategies, and Japanese TNCs are pre-eminent in this regard.

There is a large measure of personalism in inter-business, inter-governmental and business–government relationships in the ANICs and in Southeast Asia. While personalism is also prevalent in Japan, the highly bureaucratised nature of big Japanese corporations and the difficulties that many Japanese have in operating outside their own linguistic orbit can reduce the effectiveness of Japanese businesses elsewhere in the region. For these reasons, Japanese firms sometimes rely on local partners to take the lead in overseas investment in the region. For example, Ulbon Bhd is Malaysia's leading producer of high-tensile steel rods used in pre-stressed concrete (PC) construction piles and power transmission poles. Neturen, a Japanese firm, holds a minority interest in Ulbon and similar manufacturing firms in Korea and Taiwan and exclusive rights to the technology used in hardening the steel rods. Neturen, wanting to set up a PC plant in China in 1996 that would use this tech-nology, decided that Ulbon should take the lead in the China venture. Ulbon's Japanese Managing Director explained to the Malaysian press: 'For political rea-sons, the Taiwanese concern may not be able to play a vital role while Malaysia has the advantage over South Korea and Japan in terms of language. For this reason, the venture into the Chinese market will be led by the Malaysian party' (New Straits Times 1996). Following a similar strategy, Mitsubishi Motor Corporation (MMC) has formed a joint venture with its Taiwan affiliate, China Motor Corp. and a Chinese auto-maker to assemble vans in Fujian, with the engines, transmis-sions and other key parts coming from Mitsubishi. MMC's stated aim is to take advantage of China Motors' 'cultural familiarity with Fujian' (*The Nikkei Weekly* 1996a). Additional Japanese TNCs are expected to follow the same practice.

On similar logic, but for somewhat different reasons, Mitsubishi Motors formed a joint venture (Vinastar) with a Vietnamese state firm and Proton, Malaysia's national car company, in 1994 to assemble small buses and trucks in Vietnam. MMC is part-owner of and supplies parts and technology to Proton. While happy to be included in this project and to take a 25 per cent share, Proton was not involved in planning it (Interview, Malaysian auto industry insider, December 1996). It was, rather, part of Mitsubishi Corporation's 1993 Comprehensive

Master Plan for the Automotive Industry drawn up for presentation to the government of Vietnam. At the time, the Mitsubishi Managing Director said his firm was in 'an advantageous position to enter the Vietnamese market compared with other Japanese automakers because of a decade-old co-operative tie with Proton . . . [W]e benefited from the close ties between Vietnam and Malaysia' (*The Japan Times* 1994). Proton's input on its own experience with Mitsubishi was helpful to Mitsubishi in the Vietnamese government's licensing process. Presumably, this is one of the reasons that Proton was included in Vinastar. In any case, the firm is assembling completely knocked-down (CKD) kits which contain many components that are either directly or indirectly of Japanese origin. The two foregoing MMC cases represent Taiwanese and Malaysian FDI, but are examples of proxy investment based on special characteristics of the local firms. While no doubt advantageous to the Taiwanese and Malaysian partners, both result in extension of the Japan-centred regional division of labour.

Dependent investment: some examples

Proxy investment is relatively easy to identify because it can be determined by the origin of the investment decision. It can, for example, simply be assumed in the many cases of investment by wholly owned subsidiaries. Dependent investment can be more difficult to identify, as there are different types and degrees of dependence. A firm may be dependent to various degrees on one or more other firms for capital, technology, a market, materials and supplies, or some combination of these. Moreover, the distinction between proxy and dependent investment may be blurred in cases where dependent firms are making their own investment decisions in response to being 'asked' to relocate by a TNC they do subcontract work for or in a context where following such a TNC when it relocates is the only reasonable 'choice'. In any case, the most important distinction is between proxy and dependent investment on the one hand and autonomous investment on the other. ANIC and ASEAN-4 firms' Japanese proxy or dependent investment, to varying degrees, extends and consolidates Japanese corporate production networks in East Asia, while their autonomous investment, being primarily in smaller and lower-technology undertakings, does little to disperse power within it.

In many cases, even the most advanced Korean and Taiwanese TNCs remain quite dependent on imported Japanese and, to a lesser extent, American technology. According to Bloom (1993: 120), Korean TNCs Samsung and Lucky Goldstar, which have several regional production facilities in Southeast Asia, became 'global companies as a by-product of the role they came to play in the globalization of Japanese companies and in the counter-strategies of American companies in their own competition with the Japanese'. This process started when Samsung was involved in joint ventures with NEC and Sanyo and Goldstar with NEC and Alps Electric. When the Japanese partners later withdrew from these joint ventures, they entered technology licensing and OEM agreements with the latter. Both companies are still

87

tied to a system in which they are either producing as a proxy for Japanese companies . . . or helping American companies compete against the Japanese. Even where overseas sales are on an own name basis, Japanese companies benefit from supplying the higher value-added components.

(Bloom 1993: 125)

Korean high-technology industry also remains quite import-dependent. Yu (1995: 97) says that

the critical parts and components . . . as well as the manufacturing equipment and facilities necessary for the manufacture of . . . [high-tech] . . . products are still imported, mostly from Japan. This is shown in trade statistics – the more high-tech products Korea exports, the more it has to import from Japan.

Indicative of the import dependence of Korean electronics firms, for example, is a 1993 Bank of Korea study showing that only 38 per cent of the value of semiconductors was added in Korea (cited by Bernard and Ravenhill 1995: 191). Such import dependence on higher-technology components, many of them from Japan, is also characteristic of Taiwanese firms. Indeed, 90 per cent of Taiwan's imports from Japan are parts and components for manufactured products and machinery to make them with. Bernard found that while Taiwanese firms accounted for 39 per cent of world computer monitor production in 1991, 'the key component, the cathode ray tube, is procured exclusively from Japanese suppliers, and these tubes represent between 30 and 35 per cent of the cost of a monitor' (Bernard and Ravenhill 1995: 193). These are problems that the governments and leading firms of both countries are working very hard to overcome, but this remains a long-term project. In any case, when such firms set up production facilities in Southeast Asia, which in turn must rely on Japanese parts and components or Korean components with substantial Japanese content, they also serve to extend Japan-centred production networks.

A 1993 study conducted by the Singapore Institute of Policy Studies of the overseas investments of 14 manufacturing companies that were wholly- or majority-owned by Singapore citizens or permanent residents also offers several good examples of dependent investment (Lee 1994). In several cases based primarily on market dependence, companies that had been supplying Japanese TNCs in Singapore followed them to neighbouring ASEAN countries. Amtek Engineering Ltd, a maker of precision metal parts, for example, had set up two subsidiaries in Selangor and near Penang and was planning to set up a third in Johor, all in Malaysia, primarily to sell to Japanese electronics firms now located there (Lee 1994: 12–16). In other cases, firms producing on an OEM basis for corporations in Japan have relocated to Malaysia to take advantage of lower production costs. Material Handling Engineering Ltd has set up two factories in the Shah Alam, Malaysia industrial estate (Lee 1994: 57–61). One produces press bearings and press wheels, 80 per cent of which go directly to Japan on an OEM basis from Malaysia instead of Singapore. These investments originate with Singaporean firms and show up in the statistics as Singaporean FDI, but it tends to extend and consolidate rather than cut across the Japan-centred regional division of labour. This is all the more so in cases in which such firms are dependent on Japanese technology and supplies of intermediate goods in addition to their dependence on sales to Japanese TNCs.

In addition to its aforementioned involvement in truck and bus assembly in Vietnam, Malaysia's Proton entered into a joint auto assembly venture in the Philippines in 1994. Indicative of the importance of personal ties in Southeast Asian government and business affairs, the initial steps on this were taken by Malaysian Prime Minister, Dr Mahathir, and Philippine President Ramos during exchanges of official visits. President Ramos ordered relaxation of his country's restrictive national car development programme to make the project possible. The plant has been located some 200 kilometres north of Manila, in Pangasinan, Ramos's home province. Mitsubishi, which assembles cars on its own in the Philippines, was displeased with this move, as it has been with several previous independent initiatives taken by Proton (most notably exporting to the UK), but could not stop it. Mitsubishi has no capital stake in Proton Pilipinas, which is a joint venture between Proton and well-connected private firms in Malaysia and the Philippines. Nonetheless, the Philippine firm is assembling CKD kits with significant Japanese content. This Proton venture is structurally different from the one in Vietnam and could possibly result in more long-term benefits for Malaysia, but for the time being, owing to the dependence on Mitsubishi technology and components, this venture also extends the Japan-centred division of labour in the motor vehicle sector.

Conclusions: hierarchy and industrial development

What do the developments outlined to this point promise for countries in lower tiers of the regional division of labour? The advent of new regional sources of FDI has made the East Asian division of labour more complex, but it remains largely hierarchical. Wide dispersal of production sites in a hierarchically organised production network does not translate into a commensurately wide dispersal of the economic benefits of production either between countries or within them. Such benefits are determined primarily by where value is added and how it is shared. These questions are continuously at issue between countries at different levels in the regional and global division of labour as those below seek to move up and those on top seek to stay there. They are regularly joined in negotiations over such matters as localisation, technology transfer, exports, taxation, regulation and market access. The enormous asymmetry of economic power between Japan and its neighbours means that the results of such negotiations for regional states are often acceptance of benefits that are largely concessions granted on Japanese corporate terms or extracted only after extremely hard bargaining. This problem is compounded by the fact that the Japanese corporate system into which its neighbours are increasingly integrated is undergoing changes that work to the detriment of its less powerful participants. The seriousness of the long slump in Japan is altering corporate practices in ways that will be to the permanent disadvantage of small and medium-sized industries that act as suppliers (and which have, in any case, normally taken the brunt of economic downturns) and of many employees. This is reflected in Japanese corporate operations both at home and overseas.

One of Japanese TNCs' purposes in building and extending global and regional production networks has been to enhance operational flexibility in order to protect themselves from unfavourable international economic currents – most recently, the high yen. Just as these firms shifted production to Southeast Asia in response to yen appreciation, they have recently been shifting some of it back home as the yen has weakened. For example, Kyushu Matsushita Electric Co. (KMEC) transferred production of one of its popular personal fax machines from Japan to Johor when the yen reached 90 to 1 US dollar in spring 1995 and then began moving it back to Japan in early 1996 when the yen fell to 110 to 1 US dollar. Hitachi Maxell has also returned videotape production from Melaka to Japan. A company manager explained, 'it is our policy to determine how much to produce overseas and to buy imported parts according to foreign exchange rates and other conditions at the time' (*The Nikkei Weekly* 1996b). Fujitsu, which currently procures nearly all of its PC motherboards from Taiwan, plans soon to resume making 30 per cent of them in Japan (*International Herald Tribune* 1997). Similarly, this kind of flexibility makes it possible readily to shift production facilities for other reasons. Aiwa, for example, which made 90 per cent of its mini-stereo systems in Malaysia until 1995, now makes 70 per cent of them in Japan. They made this shift because they needed new key parts, developed by Sony and Sharp and available only in Japan, and it was more cost-effective to produce near the source (*FEER* 1996). While this repatriation to Japan of regional production facilities has yet to become widespread, as the Nikkei put it, in giving evidence of this capacity, 'the power of [the Japanese production] system is being demonstrated as the yen moves [down]' (*The Nikkei Weekly* 1996b). This kind of flexibility clearly enhances the relative power of those who make the decisions about location of production facilities in relation to those who host them.

The boundaries within which much of the industrial development of East Asian states takes place are carefully tended by Japanese TNCs. The extent to which this is so, of course, varies from country to country. As the introduction to this volume makes clear, the capacity of individual states and firms in the lower tiers of the regional division of labour to make effective use of technology has a major bearing on their prospects for industrial development (see also Evans 1995). It also varies from sector to sector. In any case, boundary maintenance is for the most part simply a consequence of the business strategies Japanese firms employ in expanding and deepening their regional production networks. Japanese firms may at times adjust boundaries for their own reasons, but when states or firms in lower tiers of the regional division of labour push these boundaries, Japanese firms are

THE EAST ASIAN DIVISION OF LABOUR

very likely to attempt to maintain them. This does not always work, as Proton's export programme and move to the Philippines demonstrates. Nonetheless, Japanese control over the flow of technology and the conditions under which it is used by their neighbours is the central mechanism for maintaining these boundaries. This is why so many ANIC and ASEAN firms are technologically dependent on Japan and, hence, one of the reasons that growing complexity in the regional division of labour has not translated directly into greater pluralisation and erosion of hierarchy.

M. Taylor (1995: 14) argues that the 'Japanese have long taken a strategic approach to technology transfer [and that their] firms now dominate [Southeast Asian] economies through strategic control of technology'. He reminds us that the edge Japan currently enjoys in some industries was to a large extent created with technology purchased from American firms, and contends that Japan 'is determined not to repeat American mistakes. Fearful of initiating a similar competitive backlash, Japanese firms currently investing in Southeast Asia focus on market penetration and the control of outward flows of technology'. He says that 'Japanese firms have been careful to retain control over their vital know-how when doing business in developing countries' and lists some of the methods they use for limiting technology flows in joint ventures. He says that such ventures' capital dependence and the fact that Japanese expatriates retain control of key managerial and technical positions keeps 'decisions about technology in Japanese hands . . . [so that] decisions regarding the amount and type of technology transferred depend on the Japanese headquarters' global strategies, not on local interests'. He maintains that because local employees are not trained for higher-level positions, they do not develop the capacity to implement technology independently. He further argues that 'Japan's relatively closed markets prevent Southeast Asian high-technology firms from earning the profits required for further technology transfer and from building the customer bases necessary for economies of scale' (Taylor 1995: 15–17). Much more direct forms of resistance to the independent technological advance of other regional states – such as dumping products that others have finally succeeded in localising (Yu 1995: 98), manipulative pricing practices, fragmentation of production processes, and arbitrary application of standards (Machado 1994: 309–10) – should be added to this list.

The degree to which technology flows to the rest of Asia are shaped and limited by Japanese TNCs' larger strategies is shown by a 1994 Long Term Credit Bank of Japan (LTCB) survey. They asked whether increasing production overseas would weaken Japan's technological edge, and concluded that it would not. A survey of 101 major Japanese manufacturers showed that most overseas operations mass-produce 'general-purpose products . . . [and that] most companies continue to do prototype production and mass-production of newly developed products in Japan'. Of the respondents 55 per cent said they 'expect to move their general-purpose product manufacturing abroad within three years'. Asked what operations have to stay in Japan: 87 per cent said basic research; 72 per cent, applied research; 51 per cent, prototype production; and 48 per cent, design and development. Firms in the general survey predicted that 22 per cent of their US and European operations, but only 6 per cent of their Asian operations would take over basic design for more than half of their products within three years. With respect to planned development and improvement of production technology, respondents were asked to pick from three options: first, increase technological development in Japan and transfer know-how abroad; second, have Japanese engineers perform technological development at production sites abroad; third, have local engineers perform technological development at production sites abroad. The response ratios in the order of the three options were 3:3:2 for US and European operations and 4:2:1 for Asian operations (*The Nikkei Weekly* 1995b).

The LTCB analyst concluded that it

> seems inevitable that some R&D work will be shifted abroad in the future, [but] the amount of research activity . . . [in Asia will] . . . be limited. Some design modification and development or improvement of production technologies that fall short of major technological innovation will probably be performed in Asia.
>
> (*The Nikkei Weekly* 1995b)

A Japanese analyst explains that

> by keeping the innovation capacity of critical [high-technology] parts at home, we free ourselves from . . . fear of . . . *hollowing* . . . [T]he development of high technology . . . facilitat[es] a corporate strategy in which the competitive edge is maintained by keeping and concentrating on the R&D [for] critical parts [at] home . . . [while shifting manufacturing overseas].
>
> (Kodama 1995: 41–2)

What is, however, also being shifted to other East Asian countries is a share of the costs of the key R&D work that will remain in Japan and that will perpetuate these other countries' technological dependence. It has been reported that 'to fund domestic R&D, manufacturers have begun tapping overseas subsidiaries for greater dividend payments, raising transfer prices and taking other measures to bring profits back home.' They are also said to be tapping 'royalty income from technology transfers to overseas bases' for the same purpose (*The Nikkei Weekly* 1994).

Felker and Weiss (1995: 386–9) offer an analysis of technological trajectories that helps to explain the problem faced by countries in the lower tiers of the regional division of labour. They define technology development strategies by the relative weights assigned to three dimensions of technological development: first, deepening (moving from production capabilities to process or product innovation capabilities and eventually to research capabilities); second, indigenisation (degree to which indigenous personnel have mastered technology); and third, proximity to the frontier (distance of a specific technology from the most productive or sophisticated one available). They argue that progress along one dimension is likely to be at the expense of progress along another and that the 'key strategic imperative facing developing-country governments . . . is to minimise the trade-offs between these dimensions over time' (Felker and Weiss 1995: 394). It is progress in deepening and indigenisation that builds the underpinnings for secure and self-sustaining industrial advance. Technologically dependent firms may, however, more easily approach the frontier in partnership with more advanced foreign firms than develop the capacities to get close to it on their own.

Morris-Suzuki (1992) argues that the specialisation dictated by the requirements of transnational networked production limits the possibilities for modifying and adapting technology to local needs and does little to stimulate innovation, processes that facilitate deepening. Another consequence is 'a widening gap between modern factories using imported technologies and small firms in traditional areas of man-ufacturing' (Morris-Suzuki 1992: 145). Hence, the development of backward linkages is often based on tie-ups between local and Japanese firms or outright relo-cation of Japanese suppliers rather than indigenisation. This both perpetuates technological dependence and further extends the Japan-centred regional divi-sion of labour. Some highly innovative studies in the electronics sector in Malaysia might appear to refute this argument, as they show technological advancement among Malaysian firms as a result of their subcontracting work for TNCs. Rasiah (1994) shows that local machine-tool makers advanced technologically as a result of working with TNCs. The one Japanese TNC (six were North American) included in his study, however, used its own machine-tools and was thus an excep-tion to his findings. In a more extensive survey, Nazari (1995) finds local suppliers to have benefited technologically from their ties to TNCs. While he does not sys-tematically compare results for links with TNCs based in different countries, he makes a number of observations that qualify his conclusions insofar as ties with Japanese TNCs are concerned. For example, he finds Japanese TNCs less inclined to procure locally than American and European firms. He thinks that this is because American and European TNCs tend to have Malaysian-Chinese pur-chasing managers with personal ties to local suppliers, while Japanese TNCs tend to have Japanese expatriate purchasing managers (Nazari 1995: 129–30). This is not a convincing explanation. Japanese TNC personnel assignments and procure-ment practices are based on policies intended to maintain network boundaries. If Japanese firms were interested in local sourcing in these cases, they would also hire Chinese-Malaysian purchasing managers if they thought it advantageous.

To understand how hierarchy in the division of labour is maintained and how it is eroded, when it is, it is necessary to focus on the activities at this boundary. These are primarily interactions between Japanese TNCs and local firms and gov-ernments related to the expansion of production networks. The most important of these concern the terms and conditions under which wholly owned and joint-venture firms are established and financed, the content of technology agreements, and arrangements for sourcing and marketing. Of particular interest in assessing prospects for change are identification of cases in which challenges are made to established boundaries by local firms and governments and determination of conditions that shape the outcomes. Among the most important of these conditions is the bargaining leverage of local firms and governments with Japanese TNCs. Leaders of states and firms seeking to improve their position in the international division of labour need to be aware of these realities, to co-operate among themselves to devise common strategies for advancement, and to seek leverage wherever they can find it if they are to strike the best deal they can under such circumstances. It is partly because such leverage is likely to be enhanced when Japanese firms face strenuous competition that the question of power dispersal in the regional division of labour will remain an important one. This is, in turn, why the development trajectories of TNCs based elsewhere in East Asia, while not yet leading to significant pluralisation, will be of continuing interest.

Notes

Parts of the text and three of the tables come from a paper originally presented at the annual meeting of the Western Political Science Association in San Francisco, California, 14–16 March 1996. Subsequent research in Malaysia was done with the financial support of a Fulbright–Hays Faculty Research Abroad award and California State University, Northridge as well as the institutional support of Institut Kajian Malaysia dan Antarabangsa (IKMAS), Universiti Kebangsaan Malaysia. I thank all for their support. I alone am responsible for the views expressed here.

1 Parts of this section are abbreviated and updated from Machado (1995).
2 There are many problems in comparing investments originating in different countries. FDI figures published by investing and host states often differ significantly. Host countries usually publish FDI approvals, but there are often big differences among both host and investing countries in the extent to which approvals actually become investments. In some countries, a portion of capital outflow, often quite large, is not reported to the government. FDI figures are also frequently not strictly comparable across countries as there are a number of different ways in which FDI may be reckoned. Figures presented here should be considered with these cautions in mind.
3 These tables are based on the MIDA survey of Companies in Production as at 31 December 1994 conducted in early 1995. The survey is estimated to represent about 80 per cent of the total cases. Because special efforts are made to get responses from larger companies, which are in any case administratively best equipped to respond, the survey results tend to over represent larger companies.
4 This information comes from the MIDA survey of Companies in Production as at 31 December 1994, Toyo Keizai, 1995, and Wesley Publishing Co. (1996a, b).

References

Anuwar Ali, 1992. *Malaysia's Industrialization: The Quest for Technology*. Singapore: Oxford University Press.

Aoki, T., 1986. Development of High Technology, Industrial and Trade Networks in the Pacific Region. *Asia-Pacific Economic Symposium Papers*: 42–89.

Bernard, M. and J. Ravenhill, 1995. 'Beyond Product Cycles and Flying Geese: Regionalization, Hierarchy and the Industrialization of East Asia', *World Politics*, 47: 171–209.

Bloom, M., 1993. 'Globalization and the Korean Electronics Industry', *The Pacific Review*, 6(2): 119–26.

Bonacich, E., L. Cheng, N. Chinchila, N. Hamilton and P. Ong (eds), 1994. *Global Production: The Apparel Industry in the Pacific Rim*, Philadelphia: Temple University Press.

Business Taiwan, 15 May 1995.

Business Times (Malaysia), 28 October 1995.

Cox, R., 1987. *Production, Power and World Order: Social Forces in the Making of History*, New York: Columbia University Press.

Dobashi, K., 1988. 'Restructuring of Japanese Industries and the Impact on Asian Economic Development', *Asian Perspectives* (Nomura Research International, HK) 5(4): 2–28.

Doherty, E. (ed.), 1995. *Japanese Investment in Asia: International Production Strategies in a Changing World*, San Francisco: The Asia Foundation and Berkeley Roundtable on the International Economy (BRIE).

EIU (Economist Intelligence Unit), 1993. *Japanese Motor Industry, 4th Quarter 1993*.

Evans, P., 1995. *Embedded Autonomy: States and Industrial Transformation*, Princeton, NJ: Princeton University Press.

FEER (*Far Eastern Economic Review*), 18 March 1993.

——, 29 August 1996.

Felker, G. and C. Weiss, 1995. 'An Analytic Framework for Measuring Technological Development', in Simon: 385–400.

Gereffi, G. and M. Korzeniewicz (eds), 1994. *Commodity Chains and Global Capitalism*, Westport, Conn.: Greenwood Press.

Harrison, B., 1994. *Lean and Mean: The Changing Landscape of Corporate Power in the Age of Flexibility*, New York: Basic Books.

Hollerman, L., 1988. *Japan's Economic Strategy for Brazil: Challenge for the United States*, Lexington, Mass.: Lexington Books.

International Herald Tribune, 30 January 1997.

Japan Times, 22 January 1994.

Kobayashi H. and T. Hayashi, 1993. *Asean shokoku no kogyoka to gaikoku kigyo (ASEAN Countries' Industrialization and Foreign Enterprises)*, Tokyo: Chuo keizaisha.

Kodama F., 1995. 'Emerging Trajectory of the Pacific Rim: Concepts, Evidences, and New Schemes', in Simon: 28–52.

Kono, T., 1984. *Strategy and Structure of Japanese Enterprises*, London: Macmillan.

Korea Economic Daily, 5 February 1996.

Ku, S.C.Y., 1995. 'The Political Economy of Taiwan's Relations with Southeast Asia: The Southward Policy', *Contemporary Southeast Asia*, 17(3).

Lee K., 1995. 'A Comparative Analysis of South Korea and Japanese Foreign Direct Investment in ASEAN', in D. Singh and R. Siregar (eds), *ASEAN and Korea: Emerging Issues in Trade and Investment Relations*, Singapore: Institute of Southeast Asian Studies: 33–54.

Lee T.-Y., 1994. *Overseas Investment: Experience of Singapore Manufacturing Companies*, Singapore: McGraw-Hill/Institute of Policy Studies.

Machado, K., 1994. 'Proton and Malaysia's Motor Vehicle Industry: National Industrial Policies and Japanese Regional Production Strategies', in Jomo K.S. (ed.), *Japan and Malaysian Development: In the Shadow of the Rising Sun*, London: Routledge, 291–325.

——, 1995. 'Japanese Foreign Direct Investment in East Asia: the Expanding Division of Labor and the Future of Regionalism', in S. Chan (ed.), *Foreign Direct Investment in a Changing Global Political Economy*, London: Macmillan: 39–66.

MIDA (Malaysian Industrial Development Authority), 1995. 'Seminar on Opportunities for Investment in South Nations for Malaysian Private Sector', 3 August 1995, Kuala Lumpur: MIDA.

——, 1995a. *Directory of Approved Companies in Production as at 31 December 1994 (By Industry Group)*, Kuala Lumpur: MIDA.

——, 1995b. *Directory of Approved Companies in Production as at 31 December 1994 (With Investment from Japan, Korea, Taiwan, Hong Kong, Singapore, Indonesia, Thailand, Philippines, China)*, Kuala Lumpur: MIDA.

MITI (Ministry of International Trade and Industry) Japan, 1992. *White Paper on International Trade – Japan 1992*, Tokyo: Japan External Trade Organization.

MITI (Ministry of International Trade and Industry) Malaysia, 1993. *Malaysia International Trade and Industry Report 1993*, Kuala Lumpur: MITI.

MITI (Ministry of International Trade and Industry) Malaysia, 1994. *Malaysia International Trade and Industry Report 1994*, Kuala Lumpur: MITI.

MOF (Ministry of Finance) Malaysia, 1996. *Economic Report, 1996/97*, Kuala Lumpur: Ministry of Finance.

Morris-Suzuki, Tessa, 1992. 'Japanese Technology and the New International Division of Knowledge in Asia', in Tokunaga 1992b: 135–52.

Nazari Ismail, 1995. *Transnational Corporations and Economic Development: A Study of the Malaysian Electronics Industry*, Kuala Lumpur: University of Malaya Publications Department.

New Straits Times, 5 February 1996.

Nihon boeki shinkokai (JETRO), 1993, *1993 JETRO hakusho – toshihen: Sekai to Nihon no kaigai chokusetsu toshi* (1993 Jetro White Paper – investment volume: The world and Japan's overseas direct investment), Tokyo: *Nihon boeki shinkokai.*

——, 1997. *1997 JETRO hakusho – toshihen: Sekai to Nihon no kaigai chokusetsu toshi* (1997 Jetro White Paper – investment volume: The world and Japan's overseas direct investment), Tokyo: *Nihon boeki shinkokai.*

The Nikkei Weekly, 7 November 1994.

The Nikkei Weekly, 30 January 1995a.

The Nikkei Weekly, 1 May 1995b.

The Nikkei Weekly, 17 June 1996a.

The Nikkei Weekly, 4 November 1996b.

NRI (Nomura Research Institute) and ISEAS (Institute of Southeast Asian Studies), 1995. *The New Wave of Foreign Direct Investment in Asia*, Singapore: Institute of Southeast Asian Studies.

Rasiah, Rajah, 1994. 'Flexible Production Systems and Local Machine-tool Subcontracting: Electronics Components Transnationals in Malaysia', *Cambridge Journal of Economics*, 18(3): 279–98.

RIM Studies Group, 1988. 'International Division of Labor in the Pacific Rim Area', *RIM: Pacific Business and Industries*, August: 5–19.

Rodan, G., 1993. 'Reconstructing Divisions of Labour: Singapore's New Regional Emphasis', in R. Higgott, R. Leaver and J. Ravenhill (eds), *Pacific Economic Relations in the 1990s: Cooperation or Conflict?*, Boulder, Colo.: Lynne Rienner Publishers.

Samsung, 1996. *Home Page*. http://www.samsung.com.

Simon, D. (ed.) 1995. *The Emerging Technological Trajectory of the Pacific Rim*, Armonk, NY: M.E. Sharpe.

Singapore, DoS, MTI (Department of Statistics, Ministry of Trade and Industry), 1995. *Singapore's Investment Abroad – 1990–1993*, Singapore: DoS, MTI.

——, 1996. *Singapore's Direct Investment Abroad – 1994*. Singapore: DoS, MTI, Occasional Paper 23.

Singapore, MoF (Ministry of Finance), 1993a. *Interim Report of the Committee to Promote Enterprise Overseas*, Singapore: MoF.

——, 1993b. *Final Report of the Committee to Promote Enterprise Overseas*, Singapore: MoF.

Sohn, J.-A., 1994. 'Korea's Big Rush Abroad', *Business Korea*, 12(6) (December): 30–2.

Tachiki, D., 1993. 'Striking up Strategic Alliances: The Foreign Direct Investments of the NIEs and ASEAN Transnational Corporations', *RIM: Pacific Business and Industries* III: 22–36.

Takeuchi, J., 1993. 'Foreign Direct Investment in ASEAN by Small and Medium Sized Japanese Companies and Its Effects on Local Supporting Industries', *RIM: Pacific Business and Industries* IV(22): 36–57.

Taylor, M., 1995. 'Dominance through Technology: Is Japan Creating a Yen Bloc in Southeast Asia?', *Foreign Affairs*, 74(6): 14–20.

Taylor, R., 1996. *Greater China and Japan: Prospects for an Economic Partnership in East Asia*, London: Routledge.

Tokunaga S., 1992a. 'Japan's FDI-promoting Systems and Intra-Asian Networks: New Investment and Trade Systems Created by the Borderless Economy', in Tokunaga 1992b: 5–47.

Tokunaga S. (ed.), 1992b. *Japan's Foreign Investment and Asian Economic Interdependence: Production, Trade, and Financial Systems*, Tokyo: University of Tokyo Press.

Toyo Keizai, 1992. *Japanese Overseas Investment, 1992/93*, Tokyo: Toyo Keizai.

——, 1997. *Kaigai shinshutsu kigyo soran '97* (Overseas Business Survey, '97). Tokyo: Toyo Keizai Shinposha.

Tsushosangyosho (MITI), 1991. *Kaigaitoshi tokei soran, dai 4 kai* (Foreign Investment Statistics, 4th edition), Tokyo: *Okurasho Insatsukyoku*.

——, 1994. *Kaigaitoshi tokei soran, dai 5 kai* (Foreign Investment Statistics, 5th edition), Tokyo: *Okurasho Insatsukyoku*.

United Nations Conference on Trade and Development, Division on Transnational Corporations and Investment (UNCTAD/DTCI), 1995. *World Investment Report, 1995: Transnational Corporations and Competitiveness*, New York and Geneva: United Nations.

United Nations Conference on Trade and Development, Division on Transnational Corporations and Investment (UNCTAD/DTCI), 1996. *World Investment Report, 1996: Investment, Trade and International Policy Arrangements*, New York and Geneva: United Nations.

Weidenbaum, M. and S. Hughes, 1996. *The Bamboo Network: How Expatriate Chinese Entrepreneurs are Creating a New Economic Superpower in Asia*, New York: The Free Press.

Wesley Publishing Company (WPC), 1996a. *Japanese Products and Services in Malaysia – Buyers' Guide 1996*, Singapore: WPC.

——, 1996b. *Japanese Products and Services in Singapore – Buyers' Guide 1996*, Singapore: WPC.

Yu, S., 1995. 'Korea's High Technology Thrust', in Simon: 81–102.

5

MALAYSIA'S INNOVATION SYSTEM

Actors, interests and governance

Greg Felker

Technology development depends importantly upon the institutions that support industrial firms as they invest in building their technological capabilities. Institutional support is critical because private investments in technology face significant market failures, and unfold cumulatively under conditions of imperfect information and inherent unpredictability. This is true even for developing countries seeking to industrialise using imported technology, since deeper levels of innovative capability can only be acquired through deliberate and costly local investments in technological learning. Institutions shape the incentives, both rewards and risks, which motivate firms to seek to improve their technological capabilities. They also provide assets – information, skills, services and specialised capabilities – that complement firms' in-house resources in technological learning.

A growing literature on 'national innovation systems' draws attention to the variety of public and private institutions which affect technological change, as well as to national differences in their composition and effectiveness (Freeman 1987, 1995; Fransman 1995; Mowery and Oxley 1995; Lundvall 1992; Nelson 1993; Patel and Pavitt 1994). National innovation systems are composed of institutions which 'govern' investments in various aspects of technology development by influencing the allocation of public and private resources. Major variations in the institutional environment for innovation have become increasingly apparent as globalisation narrows other types of structural and policy differences between nation-states. In turn, awareness of the link between institutions, technological development, and a nation's competitive success in the global economy has stimulated a growing 'techno-nationalism', expressed in new policies and institutions to stimulate, guide and appropriate industrial innovation (Ostry and Nelson 1995). Yet, such policies presume that economic governance arrangements, such as innovation systems, can be freely selected or created. To what extent can such systems be deliberately constructed as instruments of national industrialisation strategies?

Malaysia offers an important case study of this question. For over a decade, the Malaysian state has sought to guide the economy's transition to technology-based industrialisation through strategic industrial and technology policies. Recognising the importance of institutional support for technology development, state officials have endeavoured to build a comprehensive system of incentives, specialised technical support institutes, and public investments in R&D and technology commercialisation. These efforts, however, have thus far met only with mixed success in influencing technological development within industry. Relative to the size and sophistication of Malaysia's manufacturing sector and export profile, the local technological base is remarkably shallow (Lall, this volume). Measures of productivity growth indicate that Malaysia has lagged behind both the first-generation NICs and its regional competitors, despite striking export success in a narrow range of technology-intensive industries.[1] With a few salient exceptions, locally owned industry demonstrates minimal technological dynamism. The formation of intra- and inter-industry linkages vital to the growth of dynamic industrial clusters and enhanced value-added has been limited. At the same time, multinational corporations (MNCs) operating in Malaysia have substantially upgraded their technological levels, new foreign direct investment has flowed into higher-technology production, and some evidence of technology spin-offs to the local economy has begun to emerge. What does this juxtaposition suggest about how national innovation systems emerge in newly industrialising economies?

This chapter analyses Malaysia's national innovation system as a problem of economic governance, and explains its strengths and weaknesses in terms of the interests and capabilities of three key political economy actors – the state, local business and MNCs. Because technology development is ultimately realised through its effects on industrial production, efforts to govern the process require industrial firms' active participation, not mere acquiescence, in co-ordinated decision-making. While Malaysia's political leadership enjoys considerable autonomy in setting economic policies, substantial economic liberalisation over the past decade has required the state to seek to influence and respond to private decision-makers in technology development and industrial upgrading.

The emergence of a national innovation system has therefore hinged on the degree to which bargaining between these three actors has produced a consensus on the degree and form of co-operation in technological issues. In Malaysia, coherent and activist state initiatives have reformed technology policies and institutions in ways that complement technological upgrading *within* MNCs' local production complexes. Yet efforts to mobilise local private-sector technological investments and to encourage the diffusion of MNC dynamism to the local economy have been largely unsuccessful despite deliberate efforts. This mixture of success and failure reflects converging and conflicting interests among the state, local business and multinationals, as well as the narrow and weak character of policy networks linking the state to local business interests. An overview of Malaysia's innovation system reveals that, even in the context of a foreign-investment-led industrialisation strategy, coherent state intervention is vital in providing infrastructural support and reinforcing private-sector trends in technological development. Yet the potential for 'governing' technology development in strategic ways depends upon the interplay of state and business sectors' distinct political and economic interests.

The chapter is organised in the following way. The next section reviews political-economy perspectives on successful late industrialisation. It provides a brief analytic outline of the changing political-economy trends shaping Malaysia's industrial policies, focusing on the political interests that determine the degree of co-operation between the state, local business and MNCs. The following section discusses the various elements of Malaysia's national innovation system, and analyses institutional governance in terms of the interests and roles of the same three actors. The final section draws conclusions and considers the prospects for reform of technology policies in light of the governance possibilities defined by Malaysia's political economy.

Changing political-economy influences on Malaysia's technology development

Institutionalism and the politics of industrial governance

Attempts to explain the remarkable economic performance of various East and Southeast Asian economies have turned on the importance of 'strong' states, through strategic industrial policies as opposed to market forces in propelling rapid industrialisation. Recent efforts to synthesise this debate have employed a generic institutional logic to shed light on various types of collective action problems in overcoming development challenges (Doner 1991; Wade 1992). Neo-institutionalist approaches accept the premise that pervasive market failures beset late industrialisation, whether weak infrastructures in finance, information and human capital formation, or disadvantages inherent in latecomer status, such as the extended learning period required for infant industries to become internationally competitive. Overcoming these obstacles requires co-ordination among various economic actors, whose parochial interests, however, might conflict with long-run development goals. Institutions facilitate co-operation by defining the spheres of co-operation and competition, establishing rules for collective decision-making, and determining authority relationships for monitoring and enforcement. A range of state and non-state institutions can serve to co-ordinate developmental efforts and reconcile diverse interests with the requirements of long-term growth (Doner 1992). Recent empirical scholarship has explored a broad range of intra-industry institutions which allow private-sector actors to co-ordinate decisions and internalise market failures, including multi-sectoral business groups, buyer–supplier linkages, ethnic and other social networks, and international production chains (Friedman 1988; Hamilton 1991; Gereffi and Korzeniewicz 1994).

The 'choice' of particular institutions of economic governance reflects both technical or administrative factors and political interests and power. The technical-cum-administrative dimension of economic governance describes the organisations, procedures and informal norms that govern investment decision-making, resource allocation, and the flow of information on market conditions and economic outcomes. Technology development is a particularly challenging policy area in that, while substantial market failures create a large scope for co-ordinated investment decisions, the production-centred nature of technological learning means that successful promotional efforts must involve highly differentiated information as well as decentralised efforts and investments (see Meyer-Stamer, this volume). In short, technological learning in industry cannot be centrally orchestrated or driven by policy fiat, but only induced by information-sharing and negotiated consensus. Administrative considerations in economic governance are bounded by politics. Power relations, and the degree of convergence or conflict among key actors' interests, determine the possibilities for co-ordinated decision-making. Formal policies and institutions frequently fail because of conflicting interests, disputes over institutional authority, and struggles over the distribution of joint costs and gains.

Neo-institutionalist accounts of rapid industrialisation place less emphasis on a politically autonomous and 'strong' state and instead highlight the importance of networks or linkages between state and business actors (Okimoto 1989; Doner and Hawes 1995). In administrative terms, networks support the flow of information necessary for effective implementation. In the political dimension, policy networks allow the reconciliation of interests and negotiation of consensus under varying distributions of power between state officials and private business (Samuels 1987). The collective action logic at the core of the institutionalist approach suggests that policy networks will be more effective and functional to the extent that they involve bargaining among encompassing political and economic interests, rather than particularistic and narrow exchanges. Effective policy networks are likely to involve three features: political elites with broad and well-institutionalised political bases; private business sectors with long-term investment interests and strong organisational coherence, either in the form of large corporate groups or formal representative associations; and networks of access to policy-making which are transparent and institutionalised rather than informal and particularistic (Doner and Hawes 1995: 156).

From this standpoint, the absence or poor efficacy of much industrial policy in Southeast Asian countries has stemmed from the narrow and personalistic character of their policy networks. Some have argued that the rise of private-sector influence and the state's gradual withdrawal from many areas of intervention during the last decade has involved the creation of more encompassing policy networks and led to an increasing 'rationalisation' of economic policy-making (MacIntyre and Jayasuriya 1992). The Malaysian experience, however, partly contradicts this thesis. Recent reforms have indeed rationalised the content and administration of state industrial policies, curbed public-sector waste, and at least partly checked rent-seeking (Lall 1995). Yet, these achievements have come as a result of enhanced state autonomy, and have been accompanied by a narrowing of the scope of networks between state and business elites. In shifting the aims of economic policy-making from inter-ethnic redistribution to the promotion of rapid industrialisation, the state has concentrated its linkages to the private sector and moved them outside of formal bureaucratic channels. This tension between rationalising and extending state/business networks has shaped the form and character of economic governance in Malaysia's national innovation system.

Actors, interests and networks in Malaysian industrial policy

State interests in policy co-ordination

State elites' interests in drawing the private business sector into co-operative economic governance arrangements have evolved considerably in Malaysia during the past twenty years. The New Economic Policy (NEP) era (1970–90) saw tremendous expansion of the state's economic control through regulation, finance and production. State economic expansion and the regime's ethnic–populist coalitional base resulted in significant tension with the predominantly ethnic-Chinese local business community. Far from promoting the growth of manufacturing under national (as opposed to foreign) auspices, the state sought to control Chinese business expansion through the Industrial Co-ordination Act (ICA) of 1975. Meanwhile, however, export-oriented foreign manufacturing investment continued to be courted with the objective of increasing employment, particularly through Malay migration from rural areas to the urban manufacturing centres. Within this framework, state officials did not seek to bargain with MNCs over industrial development issues such as localisation of production, managerial control or technology transfer.

At the start of the 1980s, new political leadership under Dr Mahathir Mohamad viewed the sprawling bureaucratic involvement in economic regulation as too inefficient and unwieldy to serve an ambitious industrial development agenda (Halim 1990: 77). Authority and initiative in the policy process were centralised under the chief executive, bypassing key bureaucratic interests. His early administration featured not only a major heavy industries thrust under state ownership, but also campaigns to streamline the public sector through privatisation and budgetary controls, as well as tentative efforts to engage the private sector through the 'Malaysia Inc.' programme of formal policy dialogues. The political risks of this coalitional shift mushroomed into crisis in the years after Malaysia's sharp mid-decade recession (Crouch 1992). The Prime Minister's victory in intra-party struggles served to hasten a political realignment in which power was lodged in a coalition of political and business elites, including a cadre of ethnic Malay businessmen who had emerged through state-mediated patronage during the previous decade (Leigh 1992). The political crises of the late-1980s solidified the leadership's commitment to fostering private-sector-led growth as a formula for buttressing the political party's political support and authority. Growth secured legitimacy in the eyes of the middle class, liberalisation restored confidence among the Chinese business community, and privatisation sealed the support of large-scale business interests.

Business interests in policy co-ordination

Despite Mahathir's conscious efforts to build policy networks with the private sector, the changed context did not result in a broad-based public/private consensus on industrial development goals. Annual policy dialogues in the late 1980s and early 1990s were more useful in securing private-sector acquiescence and support for trade, investment, fiscal and regulatory liberalisation than in mobilising action on industrial upgrading, human resource development and technological development. The difficulties in mobilising consensus stemmed in large part from NEP-era legacies in the organisation and interests of local business groups. During the 1970s and early 1980s, private business influence on economic policy-making was minimal, and the business sector's collective political voice was weakened by ethnic divisions both in institutional representation and in their underlying interests in state intervention (Jesudason 1989: 137–47). While excluded from formal participation in policy-making, individual businessmen, both Malay and Chinese, prospered through personal access to political and bureaucratic leaders. Indeed, as the state's role in allocating resources grew, the value of such patronage connections increased (Sieh 1992). The ethnic-Chinese manufacturing sector therefore welcomed economic liberalisation in the late 1980s as much preferable to what it had perceived as an earlier predatory interventionist stance. Few Chinese manufacturers were directly threatened by the relaxation of foreign investment and trade rules, and even those concerned with the influx of foreign investors were unwilling to advocate greater state industrial regulation to protect national interests. As a whole, ethnic-Chinese manufacturers remained wary of government motives and procedures in allocating incentives and subsidies.

The legacies of clientelism and ethnic division also left the main business associations organisationally weak. Their collective strength and representative capacities were undermined by a divide between a set of politically connected leaders and a larger constituency of small and medium-sized firms with limited faith in their organisational representation. The Federation of Malaysian Manufacturers was better organised than most, and became a credible voice for the business sector on broad policy matters, yet as a multi-sectoral umbrella organisation, it had only limited ability to mobilise collective action on specific industrial development issues. The majority of industry-specific associations were also relatively ineffective as mechanisms of collective representation and implementation. A few exceptions were found in sectors like plastics and foundries, where small and medium-scale firms had organised to lobby the government on trade and tax issues. These associations were almost exclusively ethnic-Chinese, and ethnic political considerations rendered their very activism prone to result in tensions with bureaucratic authorities.[2] Ethnic-Malay business associations had long functioned as mechanisms by which to lobby for state privileges, and largely represented the voice of medium-scale enterprises dependent upon bureaucratic patronage. In the early 1990s, the leadership of the Malay Chambers and National Chambers of Commerce and Industry was assumed by prominent corporate figures selected by the political leadership. Charged with modernising the associations, the new leadership essentially converted them from moribund vehicles for rent-seeking into extensions of the new, high-level clientelist networks, which now figure prominently in policy-making.

The political elite recognised the constraint which business's organisational weakness places on its ability to mobilise collaboration for development goals. The Minister of International Trade and Industry announced in 1993, for example, that a Domestic Investment Initiative would (among other objectives) 'focus on ways and means to encourage strong and healthy representational organisations which can organise and co-ordinate the development of their respective sectors' (*Business Times*, 25 February 1993). During the late 1980s and early 1990s, the government sought to strengthen formal government/business dialogue process and to pressure the bureaucracy to respond to business priorities. In response, the peak associations became more professional in management and operation. However, while wishing to draw the broader business sector into networks for better information gathering and policy implementation, the state leadership has been wary of the political implications of stronger collective business influence over economic policy.[3] From 1991, peak-level policy negotiations have been channelled into the Malaysian Business Council (MBC), whose private-sector representatives are individually selected by the government, rather than in the annual dialogues between ministry officials and representative associations.[4]

The importance of the MBC in policy-making is revealing of the politics of economic governance in several ways. First, it demonstrates the continued primacy of informal or clientelist relations between the political and business elites, and the marginalisation of the bureaucracy as a political force in policy formulation. On the other hand, by giving these particularistic linkages a quasi-formal expression, the government indicated its strategy of using its links to big business to execute broader governance functions in the economy, including infrastructure development, human resource development, and, as in the case of the newly privatised automotive industry, industrial and technological deepening. In short, economic liberalisation and the rationalisation of industrial policies were not the outcome of greater business political influence and access to economic policy-making. More nearly the opposite, it stemmed from political elites' strategic efforts to de-bureaucratise policy-making and draw business into greater consultation, particularly within clientelist channels at the apex of the political party and government system.

MNC interests in policy co-ordination

Foreign multinational corporations' (MNCs') interests in participating in institutions of industrial governance have also changed significantly in recent years. In the 1970s, foreign manufacturers in the Free Trade Zones (FTZs) were relatively willing to comply with ICA ethnic employment quotas in return for generous tax incentives, subsidised infrastructure and controls on labour organisation.[5] In the 1980s, however, the heavy industries programme drew the state into a direct bargaining relationship with foreign investors over matters of industrial deepening and technology transfer, giving rise to disputes with Japanese partners in the steel and automotive projects. The state's aggressive expansion into the industrial sector combined with recession abroad to cause a significant fall in new foreign investment approvals. When the 1985–86 recession struck, the government abruptly reversed its tentative efforts to bargain with MNCs over ownership, localisation and technology transfer. NEP-era employment and equity-sharing quotas were 'suspended' in 1986, and 100 per cent foreign-equity ownership was allowed for projects exporting more than 80 per cent of output.

The reforms entailed much more than simply the state's retreat from industrial governance. In fact, authorities strove to make the industrial policy framework and bureaucracies more responsive to the requirements of foreign investors. The Malaysian Industrial Development Authority (MIDA) was empowered to serve as a one-stop investment approval agency in 1988; labour laws were amended in 1989 to facilitate the creation of in-house unions; and new incentives were offered for established MNCs that expanded their existing production facilities. Even in the midst of liberalisation, moreover, government officials remained concerned about the low levels of backward linkages and technology spill-overs from the foreign sector, and debated ways of pressuring or inducing MNCs to sink roots in the local economy. This concern was primarily expressed in exhortations and informal bargaining between top government officials and individual MNC investors. A local content measure was imposed on the electronics sector in 1990, though its provisions were limited and had a primarily symbolic effect.

The foreign direct investment (FDI) which flooded into Malaysia in the late 1980s reflected not only an increase in volume, but also profound evolution in MNCs' production strategies. Previously, the dominant motives for FDI were to access protected local markets or to transfer labour-intensive phases of production to convenient off-shore locations. In the mid-1980s, however, Japanese and East Asian corporations moved swiftly to expand, upgrade and integrate their heretofore fragmented and shallow manufacturing investments in Southeast Asia to produce sophisticated goods for regional and global markets.[6] Beyond deepening their off-shore investments, MNCs began to confer greater autonomy on their regional subsidiaries in the areas of procurement, marketing and technology development. The appreciation of East Asian currencies led Japanese and Taiwanese manufacturers to shift parts and components production and procurements to off-shore suppliers in place of high-cost imports from home countries. To meet the demands of global market competition, MNCs' Malaysian subsidiaries began to automate production, upgrade workforce skills for higher quality, and undertake more local product and process design.[7] Production engineering capabilities in the long-established semiconductor MNCs, for example, began to approach their parents' global standards, and a wave of technological upgrading in the late 1980s generated more interest in ties to local sub-contractors and sources of training and technical services (Rasiah 1995a).

MNCs' globalisation and regionalisation strategies had contradictory effects on their interests in co-operation with host-country actors in technological upgrading. As they deepened and rationalised their Southeast Asian production bases, foreign investors perceived a new interest in the quality of their host countries' base of suppliers, technical infrastructure, and workforce skills. MNCs absorbed the costs of major externalities of investments in technological upgrading, such as workforce training and developing local components supply networks, and thus were more willing to share these burdens through co-operation with local firms and supporting institutions, provided these could achieve the higher quality standards required for globally competitive production. Japanese official foreign assistance began to concentrate on developing technical and skills infrastructure in Southeast Asia as part of a broader attempt to co-ordinate the internationalisation of Japanese production (Unger 1993; Doner 1993). The extent to which MNCs favoured particular locations for higher-technology investment hinged largely on the success of host countries in responding to these requirements of their globalisation strategies. Singapore was favoured for high-technology operations, regional procurement operations and regional management headquarters due to its superb infrastructure, lack of equity or trade restrictions, and effective government action to build local technology infrastructure and to upgrade local supporting industries. Malaysia, though occupying a lower position in the emerging regional division of labour, has been increasingly selected as a site for technology-intensive operations; Singapore's rising costs have been a push factor, while the Malaysian government has striven to provide conducive infrastructure for emerging MNC clusters in industries such as disk-drives, opto-electronics, semiconductors and consumer electronics.

While MNCs' new interests thus converged to a limited degree with host-country policy-makers' desire for production deepening and technological upgrading, they quite obviously did not signify a willingness to have local governments assume greater governance authority over their decisions in these areas. Efforts to upgrade subsidiaries' technology and exercise greater regional co-ordination demanded that MNCs exercise tighter management control over decisions in procurements, technology and marketing. Thus, freedom to hold 100 per cent equity became a central issue for foreign investors. Where access to imported capital equipment and production inputs was constrained (as they were not in Malaysia's FTZs), further liberalisation was required to attract FDI in higher-value-added activities. Though producing or procuring more parts and components within the region, leading MNCs were intent upon progressively integrating their various off-shore units into a single division of labour, a goal which stood in tension with individual host countries' efforts to maximise local linkages and technology spill-overs.

MNCs naturally resisted government oversight of vendor selection and contracting. The Japanese sub-contracting system typically involves a high degree of information and technology sharing, and government intervention in vendor relations could pose a threat to strategic management of technology assets. Even when procurement of key components has been transferred from Japan for cost reasons, it has usually shifted to other Japanese suppliers also relocated to the region.[8]

Finally, locally owned supplier industries in Malaysia were technically weak, and bringing them up to the scale and quality standards necessary to supply MNCs' export operations would require a substantial investment of time and resources. While a few foreign firms became more willing to absorb some of these external-ities with the hope of capturing long-term benefits, they resisted host-government efforts to impose the costs and risks of technical assistance to local firms. In sum, MNCs' moves towards technological deepening and regional production networks enhanced their interests in local collaboration in various types of infrastructure. Yet their strengthened bargaining power, stemming from regional liberalisation and rapid technological change, made them disinclined to participate in local gover-nance arrangements which infringed upon their managerial freedoms and control over production decisions.

These political economy trends powerfully influenced Malaysia's efforts to build institutions to govern investments in industrial and technological upgrading. Economic liberalisation was achieved through a centralisation of power and authority in economic policy-making within the state. The state's leaders sought to build policy networks with the organised business sector in order to secure co-operation in implementing policies determined autonomously, while business's real access to decision-making power remained lodged in narrow, informal elite networks. MNC interests became more amenable to certain technological devel-opment goals, but foreign firms' sensitivity and resistance to national policies which inhibited their autonomy also increased.

Malaysia's national innovation system

An analytic framework

Scholars of technology development have employed several similar macro-frameworks to analyse national technological strategies. Dahlman and Brimble (1990) suggest a useful framework that groups together institutions and policies which affect *technology acquisition, technology use and diffusion, technology improvement and development, and investment in technical human capital.* Technology acquisition includes policies and institutions connected with the various modes of technology import and information gathering. The elements of national innovation systems that affect technology acquisition include:

* technology transfer regulations
* foreign investment promotion policies and agencies
* capital goods imports
* informal mechanisms such as foreign buyers' technical assistance
* reverse direct investments in developed countries to acquire or set up compa-nies as 'technological outposts'.

Technology diffusion involves efforts to use and replicate acquired technologies throughout the industrial structure, and in particular to raise average productivity levels by narrowing the gap between technology leaders and laggards. A wide range of policies and institutions, both public and private, play roles in this process:

- sub-contracting networks
- small and medium-sized industries (SMI) assistance programmes and agencies
- standards, testing, quality-control and quality-promotion organisations and programmes
- technical information organisations and services.

Technology improvement covers organised efforts to adapt, improve and innovate technology. Relevant institutions are:

- R&D facilities, including government and private institutions and firms' in-house engineering or research laboratories
- university laboratories
- financial sources for R&D, including public funds and venture-capital firms
- R&D and other innovation incentives.

Technical human capital creation involves efforts to train scientists and industrial engineers and to boost the technical skills of the labour force. It is affected by:

- universities and other higher-education programmes
- vocational and technical training institutes
- firms' in-house training activities
- specific incentives, funding and policies for technical and skills training.

A fifth, macro-level function should be added, namely *technology strategy*, which involves gathering and disseminating information on national technology development, setting strategic priorities and developing plans, monitoring implementation, and allocating funding and other resources. The technology strategy system would include:

- science and technology ministries and policy agencies
- technology foresight and priority-setting mechanisms
- bodies allocating public investments in technology
- mechanisms for consultation and feedback among public and industry representatives.

Some combination of these elements is present in all industrialising economies. Yet national innovation systems differ in the mix of institutions, in the strength and performance of various aspects of the system, and in the roles played by government and business actors. As argued above, moreover, political factors decisively influence the performance of technology policies and institutions by allowing or frustrating co-ordination in technology development. Writing about Japan, for example, Samuels (1994: 330) argues, 'national [innovation] systems are more than aggregate expressions of domestic institutions and sectoral networks. They comprise shared values and beliefs that are confirmed and reconfirmed by the intimacy of shared national experience.'[9]

The following sections of this essay examine these five functional categories in terms of the politics of economic governance, highlighting three variables: (a) 'actors' – the roles of state, local business, and MNCs in initiating and operating technology institutions; (b) 'interests' – the larger political and economic motivations which shape major actors' behaviour within the innovation system, and the extent to which these interests converge or conflict; and (c) 'governance' – the degree to which basic functions of the innovation system are managed through conscious, collective or co-ordinated strategic choices as opposed to spontaneous, disaggregated or market-driven decision-making. We begin with the macro-level governance of Malaysia's technological development, namely technology strategy and policy-making.

Science and technology strategy

Policies and institutions

The first element of Malaysia's national innovation system is the science and technology policy-making system. Throughout the 1980s and 1990s, S&T policy-making has become progressively more institutionalised and integral to government development planning. The key central government policy bodies are the inter-ministerial National Council for Scientific Research and Development (MPKSN), established in 1975, and the Ministry of Science, Technology, and Environment (MOSTE), created in 1976. In their first decade, these agencies occupied a low profile within the bureaucratic structure, with minimal budgets and authority.[10]

As development priorities turned towards industry under the Mahathir administration in the early 1980s, the government launched efforts to co-ordinate S&T policies with broader industrialisation strategies. General S&T policy goals were outlined in the 5th Malaysia Plan (1986–90) and the promulgation of a National S&T Policy in 1986.[11] Also in that year, the Industrial Master Plan (IMP) called for several general and sector-specific technology promotion measures. The appointment of a Science Advisor to the Prime Minister's Department in 1984 reflected the broader centralisation of policy initiative and authority under the chief executive's direct control, and this office became a prime mover in S&T policy reform throughout the 1980s and 1990s. The Science Advisor was the author of the Intensification of Research in Priority Areas (IRPA) programme in 1987, which centralised all public R&D allocations under the National Science Council for greater strategic control. Notwithstanding these reforms, the public policy machinery remained largely unable to achieve its ambitions for co-ordinated strategic management of the country's S&T institutional system. Despite its nominal monopoly on public R&D allocations, for example, the IRPA programme could not alter the R&D totals assigned to each government ministry under the five-year national development plans. IRPA also did not cover public research institutions' (RIs') capital budgets, and even operating R&D expenditures approved under IRPA were still disbursed and monitored by RIs' parent ministries rather than the National Science Council itself.

In recognition of the existing framework's weaknesses, the government commissioned a National Action Plan for Industrial Technology Development (APITD), which was issued in 1990. The 'Technology Action Plan' recommended creating a Cabinet Committee on Science and Technology, as well as centralising authority for all S&T policy under the Ministry of Science. Efforts to overcome bureaucratic fragmentation intensified under the new Plan and leading research institutions were transferred from other line ministries to the MOSTE. In 1989–90, the National Science Council was suspended while the new policy architecture was determined. A proposal for an extra-bureaucratic public/private National S&T Board with independent grant-making authority was rejected in favour of reforming the existing Council with enlarged private-sector representation.

Difficulties in S&T policy co-ordination and implementation were also addressed by creating extra-bureaucratic policy bodies. First, the office of the Science Advisor continued to provide strong informal co-ordination and monitoring of the policy machinery. Second, the peak-level government/business consultative forum, the Malaysian Business Council (MBC) included a working committee on industrial technology, which developed several policy initiatives which were later adopted by the bureaucracy. Finally, the Malaysian Industry–Government Group for High Technology (MIGHT) was formed in 1993 under the office of the Science Advisor and, like the Malaysian Business Council, it entailed direct consultations between top government and individual business leaders.[12] MIGHT was charged with monitoring international technological trends, identifying strategic investment opportunities for Malaysian industry, and forging a public–private consensus on needed actions. It organises ongoing consultations according to technology-specific interest groups, in sectors ranging from composite materials to pollution control. Though primarily focused on newly emerging technology areas, MIGHT has also become involved in the more mundane and essential tasks of upgrading productivity and quality standards.[13]

The paramount goal of reforms of the S&T policy machinery was to allow strategic technology 'targeting' of public investments in technological development. Both the Industrial Master Plan and the Technology Action Plan included detailed surveys of the technical strengths and weaknesses of specific industrial sectors. The Technology Action Plan identified five technology priority areas: automated manufacturing; advanced materials; electronics; biotechnology; and information technology.[14] These priority areas have guided the government's efforts to expand and reform the public research infrastructure.[15]

Reforms of the chief policy-making bodies achieved mixed success in targeting public technology investments to support industrial development strategies. Though partly attenuated, problems of bureaucratic co-ordination persisted. The National Science Council and MOSTE struggled with insufficient numbers of qualified personnel, making it difficult to execute detailed S&T policy planning and monitoring through IRPA. A second hindrance was the dearth of reliable information on national technology resources and trends, especially at the sectoral level. Intended to be a framework policy document, the APITD's list of technology priorities was something of a 'wish list' composed of broad categories based on emerging global trends, rather than an empirical evaluation of specific technological capabilities Malaysia's industrial firms presently require or might soon become competitive in.

The government persisted in its efforts to strengthen the national S&T planning process in the 1990s. One milestone came in 1992 with the establishment of MASTIC, a national S&T information centre within the Science Ministry charged with collecting data through biennial national surveys. Following its 1990 reorganisation, the National Science Council formed five technical working groups to formulate policies in each of the Technology Action Plan's priority areas (with an additional group focused on energy).[16] These panels include public and private representatives, and meet several times a year to commission studies and workshops intended to guide MOSTE's formal policy-making work. In 1994, a more rigorous priority-setting exercise was carried out in preparation for research allocations under the Seventh Malaysia Plan (1996–2000). The Science Council's technical working groups brought together relevant government agencies (including the central Economic Planning Unit, MITI and MIDA) and the major industry representative associations (e.g. FMM) to identify trends and priorities in specific industry categories. The participation of relevant business associations allowed a more direct focus on the technological needs and opportunities arising from the country's industrialisation, and provided a stronger empirical basis for future IRPA allocation decisions.[17]

In general, however, integrating detailed and reliable private-industry input into national technology planning and funding has been difficult. Private-sector representation in the National Science Council and the governing boards of other S&T institutions has not proved effective in overcoming the gaps between public S&T investments and industry demands, in part because business representatives are chosen as individual experts rather than as institutional representatives of organised business groups. In recognition of poor co-ordination with business, the MIGHT body was explicitly charged with the primary task of forging public–private consensus on technology development priorities.

If strategic priorities are to have any real impact, they must influence the allocation of technology development budgets and other resources. In Malaysia, the planning and funding functions are ostensibly integrated under IRPA which, as noted above, faced difficult informational constraints. In general, the capacity of central policy bodies to act upon industry-specific recommendations and redirect resources towards the identified priorities is limited. Malaysia has thus far eschewed the model of an quasi-independent grant-making technology board, such as Singapore's National Science and Technology Board. Yet some such body will be essential to realising current proposals for a fully contract-driven public research infrastructure. A contract-based research system would fully separate the functions of sponsoring and performing research, forcing all research institutions (public and private) to bid competitively for contracts from the government as well as from industrial clients. Such a system presupposes the capacity to link funding decisions to research agendas which outline highly specific priorities, based on industrial needs and prospects. The existing policy structure as yet lacks the analytic capabilities and full-time staff to perform these functions effectively, though ongoing efforts have begun to strengthen the system.

S&T policy-making: governance, actors and goals

Malaysia's government has sought to forge a strong central S&T policy system to develop detailed national technology strategies in support of the broader industrialisation drive. These efforts are supported by political and administrative capacities unmatched in Southeast Asia, except in Singapore. Malaysia has suffered from the weaknesses of bureaucratic overlap and inertia common to government systems around the globe, but persistent reforms have created an increasingly coherent and dynamic policy system in S&T as well as in broader industrial policy arenas (Lall 1995). More general trends in Malaysian policy-making, towards reliance on direct government–business consultations and corporatised agencies independent of bureaucratic control for implementation, have also been evident in science and technology.

Determined state leadership has achieved mixed results, however, due to the persistent gap between state and private business goals. On the positive side, S&T policy reforms have increased public investments in human resources and knowledge creation and related them in a broad way to industrial development goals. Consciousness of the goal of industry-relevance has permeated the central policy bodies, and major efforts have been made to integrate private-sector input to guide policy-making. On the other hand, the state's dominant leadership in setting S&T priorities is itself problematic, in that ambitious technology strategies still often seem disconnected from the realities and constraints facing much of Malaysia's industries. The political elite's efforts to implement more detailed S&T strategies have generated a profound paradox: policy authority became highly centralised in order to force the fractious bureaucracy to be responsive to industry, yet effective technology policies require highly industry-specific information and monitoring which is most readily acquired through more decentralised, horizontal, and consensual decision-making. This dilemma is neatly captured in the Ministry of Science's paradoxical description of the ideal public research system as 'top-down and demand-driven' (Danabalan 1994).

One result is that technology strategies have largely focused on generating entirely new indigenous products, or on fostering the growth of cutting-edge 'high-technology' industries, rather than on more routine but essential tasks – quality improvement, mastering acquired technology, minor adaptation – of evolutionary capability-building in existing manufacturing industries. One analyst has argued, 'This Plan [the National Technology Action Plan] may be *too* ambitious. While it covers comprehensively all the aspects of technological development, it seems to lack a "feel" for the real problems and needs of private industrial enterprises' (Lall *et al.* 1994: 118).

The dilemma is exacerbated by the weak private-sector role in S&T policy-making. Government efforts to engage the private sector in formal and informal consultations have been of little concrete use in guiding policy formulation. Such weaknesses are partly explained by Malaysian industry's limited interest in formal R&D and new-product innovation, yet business guidance for other policies in the areas of technical support, training, incentives, etc. has not been much more effective. A partial exception is the FMM, which has developed its analytical and advisory capabilities and made effective use of policy dialogues with the government. Individual industry associations are better positioned to gather information on technology needs and assist with policy implementation, yet only a handful have been effective in performing such functions in Malaysia.[18] Managers from leading MNCs have served on leading policy committees, including the National Science Council's working groups, and foreign business representative organisations have provided feedback on government policy initiatives. In general, however, technology is considered a 'sensitive' issue by most foreign investors, reflecting a perception of underlying conflicts of interests. While important opportunities exist for collaboration between government and foreign investors in shaping Malaysia's technology policies, it is clear that foreign business is wary of government efforts to directly guide business behaviour. These conflicts of interest have tempered government efforts to implement its strategic priorities in technology development.[19]

Technology acquisition

Policies and institutions

Malaysia records high levels of technology import through various modes. Capital goods imports have been large both in absolute terms and as a percentage (42 per cent in 1992) of the total import bill. Relatively free access to technology embodied in capital equipment has helped Malaysian manufacturing to achieve competitive levels of efficiency in a range of export industries. Much of Malaysia's capital goods imports, however, occur as part of foreign direct investment (FDI) inflows. Many local firms have less awareness of and access to advanced production technology, including automated systems. In addition, the weakness of the local capital goods industries has contributed to low inter-industry linkages and limited the user–producer interactions critical to innovation (O'Brien 1993).

Table 5.1 Technology transfer agreements 1976–96

	1976–80	1981–85	1986–90	1991	1992	1993	1994	1995	1996	Total
Sector										
E&E	69	91	159	45	38	69	44	25	59	599
Chemical	42	74	113	21	19	20	12	17	17	335
Transport equipment	26	81	53	16	28	25	21	9	16	275
Fabricated metal	37	45	71	13	6	11	4	4	7	198

Source		1975–90		1991	1992
Japan		619		92	69
USA		185		18	10
UK		215		14	14

Sources: UNDP (1993) Table 2.1; unpublished MIDA data, 7th Malaysia Plan

Malaysia's manufacturing sector has seen an increase in the number of technology licensing agreements and other contractual forms of technology transfer during the last two decades (UNDP 1993); see Table 5.1. Annual payments under official technology agreements rose from RM240 million (about US$100 million) in 1990 to an estimated RM1 billion in 1995.[20] Despite the impressive totals, the bulk of technology transfer agreements do not represent arm's-length forms of technology acquisition, but rather are extensions of MNCs' strategic decisions to transfer technology and profits across their global operations. During the period 1989–92, for example, two-thirds of all such agreements, and well over 90 per cent within the electronics sector, were signed by foreign firms or foreign-majority joint ventures.

All agreements are subject to an approval procedure in which applications are processed by the chief investment agency, MIDA, and screened by an interministerial committee chaired by MITI (Anuwar 1992: 87–94). Technology transfer regulations impose formal restrictions on inflated royalty fees, restrictive clauses and other applications of MNCs' market power, and formally link royalty rates to various criteria, including the extent to which the contract involves 'high' technology. Screening of agreements in practice is not stringent, however, and MIDA lacks the capacity to monitor the implementation of agreements *ex post* to ensure that the contract has conferred technological mastery to the technology purchaser (Rasiah 1995b). Transfer regulations have likely reduced the incidence of restrictive clauses and abuses of market power in technology agreements, but they have not served as a means of bargaining or monitoring the technology acquisition process. Informal means of technology import, such as direct relationships with international buyers of OEM products, have thus far been limited, except in certain sectors like resource-based (wood and rubber) products and finished garments. This is because the share of locally owned firms in direct manufacturing exports has been relatively small.

Instead, the dominant mode of technology acquisition in Malaysia's industrial sector is foreign direct investment (FDI). Malaysia has long encouraged (particu-larly export-oriented) FDI, even when, as during the 1970s, criticism of MNCs' impact in developing countries was widespread. As a result, Malaysia has attracted a relatively large share of manufacturing FDI flows to the developing world, though the totals have fluctuated over time (Anuwar and Wong 1993). The basic controversy over FDI centres on the extent to which it has transferred genuine tech-nological capabilities to the local economy. The South Korean and Taiwanese examples suggest that active screening of FDI, and state-supervised bargaining for technology access in exchange for entry to the local market, played an important role in helping local industry acquire technology (Mardon 1990; Dahlman and Sananikone 1990). Yet, the global trend, in which Malaysia is a leader, has been to liberalise FDI regulations to attract continued investment inflows. The facilities and incentives granted to firms in the Free Trade Zones (FTZs), while successful in attracting investment, worked against the formation of production linkages and technology spill-overs to the local economy (Rasiah 1993: 139–42; Lim and Pang 1991: 110–11). One hundred per cent foreign equity ownership is permitted for projects meeting broad export or employment conditions. Local content regula-tions on FDI apply only to the automotive sector and, as of 1990, to electronics industry projects.[21]

In recent years, however, MIDA has begun to implement positive, rather than restrictive, forms of selectivity by actively soliciting investment in specific high-technology areas and creating new incentives and criteria for high-tech investments. The criteria for these special incentives were formalised in 1994, and require that companies achieve R&D expenditures equal to 1 per cent of sales revenue within three years from start-up, and have 7 per cent of workforce com-posed of science and technical graduates. Government investment promotion missions have targeted high-technology companies in Japan, Europe and the US. Such efforts are reinforced by MITI's attempts, through incentives and informal bargaining, to encourage established foreign investors to do more R&D and design work locally. In 1994, MITI and MIDA together with the Kedah state gov-ernment opened the Kulim High-Technology industrial park, which is discussed below. The overall strategy appears to be a variation of Singapore's use of posi-tive inducements to induce foreign investment to achieve industrial and technological upgrading (Lim and Pang 1991). It is not clear that reforms of investment incentives entail any greater institutional capacity to screen and eval-uate the technological content of foreign investment projects. However, they may serve as a signalling device, reinforcing existing trends among foreign investors towards technological upgrading and enhancing the economy's attraction to high-technology operations.

Technology acquisition: actors, interests and governance

Malaysia's technology acquisition is thus largely governed by decentralised private-sector decisions within the context of an FDI-centred industrial policy. The policy stance towards technology imports is highly receptive, though passive in terms of bargaining or screening.[22] Malaysia's historic preference for foreign investment has reflected state elites' desire to avoid strengthening the ethnic-Chinese community's control over the domestic economy (Lim and Pang 1991: 36–45). The state's occasional efforts to bargain more aggressively with foreign investors over technology have not been undertaken to support the existing local business sector, but rather have taken the form of state/foreign joint ventures. Interestingly, domestic capital has been quiescent and often even actively supportive of FDI promotion. Though local ethnic-Chinese business representatives have complained of government favouritism towards foreign investors, therefore, they have usually aligned with MNCs in forums such as the Federation of Malaysian Manufacturers (FMM) in opposing specific instances of government regulation. In the mid-1990s the government became more active in managing technology acquisition, particularly by using new incentives and facilities to encourage the trend among MNCs to transfer higher-technology capabilities to local subsidiaries. These new technology-based investment promotion efforts are certainly not the determining factor in MNC decision-making, but they have allowed Malaysia to capitalise on the potential created by these firms' globalisation strategies.

The key question is whether more selective governance of technology acquisition, particularly in regulating FDI, would benefit Malaysia as it navigates the transition towards technology-intensive industry. A former high-level government planner (Abdullah 1995) articulates a common view that 'FDI cannot be relied upon to build up an indigenous industrial base which is required for long term sustainable industrialisation' and that policies should give distinct preference to local investment in manufacturing. Many observers are sceptical that more stringent regulation of FDI would benefit Malaysia. O'Connor (1993: 227) argues, for example, that 'one does not help local firms to compete by removing the competition. The sources of domestic firms' competitive disadvantage need to be identified and positively addressed.'[23] A second objection rests on the recognition that, in an era of globalised production and rapid technology change, the balance of bargaining power has shifted decisively towards MNCs, thus rendering Korea-style efforts to 'unpackage' FDI extremely risky if not altogether obsolete. Malaysia, with its small domestic market and limited indigenous industrial sector, very likely has little direct bargaining leverage *vis-à-vis* foreign investors. Moreover, the potential gains from co-operative 'Singapore-style' policies, involving inducements to MNCs to maximise technology inflows, recommend a more positive, if perhaps equally selective, governance approach.

Virtual free-trade conditions for promoted projects, together with the government's active efforts to streamline regulations and upgrade infrastructure, have indeed caused many MNCs to select Malaysia as the regional centre for more technologically sophisticated production. The leading example of the new wave of investment is the Matsushita group of companies, which established new Malaysian subsidiaries in the late 1980s to serve as regional export production centres for colour televisions and split-level room air-conditioners, and by the early

1990s, accounted for over 4 per cent of Malaysia's GDP. In some cases, MNCs' decisions to site higher-technology functions in Malaysia have come in response to the accumulation of capabilities within their long-established subsidiaries, as in the case of Motorola Penang's design centre for two-way land-based radio communication products, and Sharp Corporation's establishment of a TV design unit. The official 1994 national R&D survey reported that twenty-nine wholly- and twenty-nine majority-foreign owned MNCs engaged in formal R&D, and that their spending (US$30 million and US$16 million respectively) accounted for almost two-thirds of all manufacturing-sector R&D.

In sum, institutional governance of technology acquisition has been limited in scope and impact. Government investment promotion agencies have long lacked the technical expertise to screen and evaluate the technological content of investment projects. Underlying administrative weaknesses, however, is the absence of the nationalist political motivations which long shaped foreign investment policy in many developing countries. The state's ethnic motivations to use FDI to bypass local capital have waned, but Malaysia's perceived weak bargaining leverage has made government officials hesitant to regulate and bargain with foreign investors over technology transfer. The legacy of ethnic politics and the weakness of state/local business networks thus militate against more co-ordinated or institutionalised governance of technology acquisition. Instead, recent reforms indicate movement towards a technology acquisition strategy involving positive selective inducements to high-technology investments, which fully embraces an FDI-led industrial upgrading.

Technology use and diffusion

Policies and institutions

A chronic weakness in Malaysian manufacturing, one emphasised by the first (1986–95) and second (1996–2005) Industrial Master Plans, is the sector's dualistic nature, in which the foreign-dominated export industries remain disconnected from import-substituting manufacturing (Jomo and Edwards 1993: 320–1). Technology is a major aspect of this dualism. Foreign-dominated export-oriented industries employ modern production technologies while domestic-oriented and small-scale industries use outmoded techniques and equipment and register poor productivity growth. This persistent gap points to the economy's underlying failure to diffuse technology from the foreign sector throughout the industrial structure. Policy-makers have recognised that raising technological capabilities among local supporting industries, particularly small and medium-sized industries (SMIs), is a prerequisite to achieving a more integrated industrial structure.

MNCs' adoption of flexible manufacturing techniques, including just-in-time inventory management and greater sub-contracting, has drawn increasing attention as a promising trend for technology diffusion to local supporting industries

117

(Wong 1991; Rasiah 1994). Sub-contracting networks in Malaysia have grown notably in recent years, raising local-content levels in various industries (Aoki 1991). Contrary to the government's hopes, however, linkage growth has not resulted in widespread diffusion of technology to locally owned industry. Rasiah (1994, 1995a, 1995b) documents the emergence of dynamic backward linkages from foreign semiconductor assemblers to local machine-tool firms in Penang. However, such technology-rich sub-contracting patterns have been less evident in the major industrial areas of the Kelang Valley and Johor. Furthermore, much of the growth in sub-contracting involves linkages between foreign assemblers and foreign supplier firms. This is particularly true of more technologically complex components, while local suppliers primarily provide standardised plastic and metal parts and packaging materials (Guyton 1996). Despite some positive examples, sub-contracting networks appear thus far to be less effective in fostering technology diffusion than comparable linkages in Japan, Taiwan, Singapore and elsewhere (Lim and Pang 1991: 109–10).

Recognising the problem as a crucial obstacle to technology diffusion, the Malaysian government mounted several efforts in the 1990s to promote sub-contracting links between large local and foreign 'anchor companies' and locally owned suppliers. The first of these was a pilot vendor-development initiative begun in 1988 by Proton, the government-owned auto maker, to bring a number of new *Bumiputera* suppliers into the previously exclusively ethnic-Chinese auto-parts industry. In 1993, the concept was broadened under the Vendor Development Programmes administered by MITI and the Ministry of Finance. In these schemes, MNCs and large local companies sign agreements with MITI and designated banks to provide supplier firms with procurement contracts, technical assistance and subsidised finance. As the government signalled its seriousness, large numbers of MNCs joined the programme. By 1995, fifty-four firms, most of them foreign, had agreed to become anchor companies, supporting seventy-nine SMI vendors with RM230.4 million worth of contracts (*The Star*, 1 April 1996). The linkage-promotion effort was greatly expanded under the Second Industrial Master Plan (1996–2005) and concurrent Seventh Malaysia Plan (1996–2000).

Despite the Vendor Development Programme's high profile, it has yet to register a major impact on technology transfer through industrial sub-contracting networks (see Tables 5.2 and 5.3). One factor is the absence of clear performance measurements and monitoring of the technology transfer or assistance component of sub-contracting relationships established under the scheme. Several participating anchor companies expressed their unwillingness to devote large subsidies to assist unqualified vendors selected by the government, and complained about the lack of clear definition of their responsibilities *vis-à-vis* officially designated vendors.[24] The government, for its part, complained that the Malaysian supplier companies suffered from 'the lack of guidance and inconsistent and unreasonable volume of orders from the anchor companies . . . [who] do not give priority to the vendor development programme'.[25]

Table 5.2 Vendor Development Programme – anchor companies by year

Sector	1988–92	1993	1994	1995	Total (Dec. 1995)
Electrical/electronics	2	6	29	—	37
Wood-based	—	1	2	2	5
Automotive	1	—	1	1	3
Telecommunication	—	—	—	2	2
Building materials	—	—	—	2	2
Ship building and repair	—	—	—	1	1
Film production	—	—	—	1	1
Ceramics	—	—	—	1	1
Engineering	—	—	1	—	1
Trade and export	—	—	—	1	1
Total	3	7	33	11	54

Source: MITI Annual Report 1995/96

Table 5.3 Vendor Development Programme – vendors by activity (Dec. 1995)

Metal stamping and fabrication	18
Plastic components	18
Wood-based furniture components	13
PCB assembly	8
Automotive components	6
Moulds and dies	5
Wire cords and wire harnesses	3
Surface-mount technology operations	2
Computer diskettes	1
Rubber keypads	1
Wooden cable drums	1
Cables	1
Transformer assembly	1
Die-attach wire bonds	1
Total	79

Source: MITI Annual Report 1995/96

A related aspect of technology diffusion is Malaysia's SMI-assistance schemes, which have been a perennial feature of the country's economic development programmes. Similar industrial extension programmes have been significant in Taiwan, Singapore and other countries in helping SMIs acquire modern production technologies and improve quality and productivity (Dahlman and Sananikone 1990). In Malaysia during the NEP period, the number of SMI programmes proliferated, though virtually all were directed towards facilitating the entry of new *Bumiputera* micro-enterprises, rather than towards broad-based technological upgrading of existing manufacturers. Many of these programmes have suffered from a lack of co-ordination and overall mismanagement and waste (Chee 1986; Ismail 1990). In 1991, an effort was made to rationalise the various schemes, with

MITI's newly created SMI division co-ordinating industrial extension and the Ministry of Science and Technology having authority over technology assistance programmes. Continued dissatisfaction with the co-ordination and effectiveness of SMI programmes, frequently articulated by the Federation of Malaysian Manufacturers, led in 1995 to a decision to establish a single government agency to supervise all SMI assistance schemes.[26] Funding for financial and technology-acquisition programmes for SMIs was increased five-fold for the Seventh Plan period.

Two of the key institutions involved in SMI assistance are the Standards and Industrial Research Institute of Malaysia (SIRIM) and the National Productivity Corporation (NPC). The NPC provides training and extension programmes in 'soft technology' or management systems, such as total quality management (TQM), personnel training, etc. Like other government agencies offering technical assistance to SMIs, the NPC historically emphasised assisting small *Bumiputera* entrepreneurs in a range of resource-based and non-manufacturing industries. However, in recent years it has adopted a wider approach in line with the government campaigns to promote quality consciousness in industry, as exemplified by the annual Prime Minister's Quality Awards. SIRIM has also become more active in providing technical assistance to SMIs, often as part of MITI vendor-development activities, through its quality-practice improvement schemes and administration of ITAF (Industrial Technology Assistance Fund) matching grants (discussed below).

SIRIM is a central actor in broader technology diffusion programmes, as well. One of its key roles is in setting and certifying product and quality-system standards. Standards promotion assists technology diffusion by codifying and spreading basic technical information widely, drawing firms' attention to technical benchmarks, and setting realisable targets for incremental technical improvement. While of less concern to technology leaders, it can be important in making sure that small firms and technology followers do not fall irretrievably behind, thus raising average quality levels across industrial sectors. Active standards-setting also provides the public good of enhancing a national industry's reputation for quality, and is therefore a vital support in exporting. SIRIM has been notably effective in promoting the International Standards Organisation's quality-systems certification programme, the ISO 9000 series, and had issued 700 certificates by the end of 1995. In response to the escalating demand for the ISO 9000 certification, the government established the Malaysia Accreditation Council in 1994 to accredit private and non-profit bodies offering their own certification services. Other than mandatory safety standards for consumer items, which SIRIM administers, standards-writing and certification for specific industries is a constantly evolving task. Recently, SIRIM has begun to delegate standards-writing authority to business associations with sufficient technical competence, such as the Malaysian Plastics Association and the Malaysian Iron and Steel Industry Federation. SIRIM has also spun-off some of its technology extension functions into commercial joint ventures. One 1994 joint-venture with Sime Darby, a leading plantation-based conglomerate, offers calibration and measurement services, while another collaboration with the government-owned Malaysian Technology Development Corporation offers technology consulting at subsidised rates.

A third diffusion function is technical consultancy or assistance in technology selection, training and trouble-shooting. Such services are particularly important as firms seek to adopt automated and semi-automated production equipment for the first time. Again, SIRIM is the primary institution supporting the use of automation technologies through its Advanced Manufacturing Technology Centre and national CAD/CAM centre. Malaysia's universities have become more active in technical consultancy in recent years. Their rapidly growing services to industry centre on short-term training and specialised testing, as well as provision of mandatory environmental impact assessment studies.

Finally, several institutions serve as sources of technological information for industry – a basic facet of technology diffusion. SIRIM maintains a technical library and offers a range of information services, such as world-wide patent search and standards information, as do several sector-specific public research institutions like the Malaysian Institute of Microelectronics Systems (MIMOS). These institutes also conduct national and regional information seminars, workshops and short courses in specific technology topics. At the apex level, the government in 1992 established the Malaysian Science and Technology Information Centre (MASTIC) to generate and distribute statistical information on science and technology trends to policy makers and other consumers. The centre has thus far focused on the policy component of its role, executing the first comprehensive national survey of R&D in 1994. Industry linkages are yet to be developed significantly, though plans call for a range of information services to the private sector.

Technology diffusion: actors, interests and governance

Malaysia's innovation system features vigorous government efforts to promote, co-ordinate and strategically manage technology diffusion and industrial integration. Government policies have aimed to reinforce MNCs' own moves to create local linkages, while also expanding 'supply-side' technical assistance to raise local SMIs' absorptive capabilities. Positive examples of technology linkages and spill-overs are evident in some sectors and regions of the country. While the situation is dynamic, however, the two types of institutional governance (private/MNC sub-contracting networks and government programmes) have so far failed to coalesce effectively. The formation of technologically fruitful linkages between MNCs and local firms has been much less than desired. Notwithstanding a few individual examples, a corps of dynamic middle-range sub-contract manufacturers, capable of sophisticated OEM production and an imminent move into own-design work, has yet to emerge.[27]

Limited progress in technology diffusion reflects both the continued weakness of absorptive capabilities within indigenous manufacturing (particularly SMIs), as well as persistent conflicts of interest among state, MNC and local business actors. State activism has yielded progress in various areas, including quality control certification. Co-operation in technology diffusion between government agencies

121

and local private industry has increased, as evidenced by MITI/FMM co-operation, SIRIM's extension activities, and universities' growing linkages to industry. Yet the legacy of the inter-ethnic restructuring goals, which long dominated SMI assistance programmes, has made many ethnic-Chinese manufacturers reluctant to participate in assistance programmes for fear of increased exposure to regulatory and tax authorities. Many local manufacturers view bureaucratic discretion in SMI promotion as inevitably connected either to *Bumiputera* promotion or to political patronage. MNCs, while co-operating with formal requirements, have resisted government attempts to accelerate and directly intermediate in their formation of vendor networks. Government oversight of vendor selection threatened Japanese companies' traditional sub-contracting practices, which are based on the gradual building of trust and information-sharing. Several MNCs were alarmed to find that local vendors had invoked government intervention in negotiations over pricing and volume. In sum, the weak policy networks between government and small and medium-sized manufacturers, and MNC resistance to government regulation, frustrate the effective functioning of institutions supporting technology diffusion.

An important partial exception to this pattern is found in Penang, where closer collaboration between state government officials, MNCs and local industry has underpinned the rise of high-technology industrial clusters in semiconductors, disk-drives and related industries.[28] Here, early moves by American electronics MNCs to develop local vendors were later reinforced by the promotional efforts of the state economic development corporation, which provided infrastructure and basic assistance to local SMIs (Rasiah 1995a). Significantly, Penang has Malaysia's only ethnic-Chinese-led state government, making it easier for state officials to overcome SMIs' wariness of the motives behind government industrial extension programmes. Shared backgrounds among state government officials, university lecturers and MNC managers (many of whom were locally raised and educated) facilitated co-operation to address technical and infrastructural obstacles to greater local sub-contracting. MNCs' network formation in Penang has thus included more locally owned firms in technologically sophisticated roles, in contrast to the pattern elsewhere in Malaysia.

Technology improvement and development

Policies and institutions

Malaysia's technology policies over the past decade have focused even more strongly on the generation of new technological innovations. In particular, Malaysia has sought to boost public R&D spending and reform its system of public science and technology (S&T) institutions to better serve industrial development goals. Its efforts in this regard have been more thorough and persistent than those of any other second-generation newly industrialising economy. As with the task of technology diffusion, however, a considerable gap has been apparent between vigorous policy measures and the desired effects on industry.

The centrepiece of post-1985 technology policy has been an effort to raise the national investment in research and development (R&D). The Fifth Malaysia Plan (1986–90) for the first time included a separate budget allocation of RM414 million (approximately US$166 million then), which rose to RM588 million during the Sixth Malaysia Plan (1991–95) and RM1 billion for the Seventh Malaysia Plan (1996–2000); see Table 5.4. The 1990 National Plan of Action for Industrial Technology Development (or APITD) set ambitious targets for increased R&D expenditures of 1.5 per cent of GDP by 1995 and 2 per cent by the year 2000.

It became clear within a few years that these targets were overly optimistic, and the ten-year goal was revised downwards to 1.6 per cent. A major obstacle to raising national R&D was the lack of institutional and human resources, particularly in non-agricultural research. A survey of IRPA-funded projects in 1993, for example, indicated that the existing research infrastructure had been unable to utilise the increased R&D allocations effectively because of limited physical facilities and a shortage of qualified research personnel. This was particularly true of approved allocations for industry-sector R&D projects, of which only 46 per cent were spent during 1986–91. Continuing efforts to enhance R&D monitoring and oversight have produced higher completion rates in subsequent years.

As noted above, the government in 1986 created the Intensification of Research in Priority Areas programme, or IRPA, to gather all public R&D funding under a centralised allocation and review mechanism. Besides setting strategic technology priorities, central policy makers have used the IRPA programme to induce major changes in the management of the country's thirty-two public research institutions (RIs). The chief goal of institutional reform has been to guide the public R&D effort towards projects and discoveries that might be commercialised by private industry. Under IRPA, commercial relevance was ostensibly a major criterion for project selection, both at the level of individual research institutions as well as in the national allocation process. According to government reviews during the early 1990s, however, the process did not result in a notable increase in the number of commercial products arising from public R&D, due in part to vague selection criteria, *ad hoc* evaluation procedures, and the rigidities of a five-year budget planning cycle.

Table 5.4 IRPA – Public-sector R&D allocations in Fifth and Sixth Malaysia Plans

Sector	5MP, 1986–90		6MP, 1991–95	
	RM mill.	(%)	RM mill.	(%)
Agriculture	203.2	49	273.8	47
Industry	138.1	33	165.8	28
Medical	33.1	8	59.8	10
Strategic	39.4	10	78.6	13
Social science	—	—	10.1	2
Total	413.8	100	588.2	100

Source: MPKSN Annual Reports, various years

Frustrated with the minimal commercial impact of public R&D spending, the government in the early 1990s mounted a major reform effort to make RIs' research activities more 'demand-driven' and responsive to industry's priorities. Following the 1990 Technology Action Plan's recommendations, all RIs were required to draw up five-year corporate development plans with measures to increase commercialisation of research. General self-financing targets – 30 per cent of operating budgets to be derived from industry contracts by 1995 – were set. Similar reforms, including relaxation of limits on compensation from and time limits on outside projects for faculty, have led to the growth of innovation consultancy and extension units at each of Malaysia's universities. The most successful reform case is SIRIM, which expanded its research division, aggressively pursued industry contracts, and moved to spin off many of its service activities in commercial joint ventures.[29] The Science University of Malaysia in Penang has been equally dynamic in forging industrial linkages. Its Innovation and Consultancy Centre worked with over seven hundred corporate clients during 1981–93, and in 1995 alone obtained contracts worth RM2.3 million from six hundred companies (*The Star*, 3 February 1996). Reform of the research infrastructure has progressed towards the full corporatisation of many institutes, taking them out of the ordinary civil service system.[30]

In a bid to enhance the commercial impact of the now vastly expanded public R&D budget, the government launched the Malaysian Technology Development Corporation (MTDC) in 1993. MTDC is a public/private venture-capital company involving several of the country's largest private business groups, banks and government financial trust agencies.[31] The corporation's original mission was to search university and public-sector research institutions for commercially viable research findings, locate potential industry clients to license the technology, and in certain cases provide equity investment to resulting ventures. Its extensive efforts yielded a relatively small number (15 by the end of 1996) of contracts commercialising original innovations, and most of these are in agricultural or resource-based applications. MTDC's other roles proved more fruitful, including equity investments in established small technology-based companies and brokering international deals between foreign technology licensers and local firms. By 1995, MTDC had taken an equity stake in 28 medium-sized technology companies, and was targeting emerging fields such as LCD display assembly and semiconductor equipment manufacture. In several cases, MTDC's primary function has been to take the *Bumiputera* equity shareholding that is required of most companies above a certain size threshold, thereby allowing its portfolio firms to grow and move towards a public listing. Perhaps more than finding and nurturing new technology start-ups, MTDC's major contribution might be to shelter the growth of technology-based firms by brokering the kind of inter-ethnic investment partnerships which Malaysia's political economy requires.

A second effort to stimulate technology creation in industry was the creation of specialised technology parks to house and support private research facilities and technology-intensive companies. Technology Park Malaysia (TPM) was established

Table 5.5 Commercialisation of public-sector R&D fundings, December 1996

Sector	Number of projects
Biotechnology	4
Nuclear technology	3
Environmental technology	2
Medical and pharmaceutical	2
Scientific and industrial equipment	2
Advanced manufacturing technology	1
Non-scientific research	1
Total	· 15

Source: MTDC

in 1988 and began an incubator programme with a small number of micro-enterprises in information technology and electronics. In 1996, the TPM opened permanent facilities, including sophisticated testing and prototyping equipment, testing and training facilities, and an IT R&D laboratory. By that time TPM had assisted sixty companies with technical facilities (e.g. CAD/CAM), arranged several international technology contracts, and was prepared to expand the number of its corporate tenants. Though slow getting off the ground, by the mid-1990s the Technology Park had become a focal point for government efforts to link public technology institutes to industry. The Kulim High-Technology Park in the northern Kedah state is an equally large effort, supported with special investment incentives, to solicit technology-based foreign and local investment projects. The Kulim Park is intended to create an integrated environment for R&D and technology-intensive production, with supporting facilities (an IT centre operated by Malaysia's Science University, integrated manufacturing lab, CAD/CAM centre, training centre, incubation facility, etc.); on-site presence of the chief public RIs (MIMOS and SIRIM) and universities (Science University and the Technology University); special infrastructure (toxic waste disposal, fibre optics, redundant power supplies); and special lots for SMIs in ancillary industries. The anchor tenant was to be Malaysia's first full-scale semiconductor wafer fabrication facility, though the project has met with repeated delays. Other tenants are disk-drive, semiconductor assembly, and specialised tooling companies (many expanding investments from nearby Penang). In late 1996, the government unveiled its most ambitious infrastructural project for high-technology industry, the Multimedia Super Corridor (MSC). The MSC was to be a multi-billion-dollar zone in which special facilities and incentives would be offered to stimulate the emergence of IT development and research.

Besides reforming or expanding public-sector R&D institutions and infrastructure, the government created a range of policies to stimulate industry's own R&D investments. The 1990 Technology Action Plan, citing the swift rise of private-sector R&D in South Korea, called for a shift in the ratio of public to private expenditure from an estimated 80:20 in 1990 to 40:60 by the end of the decade.

The government offered an expanding menu of tax incentives, beginning in 1984 with a tax deduction for approved in-house R&D projects, later increased to a double deduction (see Table 5.6).[32] Other fiscal measures include tax holidays for private-contract R&D firms or new innovation-based companies, allowances for capital expenditures on R&D facilities, and double deductions for expenditures on externally contracted research. The response to the various tax incentives over the past several years was negligible prior to 1991, with fewer than ten companies a year receiving the basic double-deduction, and more recent years have seen only modest improvement.[33] Furthermore, only a quarter of the value of approved deductions for 1984–93 went to industry-related R&D, with a far greater amount being awarded to agricultural research. The low uptake of R&D incentives has been attributed to the complexity of the application process, the narrow definition of eligible research activities, and the riskiness to firms of having to win approval of expenditures *ex post*. The government continued to revamp tax incentives for R&D in a quest for greater impact, most notably in 1994 with MIDA's introduction of Pioneer Status for new investments in particular 'high-technology' activities that meet R&D-intensity and other criteria.

Table 5.6 Double-deduction tax incentive for industrial R&D, 1984–93

Ownership Category	Number	Value (RM '000)	% total value	Average per project (RM '000)
Wholly Malaysian	14	5,998	14	428
Malaysian majority	32	5,702	13	178
Majority foreign	40	7,917	18	198
Wholly foreign	38	23,382	54	615
Total	124	43,084	100	346

Source: unpublished MIDA data

Table 5.7 Industrial Technical Assistance Fund (ITAF) for SMIs, 1990–96

Scheme	No. approvals	Grants (RM mill.)
Consultancy services (ITAF 1)	422	7.2
Product development and design (ITAF 2)	145	10.8
Quality and productivity improvement (ITAF 3)	212	14.0
Market development (ITAF 4)	623	4.1
Total	1402	36.1

Source: Malaysia, International Trade and Industry Report 1996/97

Sources of specialised financial support for industrial R&D in Malaysia are relatively few, but growing in number. The chief government subsidy programme is the Industrial Technical Assistance Fund (ITAF), established in 1989 with an

RM50 million allocation, which provides matching grants to small and medium-sized industries for innovation projects (see Table 5.7).[34] Like R&D tax incentives, the ITAF programme initially met with negligible response, though subsequent efforts to streamline and publicise the scheme have increased the annual number of awards. SIRIM's role as an administrator of ITAF allows it to package the grants with its other technical assistance programmes, including MITI's vendor development programmes. Despite improvements to ITAF and a subsequent growth in grants, its impact is limited by its small scale in terms of total available funds and the average grant size, as well as by its restriction to SMIs. The absence of a broader subsidised credit or grants scheme for private-industry R&D contrasts with similar programmes in South Korea and Singapore. Significantly, a proposal advanced in the 1990 Technology Action Plan for a much broader R&D grant scheme, utilising the National Science Council's IRPA review panels and open to firms of all sizes, was rejected in favour of continued elaboration of tax incentives.[35]

In late 1996, the idea was revived – in the form of a RM100 million Industry Grants Scheme under MOSTE, which would provide matching-grant funding for joint public–private R&D projects. The scheme drew little response initially, however (*Business Times*, 9 July 1997). Under the 7th Malaysia Plan (1996–2000), several other new technology funding mechanisms were announced. These include: two RM100 million matching-grant funds administered by the MTDC, one for technology acquisition and the other for technology commercialisation; a RM200 million multimedia matching-grant scheme and a venture-capital scheme for investment in MSC-status companies; and a RM10 million venture-capital fund administered by Technology Park Malaysia.

Beyond these specialised technology-related funds, the government has launched broader efforts to encourage investment in high-technology industries. In 1994, the Ministry of Finance established an investment arm, Khazanah Holdings, to spearhead direct government investment in major strategic and high-technology sectors. Khazanah took major investment stakes in MTDC, in the chief MSC development company, and in HICOM (the privatised parent company of the national car company Proton and the troubled Perwaja steel project). Through joint ventures with foreign partners at the Kulim High Tech Park, Khazanah is also the spearhead for the government effort to establish a wafer fabrication industry. In 1997 it partnered a local ethnic-Chinese firm in an ambitious (RM4 billion) project to create a Malaysian-brand electrical-appliance conglomerate. Finally, in 1996 the government announced plans to launch MESDAQ, an automated stock exchange for high-technology firms. Unfortunately, these plans were set back by the dramatic fall of the equity markets amidst the regional economic crisis in 1997–98.

Technology improvement and generation: actors, interests and governance

The Malaysian state has strongly endeavoured to govern new technology creation through strategically co-ordinated public-sector R&D investments on the 'supply side' and efforts to stimulate 'demand-side' investments in technology development by private industry. Despite mounting efforts, the policy emphasis on technology creation and R&D has had only limited impact on actual technology development within industry. Indeed, the official national R&D survey revealed that the national expenditure on R&D has fallen far short of the large increases planned, and indeed dropped from RM611.2 million in 1994, a mere 0.34 per cent of GDP, to RM549.1 million in 1996.[36]

Somewhat surprisingly, the business sector accounted for RM400.1 million or 73 per cent of the 1996 total, a 37 per cent increase over 1994, while the government and higher education spent only 23 per cent. Business's impressive growth and share of national R&D are partly misleading, however, because they reflect growth from a small initial base as well as a sharp drop in public R&D spending in 1996. Several other factors point to the continued weakness in private-sector R&D. Business-sector spending was highly concentrated with the national oil company and quasi-privatised electric utility alone accounting for nearly one-third of total business R&D. Significantly, manufacturing companies spent less than one-half of total business R&D. In sum, the growth of private-sector R&D is a hopeful sign, but the magnitude and depth of private technology investments remains inadequate in light of the country's changing industrial structure and aspirations for NIC status.

In terms of R&D linkages between the public system and private industry, the 1996 survey reported that less than 1 per cent of businesses' reported expenditure was obtained from government sources, with an even smaller amount of spending contracted out to local universities or public research institutions. The data thus portray a persistent gap between public R&D investments and incentives on the one hand, and business's innovation efforts on the other. The far-reaching efforts to reshape the public-sector research infrastructure have not resulted in the desired growth of public–private R&D collaboration and commercialisable inventions.

Table 5.8 R&D expenditure by agent – 1992–1996 (RM million)

	1992	%	1994	%	1996	%
Government/RI	253.7	46	164.9	27	108.7	20
Higher education	50.7	9	150.9	25	40.4	7
Business	246.3	45	292.6	48	400.1	73
Total	550.7	100	611.2	100	549.1	100

Source: MOSTE – MASTIC 1996 National R&D Survey

Evolutionary theories of innovation illuminate these findings, in that most of Malaysia's locally owned industries have yet to reach a stage in which original innovation and formal R&D are major concerns, and most of business's R&D activities involve in-house efforts to apply or adapt existing technologies. Simply put, neither local nor multinational business yet shares the government's ambitions in indigenous technology creation.[37] This implies that the core thrust of much recent technology policy, boosting national R&D investments and commercialising public-sector research findings, has been misplaced. Though reforms have striven to make the research infrastructure 'demand-driven', they have implicitly assumed a linear, R&D-driven innovation model. Efforts to stimulate private business's own R&D activity were confined to largely ineffective tax measures until quite recently. Recent policy changes under the auspices of the Second Industrial Master Plan (1996–2005) seem to reflect an awareness of the difficulties in trying to drive industrial technology development through public-sector R&D spending. The Plan's guiding concept is that industries develop by gradually expanding along a 'value-added chain' from simple assembly to embrace a spectrum of design, production and marketing activities, among which formal R&D may emerge relatively late. Moreover, expanded funding for private-sector technology acquisition and R&D, along with new direct government investments in targeted high-technology ventures, point to a realisation that stimulating industry's own production-based learning, rather than attempting to commercialise public-sector research findings, is a crucial element of technology policy. However, the challenges of implementing these new, more nuanced policies are formidable, and, like earlier promotional measures, they are hampered by weak policy networks with the private sector and a lack of shared public–private interests and consensus on goals.

The new technology-related matching-grant and venture-capital schemes naturally target local companies and thus require Malaysian-majority ownership. Like the earlier tax incentive schemes, however, these mechanisms have generated only a weak response (*BT*, 9 July 1997). The funding agencies' weak links to the private sector, a general lack of awareness of the schemes, and many businesses' scepticism of involvement with government programmes are all obstacles to the new efforts to nurture government–business links in R&D. Significantly, the biennial R&D surveys document a trend among private business towards contracting R&D services from foreign sources, rather than local institutions.

Given foreign companies' leading role in Malaysian industrialisation, the country is a crucial case study in the debate as to whether multinational corporations' interests conflict with and frustrate industrialising countries' ambitions to foster technology development. The oft-heard argument is that MNCs inevitably retain their technology creation functions in home-country headquarters while limiting their off-shore subsidiaries to production, or at most, adaptive R&D. A counter-argument holds that MNCs have begun to decentralise authority and move key design and research functions to their established production bases in advanced developing countries.

Evidence from Malaysia is mixed. In the 1990s, a succession of manufacturing MNCs announced the creation of formal R&D departments and the initiation of local product design activities within their Malaysian subsidiaries. Foreign-owned and -controlled enterprises accounted for three-quarters of the tax deductions for approved R&D for 1984–93. They spent two-thirds of manufacturing business's R&D in 1994 and more than half of the sectoral total in 1996. Not surprisingly, most multinational companies' R&D involves adaptive design work rather than innovation linked to core technologies, and MNCs have shown no more demand for public-sector R&D services than have local firms.

Eventually, as Malaysian industry accumulates greater engineering and design capabilities, the anticipated conflict of interest between local and multinational actors might become more acute if MNCs shift attention to other locations for high-tech operations or crowd-out local companies' efforts to move into own-design or own-brand manufacturing. Indeed, the key electronics industry remains dominated by final assembly and testing activities, despite significant diversification and some design-for-manufacture activity. Yet, recent trends suggest that MNC subsidiaries in Malaysia are indeed taking on somewhat more important functions in their parents' overall technology development efforts. The immediate possibilities for encouraging technological deepening *within* MNC subsidiaries, as well as foreign participation in non-R&D links with local RIs and universities, might therefore be greater than commonly assumed.

Despite the general absence of shared interests in R&D among state and local and foreign business actors, the government's concerted efforts to mobilise public R&D institutions and policies to support industrialisation are far from having been wasted. Public-sector investments in research have created new stocks of physical and human capital in technology. While public RIs have commercialised few new innovations, their contract numbers and revenue figures indicate that linkages to industry have begun to grow. This contrast suggests that strenuous reform efforts have in fact succeeded in changing the incentive structure motivating public research institutions, but that the nature of industry demand and the resulting linkages are concentrated on 'shallower', non-R&D services, including information, testing and consultancy. Caught between the rather conflicting imperatives of commercialising public R&D and expanding their industry contracts, institutions like SIRIM have evolved towards a greater emphasis on supporting firms' technology acquisition and diffusion. Basic challenges for the future, therefore, are to continue to refocus policy away from an R&D-driven model in order to enhance the public system's role in technology acquisition and diffusion, while simultaneously finding broader mechanisms through which to stimulate industry's own innovative efforts.

Technical human resource development

Policies and institutions

Malaysia's comparatively strong primary education system nurtured a literate and trainable labour force, which fuelled the swift transition from an agricultural to an industrial economy. Rapid structural change in recent years, however, has far outrun the educational system's ability to supply industry with the skilled human capital it requires, ranging from vocationally skilled labour to technicians and production engineers. The skills shortage not only hampers short-term productivity growth but also has follow-on effects which are likely to seriously inhibit firm-level investments in skills formation and technological deepening.

The most serious issue is the negative effect on firms' own in-house training efforts. Salaries soared during the 1990s, accompanied by high rates of turnover and widespread complaints of excessive 'job-hopping'. A 1995 World Bank survey reported average employee turnover of between 20 and 27 per cent (World Bank 1997: 41). Quit rates for non-production workers, including engineers and supervisors, were lower, but still approached 10 per cent per annum. Rapid employment turnover creates a major disincentive for firms to invest in training, since they are unlikely to capture most of the productivity improvements which result. The same survey reported that firms that provide formal training actually experienced higher rates of workforce turnover. Among firms that did not give formal training to their workers, high labour turnover was the second most often cited reason (after a perceived lack of need). A second negative effect of skills shortages is to place smaller locally owned manufacturers at a disadvantage in the labour market. Such firms are unable to match the salaries and other benefits MNCs offer, and so have even greater difficulty attracting and retaining technically skilled staff. In this way, the skills shortage undermines efforts to boost technological capabilities among Malaysia's SMIs and foster linkages with the foreign manufacturing sector.[38] The World Bank (1997: 11) study found that only one-quarter of small firms invested in formal training, compared to half of medium-sized firms and two-thirds of large firms.

In order to encourage firms' technical training investments, the Ministry of Finance initiated a double tax deduction for training expenditures in 1986. As with R&D tax incentives, the response from industry was disappointing. In 1993, the government undertook a much more active governance role with the creation of the Human Resources Development Fund (HRDF), an industry sector-wide payroll levy and subsidy scheme.[39] Firms employing more than fifty workers[40] are required to contribute 1 per cent of their payrolls to the Fund, and may apply for reimbursement of a percentage of expenses on approved training programmes at government and certain industry-run training institutes. Companies also have the option of applying for approval of their in-house annual training plans and special training courses. The HRDF is an ambitious attempt to use mandatory contributions and public governance to stimulate private-sector training and to encourage the demand for the services of specialised training providers. Insofar as most MNC manufacturers already engage in high levels of training, the primary impact is likely to be on local industries.[41] A Human Resources Development Council governs the Fund with representation by employers' associations. Nonetheless, it drew significant business criticism in its early years for slow approvals for in-house training programmes, delays in reimbursements, confusion about documentation and allowable expenses, and the overall administrative burdens involved. Subsequent efforts have sought to streamline and publicise the Fund, and by 1995 the programme had disbursed RM74 million in reimbursements for the training of 439,016 employees (Yau 1995: 15).[42]

131

Compounding the skills shortages has been a persistent mismatch between the types of training provided by the vocational and technical educational system and the needs of industry. As recently as 1991, almost 60,000 job seekers registered with the Ministry of Human Resources could not be placed because of inadequate or inappropriate skills (Kanapathy and Abdul Rahman 1994: 5). Three different ministries and the Majlis Amanah Rakyat (MARA) share authority for the vocational education system.[43] The Ministry of Human Resources oversees the Centre for Instructors and Advanced Skill Training (CIAST) and 10 regional industrial training institutions (ITIs); 67 vocational and technical schools and 7 polytechnic schools are under the purview of the Ministry of Education; the Ministry of Youth and Sports operates a handful of youth training centres; and MARA operates 9 skills institutes and 20 skills centres around the country. A small number of private-sector institutes also provide technical training.[44] In 1990, Malaysia's tertiary enrolment ratio was only 6 per cent of the university-age population, while vocational enrolment was 7 per cent of the relevant population. The vocational education system's capacity was a mere 22,220 in 1990, though the intake volume increased to 43,100 in 1995. In 1990, the government estimated that the country would encounter shortages of 9,100 engineers, 17,930 engineering assistants and over 127,700 vocationally skilled workers by the year 2000.[45]

In line with an Industrial Master Plan recommendation, a National Vocational Training Council (NVTC) was created in 1989 in an effort to better co-ordinate all public-sector vocational training programmes, administer certification examinations, and enhance private-sector participation in curriculum reform. Bureaucratic overlap and division, however, continued to inhibit reform efforts (Rozikin 1994: 72). The ITIs under the Ministry of Human Resources are the primary source of formalised trade skills training under the National Apprentice Scheme and the Trade Skill Certification Course. According to government reviews and business representatives' evaluations, the ITIs have been largely unresponsive to changing industrial needs, in large part due to shortages of qualified instructors and outdated materials and equipment. Similar difficulties have plagued MARA's skills institutes.

Mounting concern with the skills deficit prompted the formation in 1990 of a Cabinet Committee on Training, which examined the skills training infrastructure in six industrial sectors. The Cabinet Committee's Report stressed the need to address the vocational system's rigidities, emphasise teacher training, and increase collaboration with the private sector. Despite the high-level attention to the problem, reform of the public vocational education system has progressed relatively slowly, and administrative divisions and limited interaction with industrial clients have persisted. The policy focus in the 1990s has shifted to other institutional initiatives, including joint ventures with the German, French and Japanese governments to set up technical training institutes, and the encouragement of industry-operated skills development centres modelled on the successful Penang Skills Development Centre (PSDC).

The PSDC was established in 1989 following consultations between the Penang Development Corporation (PDC) and the managing directors of several MNCs operating in the state. Its primary mission is to provide specialised skills training to help firms upgrade personnel from production workers to technical specialists and technicians, though higher-level engineering courses are also offered. It conducts short courses in a range of production operation and control skills, including use of automated assembly equipment, and consults with firms on the design of in-house training programmes. PSDC is managed by a board consisting of its corporate members with representation by the PDC, the Science University (USM), and SIRIM. The Centre operates on land donated by the PDC and utilises up-to-date equipment donated by or on loan from industry, as well as equipment purchased with government support. It carries out biannual training needs assessments in order to guide the work of the curriculum development committees, which comprise its corporate members. The PSDC's rapid growth and favourable evaluation by its business members attracted the attention of the federal government, which in 1994 called for the replication of industry-managed skills development centres in each state. In 1995, a similar centre was established with MNC participation in Selangor, the state in which the Klang Valley industrial concentration is located. The model was then replicated in other states, including Johor, Kedah and Pahang.

Malaysia's human resources gap has also spurred efforts to reform the system of higher education. Science and engineering enrolments were expanded among the established varsities, and new universities were established in Sarawak in 1993 and Sabah in 1996 with an explicit emphasis on engineering and information systems. In 1996, three major pieces of education legislation were passed. One Act was passed to recognise final degrees from private universities and permit foreign universities to open branch campuses. An amendment to the Universities Act passed that year enables the established public universities to be made into independent public corporations.[46] One specific provision of the reform of the laws governing universities allows engineering programmes to be cut from four to three years as a way of speeding the entry of graduates into the workforce. A system of private colleges also operates in Malaysia, many of them offering two-year programmes linked to subsequent degree study in overseas universities. Most of these, however, offer primarily liberal arts and professional programmes, rather than science or engineering. Finally, in the mid-1990s the government instructed the privatised telephone and power utility monopolies, together with the leading indigenous telecommunications manufacturing conglomerate, Sapura, to establish degree-granting institutions in their respective engineering fields. Universiti Telekom is tapped to train high-level technical personnel for the Multimedia Super Corridor, together with Sapura's Asia Institute of Information Technology, which is housed in the Technology Park. In 1997, a project to create a new Malaysian Science and Technology University was launched with technical assistance from the Massachusetts Institute of Technology.

Reform of the university system long posed a difficult challenge, in part due to the central role of tertiary education in achieving the New Economic Policy's goals of social restructuring: ethnic quotas have been applied to the local public varsities since shortly after Independence. A second major concern is the declining popularity of science and technical education. Though graduates in the science and technical streams increased by 42 per cent in the Sixth Malaysia Plan period (1991–95), their proportion of all tertiary graduates (degree, diploma and certificate) fell from 54 per cent to 46 per cent.[47] In general, the growth of the university system has not kept up with the country's needs and Malaysia historically sends thousands of students abroad for higher education. Overseas education is one of the central ways in which successful industrialising countries have formed technical human capital and acquired up-to-date technology. In Malaysia's case, the benefits accruing from foreign education have been somewhat mitigated by the fact that, during the 1970s and 1980s, many ethnic Chinese chose to remain abroad to build careers. Quite often, those staying abroad had degrees in sciences or engineering, and their skills secured them positions in Singapore, Australia and elsewhere. Since the Malaysian economy took off in the late 1980s and social restructuring policies were eased, this trend has apparently begun to decline. In 1994, the Ministry of Science initiated a programme to encourage Malaysian scientists and engineers living abroad to return home to public or private positions. Working with the FMM, MIDA has circulated lists of Malaysian engineering students to encourage and assist foreign companies in recruiting staff directly in their home countries.

Technical human resource creation: actors, interests and governance

By most accounts, human resources are the weakest link in Malaysia's national innovation system. The state has taken a leading role in human capital formation in Malaysia through its investments in education and vocational training. Nowhere has the tension between social restructuring and industrial development goals been more acute, however. Higher education and vocational training are fundamental components of the effort to strengthen the cultural vitality and economic participation of the indigenous *Bumiputera* population. The balance struck between these goals produced an educational system in which basic and secondary education were emphasised over the kinds of specialised higher education and training more directly linked to industrial demands. Thus, for example, Malaysia's secondary enrolment ratio in 1990 was 56 per cent compared with Thailand's 32 per cent, whereas the tertiary enrolment ratios were 7 per cent and 16 per cent, respectively. For the same year, Thailand's vocational enrolments were over 444,000 compared with 31,000 in Malaysia (UNESCO 1993).[48] Meanwhile, the public higher educational and vocational training systems have not kept up with the changing skill profile required by industry, and rapid growth and technical change has thrown the system's flaws into critical focus.

As state priorities shifted in favour of growth promotion in the late 1980s, educational reform remained perhaps the most symbolic and politically challenging issue within Malay politics. The emphasis on private or business-run training institutions in part represents an attempt to bypass the bureaucratic and political difficulties of reform. In the mid-1990s, however, the state tackled fundamental reforms in higher education, albeit from the standpoint of a market-driven approach. It is far from clear that the private sector can play the leading role in creating the workforce Malaysia needs for its next stage of industrialisation, especially in the light of the current economic downturn.

Multinational business has been a leading actor in the formation of human capital for a technology-intensive industrial structure. MNCs have intensified their in-house training programmes as their production facilities have upgraded from simple labour-intensive assembly operations. Insofar as they have continued training in the face of significant labour-force turnover, MNCs have absorbed the costs of major externalities in human capital formation, which have benefited the economy greatly. Under these circumstances, foreign investors have been willing to collaborate with Malaysian entities in building new facilities and programmes for training, as have their home-country governments in several instances. However, MNC and local interests in technical human capital formation do not wholly converge. In 1990, for example, it was alleged that Japanese manufacturers had begun to collude to limit staff turnover and salary increases.[49] Foreign firms also objected to the government's direct intervention through the mandatory HRDF, as they are naturally disinclined to bear the costs of even broader efforts to upgrade the human capital infrastructure and promote training among local industry.[50] Apart from the limitations of relying on foreign firms' in-house training, the shortage of highly technically skilled workers with high 'absorptive capacities' has hampered Malaysia's ability to capitalise on MNCs' training externalities. Foreign business representatives repeatedly stress the skills deficit as a major constraint on technology transfer.

Local business has generally been less active in reform of Malaysia's education and training infrastructure, perhaps because of the recognition of the political sensitivities of educational reform. The leading business associations have consistently observed the need for improvements in training facilities in their policy dialogues with the government, and as the political relationship between state and business became closer in the late 1980s, offered more detailed suggestions for policy reform (FMM n.d.). Several business associations have also become active in providing training programmes in both technical and managerial fields.[51] Such industry-based training efforts are positive exceptions to the generally weak investment in training among locally owned manufacturing enterprises.

In sum, technical human capital formation has been governed through a range of relatively decentralised institutions, with MNCs' in-house investments figuring prominently. The public institutional system continues to confront daunting challenges in reforming and upgrading its capabilities and responsiveness to the demands of industrialisation. Success in reforming Malaysia's human capital systems will require rapid and effective reform at the system-wide level, as well as support for targeted industry- and skills-specific training mechanisms. The ambitious educational reforms adopted in 1996, following prolonged consideration of the system's weaknesses, seek to address the first task.[52] The latter thrust demands continued efforts to foster close collaboration with foreign and local industry. The HRDF represents an important effort to mobilise and regulate greater industry-based training efforts through a national governance mechanism. Yet again, MNC resistance and local business's wariness, together with administrative difficulties, confronted the scheme's early implementation.

Conclusion

Malaysia's concerted efforts to create a national innovation system shed important light on the role of state and business actors in successful late industrialisation. The need for explicit technology-supporting institutions and investments, which arises quickly in the course of rapid industrial growth, does not generate a spontaneous response. The Malaysian experience highlights the potential importance of activist state policies to create the institutions that support industrial technology development within firms and across industries. Malaysia's post-1985 transition to a market-based development strategy has not, for example, provoked a comparable surge in business investments in technological development. Rather, state initiatives to encourage technology diffusion, quality control standards and technical training have been central to creating an environment conducive to structural transition in industry. The globalisation of MNC production strategies has in fact given rise to new possibilities for the encouragement of MNC-led local technology development and linkage formation. In a manner somewhat reminiscent of Singapore, the Malaysian government's encouragement and pressure have combined with the local accumulation of skills and experience to support MNC investments in higher-technology production operations.

Yet, the limitations to state- and MNC-led technology strategies are also evident in the Malaysian case. Notwithstanding its real achievements, Malaysia's technology development agenda has fallen well short of its own ambitious goals, particularly in encouraging the growth of genuine innovative capabilities within locally owned industry. The lack of technological dynamism across broad spectrums of locally owned industry remains the most worrying feature within a highly dynamic industrial picture. In large part, the disjuncture results from a mismatch between Malaysia's nationalist 'Korea-style' ambitions (e.g. R&D-driven innovation), outlined in its technology strategy, and its highly internationalist 'Singapore-style' FDI-reliant industrial policy. Though S&T policies have made the generation of new technologies the focus of efforts to expand local R&D, the population of local and foreign-owned industry having reached the stage of original innovation work is still quite small.

Reconciling the disjuncture between Malaysia's industrial development framework and its technology strategy implies refocusing technology strategies in several basic ways. First, the emphasis of public policies must be shifted from R&D promotion to the encouragement of technology acquisition, use and diffusion. The development strategy outlined in the Second Industrial Master Plan (1996–2005) points clearly in this direction by emphasising the importance of marketing, management and other functions besides formal R&D. Progress is evident in the small but rapidly growing linkages between a few public research institutes and universities and their industrial clienteles, which primarily involve a range of information, consulting and training services. Many state agencies, however, lack sufficient depth of industry-based expertise to foster and monitor the types of non-R&D investments that contribute to productivity growth.

Second, Malaysia's technology policies will need to focus more closely on the central role of multinational corporations as agents of the country's technological transition. Singapore's experience has revealed the extent to which targeted investments in requisite skills, supporting industries, and incentives can both induce MNCs to upgrade their internal technology development activities as well as better capture the externalities of foreign investment through training, sub-contracting, spin-offs and staff migration, and other linkages to the local economy. The Malaysian government has begun to bargain in a general way with foreign investors over technology issues, and more nuanced efforts to govern FDI to enhance technology spill-overs promise to yield larger benefits. Such government/MNC co-operation is evident in Penang state, from which the federal government has sought to generalise several policy ideas. Third, the critical importance of dramatically raising the quality and quantity of technical skills in the workforce demands far-reaching measures. Again, significant action on this front is a major portion of the agenda laid out in the Second Industrial Master Plan (1996–2005) agenda. The urgency of addressing the human capital question is clearly understood; the difficulty lies in harmonising sharp increases in human capital investments with thorough reform of the formerly unresponsive and bureaucratic education and training system. Whether the current privatisation-based approach will achieve the necessary combination of growth with quality will be a vital question for future study.

The foregoing recommendations emphasise bringing the strategically ambitious technology policy in line with Malaysia's more liberal industrial policy framework. Important consideration should be given to the opposite type of reform, namely revising industrial policy to better reflect the developmental aspirations evident in the 1990 Technology Action Plan. For all of Malaysian industry's dynamic growth, local industry participation remains weak in several leading growth industries, and there is only scattered evidence that local industry in general is advancing through a transition into OEM and more design-based production roles. Technological deepening among MNCs seems to be proceeding into design activity, but both the pace and the content of this activity might not serve Malaysia's long-run goals. MNCs' new R&D activities appear primarily aimed at cosmetic changes to create new models for local and regional markets, or design modification to suit local production conditions. Moreover, the establishment of regional R&D units in Singapore might slow the growth of similar activities within Malaysia.

The examples of Taiwan and Korea show that once locally owned industries accumulate sufficient production mastery and design capabilities, they are able to locate new, more lucrative and higher value-added roles in local and international supplier chains in co-operation with multinational corporations. Global competition drives MNCs to access the advantages of developing-country locations, not merely low wages, but conducive skills, infrastructure and institutions. Even in an age of globalisation, therefore, host countries have sources of bargaining leverage which, if applied judiciously, may accelerate the *indigenisation* of technological capabilities without permanently alienating foreign capital. The thrust of this reasoning is certainly not to argue for blanket restrictions on FDI or non-selective protection of local industry. However, it does suggest that the risks of more carefully regulating foreign investment to benefit local industry might yet be warranted in specific cases.[53] Malaysian-owned companies should indeed already be capable of more OEM production of simpler or lower product ranges in electronics, textiles, machinery and other industries than is currently evident. Insofar as foreign MNCs are slow to 'vacate' and yield these segments to local producers as product cycle theory predicts, a case might well be made for a more assertive bargaining posture.[54] Again, the evolutionary approach to innovation emphasises that such policies alone are insufficient. Infant-industry policies must be calibrated and selective, based on a realistic evaluation of the prospects for local firms to become competitive in the medium term; supply-side investments in raising local firms' skills and technological capabilities are an essential complement; and every effort must be made to maintain access to foreign technologies and markets.

In the end, options for improving the fit between technology development ambitions and industrial policy realities depend on the capacity of policy networks to support effective implementation. While technology policy *per se* is far from politically contentious, the implications of many aspects of S&T policy, including education and training reform, promotion of small and medium-scale industry, and general efforts to support the private sector have enormous political implications in the Malaysian political context. Despite profound changes, Malaysia pays an evident price for its historical legacy of adversarial government/business relations. Much of the existing population of indigenous manufacturing firms, whose accumulated production capabilities might provide a basis for further indigenous development, remain suspicious of close involvement with government promotional policies. Though political elites in the 1990s openly prioritise growth over redistribution, the state retains its emphasis on particularistic linkages to business, in part to manage inter-ethnic competition, in part to retain the political resources of patronage, and, paradoxically, in part as a response to bureaucratically controlled rent-seeking during the NEP era.

The weak private-sector response to incentives for technology development, together with the delayed emergence of an 'innovation culture' within local manufacturing, indicates the potential importance of a more aggressive programme of subsidisation of industry efforts by government. Mindful of the rent-seeking dynamics that emerged during government-financed social restructuring under the NEP, the political leadership has eschewed broad-based subsidies to industry through bureaucratic channels. Instead, the primary strategy for encouraging a locally owned corporate industrial sector has been to privatise former government industrial initiatives to a small group of entrepreneurs on the grounds that selectivity is necessary to ensure better performance and accountability. While this issue is contentious, it is clear that broader and stronger organisational interfaces between government and the mass of manufacturers are an essential prerequisite for a more nuanced industrial and technology policy which aims to bolster locally owned industry's position within MNC-dominated export manufacturing. This demands a stronger role for collective business organisations in policy-making, which in turn implies a stronger and more autonomous political role for business. Whether the recent political rapprochement between political and business elites will broaden and become even better institutionalised will determine the prospects for more successful strategic governance of technological development.

Notes

Research for this paper was conducted under the sponsorship of the Fulbright Student Research Grants Programme jointly administered by the Institute for International Educational Exchange and the Malaysian–American Commission on Educational Exchange (MACEE). Additional support for research was provided by the Center for International Studies of Princeton University through the Sumitomo Bank Fund. Invaluable logistical support was provided by the Institute for Strategic and International Studies (ISIS) Malaysia in Kuala Lumpur. Thanks are also due to the many Malaysian officials and academics who gave generously of their time and insights into Malaysian policy-making, with special thanks to Jomo K.S. for counsel and encouragement. None of these institutions or persons is responsible for the content or analysis of this paper, or for any errors of fact or interpretation contained therein.

1 Estimates of Malaysia's productivity growth vary. The Malaysian National Productivity Corporation reports that TFP growth averaged 3.2 per cent per annum from 1986 to 1995. The difficulties in estimating TFP, however, mean that this figure is not wholly reliable. The NPC's estimates do point to a trend of declining TFP growth rates during the 1990s, however.

2 An important example in 1993–94 involved the imposition of import controls over certain chemical feedstocks used by the majority of plastic products manufacturers. The controls aimed to support an infant-industry petrochemicals joint-venture involving the government and Taiwanese investors. The local plastics association and industry ministry officials argued over the project's impact on feedstock pricing and the procedures for import approvals, and the import restrictions were eventually lifted when the association enlisted the support of Singaporean chemicals suppliers, who in turn involved the Singaporean government in pressuring the Malaysian government.

3 This was underscored in the 1989–90 negotiations over the policy framework to succeed the NEP. The Malaysian Chinese Association (MCA), the ethnic-Chinese component party in the ruling coalition, successfully pushed for the establishment of a National Economic Consultative Council in late 1988 to draw up a new national development policy. The scepticism of the political leadership vitiated this attempt at broad-based quasi-corporatist bargaining over the future direction of development policy, and instead, the National Development Policy was formulated and issued unilaterally by the government (Jomo 1994).

4 The Malaysian Business Council was established in 1991. Chaired by the Prime Minister, its membership is made up of the country's leading political and business figures. In contrast to the formal policy dialogues between the line ministries (MITI and MOSTE) and the representative business associations, the MBC is an informal and

confidential forum in which the conceptual bases for policy initiatives are proposed and debated. In recent years, it has become increasingly influential in shaping the course of policy reform.

5 Foreign manufacturing investment was crucial to the state's ability to persist in industrial regulation for ethnic redistribution in the face of declining domestic private invest- ment, as well as in its programme of buying out foreign plantation companies (Jesudason 1989: Ch. 5).

6 Most important were 'push' factors: the appreciation of home-country currencies; rising labour and other business costs; and tension over bilateral trade surpluses with the US and Europe. Yet changing conditions within Southeast Asia, and in Malaysia specifically, were also important in attracting higher-technology FDI and inducing established foreign pro- ducers to upgrade their technological capabilities. These included both liberalisation of investment and import regulations and efforts to upgrade local economic infrastructure.

7 For analysis of technological upgrading within MNCs in Malaysia, see essays by Hobday, Norlela and Nazari in Jomo et al. (1999). Earlier work by Rasiah (1994, 1995) analyses technological upgrading in electronics MNCs in great detail.

8 In the latter case, an important motive was the ability to undertake transfer pricing, which in Malaysia allows profits to be shifted between affiliates to maximise tax advan- tages, especially given that group accounting is not legally recognised.

9 Samuels (1994: 53) describes the effects of political relationships on innovation in Japan in the following way

> The Japanese have constructed an elaborate system of protocols – some- times tacit, at other times explicit – to induce domestic firms, even as they compete, to negotiate constantly with their competitors and with bureau- crats to share market jurisdiction and control. These protocols can be as simple as legitimacy afforded to government advisory commissions and as complex as reciprocity accumulated over decades of interaction. They force interests as varied as the largest industrial producers, small subcon- tractors, regional industrial associations, local and national bureaucrats, and financial institutions to take account of each other's needs in shaping the economy.

10 Most public-sector research was concerned with agricultural and natural-resource pro- duction. In these areas, Malaysia's scientific and technology infrastructure performed exceptionally well, supporting technical advance in rubber and palm oil production, for example.

11 The Fifth Malaysia Plan noted that, previously, 'There was . . . an absence of overall direction and comprehensive and explicit strategies and policies on S&T'.

12 In fact, MIGHT originated as a Malaysian Business Council proposal.

13 An example is MIGHT's work in the mid-1990s in mobilising action on raising stan- dards in the construction sector, where a boom in large-scale construction projects had over-stretched the industry's abilities to maintain sufficiently high quality standards. In a series of MIGHT forums, leading construction firms were brought together with SIRIM and international experts to decide upon remedial measures.

14 Later, other strategic technologies were added to the priority list, including energy, aerospace and environmental technology.

15 For example, a National Biotechnology Directorate was established under MOSTE; an advanced materials technology park was established in Malacca; a light-aircraft manu- facturing company was established as a government corporation, all in line with the strategic priorities set down in the Technology Action Plan.

16 In addition to these formal advisory bodies, several other bodies play an informal role in setting S&T policy priorities in parallel to the formal National Science Council

structure. The Malaysian Academy of Sciences, comprised of fifty leading academics, engineers and technologists, was established in 1994 as an independent body of senior professional expertise to advise government policy-makers. While not involved in priority-setting *per se*, several non-governmental organisations and professional societies provide advice and feedback on government S&T policies, including the Malaysian Invention and Design Society (MINDS); the Confederation of Scientific and Technological Associations of Malaysia; Malaysian Scientific Association; and Institute of Engineers Malaysia.

17 In 1995, the IRPA process was reorganised in an attempt to strengthen and focus the strategic impact of the allocation process. IRPA's five allocation panels (Agriculture, Industry, Medical, Strategic and Social Science) were expanded to ten (Agro-industry, Manufacturing, Science and Engineering, Health, Energy, Environment, IT, Social and Economic, Mining, Service). The extent to which the improved priority-setting procedures have increased the contribution of public-sector R&D to national development is not yet clear.

18 The Malaysian Plastics Association and the Malaysian Auto Components and Parts Manufacturers Association are two examples which have significantly addressed technical upgrading in their respective industries.

19 An important example is the case of the Malaysian Institute for Microelectronics Research (MIMOS). The government established MIMOS in 1985 to lay the groundwork for the deepening of technological capabilities in semiconductors, the leading electronics export industry. Yet, the industry, almost wholly dominated by foreign companies, showed little interest either in collaborating with MIMOS to develop local integrated-circuit design capabilities or in deepening their own production from IC assembly and testing to the more demanding stages of wafer fabrication (O'Connor 1993). MIMOS later reorganised its mission to emphasise a broader menu of research and technical services, including information technology use, printed circuit-board design and expert-systems software development.

20 These payments included franchise and trademark agreements as well as technology licences and assistance contracts.

21 The conditions for local content in electronics are very flexible and balanced against other measures of technological investment, including employment of engineers and technicians, and 'high-value-added' activities. Interviews with MNC managers indicate that foreign firms have no difficulty in meeting two of the four criteria, as required, and that actual government monitoring is virtually absent.

22 Several important exceptions qualify this characterisation. First, government intervention in the 1970s led to a 'velvet nationalisation' of the foreign plantation houses in the primary sector. Second, the Industrial Co-ordination Act (ICA) did induce foreign investors to share equity in domestic-market-oriented manufacturing projects, though its primary impact was on the employment of *Bumiputera*. Third, the Mahathir administration's heavy-industries push in the early 1980s engaged the state in much more direct and aggressive bargaining over technology in a series of state–foreign joint ventures. The frustrations and setbacks of these efforts (see Chee 1994) were a major factor contributing to a reversion to Malaysia's historic emphasis on active promotion of FDI under comparatively liberal conditions.

23 This argument correctly points to inadequate local capabilities, or 'absorptive capacity', as the basic constraint, but does not directly address the appropriateness of regulation or bargaining over terms of investment and technology access in a manner carefully calibrated to local capabilities and matched with concomitant investments in skills, information and monitoring of firm performance.

24 Author interviews (1994).

25 Remarks by Datuk Mustapa Mohamed, Entrepreneurs Development Minister, *The Star* (10 April 1996).

26 The new entity, the Small and Medium-Sized Industries Development Corporation, became operational in May 1996.

27 It should be reiterated that this evaluation has a large relative component, based on a comparison with linkage formation and technology diffusion in Japan, Taiwan and, more recently, Singapore. It draws on available studies of sub-contracting in Malaysian manufacturing, which offer mixed assessments, including several more optimistic than this summary. See, *inter alia*, Rasiah (1994, 1995a, b, c), Guyton (1996), Capanelli (1999), UNDP (1993), Lai and Narayanan (1999).

28 See Rasiah (1995a), UNDP (1993) and Palacios (1995).

29 SIRIM added an important innovation service in 1995 when it established a rapid prototyping centre assisted by McDonnell-Douglas as part of an offset deal for Malaysia's purchase of F-14 fighter jets. Another component of the offset deal is a CAD/CAM/high-speed machining centre under SIRIM. The institute has also been a leader in reforming its management systems: in 1994 it won approval for a pilot incentive scheme in which groups of individual researchers will retain three-quarters of the net profit of each contracted research project and retain patent rights to resulting innovations.

30 SIRIM was scheduled to become a government-owned corporation in late 1996, while MIMOS (the Malaysian Institute for Microelectronics Research) was corporatised the same year. The trend towards converting public agencies from bureaucratic to corporate status extended in 1996 to proposals for a sweeping reform of higher education policies to enable universities to be corporatised.

31 MTDC's initial paid-up capital was RM51.5 million (US$21 million), later expanded to RM100 million.

32 At a time when the general trend in policy has been to reduce the number of special tax incentives while lowering overall rates, the increase in tax incentives for R&D indicates the high priority which the government places on encouraging technology development.

33 Applications increased in subsequent years following a reorganisation of the programme, which set an application deadline of six months following a project completion.

34 ITAF involves four separate schemes, supporting feasibility studies, market research, quality and productivity improvement projects, and product development and design.

35 Reportedly, the reasons why proposals for an industry grants scheme were rejected have to do with the government's fear of encouraging a 'subsidy mentality'. The point is revealing of continued political concerns with rent-seeking behaviour, and an evaluation that bureaucratic capabilities to monitor and discipline subsidy recipients is inadequate.

36 Rapid growth in GDP naturally lowered the ratio. If R&D is less a driver of innovation than an activity which emerges only after long prior technology accumulation efforts, as the evolutionary approach suggests, a low R&D ratio alone is not necessarily cause for concern, particularly for countries in the early stages of industrialisation. Nonetheless, the experience of the East Asian NICs suggests that developing countries that deepen local technological capabilities as they shift towards a higher-technology industrial structure do naturally invest a growing amount of R&D expenditure. The key point is that low R&D totals may be a symptom of slow technological development, even if not a primary cause. Thus while simply boosting public R&D spending is unlikely to produce real gains in industry's technological capacities, a stagnant or declining level of national investment in R&D is an undesirable sign.

37 In response to government exhortations to step-up R&D, local business representatives have pointed to the shortages of skilled manpower, the administrative complexity of R&D incentives and programmes, and the need for direct grants to help them assume the risks of genuine innovation. These frictions suggest that, like other promotional policies, R&D incentives suffer from the effects of historically conflictual government/business relations and the weakness of public/private policy networks. However, closer

government/business consultations over the past several years have begun to ameliorate these legacies. The more fundamental issue is the underlying weakness of industry demand for formal R&D, given the stage of technological accumulation prevailing among most of Malaysian manufacturing.

38 Skills shortages have been endemic for at least a decade, even while the industrial sector has expanded and upgraded. It might appear, therefore, that Malaysia's other attractions are sufficient to attract continued foreign investments in technological upgrading, including workforce training. Yet while industrial upgrading is indeed likely to continue in the absence of strong measures to address market failures in technical human capital, the goal of making technological change more locally-driven is likely to suffer. Industry's adoption of automation technologies, for example, may involve moves towards either multi-skilled job tasks or simplified work processes, depending upon local skill levels. Likewise, greater production linkages are affected by the ability of local SMIs to adopt sophisticated quality control techniques, which in turn demands higher skill levels in both production and managerial roles.

39 The HRDF was proposed in the Technology Action Plan of 1990, and was modelled in part on a similar mandatory Skills Development Fund operating in Singapore since the late 1980s.

40 The initial threshold of fifty employees was extended in 1995 to companies with more than ten employees but with a minimum investment capital.

41 Levies left unclaimed after two years (the initial limit was one year, and was extended in response to business objections) are forfeit. Thus, one implication of the programme is to generate a cross-subsidisation of training from low-skill employers to those with higher investments in skills.

42 As part of the 1996 educational reforms, the levy on SMIs was cut in half, and the government announced a two-to-one matching grant scheme for small employers.

43 The English translation is 'The Council of Trust for Indigenous People'. Since the late 1960s, MARA has been one of the primary agencies providing loans, training and technical assistance to *Bumiputera* seeking to enter the modern urban–industrial economy.

44 These include the Federal Institute of Technology and the Workers Institute of Technology.

45 These estimates are found in the Second Outline Perspective Plan (1990–2000).

46 The University of Malaya was the first to be corporatised, in 1997.

47 Cited in Kanapathy and Abdul Rahman (1994: Table 2, p. 9).

48 Malaysia's 1990 population was approximately 19 million, while Thailand had a population of 56 million. Thus, per capita vocational enrolment in Thailand was over four and a half times that in Malaysia.

49 While the Malaysian authorities are also concerned about the effects of high labour turnover rates on incentives to invest in training, they expressed concern about MNCs' attempt to govern the labour market through non-official restrictions. Such pacts might also have the effect of weakening incentives to train and advance local personnel as a means of attracting and retaining qualified employees.

50 Once again, Penang offers an important contrast to the general pattern. Here, co-operation between MNCs, the state government and, to a lesser extent, local business has been both proactive and broadly focused. Apart from the Penang Skills Development Centre, local and foreign business have been full participants in recent state policy committees designed to manage human resource development investments for Penang's industrial future. The high degree of trust prevailing among the actors has enabled joint action on skills development as well as labour turnover.

51 The main Federation of Malaysian Manufacturers (FMM) has Entrepreneurs' Development Centres at its Kuala Lumpur headquarters and its northern branch office in Penang. The Malaysian Plastics Association, which is composed almost exclusively of wholly locally owned companies, has a technical training facility housed on the premises

of the Penang Skills Development Centre. The Malaysian Textiles Manufacturers Association also operates a training programme.

52 It should be noted that the reforms, which entail corporatisation of public universities and the encouragement of private education, are not without controversy. Specifically, whether for-profit educational institutions are either appropriate to the normative values Malaysians place on education or capable of superior performance in creating the basic human capital the country requires are both open to debate. Nonetheless, long-standing recognition of the need for major reform has given way to concerted action.

53 Provisions of the World Trade Organization (WTO) treaty and the proposed Multilateral Agreement on Investments (MAI) place even more stringent restrictions on host-country measures such as local content or technology transfer regulations.

54 In 1996, Mahathir announced that a 'national project' would seek to capture a large share of the market for household electrical appliances. The government's chosen vehicle was the Malaysia Electric Corporation or MEC, a joint venture between the Ministry of Finance and a private company. MEC was provided with substantial government subsidies in the form of land and other industrial infrastructure, as well as undisclosed tax preferences.

References

Abdullah, Tahir (1995) 'Industrial Policy and Industrial Development: Issues and Policy Directions', in V. Kanapathy (ed.), *Managing Industrial Transition in Malaysia*, Kuala Lumpur: Malaysia, 1–12.

Anuwar Ali (1992) *Malaysia's Industrialization: The Quest for Technology*, Singapore: Oxford University Press.

Anuwar Ali and Wong Poh Kam (1993) 'Direct Foreign Investment in the Malaysian Industrial Sector', in Jomo K.S. (ed.), *Industrialising Malaysia: Policy, Performance, Prospects*, London: Routledge, 77–117.

Aoki, T. (1991) 'Japanese FDI and Forming Networks in the Asia-Pacific Region: Experience in Malaysia and Its Implications', in S. Tokunaga (ed.), *Japan's Foreign Investment and Asian Economic Interdependence*, Tokyo: Tokyo University Press.

Bardhan, P. (1989) 'The New Institutional Economic and Development Theory: A Critical Assessment', *World Politics* 17(9): 1389–95.

Capannelli, G. (1999) 'Technology Transfer from Japanese Consumer Electronic Firms via Buyer–Supplier Relations', Chapter 8 in Jomo *et al.* (1999).

Chee Peng Lim (1986) *Small Industry in Malaysia*, Kuala Lumpur: Berita Publishing.

Chee Peng Lim (1994) 'Heavy Industrialization: A Second Round of Import Substitution', in Jomo K.S. (ed.), *Japan and Malaysian Development: In the Shadow of the Rising Sun*, London: Routledge, 244–62.

Crouch, H. (1992) 'Authoritarian Trends, the UMNO Split and the Limits to State Power', in J.S. Kahn and F.K.W. Loh (eds), *Fragmented Vision: Culture and Politics in Contemporary Malaysia*, Honolulu: University of Hawaii Press, 21–43.

Dahlman, C.J. (1994) 'Technology Strategy in East Asian Developing Economies', *Journal of Asian Economies*, November, 5(4): 541–72.

Dahlman, C.J. and P. Brimble (1990) *Technology Strategy and Policy for Industrial Competitiveness: A Case Study in Thailand*, Washington, D.C.: World Bank.

Dahlman, C.J. and O. Sananikone (1990) 'Technology Strategy in the Economy of Taiwan: Exploiting Foreign Linkages and Investing in Local Capability', December, World Bank.

Danabalan, V. (1994) 'The Malaysian Government's R&D Strategies', Paper presented at the Conference on Managing and Commercialising R&D, Subang Jaya, Malaysia 6–7 September.

Doner, R.F. (1991) 'Approaches to the Politics of Economic Growth in Southeast Asia', *Journal of Asian Studies* 50(4): 818–49.

Doner, R.F. (1992) 'The Limits of State Strength: Towards an Institutionalist View of Economic Development', *World Politics* 44, April: 398–431.

Doner, R.F. (1993) 'Japanese Foreign Investment and the Creation of a Pacific Asian Region', in M. Kahler, and J. Frankel (eds), *Regionalism and Rivalry: Japan and the United States in Pacific Asia*, Chicago: University of Chicago Press, 159–214.

Doner, R.F. and G. Hawes (1995) 'Southeast and Northeast Asia', in M. Dorraj (ed.), *The Changing Political Economy of the Third World*, Boulder, CO: Lynne Rienner, 145–85.

FMM (n.d.) *Strategies for Meeting Manpower Requirements of Industry in the Nineties*, FMM Economic Paper No. 4, Kuala Lumpur: Federation of Malaysian Manufacturers.

Fransman, M. (1995) 'Is National Technology Policy Obsolete in a Globalised World? The Japanese Response', *Cambridge Journal of Economics* 19(1): 95–119.

Freeman, C. (1987) *Technology Policy and Economic Performance*, London: Pinter.

Freeman, C. (1995) 'The "National System of Innovation" in Historical Perspective', *Cambridge Journal of Economics* 19(1): 5–24.

Friedman, D. (1988) *The Misunderstood Miracle: Industrial Development and Political Change in Japan*, Ithaca, NY: Cornell University Press.

Gereffi, G. and M. Korzeniewicz (eds) (1994) *Commodity Chains and Global Capitalism*, Westport, CT: Greenwood Press.

Guyton, Lynne E. (1996) 'Japanese Investments and Technology Transfer in Malaysia', in J. Borrego, A.A. Bejar and Jomo K.S. (eds), *Capital, the State and Late Industrialization*, Boulder, CO: Westview Press.

Halim, F. (1990) 'The Transformation of the Malaysian State', *Journal of Contemporary Asia* 20(1): 64–88.

Hamilton, G. (ed.) (1991) *Business Networks and Economic Development in East and Southeast Asia*, Hong Kong: Center of Asian Studies, University of Hong Kong.

Hobday, M. (1999) 'Understanding Innovation in Electronics in Malaysia', Chapter 4 in Jomo *et al.* (1999).

Ismail Muhamed Salleh (1990) *Small and Medium Scale Industrialisation: Problems and Perspectives*, Kuala Lumpur: ISIS Malaysia.

Jesudason, J.V. (1989) *Ethnicity and the Economy: The State, Chinese Business, and Multinationals in Malaysia*, Singapore: Oxford University Press.

Jomo K.S. (1994) *U-Turn? Malaysian Economic Development Policies after 1990*, Townsville, Queensland, Australia: Centre for East and Southeast Asian Studies, James Cook University of North Queensland.

Jomo K.S. (ed.) (1995) *Privatizing Malaysia: Rents, Rhetoric, Realities*, Boulder, CO: Westview.

Jomo K.S. and C. Edwards (1993) 'Malaysian Industrialisation in Historical Perspective', in Jomo K.S. (ed.) *Industrialising Malaysia: Policy, Performance, Prospects*, London: Routledge, 14–39.

Jomo, K.S., G. Felker and R. Rasiah (1999) *Industrial Technology Development in Malaysia*, London: Routledge.

Kanapathy, V. and Abdul Rahman Mohamed Ali (1994) 'Human Resource Development and Industrial Training: An Overview', in P. Pillai (ed.), *Industrial Training in Malaysia: Challenge and Response*, Kuala Lumpur: ISIS Malaysia, 1–25.

Lai, Y.W. and S. Narayanan (1999) 'Technology Utilisation Level and Choice: the

145

Electronics and Electrical Sector in Penang, Malaysia', Chapter 5 in Jomo *et al.* (1999).

Lall, S. (1992) 'Technological Capabilities and Industrialization', *World Development*, February, 20(2): 165–86.

Lall, S. (1993) 'Policies for Building Technological Capabilities: Lessons from Asian Experience', *Asian Development Review* 11(2): 72–103.

Lall, S. (1995) 'Malaysia: Industrial Success and the Role of Government', *Journal of International Development*, 7(5): 759–73.

Lall, S., R. Boumphrey and B.J. Hitchcock (1994) *Malaysia's Export Performance and Its Sustainability*, Asian Development Bank, Manila.

Leigh, M. (1992) 'Politics, Bureaucracy and Business in Malaysia: Realigning the Eternal Triangle', in A.J. MacIntyre and K. Jayasuriya (eds), *The Dynamics of Economic Policy Reform in South-East Asia and the South-West Pacific*, Singapore: Oxford University Press, 115–23.

Lim, L.Y.C. and E.F. Pang (1991) *Foreign Direct Investment and Industrialization in Malaysia, Singapore, Taiwan and Thailand*, Paris: OECD Development Centre.

Lundvall, B. (ed.) (1992) *National Systems of Innovation: Towards a Theory of Innovation and Interactive Learning*, London: Pinter.

MacIntyre, A.J. and K. Jayasuriya (eds) (1992) *The Dynamics of Economic Policy Reform in South-east Asia and the South-west Pacific*, Singapore: Oxford University Press.

Mardon, R. (1990) 'The State and Effective Control of Foreign Capital: The Case of Korea', *World Politics* 43: 111–38.

MOSTE (1993) *Annual Report*, Kuala Lumpur: Ministry of Science, Technology and the Environment.

Mowery, D.C. and J.E. Oxley (1995) 'Inward Technology Transfer and Competitiveness: The Role of National Innovation Systems', *Cambridge Journal of Economics* 19(1): 67–93.

Nazari Ismail, Mohd (1999) 'Foreign Firms and National Technological Upgrading: the Electronics Industry in Malaysia', Chapter 2 in Jomo *et al.* (1999).

Nelson, R.R. (ed.) (1993) *National Innovation Systems: A Comparative Analysis*, New York: Oxford University Press.

O'Brien, L. (1993) 'Malaysian Manufacturing Sector Linkages', in Jomo K.S. (ed.), *Industrialising Malaysia: Policy, Performance, Prospects*, London: Routledge, 147–62.

O'Connor, D. (1993) 'Electronics and Industrialization in Malaysia: Approaching the 21st Century', in Jomo K.S. (ed.), *Industrialising Malaysia: Policy, Performance, Prospects*, London: Routledge.

Okimoto, D. (1989) *Between MITI and the Market*, Stanford, CA: Stanford University Press.

Ostry, S. and R. Nelson (1995) *Techno-Nationalism and Techno-Globalism*, Washington DC: The Brookings Institution.

Palacios, J.J. (1995) 'Multinational Corporations and Technology Transfer in Penang and Guadalajara', in E.K.Y. Chen and P. Drysdale (eds), *Corporate Links and Foreign Direct Investment in Asia and the Pacific*, Pymble, Australia: Harper Educational Publishers, 153–86.

Rasiah, Rajah (1993) 'Free Trade Zones', in Jomo K.S. (ed.), *Industrialising Malaysia: Policy, Performance, Prospects*, London: Routledge, 118–46.

Rasiah, Rajah (1994) 'Flexible Production Systems and Local Machine-Tool Subcontracting: Electronics Components Transnationals in Malaysia', *Cambridge Journal of Economics* 18: 279–98.

Rasiah, Rajah (1995a) *Foreign Capital and Industrialization in Malaysia*, New York: St. Martin's Press.

Rasiah, Rajah (1995b) 'Malaysia', in Atipol Bhanich Supapol (ed.), *Transnational Corporations and Backward Linkages*, Bangkok: ESCAP, 175–210.

Rozikin Hamzah (1994) 'The Role of the National Vocational Training Council', in P. Pillai (ed.), *Industrial Training in Malaysia: Challenge and Response*, Kuala Lumpur: ISIS Malaysia, 67–77.

Samuels, R.J. (1987) *The Business of the Japanese State: Energy Markets in Comparative and Historical Perspective*, Ithaca, NY: Cornell University Press.

Samuels, R.J. (1994) *'Rich Nation, Strong Army': National Security and the Technological Transformation of Japan*, Ithaca, NY: Cornell University Press.

Sieh, L.M.L. (1992) 'The Transformation of Malaysian Business Groups', in R. McVey (ed.), *Southeast Asian Capitalists*, Ithaca, NY: Cornell Southeast Asia Program, 103–26.

UNDP (1993) *Technology Transfer to Malaysia: Reports Phase I and II*, Kuala Lumpur: United Nations Development Program.

UNESCO (1993) *Statistical Yearbook*, New York: United Nations Educational, Scientific and Cultural Organization.

Unger, D. (1993) 'Japan's Capital Exports: Molding East Asia', in D. Unger and P. Blackburn (eds), *Japan's Emerging Global Role*, Boulder, CO: Lynne Rienner, 155–70.

Wade, R. (1992) 'East Asia's Economic Success: Conflicting Perspectives, Partial Insights, Shaky Evidence', *World Politics* 44 (January): 270–320.

Wong Poh Kam (1991) *Technological Development through Subcontracting Linkages*, Tokyo: Asian Productivity Organization.

World Bank (1997) *Malaysia: Enterprise Training, Technology, and Productivity*, Washington DC: The World Bank.

Yau De Piyau (1995) 'The Human Resources Development Fund in Malaysia', Paper presented at the World Bank conference on Enterprise Training Strategies and Productivity, 12–13 June.

6

TECHNOLOGY POLICY AND COMPETITIVENESS IN MALAYSIA

Sanjaya Lall

The global economy is undergoing sweeping technological change, altering fundamentally the methods and organisation of the production of goods and services, the pattern of international trade, and the skills, information and institutions needed for industrial competitiveness. So broad and far-reaching are these technological developments that many analysts see the emergence of a new 'industrial revolution'. This revolution involves, not only new technologies (new processes and products), but also new management and organisational techniques, new forms of linkages between buyers and suppliers, and new, tighter relations between technology and science. This is the context in which Malaysia must meet the technological challenge, at a stage where it is making a vital transition to a more mature stage of industrial development.

This context is a Schumpeterian 'gale of creative destruction', with information-based innovations transforming most economic activities. To quote Freeman and Perez (1988: 60–1),

> The new technologies are intensive in their use of electronics, both in products and processes. They also embody the use of new materials, with ceramics, fine chemicals and plastics experiencing a new burst of innovation. The 'ideal' information-intensive productive organisation now increasingly links design, management, production and marketing into one integrated system – a process which may be described as 'systemation' and which goes far beyond the earlier concepts of mechanisation and automation. Firms organised on this new basis . . . can produce a flexible and rapidly changing mix of products and services. Growth tends increasingly to be led by the electronics and information sectors, taking advantage of growing externalities provided by an all-encompassing telecommunications infrastructure, which will ultimately bring down to extremely low levels the costs of access to the system for both producers and users of information . . . The skill profile associated with the new techno-economic paradigm appears to change from the concentration on middle-range craft and supervisory skills to increasingly high- and low-

148

range qualifications, and from narrow specialisation to broader, multi-purpose basic skills for information handling. Diversity and flexibility at all levels substitute for homogeneity and dedicated systems.

The skill needs of the new system are worth stressing for Malaysia, where, as shown below, skill problems loom particularly large in its industrial transition. For mass production, where Malaysia is still specialised, skills were differentiated and directed to the fragmented tasks performed by individual workers. In the emerging system, Malaysia will need new skills for four reasons:

- to make production more flexible and responsive to rapid market changes, which calls for multiple- rather than single-tasking;
- to manage the move to lower inventories, just-in-time production systems and total quality management, which relies heavily on worker skills and discretion;
- to manage the process of continuous improvement at all levels of production, which involves close interaction between workers and management, as well as higher skill levels on the part of workers;
- finally, to handle the needs of multi-skilled teams, which are more flexible and productive than individual workers, and which, in turn, require new skills of team work and organisation.

What will determine Malaysia's competitive success in this environment? The most important factors, apart from the growing supply of skills from the educational system, will be the growth of technological and organisational capabilities in its enterprises, the abilities – technical, managerial and institutional – that allow them to utilise equipment, know-how, manuals, designs, patents and blueprints efficiently and keep them at competitive levels over time.[1] These capabilities are not the technology 'embodied' in physical equipment or in patents and designs purchased by the enterprise, though these are the basic tools of industrial activity. Nor are they the educational qualifications possessed by the employees, though the receptive base of skills is essential to learning. They are these combined with the skills and learning undergone by individuals in the enterprise as they learn to manage the technology and cope with problems, interact with other firms and draw upon external institutions and markets. Technological capabilities are essentially created by firm-level efforts, and firms themselves are the most important source of 'demand' for and 'supply' of technologies. It is at this level that technology development policies must act if they are to be effective.

The role of policies in affecting firm-level technological effort lies in the fact that firms invest in building capabilities and innovating in response to stimuli from the market and by drawing upon various tangible and intangible factors from other firms, factor markets and a variety of institutions. The markets that firms operate in and the structure of supporting institutions may suffer from weaknesses and gaps – the role of technology policy should be to fill these gaps and strengthen markets so that innovation and technological deepening is stimulated and sustained. A schematic representation of the markets relevant to technology development is presented in Lall (1996).

It is important to note, at the start, that technological development does not consist only of formal research and development (R&D) – much technological effort and upgrading consists of less formal quality control, layout, maintenance and production engineering activity. However, R&D does, over time, become an important tool of competitiveness – for absorbing and keeping up with advanced technologies, raising the sophistication of local manufacturing activity, increasing local content and reducing the costs of technology import. Even countries that are not innovating on the frontier, such as Malaysia, need to raise local R&D effort, and R&D can feed into routine engineering activity related to quality management, maintenance, adaptation and productivity raising. In the East Asian NIEs, like Korea and Taiwan, many local enterprises are approaching world technological frontiers, and autonomous R&D capacity has become essential for them to access new technologies and improve upon them to diversify their competitive advantages.

It is also important for Malaysia to develop new and stronger forms of relations between firms, and between firms and institutions. Currently, inter-firm relationships between large firms and small and medium enterprises (SMEs) are still weak and rooted in older modes of organisation, and most local firms are not integrated into export-oriented manufacturing. In the industrialised world, production organisation is moving towards flatter hierarchies within firms, and increased co-ordination, more sharing of knowledge and networking between them. The realisation of the agglomeration and specialisation benefits of industry 'clusters' allows regions or groups of related activities to internalise the spillover effects of knowledge and skill creation. To the extent that these patterns are becoming the new parameters of international competitiveness, Malaysia will have to make the effort to develop comparable systems, networks and attitudes.

The strong reliance on foreign investors by Malaysia to lead its industrialisation has till now reduced the need for local effort to generate technology and undertake R&D. However, this has not reduced the need for other kinds of technological effort – using a technology efficiently inevitably requires the development of local capabilities. Nor has it obviated the need for greater local R&D beyond certain stages of affiliate development. An affiliate's ability to conduct R&D can raise its role in terms of production and exports, wage and salary levels, local value-added and weight within the multinational corporation (MNC) as a whole. The 'deepening' of technological activity may be as important for MNC affiliates as it is for local enterprises as the industrial structure becomes more complex. This is perhaps the most important change that underlies the larger transition Malaysia has to make. Moreover, the growing non-MNC sector in industry has to invest in both technological upgrading and R&D to develop its competitive edge. SMEs constitute the bulk of the domestic industrial sector in Malaysia, and much of it is not geared to facing the technological challenges of Vision 2020.

As shown below, the progress of the Malaysian industrial sector and exports has 'outrun' the development of domestic industrial capabilities. This poses a strong challenge to boost these capabilities, and there is a large role for the government in meeting the challenge. This role includes creating the supply of and markets for the skills, information, institutions and infrastructure that are the basis of enterprise competitiveness. Because of the cumulative and path-dependent nature of technological learning, it is important for the Malaysian government to make correct policy choices at this critical juncture. The remainder of this chapter focuses on what these choices should be.

Malaysia's changing competitive position

The Malaysian economy has been one of the developing world's best performers over the past two decades, especially in terms of industrial development. It grew at 6.7 per cent per annum during 1971–90, during the first Outline Perspective Plan (OPP1) period. This growth was led by the manufacturing sector, which grew by 10.3 per cent (Malaysia 1991). Performance was even stronger in the first three years of the 1990s, when the economy grew at 8.1 per cent and the manufacturing sector at 12.3 per cent per annum (Malaysia 1993). There was impressive structural transformation of the economy, with the manufacturing share of GDP rising from 14 per cent in 1971 to 30.1 per cent in 1993.

Industrial structure

The structure of Malaysian industry can be assessed by looking at the evolution of manufacturing activities from 'light' to 'heavy' activities. Light industry comprises relatively 'easy', traditional activities, and heavy industry is more capital-intensive and complex activities; the upgrading of the industrial structure is commonly regarded as the move from light to heavy industry.[2] Figure 6.1 shows the evolution over 1970–90 of the industrial structure (percentage distribution of manufacturing value-added or MVA) in Malaysia in comparison to the four East Asian first-tier newly industrialising economies (NIEs) (Korea, Taiwan, Hong Kong and Singapore) and Japan.

In 1970, Malaysia had a fairly 'light' industrial structure, dominated by food processing, wood and textiles. Even at this stage, however, the electrical equipment industry had become the second largest contributor to MVA, led by the export boom that had started in the late 1960s in the assembly of semiconductors. There was gradual change until 1980, then an accelerating pace of deepening over the decade as electrical and electronics exports took off and other heavy process industries were set up. As a result, the rate of upgrading of Malaysian industry in the 1980s was very rapid, and, by 1990, Malaysia had a relatively advanced industrial structure, with the share of heavy industry only marginally lower than for both Korea and Taiwan.[3]

Given Malaysia's recent history of industrialisation, the complexity and rate of

151

transformation of its industrial structure is well in advance of its income levels. In particular, its specialisation in electricals and electronics (higher even than most OECD countries) gives it a strong base in the most dynamic and technology-based activities in modern industry. The modern sector also contains several heavy process industries, some in the public sector, that serve both domestic and export markets. These are also technologically proficient and up-to-date, and seem to be well placed to continue growing into the 21st century.

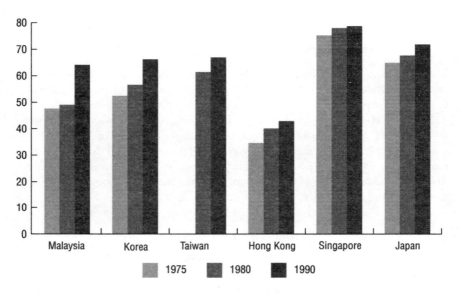

Figure 6.1 Share of heavy industry in manufacturing value-added, 1975–90 (%)
Source: UNIDO, *Industrial Development: Global Report*, 1994, Vienna

At the same time, the broad MVA figures do not show the weaknesses of the Malaysian industrial structure. First, much of the 'heavy' industrial activity in the electrical and electronics industries is concentrated at the final assembly stages of the production process, with relatively low inputs of the design, development and other advanced skills that are normally associated with such activities. Second, manufacturing activity in many heavy industries in Malaysia remains highly import-dependent and with low local supply linkages. Third, there exist 'gaps' in the industrial structure, with the largest being the lack of a local capital-goods industry. This could be an important constraint on the longer-term development of local technological capability, in that the machinery manufacturing sector is normally the 'hub' of technological progress and diffusion (Rosenberg 1986). Without such a sector, local enterprises would find it difficult to take technological progress beyond the level of adapting foreign technology.

Fourth, the large-scale modern sector is only one part of the industrial system. There is strong dualism in Malaysian industry, with a large number of SMEs comprising the bulk of the number of enterprises and accounting for the majority of industrial employment, effectively delinked from the high-technology production structure geared to export or to heavy industry. Traditional SMEs use low-productivity technologies and produce low-value products for local markets. There are, however, some exceptions: the apparel and wood products industries have large numbers of SMEs serving export markets, and these use modern technologies efficiently.

A few more sophisticated SMEs have emerged that supply high-tech components to larger enterprises, and some have become independent exporters of advanced engineering products in their own right. However, these are still a small minority – the proverbial exceptions that prove the rule. Sustained industrial development will require that the large population of more backward SMEs become more productive, competitive and outward-oriented. The government's Vision 2020 entails that wages will rise to developed-country levels, which requires that the SME sector move to the high value-added activities that their counterparts undertake in the advanced industrial countries.

Export performance

The total value of manufactured exports by Malaysia came to RM105.4 billion in 1994 (around US$42 billion). There has been an impressive expansion in manufactured exports, from US$122 million in 1970 to US$2.3 billion in 1980, US$20.7 billion in 1991, and a further doubling by 1994. The annual rate of growth over 1970–91 was 27.7 per cent per annum, with the highest growth rate (34.2 per cent) taking place during 1970–80. This is one of the highest sustained rates of export expansion recorded in recent economic history. The only comparable performances have been by Thailand and Indonesia. Of these, Thailand is now a larger exporter of manufactures than Malaysia, but Indonesia remains a much smaller exporter, with a preponderance of simple labour-intensive products.

In terms of volume, however, Malaysia still lags well behind the major East Asian exporters of Korea, Taiwan and China, each with manufactured exports of around US$70–80 billion per annum. Malaysian manufactured exports still account for a tiny share of the relevant world markets: in 1992, this came to 0.7 per cent, compared to 2.4 per cent for Korea, 2.7 per cent for Taiwan, 1.8 per cent for Singapore and 12.7 per cent for Japan. Thus, the rapid growth of its exports still leaves Malaysia a small player in the world industrial scene. Table 6.1 shows the values of manufactured exports for 1980 and 1992 (1991 for Malaysia); these exports are classified by skill levels (see below for explanation).

Thus, while the rates of growth have been high for Malaysia, the values are still relatively low. In addition, Malaysia's impressive growth performance in manufactured exports also conceals certain weaknesses. These are of five kinds:

Table 6.1 Value of manufactured exports by skill categories (US$ million)

	Malaysia		Korea		Taiwan		Singapore		Japan	
	1980	1991	1980	1992	1980	1992	1980	1992	1980	1992
Low skill	689	4642	7804	25479	10004	28873	1735	5873	11614	22796
High skill	1639	16088	7476	45051	7424	46752	6699	42523	110367	301285
Total	4308	22721	17260	72522	19408	77617	10414	50388	123961	326073

Source: Calculated from UN, *International Trade Statistics Yearbook*, various years

- There is a very high degree of *concentration*, in terms of reliance on a few manufactured products, to drive exports. In 1992, for instance, 58.5 per cent of manufactured exports came from electrical and electronic products. Such a high degree of dependence is inherently risky. The top five products (at the 3-digit SITC level) accounted for 58.9 per cent of total manufactured exports in Malaysia as compared to 39.6 per cent for Korea and 45.4 per cent for Japan.
- Second, *MNCs dominate exports*, and there is relatively low direct participation in manufactured export activity by local, especially private, firms. The main exceptions are small and medium enterprises in garment exports and public enterprises in transport equipment, petroleum products, cement and iron and steel. This high level of dependence on MNCs contains an inherent risk that if their sourcing patterns change, Malaysia would be left with little indigenous capability to continue its export-oriented growth.
- Third, the *local content of manufactured exports* is low. Apart from local resource-based products, most manufactured-product exporters have relatively weak linkages with the domestic economy. Where there has been significant increase in local content over time, it has been largely driven by foreign investment in the component sectors. Linkages with local suppliers of some components and equipment, while growing, remain quantitatively small. Thus, the MNC-driven growth has not so far created strong local 'roots' that could ensure that FDI continues to flow in at the rate needed to sustain export and industrial growth.
- Fourth, both local and foreign firms perform relatively *little R&D*, though, of these, it is the MNCs that lead private-sector technological effort (see below). Most export activities remain heavily dependent on foreign sources of technology, not just for major innovations (which is the case with all developing and many industrialised economies), but also for minor improvements, equipment, design and specialised skills. The general level of Malaysian technological capabilities, while rising in terms of process engineering, is low relative to the NIEs and its ambitious export plans. Again, the high level of reliance on MNCs to transfer technology and conduct local R&D means that if their sourcing and investment patterns change, it would be very difficult for Malaysia to sustain its technological and industrial upgrading.

• Fifth, Malaysian exporters have not developed *independent marketing capabilities*. Foreign affiliates rely on their parent companies' marketing networks and brand names. Local firms in textiles and garments sell mainly through foreign buyers.

Skill and technology composition of exports

It is useful in the context of technological upgrading to examine the composition of Malaysia's manufactured exports. Using a simple classification of manufactured exports into 'high' and 'low' skill products (made on the basis of US average wage levels in each industry, with above-average wages denoting high skills), the share of Malaysian exports in the high-skill category is very large. Figure 6.2 shows that it is higher than for Korea and Taiwan (Hong Kong data are not shown because its very large volume of re-exports makes such calculations meaningless), and just behind the high-technology leaders, Singapore and Japan.[4] Again, the main spearhead of these exports was electrical and electronics products, but chemicals and basic metals also made significant contributions.

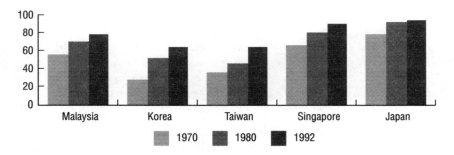

Figure 6.2 Percentage share of high skills in total manufactured exports
Source: Calculated from the United Nations, *International Trade Statistics*, various issues

The skill classification is a simple one, and does not show the competitive base of Malaysian exports. One way to assess this is to use a five-fold classification (used by the OECD) of the technological basis of export competitiveness, distinguishing between five sets of products: resource-based, labour-intensive, scale-intensive (e.g. chemicals, cement, paper, automobiles), 'differentiated' (mainly machinery and electronics) and science-based (advanced electronics and biotechnology). Figure 6.3 shows how Malaysian manufactured exports have evolved since 1970 according to these categories. It reveals sharp falls in the role of natural-resource and scale-intensive products, a gradual decline in labour-intensive products and a massive increase in the share of differentiated products. Science-based products make an appearance in 1980 and increase their role over the decade.

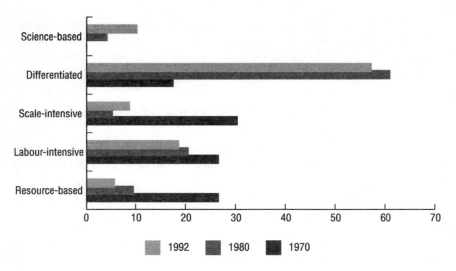

Figure 6.3 Competitive base of Malaysian manufactured exports (%)
Source: Calculated from the United Nations, *International Trade Statistics*, various issues

Science-based and differentiated products taken together normally require a strong base in R&D, and so may be considered the high-technology products of world trade. Figure 6.4 shows the shares of such high-technology exports for the region since 1970. In 1992, Malaysia had a larger share of manufactured exports in these products than all the other countries in the group, with the sole exception of Singapore. The Malaysian share of high-tech in total manufactured exports rose dramatically in the 1970s, at a rate unprecedented in the region, and perhaps in the world as a whole.

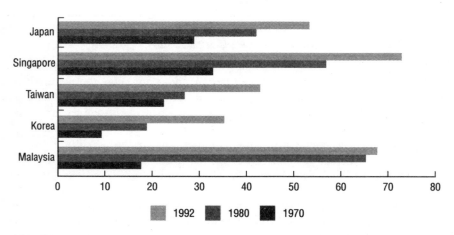

Figure 6.4 Shares of high-technology products in total manufactured exports (%)
Source: Calculated from the United Nations, *International Trade Statistics*, various issues

156

This seems a very enviable position for Malaysia to be in: a massive and rising specialisation in fast-growing high-tech exports. However, the export data are slightly misleading in that what falls under 'high-skill' and 'high-technology' products in fact include many products that are relatively 'simple' – either in their process needs (i.e. Malaysia specialises in the final assembly stages) or in their design features (Malaysia produces the simpler end of the technological scale). However, over the years, there has been significant upgrading of electrical and electronic processes and products in Malaysia (Bell *et al.* 1995), and it now deserves to be treated as a formidable force in these industries in the region. However, the structure still conceals the several weaknesses that have been noted and are explored below.

Market 'positioning' of Malaysian exports

An examination of changes in a country's share of world trade over time reveals the strength and dynamism of its exports. Changes in the country's share of world exports of particular products indicate whether it is competitive or not: rising market shares indicate growing competitiveness while declining ones indicate weakening competitiveness. While exceptions are always possible, exports of products in which a country already has a large world market share are unlikely to be able to grow rapidly in the future. Prospects for a country to expand exports in particular products also depend upon how fast world trade in those products is growing. Exports of products whose shares in total world trade are themselves declining are less likely to promote rapid growth than those whose shares are increasing. These are the criteria – market share and market growth – that individual firms often use to assess and optimise their market 'positioning'.

Table 6.2 Export product dynamism classification

Share of country's exports in world trade in a product	Share of product in world trade	
	RISING	*FALLING*
RISING	Optimal 'Rising stars'	Vulnerable 'Falling stars'
FALLING	Weakness 'Lost opportunity'	Restructuring 'Retreat'

This section considers how Malaysian manufactured exports are placed in terms of the country's world market shares and the overall dynamism of the products in which it is specialising. This is done by grouping exports according to a two-by-two matrix, based on whether they are 'competitive' or not in world markets (this is now defined in a comparative sense, according to whether the country is gaining or losing world market shares), and whether the products are 'dynamic' in trade (i.e.

if those products' own shares of total world trade are rising). Four sets of export products result (illustrated in Table 6.2):

- 'Rising stars': exports with strong competitiveness (i.e. rising world market shares) in 'dynamic' products (which are growing faster than total trade). This is the 'optimal' export positioning.
- 'Lost opportunities': exports with competitive declines (falling market shares) in dynamic products. This is the 'weakest' market position.
- 'Falling stars': exports with rising market share in non-dynamic products. This indicates competitive 'vulnerability', and so is relatively undesirable.
- 'Retreat': exports that are losing market shares in non-dynamic products. This is relatively desirable, since it shows possible 'restructuring' away from a weaker position.

The distribution of a country's exports over these categories shows its overall export positioning. How do Malaysian exports rate in terms of these groupings?

An examination of exports of Malaysia and some other countries at the 3-digit level is shown in Table 6.3. The data for export performance over 1985–92 show the shares of total manufactured exports that fall into the various groups according to changes in world market share and dynamism. They also show the 'positioning' of the two larger first-tier East Asian NIEs as well as its dynamic neighbours, Indonesia and Thailand. While the data are not complete (several exports could not be tracked in terms of growth rates), they reveal some interesting features of Malaysian performance.

Table 6.3 Dynamism of manufactured exports, 1985–92 (US$ million and %)

Country	Rising stars	Falling stars	Lost opportunity	Retreat	Total	Missing data (value and %)
Malaysia	44.0%	14.5%	41.0%	0.5%	100.0%	
	5784.9	1897	5380.5	64.1	13126.5	7684.5
	(27.8%)	(9.1%)	(25.9%)	(0.3%)	(63.1%)	(39.6%)
Korea	39.0%	12.0%	36.0%	13.0%	100.0%	
	23645.4	7429.5	21853.2	7422.7	60350.8	10473.2
	(33.4%)	(10.5%)	(30.9%)	(10.5%)	(85.2%)	(14.8%)
Taiwan	60.0%	14.0%	23.0%	3.0%	100.0%	
	37305.2	8824.3	14629.4	1538.4	62297.3	13327.7
	(49.3%)	(11.7%)	(19.3%)	(2.0%)	(82.4%)	(17.6%)
Thailand	73.0%	19.0%	9.0%		100.0%	
	10903.7	2804.5	1308.0	–	15016.2	5728.5
	(52.6%)	(13.5%)	(6.3%)		(72.4%)	(27.6%)
Indonesia	93.0%	7.0%			100.0%	
	8274.4	635.9	–	–	8910.3	7329.7
	(51.0%)	(3.9%)			(54.9%)	(45.1%)

Source: Calculated from UN, *International Trade Statistics Yearbook*, various years

Malaysia has a relatively low proportion of 'rising stars' in the group, with only Korea having a marginally lower share. Malaysia also has the largest proportion of 'lost opportunities' in the group and the second largest (after Thailand) share of 'falling stars'. It has very few products in 'retreat', which may also be seen as a strategic weakness. This relatively weak market-positioning may seem surprising in view of the technological content of Malaysian exports, but shows that within the apparently high-tech and high-skill products there are several which are not very 'dynamic', or in which Malaysia is failing to expand its market share.

These indicators are very general, of course, and need to be refined to draw firmer policy conclusions. Exports should be analysed at more detailed SITC levels and separated by destination to evaluate the exact nature of evolving competitive advantages. However, as they stand, they suggest that sustaining high rates of export growth will call for strong efforts to raise competitiveness and restructure export composition.

Malaysia's competitive base

Malaysia's export and production performance in technologically sophisticated and high-skill products, and the high weight of these advanced activities in its manufacturing value-added, would normally be associated with a far more mature industrial economy. Such 'maturity' would normally entail a diverse manufacturing base, with capital-goods manufacturing capabilities, a well-developed local supplier and subcontracting system with large 'clusters' of high-technology activities, a well-educated and technically trained workforce, and significant industrial R&D, both within and outside enterprises. Such an economy would be expected to have a diverse infrastructure of technology and training institutions, an active technology financing system and a dynamic education system geared to changing technological needs.

Malaysia has succeeded despite having few of these attributes. Its performance, practically unique in the developing world, owes relatively little to direct government policy to promote industry (Lall 1995). It is based, instead, on inflows of foreign investments into particular types of export activities. The challenge facing it now is to make a transition from this pattern, based on outside agents filling the 'gaps' in its productive base, to one where the productive base is itself able to sustain a high-technology pattern of growth. This transition is needed, not just to raise the competitiveness of domestic firms, and especially of the SMEs that dominate the domestic industrial scene, but is also necessary for Malaysia to continue to attract FDI at appropriate levels of skill and technical sophistication, to raise domestic contributions to production and technological activity, and to provide the supplier and service structure that MNCs increasingly need for competitive production.

This transition would have several features. The technological content of export production in the high-tech industries would rise, with more use of local design and development capabilities and a higher technological 'status' for the Malaysian affiliate in the multinational framework. Malaysian enterprises would enter new areas of advanced technology to diversify the competitive base and provide spillover benefits to the rest of industry. Export activity would have much greater local content and linkages, especially with SMEs. The productivity and technological levels of SMEs in general would be raised, including those in traditional low-skill, small-scale, localised activities. The technology infrastructure and universities would strike closer relations with industry at large.

The government has a vital role to play in this transition. The APITD (Action Plan for Industrial Technology Development) provides many reasons why market forces cannot achieve it by themselves. Many of the factor markets involved (capital, skills, information, technology support) suffer from deficiencies (described below). There is also a need to co-ordinate the decisions of individual economic agents in a dynamic setting with considerable externalities – market prices may not give the right signals to individual actors. The existence of important 'clustering' effects in certain industries calls for collective action.

Competitive strategy for Malaysia involves the following five factors: wages, physical infrastructure, human resources, technological effort and FDI. This takes for granted such vital factors as political stability, good macroeconomic and exchange rate management, a conducive export and private-enterprise regime, an ample natural-resource base, and a favourable geographical location. These factors, especially the trade and industrial regime, were responsible for attracting the kinds of export-oriented activities that dynamised Malaysian industry. The incentive regime has improved further, with greater liberalisation of imports and the privatisation of several public enterprises. However, there is scope for improvement in the incentive regime, and this is taken up later in the discussion of the 'enabling environment'.

Of the five factors noted, the first two do not need specific analysis in the present context. Low wages (and a well-functioning labour market with a disciplined workforce) did constitute a major competitive advantage in early industrial development in Malaysia. However, with the advent of near-full employment, rising wages and changes in employment patterns, the availability of cheap 'raw' labour is not an important competitive factor today: it is labour quality that is much more critical. The availability of good physical infrastructure in Malaysia was also crucial, and will remain an important factor in the future. However, it is more a permissive factor in industrial and technological upgrading, and does not raise particular issues in this context. Let us focus on the remaining three factors.

Human resources

Malaysia has a good primary education system, with high rates of literacy and widespread acquaintance with English. It also has rising enrolments at higher levels of secondary and tertiary education. So far this has provided a basic workforce to meet the needs of the relatively low-tech industrial development. However, this level of formal skill creation does not seem to be sufficient to meet the human resource needs of the expanding high-technology sector, or to manage the technological transformation of SMEs. There is widespread acknowledgement that there are growing skill shortages in Malaysia at all levels, particularly in technical fields. Practically the whole of modern industry complains of the constraints on upgrading and deepening posed by the lack of skills, and by high turnover rates for middle-level skilled employees.

Data on educational enrolments in Malaysia relative to other countries in the region confirm the skill gaps. Table 6.4 shows tertiary-level enrolment in general and in technology-related subjects (all science and technology areas, as well as engineering by itself), and in vocational training. Despite the fact that government education expenditure is one of the highest in the region, Malaysia's higher educational structure lacks the ability to meet the technical needs of industry.

Table 6.4 Educational enrolments

	Tertiary-level enrolment			Vocational training
	Total (% of age group)	All S&T subjects	Engineering only	
		(% of population)		
Malaysia	7	0.15	0.07	0.17
Thailand	16	0.16	0.09	0.80
Taiwan	37	0.92	0.60	2.12
Korea	40	0.96	0.58	1.93
Japan	31	0.43	0.37	1.17

Source: UNESCO, *Statistical Yearbook*, and Government of Taiwan, *Taiwan Statistical Data Book, 1994*.

Malaysian industry has been able to grow so rapidly and to compete in export markets in sophisticated activities despite these gaps for two reasons: first, the technological content of industrial activities in Malaysia has not been as demanding as in more industrialised countries, and, second, some leading firms in high-technology activities have their own training facilities to meet their skill needs. However, this is not universal in the large-scale sector, where many firms impart only fairly basic training. Meanwhile, the SME sector does very little training.

Current industrial growth has tightened the Malaysian labour market. There is now effectively full employment. In 1987, 71 per cent of reported manufacturing job vacancies were filled within the year, while in 1993 some 16 per cent of vacancies went unfilled. The country is facing an acute shortage of skilled manpower. Wages are rising and are much higher than wages in China, Indonesia, the Philippines or Vietnam (Table 6.5). There is a high rate of voluntary turnovers for several categories of skilled and professional workers (JTR 1992), reflecting growing shortages of skills.

Table 6.5 Comparative wages

Country	Average wage, 1992 (US$/month)
Malaysia	137
Philippines	118
China	45
Indonesia	25
Vietnam	20

Source: MITI, *Prospects and Challenges for Upgrading of Industries in the ASEAN Region,* 1993

However, industrial skills *have* grown significantly since the early days of labour-intensive assembly, because the complexity of local processes has risen and the range has diversified into more sophisticated products. The deployment of modern technologies in process industries and in most electronics and electrical products, even at the automated assembly and testing stages, necessitates considerable investment in skills at all levels, from shopfloor to technical, engineering and managerial. Significant capabilities have been developed in Malaysia in process engineering and improvement, capital goods adaptation and manufacture, changes to product design and even some product development for mature products (Bell *et al.* 1995). Many electronics firms have substantial proportions of technically qualified personnel, and at higher levels there is relatively low turnover of employees. The entry of second-tier MNCs, supplying complex components to the assemblers, has further deepened technological capabilities in Malaysia, with some spillover benefits to local firms and subcontractors (Rasiah 1995).

R&D and technological effort

The 1990 APITD (Action Plan for Industrial Technology Development) was based on an estimated R&D figure for the country in 1988 of 0.8 per cent of GDP, of which the public sector was supposed to account for 0.7 per cent and the private sector for 0.1 per cent. The government had originally set an R&D target for 2000 of 2 per cent of GDP, which it reduced to 1.5 per cent in OPP2, projecting that the private sector would raise its share from around 10–15 per cent in 1988 to 60 per cent of total R&D, reaching 0.9 per cent of GDP.

However, a comprehensive survey by the Malaysian Science and Technology Information Centre (MASTIC) of industrial R&D in 1992, the first of its kind, suggested that these estimates and targets were wrong. The overall level of R&D was around half of what was originally thought, at around 0.37 per cent of GDP. The private sector was, however, contributing a much larger share than expected, 45 per cent of the total (0.17 per cent of GDP) (MASTIC 1994). Thus, while the original R&D targets may not be feasible, the private sector should be able to raise its share of the (lower) total to the target of 60 per cent.

162

Table 6.6 R&D expenditure as percentage of GDP

Country	Year	Total	By enterprises
Malaysia	1992	0.37	0.17
Thailand	1987	0.2	0.03
Singapore	1992	1.0	0.6
Taiwan	1991	1.7	0.8
Korea	1992	2.1	1.7
Japan	1988	2.8	1.9

Source: UNESCO, *Statistical Yearbook*, and Government of Taiwan, *Taiwan Statistical Data Book, 1994*

Table 6.6 compares R&D in total and by industry for Malaysia (using the MASTIC) with Thailand, Japan and the leading first-tier NIEs. While Malaysia's performance turns out to be better than Thailand's, it is well behind that of the NIEs and Japan. This may be important: since the Malaysian industrial and export structure is as 'advanced' in the technological spectrum as Korea's and Taiwan's, and far more so than Thailand's, this R&D gap is a crucial problem for Malaysia.

The MASTIC survey shows that MNCs are leading the industrial research effort in Malaysia. However, the *scale* of the effort is modest. For instance, in 1992, Malaysian industrial enterprises employed a total of only 394 (full-time equivalent) researchers and 405 technicians in R&D. This was spread over 97 firms, an average of 4.1 researchers and 4.2 technicians per firm – compare this to the 500–1000 research engineers employed by each major electronics company under the leading Korean *chaebols*. The total current expenditure on R&D in Malaysia was RM125.4 million, RM1.3 million per firm, or RM0.3 million per researcher. Again, the scale of the effort was well below the minimum needed to conduct innovative research and development.[5]

Until now, the technology 'gap' has been compensated for by the lower technological level of production activity in similar industries in Malaysia, and by the substantial transfer of technology by MNCs. Does this matter? Most analysts agree that the low level of technological activity in Malaysia *does* matter and that the past pattern cannot be sustained indefinitely. The level and complexity of technological activity in the country has to rise to allow MNCs to move into more value-added activities, to deepen their 'roots' in Malaysia and to develop the capabilities of the local industrial sector. While some technological 'deepening' has taken place in the recent past, the process is still in its infancy.

Moreover, it is not certain that a natural process of evolution under market forces would lead to sufficient deepening. There is generally a discrete jump from doing process-based R&D to conducting more basic design and development work. In most developing countries, MNCs do not take the difficult and perhaps costly decision to make this 'jump' (for instance, in Mexico, which has a relatively large, mature, heavy and MNC-dominated industrial structure, R&D by the industrial sector remains at about 0.03 per cent of GDP). There are thus three reasons to argue that formal R&D capabilities in Malaysia should be increased:

- The assimilation and use of progressively more complex technologies by MNCs themselves calls for greater local design and development capability. In other words, even to keep its place as a major production centre in fast-moving technologies, Malaysia would have to develop more advanced technological capabilities than exist at present. This would involve adopting policies to increase formal R&D by MNCs.

- In order to diversify its export and industrial base, Malaysia should strengthen its ability to identify emerging critical technologies and so 'leapfrog' stages of technological development. This would allow it to tap interconnections between different technologies, and to internalise the spillover benefits of technical progress in the export-oriented sector. This requires developing strong research and monitoring capabilities in the technology infrastructure, and the development of intense links between it and industrial firms.

- It is necessary to develop the R&D base of indigenous firms to enable them to participate in international industrial activity as the economy liberalises. This will itself raise the country's attractiveness to MNCs and induce them to place more research activities in Malaysia. A strong and technologically dynamic base of suppliers and competitors to MNCs can only improve Malaysia's standing in the FDI arena. Again, given the normal constraints that face small firms that are new to R&D activity, the government would have to play a strong lead role.

In Malaysia's transition to industrial maturity, therefore, there need be no conflict between using FDI and foreign technology and increasing local R&D effort – on the contrary, these are necessarily complementary factors. Without a growing technological base, Malaysia runs the risk of losing its place in the international production hierarchy, even if it retains a heavy dependence on MNCs. The danger is not so much that international firms will pull out of their existing range of activities in Malaysia as that they will set up their more advanced facilities elsewhere as technologies continue to develop and other countries offer more advanced bases of skill and supply capabilities. Thus, the technological 'roots' of MNCs have to be strengthened to ensure that they continue to transfer their most advanced technologies to Malaysia rather than migrate to countries that have more developed technological bases.

However, the growth of R&D should be an integral part of upgrading technological capabilities more broadly. It is the latter that is the final determinant of efficiency and competitiveness, and R&D is at one end of a large spectrum of technology activity. In fact, formal R&D should follow from the perceived need of firms, once they have developed their 'routine' capabilities and see the value of starting search and experimentation detached from day-to-day production. The growth of government and university R&D should be subsidiary to and supportive of these primary objectives.

There is, at present, relatively little interaction between research and technology institutions and industrial R&D, and programmes to promote technological upgrading in the SMEs have not lived up to expectations. However, there *is* considerable scope for improving the quality and intensity of the interaction. It may be useful here to note what some East Asian NIEs did to support technology development in their SME sectors (Appendix 1). The cases noted here are Singapore, Taiwan and Hong Kong. Singapore has chosen to rely heavily on MNCs to spearhead its industrial and export thrust, but in recent years has intensified its support for local firms as suppliers and independent operators. Taiwan is perhaps the most important example of comprehensive support for SMEs. Interestingly, even *laissez-faire* Hong Kong has a large support programme for its export-oriented SMEs and provides considerable government subsidies to ensure that they keep up with changing technologies.

Each of the 'technologically minded' NIEs, Korea, Singapore and Taiwan, has set explicit national targets for R&D: Singapore and Taiwan at 2 per cent of GDP by 1995, and Korea at 5 per cent of GDP by 2000. Each has selected for promotion particular technologies, such as information technology, electronics, bio-technologies, advanced manufacturing technologies and new materials. Korea has identified 106 technologies in these fields, including machinery and telecommunications. Taiwan has selected 66 key parts, components and products and 61 new technologies in 15 industries.

Korean technology strategy has been the most interventionist in the developing world, and also the most successful in raising indigenous R&D (Appendix 2). However, it must be clearly recognised that it is not a pattern that is directly replicable by Malaysia, which has a very different pattern of industrial ownership and promotion policies. Though APITD reflects a desire to adopt a Korean-style approach in Malaysia, this is unrealistic in the Malaysian political-economic context (Lall 1995). In particular, Korea's deliberate creation of large domestic private conglomerates, the *chaebols*, to lead its export thrust, backed by heavy protection and selective credit allocation, lay at the root of its rapid increase in R&D. This strategy is not feasible in Malaysia, not just because of its heavy reliance on FDI, but also because the main tools of industrial policy used in the past in Korea cannot be used today as the international 'rules of the game' will no longer permit it. Nor does Malaysia have a strong base of indigenous industrial enterprises to take up the technological challenge. Malaysia has a long tradition of liberal and market-friendly policies, and its past success, based on FDI, has been due in large part to such policies. Thus, its approach to technology development has to be different from a country like Korea, and has to be tailored to its own political and industrial structure.

Foreign direct investment

Malaysia remains one of the main destinations for FDI in Asia. It now ranks third after China and Singapore, which, despite its small size, continues to attract large substantial investments (Table 6.7). The large East Asian tigers, Korea and Taiwan,

Table 6.7 FDI inflows into Asian economies (US$ million)

Country	1982–87 (average)	1988	1989	1990	1991	1992	1993
Hong Kong	1014	2627	1077	1728	538	1918	1667
China	1362	3194	3393	3487	4366	11156	27515
Korea	253	871	758	715	1116	550	n.a.
Singapore	1605	3655	2773	5263	4395	5635	6830
Taiwan	306	959	1604	1330	1271	879	917
Indonesia	282	576	682	1093	1482	1774	2004
Malaysia	844	719	1668	2332	3998	4469	4351
Thailand	287	1105	1775	2444	2014	2116	1715

Source: UNCTAD, *World Investment Report, 1994*

did not rely heavily on FDI inflows to sustain their technological development, and, in fact, for much of the period shown, were net outward investors. Their export thrust was largely based on the capabilities of their indigenous enterprises; this depended, as seen above, on large investments in local technological effort and human capital formation. Singapore relied heavily on FDI, but had a very pro-active set of interventions for guiding investors into high-value-added activities and for raising the local technological content of their activity, backing this up with strong investments in supply-side factors and institutional support.

In Malaysia, while FDI provided the engine for technological development and filled the 'gaps' between local technology and skills, the degree of supply-side support has been relatively low. However, given the slow pace at which domestic substitutes for FDI can develop even under optimistic assumptions, and given the dominance of MNCs in its export structure, it is very probable that Malaysia would have to continue to depend on high levels of FDI. This may not necessarily mean that the volume of FDI has to keep rising – even lower levels of FDI may be compatible with continued technological upgrading and export growth, if the new investments were concentrated in leading-edge technologies, existing affiliates invested in local R&D, and new technologies kept on being imported by non-FDI channels.

The data in Table 6.7 are reassuring as far as overall inflows are concerned. Though 1993 saw a slight decline over the previous year, this is likely to have been reversed in 1994, when there was a burst of FDI in textiles, electronics and wood products. On past trends, this level of inflows is, if maintained, sufficient to keep Malaysia on target. However, it is of interest to look at recent FDI by industrial activity. Note that these are data on approvals, not actual arrivals, of foreign investment, and they include foreign loans plus foreign equity. As such, they are not directly comparable with the UNCTAD data. The data go up to June 1995, and have been annualised by assuming that the first six months represent half of the annual figure for 1995.

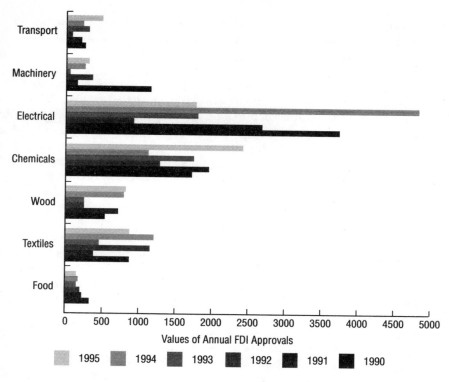

Figure 6.5 Malaysia: FDI approvals by industry, 1990–95 (RM million)
Source: MIDA, Kuala Lumpur, 1995

Figure 6.5 is based on Malaysian Industrial Development Authority (MIDA) data and shows FDI approvals in manufacturing projects for 1990–95, in seven important industries of actual or potential export interest: food products, textiles and apparel, wood and wood products, chemicals (excluding petroleum refining and products), electrical and electronics, machinery, and transport equipment. Of these, food, wood and textiles are established export activities, using local resources or cheap labour, and at the low-tech end of the spectrum. They have a strong foreign presence in the more advanced or capital-intensive end of the industry (like synthetic fibres in textiles) and also in export-oriented (low-technology) garments production.

Of the more complex industries, chemicals is partly export-oriented, with heavy process technologies and complex, but relatively slow-changing, technologies, and strong MNC presence, but also substantial local participation. Electricals and electronics are overwhelmingly foreign-owned, and enjoy the highest rates of technical change and export participation. Machinery manufacturing is a weak area of Malaysian industry, but one whose long-term growth and deepening could be of great value to local technological development in general. Transport equipment is

167

a relatively new activity in terms of exports, but has great long-term potential for technological development, 'cluster' benefits and export diversification.

The approvals data suggest the following:

- In the low-technology industries, textiles attracted a burst of interest during 1992 and 1994 in synthetic fibre capacity. The apparel sector, a much larger exporter, is getting relatively little FDI because of rising wages and the low rate of upgrading into high-value-added export items. This is unfortunate, because Malaysia is a large apparel exporter and has a long way to go, even with rising wages, before it regards apparel as a 'sunset' industry. There are many countries with much higher wages that are maintaining world market share in garments, by creating local design skills, having strong linkages between textiles and garments (in Malaysia, these are weak, and most export-oriented garment producers use imported fabric) and investing in more advanced technologies. If such upgrading of capabilities can be achieved, there could be more FDI in apparel production. In the textile sector, the local sector is weak, and in the region, Indonesia is emerging as a powerhouse of synthetic fibre production, following Taiwan. Again, there is considerable scope for technological upgrading and attracting FDI.
- The wood products industry saw declining foreign interest in 1992–93, but has enjoyed a revival since. There is considerable growth potential in this industry; the domestic wood products industry is competitive and has developed design capabilities. The food industry has a stable, low level of FDI and does not seem to be realising its full export potential in processed foods (apart from palm oil, where Malaysia is the regional leader); Thailand has a more dynamic food industry, led by large local firms, which are aggressively exporting and investing abroad.
- The chemicals industry has a fluctuating but high rate of FDI, with a large increase in 1995 that takes it above the previous peak of 1991. In terms of providing basic intermediates to Malaysian industry, it seems well placed to continue growing. The machinery sector, by contrast, is weak and continues to be a large 'hole' in an otherwise maturing industrial sector.
- Electricals and electronics continue to dominate FDI into Malaysia. There was declining interest by foreign investors after 1990, as approvals declined from RM3.8 billion to RM1 billion in 1992, followed by a revival to RM1.8 billion in 1993 and a sudden acceleration to RM4.8 billion in 1994. In 1995, approvals went back to 1993 levels. There does not seem to be any cause for concern as far as investment inflows are concerned, and if they are maintained the industry will continue to upgrade its facilities and maintain its position in export markets. The recent rise in the yen should provide another fillip to Japanese FDI in this industry. The main constraint will arise from the skill shortages noted above.
- Transport equipment attracts relatively low values of FDI, given the prominent position of the public sector in the export-oriented part of the industry.

There would appear to be plenty of scope for increasing foreign participation in high-tech components without damaging the prospects for increasing local linkages in simpler products.

Figure 6.6 shows the percentage breakdown of total FDI approvals during 1990–95 by the technological categories used earlier, including petroleum and gas.[6] Figure 6.7 shows the FDI breakdown without petroleum and gas, and relates this to the breakdown of non-oil and gas manufactured exports in 1992 (as shown earlier).

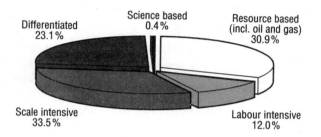

Figure 6.6 Malaysia: shares of 1990–95 FDI approvals by technological categories
Source: MIDA, Kuala Lumpur, 1995

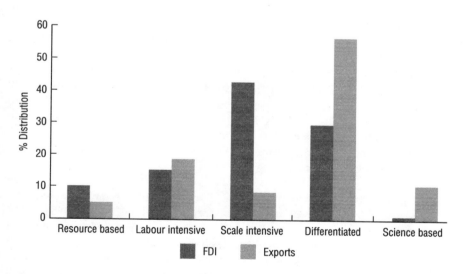

Figure 6.7 Distribution of 1990–95 FDI approvals and 1992 exports in non-oil and gas manufacturing

Sources: Author's calculations from UN, *International Trade Statistics*, various issues; MIDA, Kuala Lumpur, 1995

These breakdowns show that, if oil and gas are included, resource-based and scale-intensive sectors together account for the bulk of recent FDI approvals by MIDA. If oil and gas are excluded, the bulk of FDI goes into scale-intensive activities, followed by differentiated activities (i.e. mainly electricals and electronics). The distribution of manufactured exports is rather similar to that of FDI approvals in resource-based and labour-intensive activities, but lags well behind FDI in scale-intensive activities and exceeds FDI in differentiated and, to a lesser extent, in science-based industries (though some science-based exports are from what are classified under 'differentiated' FDI). These differences are not necessarily undesirable, as long as less export-oriented, scale-intensive FDI is technologically efficient and competitive. These activities, chemicals and steel for example, provide the intermediates that will feed into export activity as long as local linkages are increased and the activities themselves move into export.

Thus, the FDI scene seems quite healthy in Malaysia. The rise of China as a major magnet for MNCs has not (as was feared) affected their interest in Malaysia – clearly, the two are not as yet competing at the same technological level. MNCs have large sunk costs in Malaysia in terms of skills, capabilities and supplier systems, which continue to attract further high-value investments. However, whether or not this will be sufficient, in the longer term, to maintain high volumes of high-quality FDI depends on whether Malaysian skill and supplier bases can provide more advanced skills and technologies.

Conclusions

A rationalised approach to technology development must start with a systematic evaluation of the industries and products that are likely to propel Malaysia's future exports. It would be desirable to set up a system for the continued monitoring and identification of new technological opportunities, able to disseminate relevant information to Malaysian industry. The APITD made a start with the five generic technologies it identified, but the process must be more detailed, continued over time, and related to the emerging industrial structure and performance in the country. An effective policy for the purposes of technology development in Malaysia must differentiate its instruments according to the differing needs of the following four such groups:

- *Export-oriented MNCs.* These large firms have free access to the technological resources of their parent companies, 'deep pockets' and credit facilities to finance investments in technology, the ability to tap the skill and training resources of their company networks, and the knowledge of how to invest in deepening their technology base in Malaysia. In other words, they face far fewer market failures in technology development than their local, especially smaller, counterparts. These firms are already the leaders in R&D investments in the Malaysian private sector, and targeting their performance should be a major strategic focus of any technology strategy. The main problem is that the level and content of their local R&D tend to be well below what is needed for long-term technology development. The main thrust of policy thus has to be to encourage MNCs to transfer more advanced technologies as well as to build up local capabilities for more and more advanced design and research in Malaysia. However, given the integration of affiliate operations into a global framework of production, and given the opportunities for the parents to locate technological activities in many other countries, such policy has to be carefully designed to balance the need to maintain a favourable investment environment in Malaysia with that to induce greater technological content and upgrading.

- *Large local firms.* Some large Malaysian manufacturing firms are emerging as major exporters, with technology licensing agreements with international firms, growing in-house R&D capabilities and good training programmes. The policy need here is to encourage their research and training efforts, not necessarily to achieve frontier innovation, but to develop the capability to keep up with and adapt state-of-the-art technologies to diversify their own competitive base (rather like the efforts of local firms in Korea and Taiwan). The main deficiencies are in the skills and knowledge required for R&D, rather than in finance or basic technical skills. The technology import process may need to be revamped to ensure that imported know-how is fully absorbed and used as a base, rather than as a substitute, for local technological effort.

- *Modern SMEs.* There is a growing, but still small group of modern SMEs that are integrated into the modern sector. They use modern technologies, and act as subcontractors and suppliers to export-oriented MNCs (and are often set up with their active assistance). Their technological upgrading may face financial as well as skill and information constraints; an active venture-capital industry would be particularly valuable here, combined with good contract research facilities at research institutes and universities. Since most of these firms would remain too small individually to mount meaningful R&D effort, the effectiveness of the supporting technology infrastructure would be of critical importance, along with efforts made via industry associations and joint research projects between firms.

- *Traditional SMEs.* The bulk of the Malaysian industry sector consists of small traditional firms using low-technology and low-skill technologies. The upgrading of the technological capabilities of these firms faces the most difficult challenges, in all the relevant markets – finance, information, skills, technical assistance, marketing and so on. Yet, these are just as important to the technological upgrading of Malaysia as the more glamorous high-tech efforts of the large modern firms. The instruments needed for the traditional SMEs have to be very different from those needed for the latter, and, for the time being, should focus on promoting greater technological mastery rather than innovation.

171

An industrial policy which will support all these different groups of industries should be put in place. This policy may comprise many of the elements that have been shown to work in the East Asian NIEs, with the major caveat, noted earlier, that some major tools of intervention will no longer be permissible – in particular selective protection and credit subsidies. However, this does not mean that all instruments of industrial policy are ruled out. Singapore, for instance, has effectively used a variety of measures to guide and upgrade FDI in a free-trade setting, with the government taking a very interventionist and pro-active stance to create 'winners'. On the supply side, most NIEs have intervened very actively and selectively to create the conditions for technological progress and capability development. There are many things that the Malaysian government can and should do. And the evidence suggests that these have often to be selective, since intervention resources are limited and market forces by themselves may not be able to guide industry into the kinds of genuinely high-technology activities where Malaysia should be heading to use its accumulated base of industrial capabilities.

This analysis poses a significant contrast with neo-liberal prescriptions, such as those offered by the World Bank, which dismisses both the importance of selective industrial policies and the capacity of most governments, Malaysia included, to implement them successfully. In this view, Malaysia's current success has resulted solely from its adherence to liberal economic policies. By way of conclusion, then, we review the contribution selective industrial policy has made to Malaysia's development thus far.

The World Bank has argued that industrial policy in Malaysia has been largely a failure.[7] Malaysian 'industrial policy' is defined by the Bank to be the state-led, heavy-industry drive of the 1980s, and its failure is taken to be established by the government reversing its policy on state ownership once the high costs of the drive became evident (World Bank 1993: 310–11). The Bank attributes Malaysian (and East Asian) industrial success to conformance to free market forces in an export-oriented, stable macroeconomic setting, and to 'functional' (non-selective) interventions in infrastructure and human capital formation. There is certainly an element of truth in this as far as Malaysian success goes, as the above discussion suggests. However, the Bank's neo-liberal approach can be overdone.

The deficiencies of the neo-liberal argument in the case of the first-tier East Asian NIEs and Japan have been considered elsewhere (Lall 1996). As far as Malaysia goes, we accept that stability and export orientation, combined with a basic set of skills, were important in industrial success. However, there were other elements that have to be considered before a general conclusion on the inefficacy and redundancy of selective interventions is drawn.

First, the early growth of manufacturing in Malaysia was fostered by import substitution and provided much of the impetus for industrial growth up to the 1970s. The benefits of this era of industrial policy have to be taken into account. The later phase of industrial policy – state-led entry into heavy industry – did have higher costs. However, the subsequent reduction of the role of the Malaysian state in industry, precipitated by the macroeconomic crisis of the mid-1980s, does not establish the failure of industrial policy. All it shows is that the particular form of industrial policy in the 1980s may not have been well designed. The Malaysian heavy-industry drive lacked many of the critical elements of East Asian policies in overcoming market failures in industrial deepening. Malaysia's political economy at the time dictated a different, and apparently less effective, set of interventions. But direct state ownership was not really necessary for industrial policy, since interventions could (as in Korea) have been just as pervasive without it. The reduction of state ownership and the imposition of market discipline, which the World Bank sees as a renunciation of interventions, is in fact an improvement of industrial policy.

Second, the experience of Japan and Korea suggests that the time period over which heavy industry policy should be judged must be longer than allowed in the Malaysian case. The development of a complex activity like automobile manufacturing can take one to two decades if there is to be significant local content and design, even in countries with long industrial traditions (as in Latin America). In a country with a relatively shallow industrial base like Malaysia, it is creditable that Proton has done as well as it has in its relatively short life (it started in 1983). It has increased local content significantly, with greater scale economies for components manufacturers; in the process, it has fostered a large number of local suppliers with an active technology transfer programme. It has mounted a successful export drive, introduced new models with increasing local design content, and created new engineering capabilities in the country. Its long-term success remains to be established, but it is certainly too early to write it off as a costly failure. There are a number of other heavy industries that have also established an export capability and shown signs of 'growing up' from infancy.

Third, functional interventions and a stable macro framework were certainly central to Malaysia's success in attracting export-oriented FDI. However, it must be noted that selective targeting by MIDA was important in getting the electronics-based boom started. In addition, there was a strong element of luck – Malaysia's legacy of good physical and legal infrastructure, its location next to Singapore and its entry into electronics at the height of the semiconductor assembly boom. These benefits are not available to other developing countries that are liberalising today and seek to attract export-oriented FDI. The pattern of investment is thus very different, and Malaysia looks increasingly unique in its leap into high-technology exports.

Fourth, many of the factor market interventions needed to maintain industrial growth in Malaysia have to be selective, rather than functional. Thus, the creation of specific skills for electronics design, biotechnology or automobile design is necessarily a selective process. So is the setting up of technical support services for textiles or food processing, or the encouragement of R&D in the strategic technologies identified in the technology plan. Such selectivity in factor market interventions, currently under way in Malaysia, is a manifestation of improved industrial policy in Malaysia, not its renunciation.

SANJAYA LALL

Fifth, the Malaysian government is setting up the mechanisms for the kinds of private–public co-operation and interaction that were so effective in East Asia. The launching of the concept of 'Malaysia Incorporated', with a forum for regular consultation between the government and private business, marks an important step forward in mounting effective design, monitoring and implementation of interventions.

Finally, it is also relevant to note that Malaysia is reaping the benefits of industrial policy undertaken earlier by other countries in the region, in particular Japan, Taiwan, Singapore and Korea (Wade 1994). A large part of its export growth is fuelled by the capabilities that selective interventions in these countries fostered, which then spilled over to neighbouring countries that offered cheaper labour and a conducive investment climate, or, as with Singapore, from policies to encourage MNCs to move their lower-value-added facilities overseas. The market forces that Malaysia's 'market-friendly' policies tapped were thus themselves the creatures of industrial intervention. While this is not of direct concern to Malaysia (except as models on which it draws), it *is* relevant to the debate on industrial policy more broadly.

To conclude, therefore, the evidence suggests that while much of Malaysia's growth in recent years was driven by FDI and market-friendly policies, neo-liberal conclusions – that selective interventions were irrelevant or positively harmful in Malaysia – seem unwarranted. Industrial policy in Malaysia did play a role, and has an important role to play in the future, though its pattern has differed greatly from that in the first-tier NIEs. The need for selective as well as functional interventions to strengthen the local skill and technological base is correctly, and strongly, recognised by the government. The change in direction of the government in recent years, combining liberalisation of trade with more targeted selective interventions in both trade and factor markets in concert with the private sector, shows an improvement in industrial policy, rather than its absence. Finally, the benefits that are spilling over to Malaysia from industrial policy in the first-tier NIEs and Japan should be counted as benefits of intervention rather than of free markets.

Appendix 1: Technological support services in Singapore, Hong Kong and Taiwan

The Singapore Institute of Standards and Industrial Research (SISIR) is responsible, not only for promoting and certifying quality standards (which is extremely successful, since Singapore has the highest number of ISO 9000 certified companies in the developing world), but also for testing and metrology services and providing monthly information to firms on new technological developments. SISIR aggressively uses standards as a tool to force local firms to move to higher-quality products and processes. The Technology Development Centre helps local firms to identify their technology requirements and purchase technologies; it also designs technology upgrading strategies. Since its foundation in 1989, the TDC has pro-

174

vided over 130 firms with various forms of technical assistance. It also administers the Small Industry Technical Assistance Scheme and Product Development Assistance Scheme to help firms develop their design and development capabilities. It has given grants of over $1 million for 29 SITASs in the past 5 years, mainly to local enterprises. Its earnings have risen to a level where its cost-recoverable activities are self-financing.

The Economic Development Board encourages subcontracting to local firms through its 'Local Industries Upgrading Programme', under which MNCs are encouraged to source components locally. In return for a commitment by the MNCs to provide on-the-job training and other assistance to subcontractors, the government provides a package of assistance to the latter, including cost-sharing grants and loans for the purchase of equipment or consultancy and the provision of training.

The Hong Kong Productivity Council (HKPC) which was the first such institution in the region, started in 1967 to help the SMEs that constitute the bulk of the industrial sector. It provides information on international standards and quality and gives training, consultancy and demonstration services on productivity and quality to small firms at subsidised rates. It also acts as a major technology transfer agent, and over time has developed specialised technical services for all the main industrial sectors in Hong Kong. It employs over 600 highly trained consultants and staff and operates its own laboratory. Its demonstration centre can show the application of new technologies in CAD/CAM, advanced manufacturing technology, surface mount technology, micro-processor technology, rapid prototyping and so on. In 1991–92, it undertook 1255 consultancy projects, trained over 14,000 people and provided support to 2112 firms. The HKPC has always subsidised the costs of its services to SMEs. Despite the growth in the share of revenue-earning work and its withdrawal from activities in which private consultants have appeared, the government still has to contribute about half of its budget.

In addition, the Hong Kong government has supported local design capabilities by joining the private sector in starting a school of design and setting up the Hong Kong Design Innovation Company. The latter was started with seed money from the government because private-sector design services were lacking and local firms were not aware of their value. Over the four years of its existence (mainly on government financing), this value has been recognised, but the HKDIC (now under the HKPC) is still not financially self-supporting.

Taiwan also has a preponderance of SMEs specialised in numerous skill-intensive operations aimed at world markets (at technological levels generally higher than their Hong Kong counterparts), but mostly too small to conduct their own R&D. The government has helped them with a wide range of technological support measures. One has been to transfer production-ready technology that the government has imported and adapted. Another is to encourage industry to contract research to universities; half of the National Science Council's research grants of about $200 million per year funds such contracts, with enterprises providing matching funds. The Industrial Technology Research Institute (ITRI) conducts R&D in areas considered too risky or large-scale for private industry, with an annual budget of $450 million. The country's flourishing integrated circuit industry was spun off from research done at ITRI, and its Electronics Research Service Organisation (ERSO) is its main branch. The government also sets up public enterprises to enter high risk areas of investment like D-RAM memory chip manufacture, where it lags behind Korea, and co-ordinates the R&D and investments of related private firms to develop an integrated industry strategy.

The development of SMEs in Taiwan has been encouraged by local-content measures and other incentives to MNCs. But more effective have been measures to raise the efficiency of local firms by programmes of technical assistance and quality enhancement. A number of institutions provide credit, technology and marketing assistance: the China Productivity Centre (CPC) is the best known for its promotion of automation in industry to increase precision and quality. The CPC sends out teams of engineers to visit plants throughout the country and demonstrate the best means of automation and solve relevant technical problems. Over two years, the CPC visited over 1000 plants and made over 4000 suggestions for improvement. It also carried out more than 500 research projects on improving production efficiency and linked enterprises to research centres to solve more complex technical problems.

Taiwan has set up a science town in Hsinchu, with 13,000 researchers in two universities, six national laboratories (including ITRI) and a huge technology institute, as well as some 150 companies specialising in electronics. The science town makes special efforts to attract start-ups and provides them with prefabricated factory space, five-year tax holidays and generous grants. Since 1980 the government has invested $500 million in Hsinchu.

Appendix 2: Encouragement of technological activity in Korea

Korea has the best example of strategic industrial policy to develop indigenous technological capabilities. It combined import-substitution with forceful export promotion, selectively protecting and subsidising targeted industries that were to form its future export advantage. In order to enter heavy industry, promote local R&D capabilities and establish an international image for its exports, the government promoted the growth of giant local private firms, the *chaebols*, to spearhead its industrialisation drive. Korean industry built up an impressive R&D capability, drawing extensively on foreign technology in forms that promoted local control. Thus, it was one of the largest importers of capital goods in the developing world, and encouraged its firms to access the latest equipment (except when it was promoting particular domestic products) and technology. It encouraged the hiring of foreign experts. FDI was allowed where considered necessary, but foreign majority ownership was discouraged unless it was a condition of having access to closely held technologies, or to promote exports in internationally integrated activities. The government intervened in major technology contracts to strengthen domestic buyers, and sought to maximise the participation of local consultants in engineering contracts to develop basic process capabilities. In 1973, it enacted the Engineering Service Promotion Law to protect and strengthen the domestic engineering services sector, and the Law for the Development of Specially Designated Research Institutes to provide legal, financial and tax incentives for private and public institutes in selected technological activities.

Technological effort in Korea was supported by the government in several ways. Private R&D was directly promoted by a number of incentives and other forms of assistance. Incentive schemes included tax-exempt TDR (Technology Development Reserve) funds, tax credits for R&D expenditures as well as for upgrading human capital related to research and setting up industry research institutes, accelerated depreciation for investments in R&D facilities and a tax exemption for 10 per cent of cost of relevant equipment, reduced import duties for imported research equipment, and a reduced excise tax for technology-intensive products. The KTAC (Korea Technology Advancement Corporation) helped firms to commercialise research results; a 6 per cent tax credit or special accelerated depreciation provided further incentives. The import of technology was promoted by tax incentives: transfer costs of patent rights and technology import fees were tax-deductible; income from technology consulting was tax-exempt; and foreign engineers were exempt from income tax. In addition, the government gave grants and long-term low-interest loans to participants in 'National Projects' (see below), which gave tax privileges and official funds to private and government R&D institutes to carry out these projects. Technology finance was provided by the Korea Technology Development Corporation, and later a large number of venture-capital companies came into being; Korea now has the largest venture-capital industry in the developing world.

SMEs were helped in various ways. They were given shopfloor technological advice and guidance by the Korea Production Technology Corporation, which complemented the Small and Medium Industry Promotion Corporation, providing technical, training and other services to SMEs. SMEs were further assisted by the Korea Academy of Industrial Technology and by 'technology guidance systems' operated by government research institutes. The government also 'reserved' over 1000 products for production by SMEs, and encouraged the *chaebols* to increase subcontracting to strengthen SME technological capabilities.

The government invested in a large array of technology infrastructure institutions, and spending on the R&D infrastructure rose rapidly over the 1980s. In 1966, the Korea Institute of Science and Technology was set up to conduct applied research for industry. In its early years, KIST focused on solving simple problems of technology transfer and absorption. In the 1970s, the government set up other specialised research institutes on machinery, metals, electronics, nuclear energy, resources, chemicals, telecommunications, standards, shipbuilding, marine sciences, and so on. These were largely spun off from KIST, and, by 1980, there were 16 public R&D institutions. In 1981 the government reduced their number to rationalise their operations. The institutes were merged into 9 under the supervision of the Ministry of Science and Technology. KIST was merged with KAIS (Korea Advanced Institute of Science) to become KAIST, but was separated again – as KIST – in 1989.

The government launched National Research and Development Projects in 1982: large R&D projects regarded as too risky for industry to tackle alone but considered to be strategically important. National Projects were conducted jointly by industry, public research institutes and the government, on semiconductors, computers, fine chemicals, machinery, material science and plant system engineering. 'Centres of Excellence' were formed in these fields to boost competitiveness. In these projects, the government orchestrated the actors involved, provided large grants, underwrote a large part of the risks, and directly filled in gaps that the market could not remedy. National Projects were government- or industry-initiated (and carried out jointly with research institutes). The total expenditure on these projects came to US$680 million over 1982–89, with the government accounting for 60 per cent. The sums involved increased steadily each year, from US$25 million in 1982 to US$151 million in 1989. Several National Projects continue today.

Science Research Centres and Engineering Research Centres were set up at universities and around the country to support R&D activities and the common utilisation of R&D facilities. Science towns were built to capture the 'cluster' effects of R&D, with research institutions, universities and industry locating together. Daeduk Science Town started in 1974, and a large number of R&D and educational institutions are now operating there. Kwangju Science Town has also started; others are in the pipeline.

Notes

1 On technological capabilities see Lall (1993). MOSTE (1990) also has a good analysis of the central role of technology and what technological effort involves in a developing country.
2 However, simply building heavy industry may not be efficient, as the experience of Eastern Europe and some import-substituting countries shows. The facilities set up should realise economies of scale and use the complex capital-intensive technologies involved efficiently. This usually requires that the structural transformation of industry take place in an open, competitive framework, as was mostly the case with Malaysia.
3 Singapore developed a much 'deeper' industrial structure by targeting advanced electronics industries and attracting FDI into them. Given its small size and export specialisation, it has a larger weight of heavy industry than the other NIEs or even Japan.
4 These and most of the following calculations are taken from Lall et al. (1995).
5 The largest current R&D expenditure by the industrial sector was in the electrical and electronics industry (66 per cent of total industry R&D), spread over 25 enterprises (RM3.3 million per enterprise) and 210 researchers (or 8.4 researchers per firm, with RM394 thousand per researcher). These are very small sums for research. While the effort is likely to be very unequally distributed between firms, and some firms are making genuine technological contributions in terms of process engineering, most seem to be doing relatively minor jobs that would not normally be counted as R&D.

6 The industries are classified as follows: *resource-based*: food, beverages, tobacco, wood, furniture, petroleum, gas and rubber; *labour-intensive*: textiles and products, leather and products, plastic products, fabricated metals and miscellaneous; *scale-intensive*: paper, chemicals, non-metallic minerals, basic metals and transport equipment; *differentiated*: machinery, electricals and electronics; and *science-based*: scientific and measuring equipment.

7 See World Bank (1993). For a longer analysis of the Malaysian case see Lall (1995), and for a critique of the *Miracle* study see Lall (1994).

References

Bell, M., Hobday, M., Abdullah, S., Ariffin, N. and Malik, J. (1995) 'Aiming for 2020: A Demand-driven Perspective on Industrial Technology Policy in Malaysia', Final Report for the World Bank, Science Policy Research Unit, University of Sussex.

Freeman, C. and Perez, C. (1988) 'Structural Crises of Adjustment, Business Cycles and Investment Behaviour', in G. Dosi, C. Freeman, R. Nelson, G. Silverberg and L. Soete (eds), *Technical Change and Economic Theory*, London: Pinter.

JTR (1992) *Employment Turnover Survey, 1992*, Jabatan Tenaga Rakyat, Malaysia.

Lall, S. (1993) 'Understanding Technology Development', *Development and Change*, 24(4): 719–53.

Lall, S. (1994) '"The East Asian Miracle" Study: Does the Bell Toll for Industrial Strategy?', *World Development*, 22: 645–54.

Lall, S. (1995) 'Malaysia: Industrial Success and the Role of Government', *Journal of International Development*, 7(5): 759–74.

Lall, S. (1996) 'Paradigms of Development: The East Asian Debate', *Oxford Development Studies*, 24(2): 111–31.

Lall, S., Baert, F., Carroll, A.-M., Khanna, A., Finnegan, R. and Shetty, R. (1995) 'Malaysia's Export Performance and Its Sustainability, Phase II: Competitiveness', Asian Development Bank, draft.

Malaysia (1991) *Second Outline Perspective Plan, 1991–2000*, Kuala Lumpur: Government Printers.

Malaysia (1993) *Mid-Term Review of the Sixth Malaysia Plan*, Kuala Lumpur: Government Printers.

Malaysian Science and Technology Information Centre (MASTIC) (1994) *1992 National Survey of Research and Development*, Ministry of Science, Technology and the Environment, December.

MOSTE (1990) *Industrial Technology Development: A National Plan of Action*, Kuala Lumpur: Ministry of Science, Technology and Environment, Malaysia.

Rasiah, R. (1995) *Foreign Capital and Industrialisation in Malaysia*, London: Macmillan.

Rosenberg, N. (1986) *Perspectives on Technology*, Cambridge: Cambridge University Press.

Wade, R. (1994) 'Selective Industrial Policies in East Asia: Is *The East Asian Miracle* Right?', in A. Fishlow, C. Gwin, S. Haggard, D. Rodrik and R. Wade, *Miracle or Design? Lessons from the East Asian Experience*, Washington, DC: Overseas Development Council.

World Bank (1993) *The East Asian Miracle*, Oxford: Oxford University Press.

7

MALAYSIA'S NATIONAL INNOVATION SYSTEM

Rajah Rasiah

The notion of national innovation systems (NISs) is now gaining attention as a framework to conceptualise the development of innovative capability and its support of productive activities. Elements of the approach can be traced to Frederich List's (1885) arguments in support of industrial policy to create dynamic comparative advantage. Dynamic national innovation systems have helped nations transform comparative and competitive advantages (Gerschenkron 1962; Kaldor 1979; Porter 1990). Adopting a broad definition of technology which includes qualitative and intangible attributes, pioneering works in this field have deliberately left the concept's empirical boundaries open, with various agents (including firms and organisations) potentially interacting and playing mutually supportive roles in developing nations' productive capacities (Lundvall 1985; Freeman 1987; Nelson 1985; Dosi 1984). Innovation, also broadly defined, includes both rare path-breaking inventions and the commonly recorded introduction of manufacturing designs and processes, including minor improvements, that are new to a firm, if not to the world. Firms typically move from acquiring existing technologies, often through import from abroad, through stages of adapting and developing to finally innovating new processes and designs. Thus, involvement in research and development (R&D) comes at the end of a sequential learning process (Pavitt 1984). The potential capacity of a national innovation system to stimulate innovations will depend on the development of technology-supporting organisations and their effective co-ordination with firms. Proponents of NISs make the Schumpeterian assumption that firms actively and strategically shape the technology frontier, and therefore differ from the Marshallian view that firms operate as passive recipients of serendipitous technology breakthroughs.

This chapter is divided into two main sections. The first offers a conceptual framework for understanding national innovation systems, while the second employs it to assess Malaysia's NIS. The conceptual framework draws on the theoretical literature related to NISs, as well as a comparative perspective garnered from similar works on other economies, to identify key agents and their co-ordinating roles. The second part critically dissects Malaysia's national innovation system and examines potential weaknesses in its institutional set-up and co-ordination mechanisms.

The national innovation system framework

Put simply, the NIS refers directly to innovating agents and indirectly to the enabling environment that stimulates innovations. An empirical analysis must identify the system's indirect and direct agents, and the co-ordination relationships between them. Direct agents are generally firms, and their gains or losses are affected by their capacity to generate cheaper and better products and services than their competitors. Indirect agents refer to supporting organisations that constitute the enabling environment. The key enabling agents – e.g. human capital generators, funding organisations, transport and marketing networks, research and development institutes, incentive structures and regulatory frameworks – set the parameters within which firms access input and output markets and engage in efforts to improve production. Indirect organisations themselves are conditioned by other institutions (e.g. cultural norms) and by the firms with which they interact, so that all the nation's organisations may be networked within the NIS. It is an open system that enjoys inter-relationships with foreign organisations and firms. The prime difference between the NIS and other national systems (e.g. economic, security or welfare) is that it generates innovations and its direct agents are usually productive firms. NISs are increasingly inter-connected, so that knowledge and innovations flow internationally. Firms in even the most developed NIS access knowledge and innovations from other NISs. When national capacities are underdeveloped, competitive firms access foreign sources even more often. When local subsidiaries of foreign multinational corporations (MNCs) are involved, a large proportion of inputs (especially technology inputs) are sourced from abroad. With any system, synergies are maximised when a systematic, cohesive and dynamic structure emerges to co-ordinate relationships within and between institutions and firms to meet existing and future demands. For the system to be dynamic, it must be flexible and receptive to change. Finally, while both indirect and direct agents generate innovations, a nation's competitiveness is ultimately manifest in innovations generated by direct agents, particularly industrial firms.

Since the NIS encompasses a complex myriad of social agents and organisations – all of which are inter-connected – it is difficult to assess *in toto*. Thus, we limit our assessment to certain key organisations: institutions creating human resources, financial support for innovation, R&D institutions, cultural norms, government promotion efforts and incentives. Human resources provide the critical fuel for scientific inquiry and technical change, and are vital to manning both support institutions and firms. Schooling and other modes of learning, both general education and the technical training known as 'pre-employment education', are critical in providing human resources for employment and making workers receptive to absorbing instructions and in-firm training. Subsequent human resource development occurs through in-firm and work-related training designed to raise workers' productivity. Given the broad-based nature of pre-employment training – from primary to tertiary education – few, if any, manufacturing firms involved directly fund such programmes. Government participation is economically justified when, as in education, social returns exceed private returns. Private education is often determined by government incentives. Particularly in the initial stages of growth, when labour markets are underdeveloped, public investment in education tends to be much larger due to the lumpy and risky nature of such investments. Private institutions' role in general education only tends to rise as economies mature.

Firms' investments in human resource development tend to be stronger in enterprise training undertaken in-firm or in specialised organisations. The likelihood of government failure is higher here due to information asymmetry problems and conflicting interests. However, as in Korea and Singapore, governments often stimulate such training by intervening to remove market imperfections. Only as firms negotiate the technological trajectory from wholly externally sourced technologies to original equipment manufacturing (OEM), original design manufacturing (ODM) and original brand manufacturing (OBM), will substantial demand for R&D technologists and scientists emerge. Until then, the primary focus of human resource development will be on absorbing staff for production activities (Pavitt 1984). While external educational organisations employ R&D technologists and scientists, firms generally utilise them in limited and specific ways, either through contract research or by employing them directly. Most firm employees engaged in R&D participate largely in product and process improvement, rather than in basic research. The Japanese success in catching up with the United States, *inter alia*, involved a substantial contribution by process development (Best 1990, 1995) – a significant share of this was made by personnel not officially classified as R&D scientists or technologists.

The availability of finance for innovators and their supporting agents has also been critical. The classical Keynesian link of savings with investment can only stimulate growth if the capital is used productively (Rasiah 1995c; You 1995). Hence, the savings and investment structure – and not just their relative shares – is critical. Financial institutions must effectively service those agents directly or indirectly engaged in innovation. Interestingly, the East Asian experience has involved a strong link between corporate savings and investment. Also, a strong positive relationship between profits and investment has ensured a continued symbiotic relationship between high returns and investment in profitable sectors (Akyuz and Gore 1994; Rodrick 1994). Japan, Korea and Taiwan regulated their financial sectors tightly so that prioritised institutions and firms obtained subsidised loans substantially below curb (black) market rates. Intervention to direct resources to potentially productive target uses, taking into account information asymmetries (including scale economies and complementarities), has been critical in late industrialisers (Amsden 1989; Chang 1994; Rasiah 1996b).

Investments in R&D are not the most critical factor in generating competitiveness or even innovations. The share of governments' and firms' R&D investments in broader resource flows has been very small in most economies, irrespective of their level of development (see Nelson 1993). Nevertheless, R&D investments are an important component of the national innovation system. Applied R&D, in particular, is critical for generating inventions. Though basic R&D is an important part of innovation, firms rarely do it because it yields negligible monetary gains to the firm.

Cultural institutions have often been used to explain the success of particular communities in motivating and directing accumulation-oriented technical change. Examples of such arguments include the Protestant ethic in the rise of capitalism in Europe (Weber 1930), and the pursuit of knowledge and meritocracy stressed by Confucianism for the East Asian 'miracle'. As Johnson (1982), Dore (1986: 250) and Chang (1994: 87–8) have argued, the functional equivalent of specific cultural traits can be adapted to and adopted in different settings. Within the NIS framework, ethics are important, but not necessarily only as manifested in religion. More importantly, cultures are interpreted dynamically so that changes necessary for the advancement of scientific and technical knowledge and physical accumulation can be deliberately introduced.

Unlike European capitalist development, late industrialisation in the East Asian experience has shifted the emphasis from individualist to collectivist work ethics. These collaborative relationships, which grew with the medieval European guilds system, are re-emerging in new settings in Europe and North America (Best 1990). Such teamwork-based organisational innovations reorganise the labour process, including industrial relations, so that interdependent and group-work characteristics emerge to tap the innovative potential of the entire labour force. In such a system, unit costs and processes – not labour costs or workers – become the subject of control (see Best 1990; Lazonick 1989).

Most innovations are realised in firms through the introduction of new products and processes. While indirect agents who support firm operations are vital, firms eventually generate and apply most appropriable innovations. Drawing on available innovative capacities – both their own formal R&D and non-R&D facilities, and capabilities generated by support institutions – firms appropriate innovations. A significant amount of innovation emerges from the production floor, where learning enhances product and process improvement capacities. Incremental engineering, even through minor improvements, has been vital in late industrialisation (Rosenberg 1982). As the prime direct generators of products and services, firms' innovations are maximised when efforts are co-ordinated, both among themselves and with supporting institutions, to maximise synergies.

Governments generally lack a business orientation, and so face a high risk of failure. Markets, too, generally fail when price signals occur in underdeveloped structures, and when scale economies and complementarities are involved (Kaldor 1979). Hence, in addition to investing in some basic and applied research institutions, and in human resource development programmes, governments also actively create the enabling environment to stimulate indirect agents' and firms' participation in innovative activities. By prioritising investment, human resource development, research activities and other supporting activities, most East Asian NIEs have successfully developed strategic and complementary industries. Intra-industry institutions have been far more significant in stimulating innovative activities in Japan, Korea and Taiwan than government programmes. As noted earlier, governments' direct involvement as a share of overall R&D activities has traditionally been small, irrespective of development levels (see Nelson 1993).

Nonetheless, smooth co-ordination between the government, other support institutions and firms – including helping overcome market failures – have been critical in stimulating competitive innovative activities. In addition, latecomers have generally absorbed and adapted foreign technologies through both formal and informal relationships with foreign firms. The correct mix and orientations of indirect and direct agents can stimulate greater absorption of technology by local firms from foreign firms. Proactive governance to stimulate transfers through technology transfer agreements (TTAs) have been a critical pillar in Japan's, Korea's and Taiwan's success in technology accumulation (Johnson 1982; Amsden 1989; Wade 1990).

Malaysia's innovative capacity

This section examines the emergence and functioning of these key institutions – human resource development, financial resources, R&D institutions, cultural norms, as well as government promotion and incentives – in the evolution of Malaysia's NIS. The institutional context for capitalist growth in Malaya emerged during colonialism (Jomo 1986; Rasiah 1995e: Chapter 2). The colonial system was, however, largely geared towards primary production of raw materials for export. Tremendous advances were recorded in tin mining and smelting as well as rubber cultivation and processing, through incremental improvements in production. Rubber cultivation (especially high-yielding varieties) and processing particularly benefited from government research (e.g. see Lim 1967).

Expansion of the primary sector helped create the basic enabling environment for manufacturing to evolve. Railways, roads, wage labour, health and education, effective demand, administrative structure, and law and order were funded by revenue extracted from the primary sector which grew substantially in the colonial period. Primary product processing, consumer and support manufacturing industries began to emerge as a consequence (Rasiah 1995a). The government's generally *laissez-faire* approach to industrialisation limited the development of modern manufacturing. Hence, although the infrastructure created to serve the primary sector also stimulated some modern manufacturing, the colonial state's emphasis on primary production stunted manufacturing growth in the colony.

The institutional capacities that emerged during colonial rule were sustained in independent Malaysia. Rubber and tin, and, later, palm oil continued to be the main revenue generators until the 1980s. Tin's significance faded sharply after 1980 (Jomo 1990b). Rubber's contribution declined gradually, while palm oil has continued to be important. Oil became the most significant primary commodity from the late 1970s. Strong R&D efforts have continued in rubber, palm oil and petroleum activities. Research on rubber and palm oil, both in-firm and in the Rubber Research Institute of Malaysia (RRIM) and the Palm Oil Research Institute of Malaysia (PORIM), have reached their global technology frontiers. Palm oil research, for example, has generated considerable spin-offs as downstream manufacturing activities have developed strongly (Chantasmary 1994). R&D in

184

petroleum activities is still confined to process technology activities – largely spin-offs from production ventures by Shell and Exxon.[1]

The primary sector's relative significance in the national economy has, however, shrunk from the 1970s, and especially since the late 1980s. While tin and rubber have faced absolute declines from the 1980s, petroleum, timber and palm oil have remained major primary exports. The biggest growth, however, has been recorded in manufacturing, which overtook the primary commodities as the major export category in the late 1980s. Manufacturing's share of GDP had remained stagnant at 9.0 per cent between 1960 and 1965 (World Bank 1985), but grew rapidly thereafter from 13.9 per cent in 1970 to 31.6 per cent in 1994 (see Table 7.1). Manufacturing has also overtaken agriculture in terms of employment generation, contributing 24.6 per cent to the national total compared to 19.9 per cent by the latter.

Table 7.1 Malaysia: employment, output and export for selected sectors, 1970–94

	Employment			Output			Exports		
	1970	1980	1994	1970	1980	1994	1970	1980	1993
Agriculture	n.a.	39.7	19.9	29.0	22.9	14.6	63	n.a.	21
Mining	n.a.	1.7	0.5	13.7	10.1	7.5	30	n.a.	14
Manufacturing	n.a.	15.6	24.6	13.9	19.6	31.6	7	n.a.	65

Sources: Malaysia (1991, 1996); World Bank (1995: 191)
Note: n.a. – not available

Manufacturing has also undergone significant structural change. The share of capital goods in manufacturing exports rose from 5.8 per cent in 1968 to 69.0 per cent in 1994 (see Table 7.2). The electric/electronic sub-sector has expanded most, with its export share rising from 0.7 per cent in 1968 to 64.6 per cent in 1994. Capital goods output rose from 5.5 per cent in 1968 to 34.8 per cent in 1990 (see Rasiah 1995e: Table 5.3). The electric/electronic industry's share of employment and output rose from 2.0 per cent and 8.0 per cent respectively in 1968 to 30.2 per cent and 25.4 per cent respectively in 1990.

Unfortunately, the rapid growth of the manufacturing sector has not been very balanced, as reflected in several performance indicators. Burgeoning trade imbalances, high import shares to meet domestic demand and heavy concentration of production in narrowly defined segments of product chains have threatened to limit further structural change. As shown in Table 7.3, manufactured imports to meet domestic demand have continued to rise, while the manufactures trade balance has remained negative. A significant share of the profits realised by foreign firms have been repatriated as factor payments abroad as the overall current-account balance has worsened. The economy is now at a cross-roads, where the supply of resources, such as labour and infrastructural support, is increasingly strained. In fact, the growing reliance on foreign labour in the face of labour-supply constraints has slowed down the transition to higher skill and technology production.

Table 7.2 Malaysia: manufacturing export structure, 1968–94 (percentages)

	1968	1973	1980	1985	1990	1994
Food, beverage and tobacco	27	22	8	6	4	3
Textiles, clothing and footwear	3	9	13	10	9	5
Wood	7	11	7	3	3	5
Rubber	18	15	1	1	3	2
Chemicals	6	5	3	5	4	4
Petroleum manufactures	n.a.	n.a.	3	8	3	2
Non-metal minerals	3	3	1	1	2	1
Iron, steel and other metals	26	23	4	3	4	3
Electric/electronic including machinery	3	8	48	52	57	64
Transport equipment	2	3	4	5	4	5
Other manufacture	n.a.	n.a.	8	6	8	6
Total	100	100	100	100	100	100

Sources: Malaysia (1995: Statistical Table 3.5); Rasiah (1995: Table 5.3)
Note: n.a. – not available

Table 7.3 Malaysia: trade performance and balance of payments, 1973–92

	1973	1979	1985	1992
Manufacturing imports/ domestic demand[1]	0.407	0.358	0.339	0.611[2]
Goods trade balance[3]	−0.436	−0.189	−0.224	−0.182[2]
Current account balance[4]	−RM727m[5]	−RM1991m	−RM5434m	−RM6419m
Investment income[6]	−RM1187m[5]	RM2033m	−RM1522m	−RM4400m

Sources: Rasiah (1995, 1995a); *BNM* (1988, 1993)
Notes: 1 domestic demand measured as output + imports – exports;
2 1991 figures;
3 measured as [exports – imports]/[exports + imports];
4 comprises goods, transfers and service accounts;
5 1975 figures;
6 net flow of undistributed profits

To better understand the limitations of the existing mechanisms of technical change, it is pertinent to examine the nature and structure of the direct and indirect agents of innovation in the national economy. This task is undertaken using the framework introduced above, with only key agents assessed here. Also, given data constraints, the firm-level assessment of direct agents is largely limited to electronics firms.

Rasiah and Osman (1995: Table 1) reported labour supply and worker quality as the prime deficiencies confronting manufacturing firms in Malaysia. Indeed, serious shortages have been reflected in the high wage premiums enjoyed by skilled occupational categories (World Bank 1995). The sector is thus gripped by serious shortages in the 'critical mass' of employees who drive innovations. All 231 firms interviewed in 1995 identified skilled-worker shortages as their biggest problem.[2] The critical nature of this problem becomes clear when comparisons are made across economies. Malaysia's participation rates in education fall short of those of Korea and the developed economies, especially at the tertiary level (see Table 7.4). Shortages in the supply of technical graduates have been more serious, with only 2 per cent of secondary-school students enrolled in technical fields compared to 19 per cent in Korea (Table 7.5). Even Indonesia – which is less developed than Malaysia – has a 12 per cent share of secondary-school students in technical education. Systematic government promotion of technical education in Taiwan led to the transformation of the ratio of vocational high school (VHS) graduates to academic high school (AHS) graduates from 1:1.7 in 1950 to 1:1 in 1975 and 2:1 in 1988 (Lee 1994: 5–6).

Table 7.4 Selected economies: educational enrolment, 1970–92

| | % of age group enrolled in educational institutions | | | | | |
| | Primary | | Secondary | | Tertiary | |
Country	1970	1992	1970	1992	1970	1992
Japan	99	102	86	n.a.	31	32
United States	n.a.	104	n.a.	n.a.	56	76
Sweden	94	101	86	91	31	34
Germany	n.a.	107	n.a.	n.a.	27	36
France	117	106	74	101	26	46
Canada	101	107	65	104	42	99
United Kingdom	104	104	73	86	20	28
Korea	103	105	42	90	16	42
Turkey	110	112	27	60	6	15
Brazil	82	106	26	39	12	12
Malaysia	87	93	34	58	4	7
Thailand	83	97	17	33	13	19
Indonesia	80	115	16	38	4	10
Jamaica	119	106	46	62	7	9
Kenya	58	95	9	29	1	2
Bangladesh	54	77	n.a.	19	3	4

Source: World Bank (1995: 216–17)
Note: n.a.– not available

R&D activities have not been very significant. As shown in Table 7.6, Malaysia only had four R&D scientists and technologists per 10,000 people compared to 22 in Korea in 1988–90. Investment in R&D in 1992 was only 0.4 per cent of GNP compared to 2.1 per cent in Korea and even higher figures in the more industrialised economies. Malaysia's relatively low R&D endowments place it at the bottom of the technology trajectory. We noted earlier that the depth and width of R&D participation is generally a function of the structure and level of

Table 7.5 Selected economies: public education and technical orientation

Country	Public education as % of GNP		Secondary technical enrolment as % of all levels	Tertiary natural and applied science enrolment as % of total tertiary	Science graduates as % of total graduates
	1960	1990	1988–91	1990–91	1988–90
Japan	(4.9)	3.7 (5.0)	28	26	26
United States	(5.3)	5.5 (7.0)	n.a.	14	15
Sweden	5.9	6.5 (6.5)	73	43	26
Germany	(2.4)	4.0 (5.4)	80	42	32
France	(3.6)	5.4 (6.0)	54	31	27
Canada	(4.6)	(7.4)	n.a.	14	16
United Kingdom	3.4	5.3	20	39	26
Korea	2.0	3.6	19	42	29
Turkey	2.6	n.a.	25	33	36
Brazil	1.9	4.6	n.a.	31	19
Malaysia	2.9	6.9	2	30	28
Thailand	2.3	3.8	19	22	18
Indonesia	2.5	n.a.	12	n.a.	11
Jamaica	2.3	6.1	4	35	19
Kenya	4.6	6.8	2	32	24
Bangladesh	0.6	2.0	1	27	16

Source: UNDP (1995: 158–9, 192–3)

Table 7.6 Selected economies: research and development statistics

	Scientists and technologists per 1 000, 1986–90	R&D scientists and technologists per 10,000, 1986–89	R&D expenditure as % of GNP, 1987–92
Japan	110	60	2.8
United States	55	n.a.	2.9
Sweden	262	62	2.8
Germany	86	47	2.9
France	83	51	2.3
Canada	174	34	1.4
United Kingdom	90	n.a.	2.3
Korea	46	22	2.1
Turkey	26	4	na
Brazil	30	n.a.	0.6
Malaysia	n.a.	4	0.4
Thailand	1	2	0.2
Indonesia	12	n.a.	n.a.
Jamaica	6	0	n.a.
Kenya	1	n.a.	n.a.
Bangladesh	1	n.a.	n.a.

Source: UNDP (1995); MASTIC (1994)
Note: n.a.– not available

development of an economy. Malaysia's economic structure is not very different from that of Taiwan or Korea, but remains laggard in terms of R&D investments. The economy does not currently face serious demand constraints on R&D activities; serious labour shortages in Peninsular Malaysia attest to that. Except for a handful of firms, the available evidence does not suggest serious supply constraints either, despite the limited number of R&D personnel. As noted below, most firms do not have many R&D activities, and therefore do not invest in such activities or seek R&D scientists and technologists.

Why then should there be more emphasis on R&D activities? Two major reasons can be advanced. First, given the risks and long-term nature of returns associated with R&D activities, the *status quo* – reflected in current R&D supply–demand conditions – cannot be the yardstick for planning. Especially for local firms in a developing economy such as Malaysia, demand has to be created to 'shake' them in the Hirschmanian sense (Hirschman 1957). Second, foreign firms involved in leading-edge products generally access home-site NISs for their R&D activities. For example, electronics firms generally retain their key innovation-related work at their home sites. Access to external NISs to enhance Malaysia's NIS can be beneficial. Successful latecomers have successfully accessed such technology. However, continued reliance on external technology sources without significant local technological effort has contributed little to strengthening Malaysia's NIS. As we discuss below, several institutional weaknesses have restricted the country's technology absorption capacity. Hence, the critical stages in major export-oriented firms' value-added chains continue to remain located at foreign sites.

The organisation of savings and investments in Malaysia reveals a fairly strong nexus between savings and investments as the investment of corporate savings has been substantial. Malaysia has traditionally enjoyed high savings levels – rising from 27 per cent in 1960 to 38 per cent in 1993 (World Bank 1985, 1995) while domestic investments rose from 14 per cent in 1960 to 33 per cent in 1993. Malaysia's resource balance has remained positive, at 4 per cent in 1960 and 5 per cent in 1993, and its financial environment has thus been stable. It has also managed to attract significant amounts of foreign direct investment – which accounted for 24 per cent of gross domestic investment in 1994 (UNCTAD 1995). The manufacturing sector in Malaysia also obtained 41.1 per cent of its direct loans from foreign sources in 1991 (MIDA 1992). While this evidence does not allow clear conclusions on the productivity of investments, the significant roles of corporate reinvestments and external loans suggest high returns to investment.

Have incentives and investments been co-ordinated and directed towards innovative activities? Has the regulatory framework in the economy stimulated innovations? These are difficult questions to answer as innovations are difficult to define and trace. The evidence we have allows some assessment, albeit tentative, of both questions. Regulation in the financial sector, *inter alia*, has included the provision of RM80 million for investment activities, with 50 per cent reserved for Bumiputera[3] undertakings (Landau *et al.* 1995). Special programmes offer R&D activities indirect funding. The Intensification of Research in Priority Areas (IRPA) and Industrial Technical Assistance Fund (ITAF) programmes offer funding for innovative activities. In addition, the Malaysian Technology Development Corporation (MTDC) has been set up to help fund promising firms in order to expand their technological capacities. The Credit Guarantee Scheme (CGC) – operated by the central bank, Bank Negara – allows small and medium industries (SMIs) to access loans at subsidised rates and without commensurate collateral. Much of the internally generated savings from wage incomes – including Employees Provident Fund (EPF) contributions – has been directed to government institutions. A significant proportion of household investments has been absorbed into Bumiputera trusts.

As noted earlier, primary-sector R&D institutions, such as the Malaysian Agricultural Research and Development Institute, PORIM and the Rubber Research Institute, have continued to support agriculture at the technology frontier. Government efforts to stimulate R&D in manufacturing began in the 1980s. Among institutions created to support such activities are the Malaysian Institute of Microelectronics Systems (MIMOS)[4] and technology parks. Complementary institutions, such as the Standards and Industrial Research Institute of Malaysia (SIRIM) and the National Productivity Corporation (NPC), were established earlier to test and validate products for quality maintenance, and to help improve productivity. SIRIM's role from the late 1980s has been commendable as it has attempted to infuse, establish and maintain higher quality standards in firms. Interviews found that many firms have registered under the International Standards Organisation (ISO) 9000 to enhance their export potential. By promoting standards maintenance, SIRIM has played an indirect role in upgrading quality practices, especially among locally controlled firms.

The NPC appears to be less equipped to achieve productivity improvements in firms and institutions, largely due to a lack of private-sector and technical orientation. It has mainly carried out motivational programmes and aggregate productivity studies. For example, its efforts at estimating total factor productivity (TFP) reveal little dynamic understanding of firms;[5] such studies have offered little understanding of innovation and cost structures in firms. A more useful role for the NPC – which it has not yet assumed – would be to estimate and examine the performance of local firms enjoying government promotional rents, e.g. tariffs and financial incentives, to develop more performance criteria for more effective infant-industry industrial policies. For example, real operating margins and increases in unsubsidised export shares can be useful indicators for appraising performance.

There is relatively little evidence of dynamism in the formation of technology parks in the country. Aggressive promotion by the government – e.g. through direct approaches to identified transnationals – has helped attract a large number of firms to the Technology Park at Bukit Jalil and the High Tech Park at Kulim. Interviews show that the majority of firms have yet to use their investments to promote technology development. Unlike the Hsinchu Science Park of Taiwan, where effective co-ordination has led to participation by proven local firms, the rush to fill

190

space in Malaysia's technology parks seems to have even attracted firms only interested in undertaking minor process improvements. Hence, unless a major reorientation takes place, much of the innovation activity in the country will be undertaken outside the technology parks. Local firms – especially those backed by the government – are likely to operate in these parks, but without significant movement towards the technology frontiers. MIMOS announced plans in 1995 to start wafer fabrication facilities in Kulim. Its success will depend, to a large extent, on its ability to attract the requisite technical manpower and R&D technologists and to co-ordinate effectively with private firms and other supporting institutions.

Direct government monitoring of technology transfer in manufacturing can be traced to the Industrial Co-ordination Act (ICA) of 1975. However, the ICA has only provided a legal framework for formally registering technology transfer agreements (TTAs), involving foreign sources. The electric/electronic industry has been the biggest recipient of foreign technology through TTAs (see Table 7.7). Among foreign sources, Japan has been the most important. Given the importance of employment and investment generation in Malaysian industrial policy until the end of the 1980s, labour-intensive firms were preferred (Rasiah and Anuwar 1995). This trend, which began with the Industrial Incentives Act 1968, has continued with the enactment of the Promotion of Investment Act of 1986. It has only been since serious labour shortages have affected the Western (Peninsular Malaysia) industrial corridor in the 1990s that official emphasis slowly shifted away from employment generation (Malaysia 1994a). However, unlike the Northeast Asian economies, where the creation of an effective enabling environment as well as government vetting, monitoring and appraisal have achieved substantial diffusion of innovative capacities from home-site NISs to host-site NISs, environmental and governmental weaknesses in Malaysia have undermined effective transfers. The only visible regulatory activity undertaken in Malaysia has been *ex ante* vetting which has been poorly implemented, largely due to the lack of proficient bureaucrats (Anuwar 1992). Furthermore, there has not been a trend of transfers to local firms. Informal interviews found that around 90 per cent of the TTAs for the manufacturing sector have involved intra-foreign transnational firm transfers.[6] Virtually no monitoring or *ex post* appraisal is carried out. Hence, institutions governing TTAs in the country, especially the Ministry of International Trade and Industry, have hardly grasped the technology issue, let alone effectively bargained for its transfer from foreign licensers to local licensees.

Efforts have been taken since the inception of 'Malaysia Incorporated' in 1983 to improve government–business co-ordination. Government officials have been sent to Japan and Korea to better understand the nature of public/private co-operation in industrial policy implementation. Also, consultative committees have been formed between the private and public sectors. The MTDC – formed in 1992 – has begun commercialising R&D and advancing technology (Malaysia 1994a: 117). By the end of 1993, it had invested RM16 million in 12 firms (Malaysia 1994b: 300, 303). A broader collaborative umbrella, the Malaysia Industry–Government Group on High Technology (MIGHT), was launched in 1993 to promote technology prospecting and mechanisms to identify new markets, businesses and investment opportunities for R&D and technology development. While it may be too early to assess their roles, a few flaws can be identified. First, insufficient effort has been made to achieve genuine private-sector involvement, since nominal private-sector representatives are usually government selected, often from among former public officials, either appointed as corporate advisers following retirement from the civil service, or from privatised public corporations. Second, government officials' participation in private-sector decision-making has been largely ineffective, as their roles have not been clearly defined. Third, most public-sector officials seconded to the private-sector have been limited to parastatals while some officials have moved to privatised institutions merely to improve their employment benefits. Even here, not many have been involved in the business and technical aspects of production. Mistrust of government officials among businessmen – a consequence of the political economy of ethnic relations (see Jomo 1986; Rasiah 1996a) – and weak understanding of technology and business by government officials have fettered effective co-ordination between the public and private sectors.

Table 7.7 Malaysia: technology transfer agreements by industry, 1975–95

	1975–77	1978–80	1981–83	1984–86	1987–89	1990–92	1993–95
Electric/electronic	31	55	50	53	106	124	143
Chemical	7	38	41	48	74	64	54
Transport equipment	9	22	34	52	20	62	56
Fabricated metal	16	29	43	34	45	33	20
Food	13	24	40	24	45	12	15
Rubber	7	15	23	22	48	26	12
Non-metallic mineral	8	13	29	31	26	26	17
Basic metal	8	15	28	7	8	13	9
Textile and garment	15	12	12	14	12	20	7
Plastic	3	8	9	11	8	17	22
Wood	11	9	5	10	1	11	2
Paper	0	0	0	7	4	10	8
Others	16	43	42	25	61	48	52
Total	144	283	356	338	458	460	417

Source: MIDA (unpublished data), Malaysia 1996

To stimulate the growth of SMIs, three important programmes have been introduced. First, the umbrella concept of marketing (UCM) emerged in 1984. The remaining two – the subcontract exchange (SEP) and anchor company (ACP) programmes – were introduced in 1986 and 1992 respectively (Vijaya Letchumi 1993). Besta Distribution, Guthrie Furniture and Guthrie Malaysia Exchange Programme were UCM pioneers, acting as marketing support organisations for Bumiputera SMIs. Bumiputera equity has also been strongly emphasised in ACPs involving state-sponsored firms such as Proton. The SEP generally acted as a mechanism for matching foreign transnationals with local SMIs. SMIs – including those engaged in these three programmes – have been encouraged to access the ITAF, launched in 1990 to facilitate feasibility studies, product development and design, productivity and market development (Malaysia 1994a).

Despite active promotion and assistance from complementary institutions (e.g. SIRIM, Bank Pembangunan and MATRADE), SMIs have yet to develop effective capacities (Anuwar 1992; Rasiah and Anuwar 1995). Production linkages have been strongest with state-sponsored anchor firms due to the captive rents offered by government-controlled managements. But, even here, linkages with local enterprises have only grown superficially. For example, Proton was reported to have sourced 80 per cent of its components locally in 1995, but as our interviews suggest, that figure would dip below 30 per cent if imports by local supplier firms are taken into account.[7]

Five important reasons account for the general weakness of the SMI support mechanisms. First, a significant number of the SMIs engaged in support programmes have been start-ups begun largely to boost Bumiputera participation in industry. Their lack of entrepreneurial experience has often led to poor management. Second, the rents offered by state-sponsored anchor firms have not been tied to time-bound performance standards. Hence, there has been little pressure to improve efficiency, and poor performers have continued to be supported by the anchor firms at the expense of their own competitiveness. Third, the 30 per cent domestic-sourcing condition for firms applying for pioneer status and the investment tax allowance have become redundant for strategic industries, and this has created serious loopholes. Fourth, the 30 per cent domestic-sourcing condition has not discriminated against foreign-owned firms. Thus, several transnationals meet the domestic-content requirement by purchasing partially processed or assembled inputs from their subsidiaries operating in Malaysia. Fifth, quasi-government participation in learning or spin-off processes, so as to match the right SMIs with the transnationals, has not been strong. Only in Penang – where a combination of a relatively autonomous Chinese-dominated state government, transnationals, and Chinese-owned SMIs prevails – have relatively strong government–business relationships led to the growth of competitive production linkages. Most such linkages have emerged in the electronics, machine tools and plastics industries where, *inter alia*, the inherent need for flexibility has strengthened production linkages between foreign and local firms (Rasiah 1994). From 45 firms in 1989, the number of such support firms rose to 250 in 1993.[8] A state entity, the Penang Development Corporation, has been an important intermediary stimulating such developments.

Labour relations in production processes involve generally weak worker participation in innovative activities. Rasiah and Osman's (1995) study of 2200 firms found a generally significant relationship between unions and training, though draconian labour regulatory measures have limited unions only to bargaining minimal working conditions and wages (Jomo and Todd 1994; Rasiah 1995b). Innovative activities are still largely limited to the management level in most industries. Workers generally only perform operational tasks, with little effort aimed at

RAJAH RASIAH

maintaining or improving the production process. Employee relations until the mid-1980s were generally hierarchical, with strict job definitions and labour control. In several industries – including garments, rubber products, furniture and beverages – such a hierarchical organisation of labour has continued.

From the mid-1980s, however, greater employee participation has emerged in some high-technology export-oriented industries. Particularly in semiconductor assembly and testing, state-of-the-art process techniques such as total productive management (TPM), total quality management (TQM), statistical process control (SPC), just-in-time (JIT) and quality control circles (QCCs) have considerably transformed organisational structures, breaking down old demarcations and hierarchies in the process (Rasiah 1995a).[9] The successes achieved in these firms have spilled over to a number of firms in other industries. The lack of either a nation-wide framework, as in Sweden and Germany, or a firm-level framework, as in Japan, for industrial relations linking unions with training and innovation has, however, limited the participation of employees in innovative activities on a national scale.

Campaigns to instil entrepreneurship and work discipline cultural attributes on a national scale have become particularly significant since Mahathir came to power in 1981. The administration's early 'clean, efficient and trustworthy' motto was followed by the introduction of the 'Malaysia Incorporated' concept in 1983. Efforts to raise participation in science and technical fields, and greater pursuit of competitive strategies have become conspicuous only from the late 1980s. Awards for excellence, quality, scientific achievement and the like as well as MASTIC's (Malaysian Science and Technology Information Centre) creation to collect and disseminate technology information across the economy have been examples of nationally co-ordinated programmes to raise awareness of and participation in innovative activities. Many of the institutions involved in such information generation, dissemination and promotional activities have only been introduced in the 1990s, however, and information barriers still plague the local manufacturing sector.

Finally, have innovative activities become significant in Malaysia's manufacturing sector? Private-sector expenditure on R&D activities only accounted for 0.17 per cent of the GNP in 1992 (MASTIC 1994). From the earlier discussion, two major reasons seem to explain why the extent of innovative activities in the country has been far less than what one might expect from its industrial structure. First, foreign firms generally access much of the innovative know-how generated from their plants located in home-site NISs. Second, weaknesses in domestic institutional support mechanisms have limited the absorptive capacity of local firms. Table 7.8 shows R&D expenditure in selected industries in Malaysia in 1992. It can be seen that the electric/electronic sub-sector had the highest amount of investment in R&D activities, followed by transport equipment. The former is dominated by foreign firms, while the latter has been entirely one local firm, the state-sponsored Proton. Another state-sponsored firm has gone into automotive R&D activities following its establishment in 1994.

194

Table 7.8 Malaysia: R&D expenditure in selected industries, 1992 (RM million)

Industry	Local[a]	Foreign[b]	Total
Electric/electronics	9.7	102.7	112.4
Transport equipment	82.0	0.0	82.0
Food	14.8	1.3	16.1
Rubber	1.2	1.4	2.7
Textiles	0.4	0.4	0.9
Chemicals	1.9	11.7	13.5
Total	123.7	122.6	246.3

Source: MASTIC, *1992 National Survey of Research and Development*, 1994
Notes: (a) Local ownership exceeding 50 per cent
(b) Foreign ownership exceeding 50 per cent

Rasiah's (1995d) survey of 82 electronics firms in 1993 (29.3 per cent of the firms in the industry) showed that 9 firms had formal product R&D activities. Only one firm participated in new-product development – locally owned Sapura. Despite its breakthrough in certain products – e.g. developing the world's first voice-activated telephone – it is still far from the technology frontier in most other products. The remaining firms – all foreign-controlled – have been involved in product extension, customisation or redesigning. Twenty-one firms were formally involved in process R&D, 18 of which were foreign-controlled. A much higher share of firms – 73 of the 82 – reported incremental innovations, though most did not have any formal R&D activities. Foreign-controlled firms accounted for 64 of the 73 firms that reported minor innovations. Although few firms had been directly involved in formal R&D operations, the incidence of minor innovations in the industry – especially among foreign firms – has been high. Two major reasons explain this tendency. First, export-oriented electronics are in highly competitive markets where products and processes change rapidly, hence requiring quick responses from firms at all stages of production. Second, with considerable experience of the industry, the labour force is better equipped to absorb, generate and apply innovations. However, no electronics firm – including foreign firms – has been involved in 'blue sky' research in Malaysia. The most sophisticated designing activities undertaken in foreign firms have generally been limited to second- or third-order technologies – to improve performance and enhance the uses of maturing products. For example, local engineers have redesigned 386 microprocessors in Intel and 256 DRAM chips in Hitachi.

Conclusions

This chapter has presented a conceptual framework for examining Malaysia's NIS, and critically assessed the contributions of the direct and indirect agents supporting innovations. Although not exhaustive, the assessment reveals some of the more salient features of Malaysia's NIS.

Malaysia's industrial structure seems atypical when the composition of output and exports is compared to the country's innovative capacity. The country's ability to export high-technology products is largely a consequence of foreign firms' participation. Foreign firms have generally accessed their home-country NISs for much of their innovation. Most of their innovation activities undertaken in Malaysia have been confined to minor process improvements, regional customisation and redesigning mature products. Local firms have generally participated in production activities with little innovative capacity while the few local firms that have developed their innovative faculties are still far from the technology frontier. Only in resource-based agro-processing activities have local firms shaped the technology frontier.

Recognising this reality, the government has embarked on an ambitious programme to strengthen Malaysia's NIS. However, existing institutions and co-ordination mechanisms have not been adequately organised to effectively generate knowledge and innovations. As an economy which enjoys substantial resources and savings, Malaysia does not suffer from funding problems. It does, however, require effective governance of the development of absorptive capacity and technology transfer. This will inevitably mean strengthening the enabling environment so that the direct and indirect agents and their interactions are effectively co-ordinated to quicken knowledge and innovation generation for productive use.

Notes

1 Interviews conducted in 1995.
2 This unweighted sample had firms from all industries at the 3-digit standard industrial classification (SIC) level, located in all states except for Kelantan, Terengganu, Perlis and Labuan.
3 Literally 'sons of the soil', Bumiputera generally refers to the indigenous peoples of the country.
4 Initially placed in the Prime Minister's Department, MIMOS was subsequently moved to the Science, Technology and Environment Ministry (MOSTE) until its recent corporatisation.
5 See Singh (1995) for a useful discussion on the TFP measure.
6 Interviews conducted by the author in 1994.
7 Interviews by the author in 1994.
8 Personally identified by the author. The actual number can only be more.
9 See Rasiah (1987) for an account of the factors that have stimulated the introduction of such process techniques.

References

Akyuz Y. and Gore, C. (1994). 'The Investment–Profit Nexus in East Asian Industrialization', UNCTAD Discussion Paper No. 91, Geneva.

Amsden, A. (1989). *Asia's Next Giant*, New York: Oxford University Press.

Anuwar Ali (1992). *Malaysian Industrialisation: The Quest for Technology*, Kuala Lumpur: Oxford University Press.

Best, M. (1990). *New Competition*, Cambridge, Mass.: Harvard University Press.

—— (1995). 'Technology Diffusion and Regional Manufacturing Strategies', Sir Charles Carter Lecture, Belfast, May 12.

BNM (1988). *Quarterly Economic Bulletin*, Kuala Lumpur: Bank Negara Malaysia.

—— (1993). *Quarterly Economic Bulletin*, Kuala Lumpur: Bank Negara Malaysia.

Chang, H.J. (1994). *The Political Economy of Industrial Policy*, London: Macmillan.

Chantasmary, M. (1994). 'Impact of Trade AFTA on the Palm Oil Industry in Malaysia', report submitted to the Thailand Development Research Institute, Bangkok.

Dore, R. (1986). *Flexible Rigidities: Industrial Policy and Structural Adjustment in the Japanese Economy 1970–80*, London: Athlone Press.

Dosi, G. (1984). *Technical Change and Industrial Transformation*, London: Macmillan.

Freeman, C. (1987). *Technology Policy and Economic Policy: Lessons from Japan*, London: Frances Pinter.

Gerschenkron, A. (1962). *Historical Backwardness in Historical Perspective*, Cambridge, Mass.: Harvard University Press.

Hirschman, A. (1957). A *Strategy of Economic Development*, New Haven, Conn.: Yale University Press.

Johnson, C. (1982). *MITI and the Japanese Miracle*, Stanford, Calif.: Stanford University Press.

Jomo, K.S. (1986). *A Question of Class*, Kuala Lumpur: Oxford University Press.

—— (1990a). *Growth and Structural Change in the Malaysian Economy*, London: Macmillan.

—— (1990b). *Undermining Tin*, Sydney: Transnationals Research Project.

Jomo, K.S. and Todd, P. (1994). *Trade Unions and the State in Peninsular Malaysia*, Kuala Lumpur: Oxford University Press.

Kaldor, N. (1979). 'Equilibrium Theory and Growth Theory', in M.J. Boskin (ed.), *Economics of Human Welfare: Essays in Honour of Tibor Scitovsky*, New York: Academic Press.

Landau, D.F., G.J. Schinasi, M. Cassard, V.K. Ng and M.G. Spencer (1995). 'Effects of Capital Flows on the Domestic Financial Sectors in APEC Developing Countries', in M.S. Khan and C.M. Reinhart (eds), *Capital Flows in the APEC Region*, Occasional Paper 122, Washington D.C.: International Monetary Fund.

Lazonick, W. (1989). 'Business Organization and Competitive Advantage: Capitalist Transformation in the Twentieth Century', paper presented at the conference on The Process of Technological Change, New School for Social Research, New York.

Lee, J.S. (1994). 'The Role of the State in Economic Restructuring and Development: The Case of Taiwan', Occasional Paper series no. 9403, Chung-Hua Institution for Economic Research, Taipei.

List, F. (1885). *The National System of Political Economy*, London: Longman.

Lim, C.Y. (1967). *Economic Development of Modern Malaya*, Kuala Lumpur: Oxford University Press.

Lundvall, B.E. (1985). *Product Innovation and User-Producer Interaction*, Industrial Development Research Series, Vol. 31, Aalborg: Aalborg University Press.

Malaysia (1991). *Second Outline Perspective Plan, 1991–2000*, Kuala Lumpur: Government Printers.

—— (1994a). *Ministry of International Trade and Industry Report*, Kuala Lumpur: Government Printers.

—— (1994b). *Mid-term Review of the Sixth Malaysia Plan, 1991–1995*, Kuala Lumpur: Government Printers.

—— (1995). *Economic Report, 1995/1996*, Kuala Lumpur: Government Printers.

—— (1996). *Seventh Malaysia Plan, 1996–2000*, Kuala Lumpur: Government Printers.

MASTIC (1994). *1992 National Survey of Research and Development*, Kuala Lumpur: Malaysian Science and Technology Information Centre.

MIDA (1992). *Statistics on the Manufacturing Sector*, Kuala Lumpur: Malaysian Industrial Development Authority.

Nelson, R. (1985). 'Institutions Supporting Technical Advance in Industry', *American Economic Review*, 75: 186–9.

—— (ed.) (1993). *National Innovation Systems*, New York: Oxford University Press.

Pavitt, K. (1984). 'Patterns of Technical Change: Towards a Taxonomy and a Theory', *Research Policy*, 13(6): 343–73.

Porter, M. (1990). *Competitive Advantage of Nations*, New York: Free Press.

Rasiah, R. (1987). *Pembahagian Kerja Antarabangsa: Industri Semi-konduktor di Malaysia*, Kuala Lumpur: Malaysian Social Science Association.

—— (1994). 'Flexible Production Systems and Local Machine Tool Subcontracting: Electronics Component Transnationals in Malaysia', *Cambridge Journal of Economics*, 18(3): 279–98.

—— (1995a). 'Laissez Fairism and Industrial Development in Colonial Malaya', *Journal of Contemporary Asia*, 25(4): 524–38.

—— (1995b). 'Labour and Industrialisation in Malaysia', *Journal of Contemporary Asia*, 25(1): 73–92.

—— (1995c). 'Macroeconomic Management and Economic Growth in Developing Economies', paper presented at the Malaysian Social Science Association convention, Universiti Sains Malaysia, Penang.

—— (1995d). 'Institutions and Innovations: Technological Learning in Malaysia's Electronics Industry', paper presented at the conference on Innovation Networks: East Meets West, Sydney, 30–1 July.

—— (1995e). *Foreign Capital and Industrialisation in Malaysia*, London: Macmillan.

—— (1996a). 'Political Economy of Malaysia', mimeo, Murdoch University, Perth.

—— (1996b). 'Foreign Capital and Domestic Spillovers: Lessons from East Asia', paper presented at a Malaysian Economic Association (PEM) conference, Petaling Jaya, 14–17 May.

Rasiah, R. and Anuwar Ali (1995). 'Governing Industrial Technology Transfer', paper presented at the conference on Governance Mechanisms and Technical Change in Malaysian Manufacturing, Bangi, 14–15 July.

Rasiah, R. and Osman-Rani H. (1995). 'Enterprise Training in Malaysia's Manufacturing Sector', paper presented at the World Bank conference on Enterprise Training and Productivity, Washington, D.C., 12–14 June.

Rodrick, D. (1994). 'Getting Interventions Right: How South Korea and Taiwan Grew Rich', NBER Working Paper, No. 4964, Boston.

Rosenberg, N. (1982). *Inside the Black Box*, Cambridge: Cambridge University Press.

Singh, A. (1995). 'How Did East Asia Grow so Fast? Slow Progress towards an Analytical Consensus', UNCTAD Discussion Paper No. 97, Geneva.

UNCTAD (1995). *World Investment Report*, Geneva: United Nations Conference for Trade and Development.

UNDP (1995). *Human Development Report 1995*, New York: Oxford University Press.

Vijaya Letchumy (1993). 'SMI Development Programmes', paper presented at MITI/MIDA/FMM seminar on Domestic Investment in the Manufacturing Sector, Penang.

Wade, R. (1990). *Governing the Market*, Princeton, NJ: Princeton University Press.

Weber, M. (1930). *The Protestant Ethic and Spirit of Capitalism*, New York: Charles Scribner's Sons.

World Bank (1985). *World Development Report*, Oxford: Oxford University Press.

—— (1995). *World Development Report*, Oxford: Oxford University Press.

You, J.I. (1995). 'Income Distribution and Growth in East Asia', paper presented at the UNCTAD conference on Income Distribution and Development, Geneva, December.

8

IMPROVING MALAYSIAN INDUSTRIAL TECHNOLOGY POLICIES AND INSTITUTIONS

Masayuki Kondo

Malaysia grew rapidly in the 1990s, with its real GDP growing at an annual rate of 8 per cent or higher. However, as its economy has grown, labour costs have increased. Malaysia needs to move to a new stage of industrialisation, producing higher value-added products. The Malaysian government has determined that industrial technology development is key to entering this new stage of industrialisation. The government has formulated an ambitious Action Plan for Industrial Technology Development (APITD), to complement the Industrial Master Plan (IMP). While parts of these plans have already been implemented effectively, Malaysia needs to do many more things to develop industrial technology because industrial technology development is relatively limited in the country, as seen in the low level of R&D expenditure (see Table 8.1).

The need for technology development is emphasised by total factor productivity analysis. According to a recent study done by the National Productivity Corporation (NPC), Malaysia has had little total factor productivity growth.[1] The study found that labour productivity in terms of value-added per worker has been improving and that the rate of increase of capital per worker has been much larger than the rise in labour productivity. These findings suggest that capital equipment has not been used efficiently. To improve total factor productivity, more efficient use of production equipment – that is, production technology development and increased value-added products through quality improvement and other means, such as better designs – are needed.

This chapter consists of five parts. The first section reviews the national science and technology management system, discussing problems common to developing countries as well as existing organisations and related issues. The next section discusses how technology development is promoted in Malaysia, covering financial and fiscal incentives, technology transfer regulations and human resource development. The third section discusses technology policies for small- and medium-sized industries (SMIs), covering the Vendor Development Programme and the Industrial Technical Assistance Fund (ITAF). Section four discusses quality improvement activities, including awareness campaigns and the role of public procurement. The final section discusses technology development support activities, such as metrology, standards, information services and intellectual property rights protection.

National science and technology management

Problems in developing countries

There are some common problems faced by developing countries pursuing technology development. They include the confusion of science with technology and the tendency to have government-led approaches.

Science versus technology. Many government discourses do not clearly distinguish between technology policy and science policy. They often promote academic scientific research, which is valuable for science *per se*, but is rarely relevant to industrial development including technology development in the short run, under the name of technology policy. Science and technology are quite different from each other in nature, though science and technology are often dealt with as a set, as in the term 'science and technology'. Science pursues truth or theories, while technology seeks pragmatic solutions. In many cases, technology employs scientific discoveries, and in many other cases, it finds solutions without using new scientific discoveries. A caricature is that science creates knowledge using wealth while technology creates wealth using knowledge.

Technology policy, rather than science policy, should have priority for industrial development. Industrial technology policy should be formulated for industry by people involved in industrial development. In some developing countries, technology policy is formulated and implemented by science policy makers and scientists as if it were the same as science policy, partly, but only partly, because these countries lack technology policy makers. Technology, rather than science, should also have priority in human resource development. Educating technicians and engineers, rather than scientists, should have priority. At the university level, East Asian countries have correctly strengthened engineering departments, rather than science departments.

Science policy is important for long-term industrial development, and as a basis of technology development. Science promotion is needed to train teachers and to raise the general level of scientific knowledge among the people. However, science policy should be formulated and implemented distinctly from technology policy, though some co-ordination between science and technology policies is needed.

In Malaysia, the distinction between science policy and technology policy is not clearly understood. For example, the Academy of Science Malaysia and the National Council for Scientific Research and Development (MPKSN) have been created, but neither an Academy of Engineering nor a National Council for (Industrial) Technology, though the immediate national needs are to promote technology development for industry. The Intensification of Research in Priority Areas (IRPA) grants are given to universities where researchers are evaluated by the number of papers they write, but not given to firms that compete in the market.

Public versus private. The main context for industrial technology development is firms, not public institutions, which should support and facilitate technology development in industry. Technology capacity-building in industry is important for industrial development and the government needs to support this. However, in some developing countries, technology development in the public sector is carried out virtually without involving the private sector and technology policy is discussed almost exclusively by public officials.

In Malaysia, a strong public-sector presence is to be seen in technology development and most R&D is carried out in the public sector (see Table 8.2). R&D funds are not given to the private sector except through the Industrial Technical Assistance Fund (ITAF) for small and medium industries (SMIs). Public R&D funds need to flow to the private sector to encourage R&D in that sector.

The strong presence of the public sector is also seen in MPKSN, the highest advisory council on science and technology in the nation. The majority of MPKSN members are from the public sector. The private-sector presence should be increased. In fact, all members should be selected from the private sector and from research organisations, and the ministries should have a joint secretariat to listen to and act upon members' opinions. A review committee meeting to monitor APITD is held quarterly, but the private sector seems to be little involved. The Technology Committee of the Federation of Malaysian Manufacturers (FMM) is not involved in the review, though this committee provided various inputs when APITD was formulated.

Table 8.1 R&D expenditure in Malaysia, 1992

Establishments	R&D expenditure (RM million)
Government and public research institutes	75.53
Higher education institutions	11.18
Business enterprises	211.66
Total	298.37

Source: MASTIC/MOSTE, *National Survey of Research and Development, 1992*

Table 8.2 Researchers by sector in Malaysia, 1989

	Doctorate		Masters		Bachelors		
	Public sector	Private sector	Public sector	Private sector	Public sector	Private sector	Total
Manufacturing	142	7	486	18	585	115	1,353
Computer	33	0	138	1	40	30	242
Medicine	87	0	134	0	112	0	333
Agriculture	347	19	528	15	210	43	1,162
Basic science	491	9	484	32	482	134	1,632
Others	154	0	411	0	250	0	815
Total	1,254	35	2,181	66	1,679	322	5,537

Source: Government R&D Human Resource Survey

Some policies seem to be formulated for the public sector, rather than for the private sector. For example, the Malaysian Science and Technology Information Centre (MASTIC) places priority on support for the Ministry of Science, Technology and Environment (MOSTE). Some university innovation and consulting centres function for their universities, rather than their prospective clients. The Malaysian Technology Development Corporation (MTDC) finances public research institutes and government universities, but not individual researchers in the private sector, though. MTDC subsidiaries do invest in firms. The government advocates demand-driven policies, but demands are often defined by the public sector, rather than by the private sector.

National-level organisations

Malaysia has established organisations for national science and technology management (see Figure 8.1). A Cabinet Committee on Science and Technology has been set up in the government for policy co-ordination among science- and technology-related ministries and agencies. However, policy co-ordination among those ministries and agencies is weak at the working level, partly due to the institutional weakness of MOSTE.

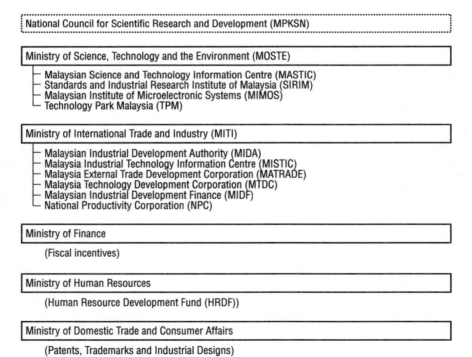

Figure 8.1 Science and technology policy organisations in Malaysia

The National Council for Scientific Research and Development (MPKSN) has been established as the highest national advisory body on science and technology. The presence of industry in its membership is weak, though this has improved recently. Its name should bear the word 'technology' to emphasise the importance of technology to the public and if this council is to seriously deal with technology development. It also needs to have separate committees on science as distinct from technology. Issues of science and technology should be discussed separately, though the two kinds of issues should be co-ordinated.

The Malaysian Academy of Sciences has also been established recently, though its intended function is not yet clear. In the United States, there are both an Academy of Science and an Academy of Engineering. It is desirable to develop engineering academic associations with close contacts with industrial associations under an Academy of Engineering in Malaysia, if created. Company engineers, engineering faculty staff and engineering researchers should exchange information and develop social networks through such associations.

Ministry of Science, Technology and the Environment (MOSTE)

The institutional weakness of MOSTE partly comes from its staffing problems. MOSTE has three types of staffing problems. First, it has a high staff vacancy rate of 44 per cent. MOSTE needs to reduce this vacancy rate quickly to function effectively.

Second, many of its officers, including some managers, are technical staff from research institutes. They are not trained as administrators, and hence are not good at negotiating and co-ordinating with other ministries and agencies. They come to the MOSTE headquarters for two to three years and then return to their original institutions so they hardly have time to build up personal networks among ministries. The poor communications involving MOSTE may be due to this. If MOSTE needs science and technology expertise, the government should recruit staff with a background in science and engineering education as administrators and train them as administrators. When the government recruits technical staff from research institutions to the MOSTE headquarters, they should work as advisers or supporters, but not as line managers.

Third, MOSTE does not seem to be attractive to civil servants. MOSTE needs to develop an attractive career path for administrators to attract competent officers. It is doubtful whether it is worthwhile to send administrators overseas for Ph.D. courses for three years. Relevant administrative training and experience is required more than Ph.D. degrees. It is more worthwhile to have relevant work experience in the area of science and technology policy overseas. If MOSTE needs more theoretical knowledge on science and technology policy, it should send its staff for short courses provided by overseas universities, appoint advisers and hire consultants.

Promoting technology development

Technology acquisition

In Malaysia, technology is largely acquired from overseas. Multinational companies (MNCs) bring in their technologies when they invest in Malaysia. Technology is also transferred through education and training, through licensing agreements and by foreign experts (see Table 8.3).

Table 8.3 Technology transfer to Malaysia, 1989–93

Type	1989	1990	1991	1992	1993	Total
Technical assistance	64	72	93	80	85	394
Licensing and patents	35	17	28	14	44	138
Trademark	18	19	9	12	14	72
Know-how	3	12	10	21	23	69
Joint venture	15	15	11	7	7	55
Services	12	6	4	4	9	35
Management	12	5	6	2	2	27
Sales, marketing/distribution	6	5	0	0	0	11
Supply and purchase	6	2	0	0	0	8
Turnkey and engineering	0	1	1	0	1	3
Others	17	1	3	0	0	21
Total	188	155	165	140	185	833

Source: J. Jegathesan, 'Malaysia – Experiences with Transfer of Technology', APEC Technology Transfer Seminar, December 1994

Technology transfer from overseas is not free to Malaysia. Every technology agreement, especially those involving royalty payments, is reviewed, and the number of foreigners in a firm is regulated by the Malaysian Industrial Development Authority (MIDA) under the Ministry of International Trade and Industry (MITI). Approved royalty rates range from 1 to 5 per cent. In the case of high-tech, 8 per cent may be approved. Though MITI claims that no complaints have been made about the limits on the number of foreign personnel, some MNCs have expressed difficulty in bringing in foreign personnel.[2] This regulation needs to be relaxed to increase technology transfer from abroad.

According to a survey (Danaraj and Chan 1993) done by the Malaysian Institute of Economic Research (MIER), the majority of firms surveyed preferred technology transfer from Malaysian firms: they acquired technology by observing competitors' products and production methods, and through suppliers. Malaysian firms have not given high priority to royalty payments through licensing agreements. Incentives, such as tax incentives, for technology licensing and other agreements should facilitate more formal technology transfer.

R&D promotion

R&D activities in industry have been growing in Malaysia. For example, a Japanese MNC established an R&D company for air conditioners; a US electronics MNC has created an R&D department; Proton has started car design; and the Malaysian Design Council has been established. To further increase industrial R&D activities in Malaysia, more public support is necessary.

The most important thing in promoting industrial R&D is to make industry carry out R&D and learn by doing R&D. Public financial assistance is useful in encouraging private-sector R&D. However, the Malaysian government does not provide financial assistance to industry for R&D, except tax incentives and a grant scheme for SMI technology development. The government needs to provide grants or conditional loans for R&D carried out by industry. Financial assistance is most needed at the stage of engineering development or pilot plants, and conditional loans should be available at this stage.

Grants. Though the IRPA programme has identified industrial R&D as one of its four priority areas, its grants only go to public research institutes or government universities, but not to firms. The MPKSN identifies the system of R&D classification as a major problem for IRPA. The real problem, however, is that industry cannot use IRPA funds and not how administrators or council members classify projects. Creating a scoring system for industry representatives to evaluate IRPA projects is more appropriate. If an applicant for IRPA funds must find a partner in industry willing to finance 30 to 50 per cent of a project, IRPA projects would become much more industry-relevant. In Germany, the Fraunhofer Institutes have to find such clients to qualify for grants from the government.

Tax incentives. The government started a tax incentive system for collaborative R&D between firms, but abolished it because no firms applied for this incentive. This outcome reflects (i) the lack of communication between the government and industry, (ii) the fact that government policy formulation is not responsive to industry conditions and needs, and (iii) government inability to encourage firms to undertake R&D.

The government initiated a tax incentive scheme for R&D and R&D companies in 1993, but the definition of R&D for taxation purposes is not clear and the scheme is difficult to qualify for. Incremental innovations of production technology should qualify. Production technology determines product cost, quality and delivery time and is a critical factor in achieving international competitiveness and it is difficult to develop.

Venture capital. The MTDC has been created for venture-capital financing. However, its funds are limited, and it focuses on the commercialisation of the R&D results of the public sector until these results are accepted for use by firms. It is better to finance engineering development also. If created, conditional loans would facilitate joint engineering development between firms and universities/research institutes after the R&D results of universities/research institutes are accepted by firms.

Linkages between universities, public research institutes and industry

The government is trying to strengthen the linkages between public research institutes and industry, as well as between universities and industry. In universities, industry liaison offices have been established to facilitate interactions with industry. Contract R&D and consulting services are encouraged. Some universities, such as the Science University of Malaysia (USM), are good at collaborating with industry. USM asks industry to make suggestions on curricula, and has established 'technology incubators' on campus. The success of university–industry collaboration largely depends on the attitudes and practices of these industry liaison offices.

Universities need to make some effort if they want to serve industry. First, they need to diffuse information on their capabilities. One suggestion is to hold 'open houses' regularly to let industry know their facilities and what they do. The Standards and Industrial Research Institute of Malaysia (SIRIM) has an open house day on 14 October, World Standards Day, every year. They may also need to establish a central clearing house to inform industry of which university has what facilities and expertise. Second, they need to develop a business culture in handling contracts and applications, understand that 'time is money' and shorten the time needed to process documents by simplifying forms and procedures. They also need to heighten awareness of the need for confidentiality.

The corporatisation of some public research institutes in Malaysia is planned. If corporatised, they should have to go to industry to raise their revenue. Thus, the linkage between research institutes and industry will be strengthened. On the other hand, the research institutes will be able to set the salaries of their staff more freely, depending on their profits and their ability to attract researchers to work in the research institutes.

SIRIM is a pioneer in such corporatisation in Malaysia. Their calibration and standards-related services are already well appreciated by industry. Now, its R&D section is quite active in marketing its services. The staff of the R&D section do not sit in their offices waiting for clients. Instead, they knock on the doors of manufacturers to offer their services. However, even SIRIM cannot be financially independent from the government, at least in the short term.

The government must be careful about the division of labour between corporatised research institutes and private firms, and the level of financial support to be given to corporatised research institutes. In the case of SIRIM, both SIRIM and private firms provide testing and calibration services. If SIRIM provides the same services as other firms do using equipment financed by the government, SIRIM's services would unfairly crowd out private services.

Human resource development

Human resource development is key to successful technology development. The Human Resource Development Fund (HRDF) has been established to encourage the training of employees. Firms with more than 50 employees contribute 1 per cent of their payrolls to the Fund. Training is eligible for financing from the Fund when firms are registered with the Fund for in-house training or if registered courses are used for outside training. Consulting by registered consultants to make annual training plans is also eligible for financing by the Fund.

Malaysia has two major problems involving technical human resources, namely the shortage of skilled workers, and job hopping among skilled workers, which discourages employers from training employees. To address the shortage of skilled workers, several efforts have been made. The Penang Skill Development Centre (PSDC) is a successful example, basically managed by large firms, mostly MNCs, reflecting the real needs of industry, as representatives of member firms determine the training curricula. The PSDC's training fees are around half of those of commercial institutions. Its building is essentially free, being contributed by the Penang state government. Up-to-date equipment is on free loan from machine vendors as the member firms are their customers. By training workers to work on their latest equipment, the vendors hope to induce their customers to buy such equipment.

Another example of a skill training centre is the Germany–Malaysia Institute (GMI), which has heavier public-sector involvement. Two other institutes – the Japan–Malaysia Technical Institute (JMTI) and the France–Malaysia Institute (FMI) – are being planned.

Another problem is that many students prefer to be accountants rather than engineers. Scholarships for engineering students are not fully taken up because of the perceived difficulty and comparatively lower salaries than accountants and hence unpopularity of engineering courses. If firms and public agencies really need engineers, they should work together to improve the salaries and career paths of engineers to change the social perceptions of engineers.

SMI technology development

SMI agencies

Currently, Malaysian SMI policies are managed by 5 ministries after consolidating SMI policy functions from 13 ministries. The 5 ministries are MITI, the Ministry of Finance, the Ministry of Human Resources, MOSTE and the Implementation and Coordination Unit (ICU) of the Prime Minister's Department.

A one-stop office to handle all SMI policies is needed for the SMIs. The Malaysia Industrial Technology Information Centre (MISTIC) within MITI is a good candidate for this because it is already a one-stop agency providing information on SMI policies. The function of this Centre should be strengthened by preparing various forms and by assisting SMIs in filling out these forms. Some SMIs complain that they have to fill out so many forms to get licences and permission from the federal government and local governments to start new businesses. The Centre should also introduce a feedback system, similar to customer opinion cards used in airline companies and hotels. Some SMI managers complain that MISTIC has not been responsive to their suggestions and requests.

Since most large firms in Malaysia are MNCs, and 93 per cent of manufacturing establishments are SMIs, the government must make special efforts to assist SMIs to develop technology. Two MITI policies in this area can be distinguished, namely the Vendor Development Programme (VDP) and the Industrial Technical Assistance Fund (ITAF). These policies are well known and successful to some extent, but there have been some problems in implementing them.

Venture capital and other start-up financing facilities are poorly developed in Malaysia. Some engineers with long experience in MNCs cannot find public finance to start their own businesses. Start-up financing facilities should be strengthened by widening the category of MTDC customers to include 'middle-tech' firms and by increasing its funds or by creating another scheme.

Vendor Development Programme (VDP)

The VDP has started to make SMIs more reliable and competent manufacturers by linking them up with large firms including MNCs. This programme is modelled on the Japanese *keiretsu* system. Inter-industry linkages in Malaysia are limited according to the input–output tables for 1983. In non-resource-based industries, only 40 per cent of inputs came from domestic sources.

Under this programme, a large firm, called an 'anchor firm', provides technical assistance to its vendors to improve technological levels as well as markets. Anchor firms receive no financial assistance, while vendors under this programme receive financial assistance from the government in the form of soft loans and advances against payments as well as technical assistance. In 1993, a new concept of a 'tripartite arrangement' was introduced, and financial institutions started to be involved in the programme.

Proton was the first anchor firm in this programme. In 1988, the Proton Component Scheme in the automotive sector started. In 1992, the Electrical and Electronics Component Scheme started with the participation of Sapura and Sharp-Roxy. As of March 1994, 20 large firms and 6 financial institutions were participating in the programme.

Proton succeeded in developing its vendors with tremendous efforts. Proton first had to find potential vendors. It checked MIDA's list of firms and put an advertisement in the newspapers. After identifying potential vendors, it examined their technological potential, provided technical assistance and monitored their performance. Proton has 120 staff in its procurement section, 80 of whom are technical staff and 48 of whom visit 128 vendors all the time. It is costly to foster and monitor vendors, and it is too much to ask large firms to participate in this programme based on their goodwill alone. Some financial assistance to anchor firms is needed to accelerate this programme as in Indonesia.

Technology transfer from overseas plays an important role in the technology development of SMIs. Among the 128 Proton vendors, 87 had received technical assistance from foreign firms, 15 of which were joint ventures with foreign firms. The government needs to facilitate technology transfer for SMIs co-operating with anchor firms. The Joint Venture Promotion Project with the Japanese Ministry of International Trade and Industry – which aims to bring together potential joint-venture partners in Malaysia and Japan – is helpful in this regard.

One of the problems for Proton in fostering its vendors is that the Malaysian market is small. Proton cannot effectively foster vendors supplying parts, even if they are key components, if sufficient economies of scale are not attained. Proton also cannot foster multiple vendors for the same component because of the size of the market Proton can offer. Such vendors may enjoy monopolies, but, as a monopsonist, Proton can control the price and quality of the products. Industrial policy to enable these vendors to become exporters is needed to strengthen these supplier industries.

Group efforts as well as individual efforts by vendors have been made to improve their technology levels. Proton vendors have established the Proton Vendors Association, which holds seminars and workshops, and organises study tours. Another large firm organises a similar association of its vendors, and arranges group training and consultants for association members; however, the government does not recognise this activity as a VDP activity because the firm purchases only a small amount of parts from each vendor due to the nature of the firm's products. The VDP should be widely interpreted to include any programme that upgrades the technological levels of SMIs. Furthermore, the main objective of the VDP should shift from providing markets to upgrading technology.

Industrial Technical Assistance Fund (ITAF)

ITAF is a 50 per cent matching grant scheme for SMIs which engage in technology development activities. ITAF consists of four components: (i) consultancy service scheme, (ii) product design and development scheme, (iii) quality and productivity improvement scheme, and (iv) market development scheme. ITAF is under MITI, but implemented by three agencies: the first scheme is implemented by Bank Pembangunan Malaysia Berhad (BPMB); the second and third schemes are implemented by the Standards and Industrial Research Institute of Malaysia (SIRIM); and the fourth scheme by the Malaysia External Trade Development Corporation (MATRADE).

ITAF has not been fully used by the SMIs. Only RM12 million out of the RM50 million allocated has been used. One of the reasons why ITAF is not used much is that some SMIs are afraid that information about their projects will be leaked to competitors. Public officials need to be trusted by industry to keep trade secrets, and the government needs to establish a procedure for firms to quickly receive compensation if their competitors make profits by stealing trade secrets. Besides confidentiality, some industrialists think it is not worthwhile to apply for ITAF grants because the application procedure is cumbersome, and it takes a long time to get grants. Instead, they prefer bearing the costs of their projects by themselves because time and opportunity cost are important factors for competing in the market. MITI has been reviewing the ITAF procedure.

Management and monitoring should be minimal at this stage. Subjecting SMIs to quality improvement and productivity enhancement efforts using consultants should be a priority. If the number of applications increases dramatically and the required amount of grants exceeds the funds available, management and monitoring of ITAF should be tighter. Though ITAF does not cover production machinery, Malaysian Industrial Development Finance (MIDF) provides low-interest (4 per cent) loans for SMIs to purchase machinery for modernisation and automation.

Quality improvement

Training and consulting

Employee training to improve quality and productivity is fairly widespread, and union leaders are generally found to be co-operative in Malaysia. Most courses provided by the National Productivity Corporation (NPC), which is a major provider of training for quality and productivity improvement, are fully subscribed. Among its courses, those on productivity measurement and quality control circles (QCCs) are most popular.

The National Advisory Committee on Total Quality Control (TQC) has been established to promote QCC activities, with the NPC as a secretariat. This committee hosts a national QCC convention, regional QCC conventions and mini-QCC conventions every year.

Quality improvement methods like QCCs and 5S (the five basic activities of quality control as expressed in Japanese) are widely practised at the factory level, even in US MNCs, partly because many Japanese MNCs have invested in Malaysia. Still, 40 per cent of Japanese firms in Malaysia think they have problems with quality management.[3]

Quality Improvement Practice scheme. The Quality Improvement Practice (QIP) scheme has started in SIRIM to help SMIs improve the quality of their products. SIRIM staff provide consulting services to SMIs on quality management systems. SIRIM tries to get the SMIs to satisfy 70 per cent of the requirements of the ISO 9000 standards, and expects them to register as ISO 9000 qualified firms within two years of finishing receiving SIRIM advice. The intention of the programme is good, but SIRIM seems to face a conflict of interests as the registration body for ISO 9000 standards. Consulting services should be provided by an agency independent of SIRIM.

Implementing the QIP scheme for groups of firms in the same sub-sector has generally been effective in enhancing its impact; and the plan to implement it through the umbrella scheme, which promotes technical improvement in a certain sector, is a good idea. If the government encourages SMIs to organise industry associations or to establish groups in existing associations, and works with these associations or groups, quality improvement activities can be diffused faster as such similar firms often have common technical problems.

Raising awareness

Unfortunately, consumer awareness of the quality of goods does not seem high. To remedy this situation, the government has created Regional Quality Centres, which are joint efforts between SIRIM branch offices and NPC branch offices, to raise quality awareness among the public, including workers and managers. The staff of these Centres go to secondary schools to educate students on quality. The Centres also hold seminars and training courses at subsidised fee rates and distribute free posters to raise quality awareness. In addition, the Centres have produced books and videos on quality in both Malay and English.

At the national level, October has been designated as a Quality Month with various activities carried out during that month. National quality awards are given during the month to outstanding firms and organisations in three categories: (i) central government organisations, (ii) manufacturing and service firms, and (iii) state government organisations. The secretariat is located in the Ministry of Youth and Sports.

Government procurement

Government procurement is a good means to set and diffuse Malaysian standards and to enhance the quality of Malaysian products. For government procurement, Mauritius provides a 10 per cent premium for Mauritius standards-certified products. Japan and Korea also have systems of preferential treatment in public procurement for standards-certified goods. Malaysia also needs to develop such a programme.

The government first needs to develop Malaysian standards for goods procured by the government and to diffuse these Malaysian standards through specifications used by the government procurement agency. Further details of product specifications may still need to be developed by the government procurement agency in addition to the more generalised Malaysian standards. In this case, SIRIM needs to help the agency set detailed technical specifications to comply with Malaysian and international standards. Furniture and stationery are areas to start with because the manufacturers of these goods are already under the Umbrella Scheme. A step-by-step approach, by setting up several partial standards as intermediate steps, is suitable for this programme.

As a major consumer/user, the government can provide good feedback to suppliers by setting standards and providing test results. For example, specifications for policemen's boots regarding size, durability, etc. could be developed in some public research institute in co-operation with manufacturers and SIRIM, while user evaluation by policemen could be conveyed back to the manufacturers.

Supporting technology development

Metrology and testing

In Malaysia, the Standards and Industrial Research Institute of Malaysia (SIRIM) plays a central role in metrology and standards. SIRIM maintains primary (physical) standards for Malaysia, and provides testing and calibration services which are well used by industry. Because of the heightened interest in the ISO 9000 series of quality system standards, the demand for calibration services has increased rapidly.

A national laboratory accreditation scheme, called the Laboratory Accreditation Scheme of Malaysia (SAMM), has been established to assure the quality of testing and calibration services. This scheme is managed by the National Accreditation Council (NAC), which has been established relatively recently, and now only works on laboratory accreditation. SIRIM is one of six SAMM assessment agencies and has accredited 42 laboratories, but has not yet been accredited itself.

Though the demand for testing and calibration services is increasing, firms have less interest in investing in testing equipment than in production equipment. Special incentives are needed to encourage medium and large firms to purchase testing equipment. For SMIs, up to 30 per cent of the ITAF grants can now be used for the purchase of testing equipment.

SIRIM. SIRIM's SAMM assessment section differs from the section for testing and calibration services, but these two functions should not exist under the same management. This arrangement implies a conflict of interests. Accrediting other laboratories would mean creating competitors to SIRIM. The best way to solve this problem would be to make the two sections independent organisations. The NAC needs to at least establish a mechanism to solve the grievances of assessed laboratories, and SIRIM needs to be assessed by a third party in order to be accredited. Another way out is to give SIRIM a special status in the Malaysian metrology system and to prohibit SIRIM from providing the commercial services that are provided by private laboratories.

The government should be careful about the corporatisation of SIRIM, which should be encouraged to provide better services to industry by giving it the incentives and freedom to use its facilities and expertise. Since SIRIM plays an important public role in metrology and standards, including the ISO 9000 series, conflicts of interest and its relations with private institutions that provide calibration, testing and quality improvement services, must be carefully examined when SIRIM is corporatised.

Standards

The national system of industrial standards is now fairly well established in Malaysia. SIRIM drafts standards, serving as a secretariat; the Standards Committee (STANCO) approves them and the SIRIM Council finally sets the standards. A total of 1908 Malaysian standards have been approved. This number is fairly large compared with Singapore, which has around 500, though, of course, the point is not the number of standards, but how the standards are implemented.

All Malaysian standards are written in English. On the one hand, this is a great advantage in being readily understood internationally. On the other hand, diffusing standards in Malaysia may be difficult for Malaysians who do not understand English well.

SIRIM should not give priority to writing standards, but to diffusing standards, and has already started to decentralise standards writing. The Malaysian Plastics Manufacturing Association has been approved to draft standards for the plastics industry. This is good in that industry needs will be well reflected in the standards. Thus, the probability of the standards being used by industry will be high. It would be better if these standards were used as industry association standards for a while before they become Malaysian standards. SIRIM should provide guidelines and consulting services on how to set company or industry association standards.

When SIRIM prepares standards, it needs to focus on some areas of standardisation based on policy needs. An example would be a group of products procured by the public sector. The standardisation of foods, furniture and stationery has priority if they do not already have standards, because the government is fostering SMIs producing these goods under the Umbrella Scheme.

Three kinds of certification are done by SIRIM: Malaysian standards certification, foreign-country standards certification, and compulsory regulation certification. SIRIM allows 'MS' marks to be put on products certified for Malaysian Standards, certification marks on products which have met foreign-country standards, and control labels on products which have qualified for technical regulation. A factory that produces certified products is required to designate an employee as a quality officer. It is not clear how strictly SIRIM inspects products and factories, or how strictly it punishes violators of either compulsory or voluntary standards. Proper implementation of existing standards is critical for further implementation of new standards and other quality improvement activities; and proper technical regulation is critical for public safety and health.

Malaysian standards are still not well diffused, though the number of product certifications has increased from less than one hundred a year between 1989 and 1992 to 161 in 1993. The problem is that consumers do not seem to pay much attention to the MS marks, and prefer cheaper goods rather than quality goods.

ISO 9000. Many Malaysian firms are now interested in the ISO 9000 series of quality system standards, as is already the norm in many other countries. These standards are a good introduction to industrial standards and quality improvement activities. The problem is that most firms eager to be registered as ISO 9000 firms consider that registration itself is the objective. To improve product or service quality, firms need to start quality improvement activities based on the ISO 9000 standards and to link quality assurance procedures stated in the ISO 9000 standards with production technology improvements.

SIRIM is the only registration body for ISO 9000 standards in Malaysia. A total of 300 firms had registered by the end of 1993. SIRIM's ability to audit quality systems has gained international recognition because the British Standards Institution (BSI) has appointed SIRIM to carry out joint audits, on its behalf, of Malaysian firms seeking BSI registration of ISO 9000 standards. However, the extent and level of international recognition of the Malaysian ISO 9000 standards system are not known.

SIRIM also functions as the secretariat for the Quality System Consultants Registration Scheme (QSCRS). This voluntary scheme aims to control the quality of consultants on ISO 9000 standards. It is good to ensure the quality of consultants because the ISO 9000 is in fashion in Malaysia and unqualified consultants may appear. A total of 9 firms and 14 individuals have registered under this scheme. SIRIM claims that it does not provide consulting services directly related to ISO 9000 standards because this would involve a conflict of interests as it is the registration body for ISO 9000 standards.

Technology parks

Several technology parks have been planned and some are in operation to assist technology-oriented venture businesses. SIRIM and some universities are also developing their 'incubators' to assist technology-oriented venture businesses.

Technology Park Malaysia near Kuala Lumpur is a technology park under MOSTE. This technology park is located in a temporary building and has not started co-operation with universities and public research institutes. Yet, all the facilities are fully occupied, and many firms are waiting to enter the technology park. The tenants have mainly come to the park because of the lower rents charged compared with commercial buildings.

Venture businesses need financing or low-cost factory space at the time of start-up. The government needs to meet these demands, and constructing technology parks is one solution. The effectiveness of technology parks in providing technical assistance needs to be studied after one of the technology parks starts full operation.

Science and technology information services

Information services are provided by various organisations in Malaysia. Information on the manufacturing sector is not centrally available, and has to be obtained from specialised institutions serving specific industrial sub-sectors. For example, the Forest Research Institute of Malaysia (FRIM) provides information on wood-processing technology. Patent information is obtainable from SIRIM and the Ministry of Domestic Trade and Consumer Affairs, while standards information is obtainable from SIRIM. SIRIM has also been designated as a National Inquiry Point for Malaysia, as required by the General Agreement on Tariffs and Trade (GATT).

The Malaysian Science and Technology Information Centre (MASTIC) has been established in MOSTE as the central science and technology information centre. However, this centre mainly serves policy formulation and policy follow-up, and is not an information service institution for industry, let alone for the SMIs, which need one. The role of MASTIC has not been clearly established. While it is supposed to be research-oriented and is expected to provide information, it is not clear what information it should provide and what information requests will be referred to others. Surprisingly, international connections with information centres overseas are not planned.

The government needs to develop technology information service centres as extension service centres, especially for SMIs, not unlike the manufacturing technology centres in the United States. These centres should also provide consulting services on what technologies are available internationally, how to select equipment and how to train workers to better use equipment.

Intellectual property rights protection

Intellectual property rights (IPRs) protection systems are fairly well established in Malaysia except for trade secrets and integrated circuits (ICs). The Ministry of Domestic Trade and Consumer Affairs administers patents, including utility models, trade marks and industrial designs. It has 14 examiners for patents and 37 examiners for trademarks. As for industrial designs, Malaysia has not examined them as yet, but this will be changed soon and the Ministry is preparing for it. Currently, if industrial designs are registered in the United Kingdom, they are automatically registered in Malaysia.

Two concerns about patents law are expressed by industrialists. One concern is that only individual innovators can apply for patents. Though employers can be owners of patents, they are afraid that there might be legal disputes if the innovators move to other firms. The other is that patent rights are not effective during the period of examination even if they are granted later. Thus, competitors can sell goods using the technology of a patent being examined during the period of examination, if the competitors obtain the technology through some other means.

Table 8.4 Patents and utility models granted in Malaysia, October 1986 to August 1994

USA	1990
Japan	1193
UK	634
Germany	232
Switzerland	210
Australia	189
France	159
Netherlands	124
Malaysia	100
Sweden	82
Others	435
Total	5248

Source: Ministry of Domestic Trade and Consumer Affairs

Malaysians have not acquired many patents and utility models (see Table 8.4). Only 1.9 per cent of all patents and utility models granted went to Malaysians between October 1986 and August 1994. More than a third of the patents and utility models were granted to American nationals, followed by Japanese nationals, British nationals and German nationals. One of the reasons for the low ratio of Malaysians is that only a few utility models are applied for, though utility models are easier to create than patents.

The basic problem is that awareness of intellectual property rights is low, and Malaysians do not mind copying products. The government could change these practices by encouraging Malaysians to apply for utility models and by strengthening intellectual property rights protection in cases of infringement.

Trade secrets are another serious issue among industrialists. When industrialists apply for grants or some other incentives, they have to give the details of their projects, and are afraid that this information may be leaked to others. Even if a firm appeals to the courts, it would take so long and cost so much to settle a case that the firm may be bankrupt by the time compensation is paid.

Concluding remarks

Malaysia is moving in the right direction in the area of technology development. Unfortunately, the government overemphasises high technology because it is attractive and appealing. Developing the basic manufacturing technology capability to produce key parts is generally more critical and deserves more attention for technology development than 'fancy hi-tech'. High technology cannot survive and supporting industries cannot flourish without basic manufacturing technology, such as precision machining and precision mould-making.

Technology policy in Malaysia has two major problems. One problem is that technology policy is often academically- or science-oriented. Since industrial engineers are not yet very influential because of the recent history of industrialisation, academics and scientists dominate the positions influencing the content of technology policy. As a result, academic or scientific influences appear to be strong in technology policy when science and technology policy is formulated and policy makers are not conscious enough of the difference between science and technology. Another reason why technology policy is academically- or science-oriented is because the government strongly emphasises high technology.

The other problem is that technology policy is formulated mostly by and for the public sector. The presence of industry in formulating and assessing technology policy is low; grants and venture capital are mainly designed for the public sector; and incentives offered are not used very much by industry because of the onerous conditions imposed. More networking between the public and private sectors in policy formulation as well as policy implementation is needed to make technology policy more industry-oriented and more effective in enhancing industrial competitiveness.

Notes

The views expressed in this chapter are my own and do not reflect the views of either the Japanese Ministry of International Trade and Industry or the World Bank. I visited Malaysia as an industrial economist of the World Bank to review its industrial technology policy during 14–29 September 1994. I visited various institutions and firms in Kuala Lumpur and Penang as arranged by the Ministry of Science, Technology and the Environment (MOSTE) during this stay in Malaysia, and I studied existing reports on industrial technology policy in Malaysia.

This chapter is based on the author's paper (1996) 'Industrial Technology Strategy of Malaysia to Enhance Industrial Competitiveness', *Development Engineering*, 2: 77–95.

1 Krugman (1994) points out that the economic growth in East Asia was driven by capital growth but not by productivity increase.
2 Japanese MNCs tend to require more foreign engineers than other MNCs because (i) they pursue perfection in quality and productivity to compete with other Japanese MNCs and (ii) their product development cycle is shorter than the cycles of other MNCs and they allow for less trouble – than other MNCs do – in starting new product production.
3 See JETRO-Kuala Lumpur (1994).

References

Danaraj, N. and Chan Kok Thim (1993) 'An Appraisal of Corporate Strategy and Technology Policy in Malaysia', MIER 1993 National Outlook Conference, Kuala Lumpur, 7–8 December.

JETRO-Kuala Lumpur (1994) 'Survey of Japanese Manufacturers in Malaysia 1994' (in Japanese).

Krugman, Paul (1994) 'The Myths of Asia's Miracle', *Foreign Affairs*, November/December, 62–78.

9

MANAGING RESEARCH
UTILISATION IN MALAYSIA

K. Thiruchelvam

Public support for research and development (R&D) activities in Malaysia has grown dramatically in recent years. Despite the large financial outlays, the returns from the massive investment have been disappointing (*Business Times*, 1992). Spending more on R&D alone does not necessarily guarantee success. Of far greater importance are efforts to ensure that investments in R&D are deployed effectively and efficiently to achieve stated objectives. Improved research utilisation has major implications for the management of public-sector R&D.

This chapter examines the management of research utilisation in the Malaysian public sector and in industry. First it describes key results from a survey of management practices in selected public research institutions (PRIs), universities and industry. Then it examines the managerial and policy implications arising from the adoption of these practices, particularly in PRIs and universities. A broad categorisation of the differing research management practices adopted by PRIs, universities and industry is provided. A central theme of the analysis is that the management of R&D cannot be left to chance, but must instead be purposive in order for it to contribute meaningfully to the organisation's objectives as well as to the nation's economic well-being.

Public-sector R&D management in Malaysia:
an overview

The salient weaknesses of Malaysia's public R&D system can be briefly summarised as follows:

- it is essentially a bottom-up system, where most of the project proposals are defined by the researchers themselves;
- it is largely science-driven, with emphasis on the 'R' and not on the 'D';[1]
- it is characterised by weak linkages with industry;
- it is marked by poor management practices, at both institutional and national levels;
- there is an absence of clear and specific articulated national research/technology targets to guide the research, particularly at the institutional level;

- the system is largely dominated by funding for agricultural research;
- performance in transforming and transferring research findings generated from this system to industry is poor.

The government has launched a number of initiatives to address these weaknesses. These include:

- the corporatisation of research institutions and universities;
- the revamping of IRPA,[2] the government's chief R&D funding mechanism, to become more focused, competitive and industry-oriented;
- the establishment of a technology development corporation which provides funding for commercialising promising research findings;
- the provision of fiscal incentives for industry to utilise the services of public research institutions (PRIs) and universities; and
- the training of senior research managers in research management.

It is still too early to evaluate the success of some of these measures. However, the common factor underlying all these deficiencies has been the quality of R&D management. The importance of the managerial dimension in shaping the success of research efforts is demonstrated by the in-depth analysis presented below.

Managing research utilisation

My study[3] of the impact of research management practices on research utilisation in selected PRIs, universities and firms in Malaysia revealed that successful research does not happen by chance or through the ungoverned exercise of scientific creativity. Instead, a number of key management practices are critical to ensuring that the research effort is navigated successfully from the stage of idea-generation to adoption by the end-user. According to the study, best-practice research management principles are broadly similar, irrespective of the organisation or sector in which the research is performed, whether PRI, university or industrial firm. However, some practices are more prevalent in certain sectors or organisations. The significance of each of these research management practices is briefly sketched in turn, while case studies illustrate their use in the Malaysian context.

Focused research

For effective utilisation of research findings, it is essential that the end-user's needs are correctly identified and incorporated as early as possible into the project's life cycle. Correct identification means that the end-user's needs must be clearly understood. Clarity in project definition prevents the work from drifting aimlessly or, worse still, achieving nothing significant at all. Attaining focused research, however, is dependent on how much prior work has gone into planning the research project.

219

The research management process adopted by firms begins with the integration of inputs from the research, production and marketing divisions at the beginning of a project. This convergence of inputs is essential to ensure that what is being developed at the upstream end of the research spectrum is in harmony with the requirements of the downstream sector, i.e. production and market needs. Research projects, particularly in the universities, have been and still are being undertaken on a sequential or pipeline basis: that is, researchers will come up with an idea and subsequently test its technical viability. The parameters that govern its introduction into industry are seldom explored since such efforts are left to industry. Failure to adopt a holistic approach to research has undermined the potential of a number of promising research projects generated by universities. Adopting such an approach has implications for how a research project is managed and funded – an aspect which I will address later.

Case study – SIRIM and the development of an automated sealing and capping machine

Care Food Industries Sdn Bhd's *sambal* (local fish paste) tastes good, but according to the firm's owner/managing director (MD), Mickey Quah, the company had difficulty selling the product, initially because of packaging problems. The firm experimented with various machines and techniques, but to no avail, since the product required special packaging. The MD contacted the Standards and Industrial Research Institute of Malaysia (SIRIM), a government research laboratory that had previously completed a project for the company. After almost 18 months of research, SIRIM developed a five-part automatic sealing and capping machine (ASCM) to trim, seal, cap, label and package the food products. The machine consists of a receiving station, a sealing-cum-trimming station and a capping station linked by a material-handling robot. The whole system is controlled by a programmable logic control.

The basic skills to design the machine were available within SIRIM. The project leader visited some local food-industry exhibitions to obtain ideas for the machine. Although the firm lacked the technical knowledge, they provided valuable inputs to SIRIM on the problems they faced with earlier machines. After the machine was commissioned, SIRIM continued to provide technical support in order to ensure that the machine was running smoothly. Both parties benefited from this joint project. The firm gained from automated packaging of its product while SIRIM acquired expertise in developing customised equipment for an automated vacuum-sealed packaging line. Now, the firm's food pastes are exported to Japan, Canada and Australia. This is a major achievement considering that it is a newcomer to the food-processing industry, having started in the business in late 1989. This project reveals how, with active end-user participation, a public research institution can effectively assist a small-scale manufacturer to enter the export market.

Extensive preparation

Extensive preparatory activities are essential for formulating a sharper project definition, gaining greater insights into end-users' needs, and reducing uncertainties surrounding the project. The more uncertainties are resolved, the greater the chances of project success. Indeed, as Baker *et al.* (1986: 34) assert, if uncertainties are not reduced during the lifetime of the project, the project is unlikely to succeed. Despite their importance, such preparatory measures were seldom initiated by the PRIs and universities. The first case study below, involving Universiti Teknologi Malaysia's (UTM) decision to provide specific funding for research preparation, suggests what is possible when this management practice is adopted. In private industry, by contrast, extensive pre-research preparation is the norm, as firms seek to ensure that projects actually satisfy customer needs before full-scale production begins, as the second case study indicates.

Design and scale-up of vacuum distillation process for the de-acidification of crude palm oil

A predicament faced by Malaysian palm-oil refiners was the unavailability of basic performance parameters for structured packing in the physical refining of crude palm oil. UTM researchers undertook an extensive feasibility study with the aim of examining opportunities for energy conservation in the distillation process. After extensive observations and visits to industry and suppliers, they noted that process efficiency could be enhanced by changing characteristics of the packing material as well as modifying the design of the distillation column. These initial studies were funded by 'seed money' from UTM, and the results of these studies were used as the basis for the submission of a research proposal for IRPA funding. A sum of RM1.8 million was approved for this project. Because of the extensive preparatory work, the project definition was clear and targeted at solving a specific industrial problem. The research team developed the specifications for a pilot plant using improved glass and engaged an experienced local contractor to undertake the task. The pilot plant was installed and trial runs were successfully undertaken. The client, a state-owned corporation is presently testing the efficiency of using this modified distillation plant. A foreign manufacturer of distillate packing materials has asked UTM to test its packing. This project demonstrates that if projects are clearly defined and sound preparatory work is undertaken, the chances of success are enhanced.

Development of soy sauce

Ajinomoto (Malaysia) is the leading manufacturer of monosodium glutamate (MSG) in Malaysia. In recent years, the company has begun to diversify its product range, and at one point was commissioned by a particular client to develop a soy sauce product. The broad product specifications were discussed extensively between the client and Ajinomoto's research team. Samples were developed and tested by the client, who asked for further refinement. This process of multiple testing and continuous interaction with the client is especially important for the food industry, since unlike other products, there are no fixed industry standards for aroma or taste. For this particular soy sauce product, Ajinomoto spent some eight months testing the product. Such repeated testing ensured that the product was finally acceptable to the client. This project demonstrates a number of points. First, it underscores the importance of developing test samples prior to production in order to obtain the client's satisfaction. It also emphasises the need for clear specifications before a project is implemented. Additionally, this project also demonstrates the importance of constant interactions with the client throughout the project.

Funding for development work

To be effective, research findings must be developed to a point at which they can be readily utilised by the client. Extensive development work is particularly important in developing countries since their industries (especially small or medium industries – SMIs) often lack the technical capabilities and investment resources to develop pre-commercial research findings into marketable products. The failure of many university R&D projects, as the case study below illustrates, underscores the importance of funding for activities such as development and prototyping. Development activities are expensive. According to Frumerman (1992: 204), as products advance through successive stages of development and into manufacture, each step becomes more costly by roughly a factor of ten. Accordingly, decisions on these activities must be carefully made and preferably undertaken in partnership with the end-user to ensure success. The success story of the automatic sealing and capping machine described above attests to the importance of end-user financing in order to ensure their commitment to the project.

Malaysia's IRPA R&D funding mechanism, however, does not provide support for such development activities, and this deficiency undermines the likelihood of success of research efforts by PRIs and universities, particularly the latter. Funding is only provided to cover the costs of the research component of the project and not subsequent development for adoption by the end-user. Such limited funding is compounded by existing procedures that do not permit heads of PRIs and universities to shift surplus funds from other research projects to finance development activities.

Automated post-bond wire inspection in integrated circuit assembly

Wire bonding is a step in integrated circuit (IC) assembly in which physical connections are made between the integrated circuit and the package leads using wires. Despite the dramatic improvements that have been made in the design of mechanical bonding machines, a significant number of faults can still occur due to incorrect bonding and breakage in the bonding wire. As a result, IC assemblers must undertake careful inspection procedures to meet exacting customer standards. The current trend towards miniaturisation and denser packing, however, makes inspection tasks even more difficult.

Given this problem, a research project was proposed to develop an automatic visual inspection system to inspect the quality of wires in the IC assembly process. The project was funded by the IRPA mechanism and also received a grant of RM30,000 from Intel Technology Malaysia. The firm was not involved in the formulation of the project, but participated actively by providing components for the new inspection system as well as samples for testing. The research achieved satisfactory results at the laboratory level, but Intel expected much further work to be undertaken before possible application. Funding limitations meant that a full-scale working model had not been developed. The researcher was planning to submit a proposal for funding to cover further development work on the system. This case illustrates the need for researchers, particularly in developing countries, to develop complete systems or working models before they can expect industry to utilise their findings.

Demonstration facilities

Provision of demonstration facilities is particularly important in the transfer of research findings to SMIs, as revealed by the experiences of the Rubber Research Institute of Malaysia (RRIM) and the Malaysian Agricultural Research and Development Institute (MARDI). Demonstration projects are helpful since most SMIs do not have funds to undertake extensive trial runs before embarking on actual production. The success of such projects rests largely on the research institution's intimate knowledge of industry requirements. Efforts to expand provision of such demonstration facilities will have implications for both management and policy, particularly in terms of funding and strategy.

Interactions / linkages

Successful research utilisation is characterised by a continuous flow of interactions and feedback from the various parties involved in the venture. Besides facilitating the actual transfer of the research findings, close interactions enhance the end-user's commitment to the project's success. Strengthening interactions with suppliers, dealers and industry associations is also vital in obtaining invaluable market information to guide the research agenda. The next case study reveals how one company used market information obtained through its dealer network to create a new niche in the power protection equipment sector.

Taking research from conception to adoption by the end-user involves a multitude of skills that are rarely found in one individual. Indeed, such diverse skills are seldom available within one organisation. In the second case study below, a university laboratory with excellent scientific research capacity lacked the applied engineering skills required to translate its findings into a form acceptable to a potential user. Such skills could have been obtained from close linkages with other organisations. Unfortunately, current civil service regulations do not encourage staff mobility between agencies. This seriously constrains PRIs and universities in extra-mural research co-operation.

Development of uninterruptible power-supply (UPS) system

Since 1984, P. K. Electronics (or PK) has developed a range of power protection products for the local market, including those specifically designed for high-end applications with high power requirements. In 1992, PK embarked on the development of a large UPS system. It had earlier received feedback from its dealers that many of the large UPS systems then were too heavy and not easily portable. Also, they did not provide opportunities for expansion. Customers, according to the dealers' feedback, would welcome a product that was not only portable but also easily expandable. PK's response was to develop a system based on existing technology but with a modular configuration to make the system more portable. The modular system also allowed for easy expansion to cater for increased workloads. Technical specifications were developed by the research team, while product design was contracted to an overseas specialist firm, since PK did not possess such capabilities in-house. The new product was successfully launched on the market after almost a year of development work. This case study demonstrates how sensitivity to market feedback can be crucial in creating new niches in product development.

Utilisation of peat for industrial purposes

A team at Universiti Sains Malaysia undertook some research with the main objective of diversifying peat use in the country. After a year of experimentation, the team focused on the potential use of peat as a filtration medium for palm-oil mill effluent (POME) treatment. Effluents from palm-oil refining factories constitute a serious environmental problem in Malaysia, despite the use of anaerobic digestion pond methods to process the waste. The research team designed a system to complement the pond system for the treatment of secondary POME. When treated with sulphuric acid and used in fresh form, peat from a particular source was found to be a good absorbent, converting the dark brown colour and foul smell of secondary POME into a clear colourless solution with less smell. Despite the promising potential of the research findings, the project failed to garner interest from industry. One problem was the failure of the research team to seek industry participation from the outset of the research project. Also, the research team failed, for lack of relevant engineering expertise, to build a pilot-scale demonstration plant of the laboratory-scale system they had designed. Potential users, it seems, needed to be convinced that success at the laboratory scale could be replicated on a full-scale working model. The research team also failed to work out the net benefits of using this new system as compared with existing modes of filtration.

Industrial extension/marketing activities

Industrial extension activities are poorly developed among Malaysian PRIs. According to Blackledge (1985: 44), these activities not only contribute to commercialisation, but also generate ideas for new projects for the research institute, improve institution–industry relations, and assist small-scale industry in solving operational or management problems. Universities undertake marketing of research findings through the Innovation and Consultancy Centres (ICCs) each has established. However, these ICCs vary widely in performance – from the dynamic operations of the ICC in USM to the more passive roles of others. This spectrum of dynamism in operations reflects the different degrees of management commitment to industry outreach. Ultimately, whatever institutional efforts are made to disseminate R&D results, the researchers themselves must also be pro-active in marketing their findings. Yet, Henault (1991: 6) reminds us that 'Researchers seldom feel inclined to make the extra effort of selling their results. Many find even the initial act of disseminating the results of their work already too arduous a task.'

Swiftness to market

Research projects undertaken by industrial firms in the study were largely dominated by concerns of profitability. Swiftness to the market was a key consideration in both project selection and implementation, since rapid commercialisation enabled the firm to reap higher profits. Moreover, the product might be further improved following market feedback. Because of these considerations, private firms largely focus on adaptive research projects, which are often less risky, less time-consuming and, more importantly, quickly result in commercial gains for the organisation. Adaptive research, however, is by no means 'easy'. It requires an ability to spot promising developments as well as a combination of technical and business expertise (Nath and Misra 1988: 7). Such scanning abilities underscore the importance of forging linkages with a variety of information sources – a point discussed earlier.

As PRIs increasingly shift towards income-generating activities, adaptive research may prove more attractive and viable. However, to be effective in this area, PRIs must improve their ability to respond swiftly to industry needs. Swift response has thus far not been common among PRIs and universities due to their structural impediments and also due to what Vitta (1992: 225) refers to as, '"not for profit" nonchalance'. It is critical, therefore, that PRIs and universities demonstrate sensitivity to the premium on timely and rapid project cycles in order to interest business clients.

Non-technical factors

Non-technical factors include the cost-effectiveness of research findings in commercial terms as well as the research institutions' provision of supporting technical services. Sensitivity to such factors is crucial in facilitating the target group's utilisation of research findings. For example, it is futile to develop a novel innovation when its cost is beyond the reach of the intended beneficiary. Provision of technical services is also critical for facilitating the adoption of research output. For example, the smooth adoption of the automatic labelling, sealing and capping machine by Care Industries (described above) would not have been possible if the developer of the machine – SIRIM – had not provided extensive training to staff members on how to operate as well as maintain the equipment. Often, relationships and 'word of mouth' reputations are built on how one responds to and assists the customer in 'after-sales service'. Research does not stop when the product or process has been transferred to the user. In fact, besides enhancing long-term relationships, providing personal assistance to the customer is a far more effective means of obtaining feedback on the research output transferred than merely conducting market surveys.

Top-management leadership

Unquestionably, the success of the research effort, at both project and organisational levels, is determined by the quality of managerial leadership. Without leadership and commitment, even the most promising of research projects will fail miserably. Poor leadership not only wastes scarce resources; worse still, it undermines the enthusiasm of other team members. A wide gulf in research management practices exists, particularly among PRIs and universities. All the PRIs and universities have some type of project selection and monitoring system to guide the research process. While some organisations have adopted structured approaches to vetting, monitoring and evaluation of projects as well as to enhancing linkages with industry, others have been more indifferent in their attitudes. Such contrasts are partly a consequence of the non-competitive nature of the national public research funding mechanism (IRPA), which has fostered the impression that research funding is easy to obtain.[4] More importantly, differences in research management practices among the organisations reflect the different degrees of commitment of the top managers concerned to research efforts. Despite being exposed to a similar civil service regime as other organisations, the initiatives adopted by SIRIM underscore how commitment from the top can influence the scale and pace of change in an organisation.

Managerial implications

The previous discussion suggested that much can be done to enhance research utilisation, particularly in PRIs and universities. The managerial implications of adopting sound research management practices can be examined in terms of disciplined research management, building partnerships in R&D, and a holistic approach towards research utilisation and leadership.

Disciplined research management

A striking feature of my organisational survey (Thiruchelvam 1995) is the uneven-ness in research management practices among PRIs, universities and firms, which reflected differences in orientation and priorities. Table 9.1 provides a broad cate-gorisation of various research practices adopted by these organisations. Industrial firms' research operations were characterised by swiftness in decision-making and stringency in project selection due to the overarching need to generate profits. These characteristics were absent in both PRIs and universities since they did not operate along business lines. Also, PRIs and universities were constrained from adopting more responsive research management practices by the civil service reg-ulations under which they operate.

The study also revealed a wide disparity in research management practices among PRIs and universities despite their similar environments. While research management in some institutions such as SIRIM can be described as sound, the sit-uation in most other organisations was less than satisfactory. For example, systems in place to appraise research proposals were poorly structured and weakly imple-mented. Additionally, public bodies seldom critically evaluated how research projects would contribute to an organisation's current and future goals. Finally, there was typically a lack of discipline in monitoring and performance evaluation.

Discipline is clearly essential if research projects are to be carefully planned, selected, monitored, evaluated, and ultimately transferred to the end-user. The organisational survey revealed that only SIRIM and UTM among the selected PRIs and universities have institutionalised pre-technical work as part of their research approval process. In the case of SIRIM, industry surveys were undertaken to identify actual industry needs, and research proposals are submitted based on such feedback. UTM directed all applied research projects to furnish documentary evidence from industry to ascertain their relevance, particularly in solving indus-try's problems. In some cases, it provided funds for researchers to engage in pre-technical activities before submitting proposals for IRPA funding. In industry, by contrast, extensive testing activities were undertaken, particularly in the food industry, in order to ensure that the client's needs were satisfied prior to production. These examples demonstrate what management, especially in PRIs and universi-ties, can do to enhance the research utilisation process in their respective organisations.

Management must ensure that research projects are carefully scrutinised before they are selected for funding. Project selection must be guided by sound inputs of information and not on biases or intuition. In industry, criteria for selection of pro-jects were sharply defined, i.e. projects were selected only when both technical and financial criteria were met. Such unambiguous criteria were absent in the selection mechanisms in PRIs and universities, where projects were often chosen on the basis of vague notions of technical 'soundness' or relevance to industry needs. Again, as in other spheres, the effectiveness of whatever system that is used is largely depen-dent on the commitment of top management to its proper implementation.

Table 9.1 Malaysia: summary of research management practices among firms, public research institutions and universities

	Firms	Public research institutions	Universities
Strategy	No explicit research plan; Ideas for projects actively sought from various sources; Participation by all sections of an organisation in a research proposal before approval.	Corporate plan prepared, but varied in detail among the PRIs; Planning of projects a mixture of both 'top-down' and 'bottom-up', i.e. from top management as well as from researchers. Discussions seldom held with end-users except for joint projects or contract research.	No explicit research plan; Projects initiated largely by researchers themselves, i.e. 'bottom-up' process.
Structure	Separate unit to undertake as well as organise the research function; Decision-making swift to respond to changing conditions; Research findings transferred to market by marketing arm of the organisation.	Separate unit to organise the research function; Decision-making slow due to need to adhere to civil service regulations; Extension activities only undertaken to a small extent in MARDI, and not institutionalised in others.	Separate unit formed to co-ordinate the research function; Decision-making slow, as in the case of PRIs; Transfer of research findings undertaken by Innovation and Consultancy Centres in each university. But performance of these centres very uneven.
System	Selection of projects based on meeting technical and financial criteria; Pre-feasibility studies and testing integral components of the research process.	Selection of projects based on soundness of proposals; Pre-feasibility studies seldom undertaken; Selection, screening and monitoring systems formalised.	Selection of projects based on soundness of proposals; Pre-feasibility studies seldom initiated; Selection, screening and monitoring systems formalised, but degree of implementation varied greatly.
Staff	No explicit reward system; outstanding staff rewarded through annual salary exercise.	Governed by civil service reward system not appropriate for research environment.	Governed by civil service reward system.
Style	Informal operations, but discipline in purpose and implementation.	Focused research management, but degree of commitment varied among organisations.	Generally *laissez-faire* style of management; Wide disparity in commitment towards research effort.

Source: Thiruchelvam (1995: 150)

Discipline in the research effort would also be strengthened if evaluation and research audit exercises are instituted as integral aspects of the research process. These practices transmit signals to researchers regarding their research, and also provide a forum where experiences can be shared and learned. Only UTM has institutionalised systematic research evaluation, enabling top management to keep abreast of the progress of the organisation's research projects.

Private industry's bottom-line considerations generate pressure to get research results to the market as swiftly as possible. Since PRIs' and universities' survival and access to future funding are not dependent on rapid commercialisation, most have failed to improve their abilities to conduct research according to tight budgets and time schedules. Private industry places a premium on making sure that things work and are delivered on time rather than on developing 'perfect' solutions that nobody requires. SIRIM has recently adopted a project budgeting system whereby costs of all inputs are captured, including the time spent by researchers, in order to enable it to objectively assess the cost of a project. Such management systems, if adopted by other PRIs and universities, would help impose cost and time discipline on researchers, regardless of whether projects are commissioned internally, by industry, or by other clients.

Building partnerships in R&D

Evidence from the study revealed that the more enterprising PRIs and universities have initiated contracts and collaboration with industry which have already yielded profitable research agreements and consultancies. Nonetheless, not one public organisation has yet approached collaboration as basically a strategic issue. However, SIRIM's efforts to assess industry's capabilities in particular sectors and to forge tripartite collaboration with industry and universities are efforts in this strategic direction. Continuous interaction and integration of R&D efforts between public and private sectors would enhance the knowledge-building activities of both these sectors (Cooray 1985: 94). Collaboration between PRIs and universities are also crucial to combining a range of expertise to achieve inter-disciplinary research objectives, to foster appropriate specialisation, and to reduce wasteful duplication of research efforts.

Collaboration will only succeed if it promises potential benefits to participating organisations (Kodama 1992: 71). The success of joint research projects attests to the importance of commitment from all the participating parties in the research effort. Moreover, they will only arise through deliberate management action. UTM, for example, has devised a reward system that encourages its researchers to work with industry by according equal consideration in staff evaluation to contract research as to academic publication. Finally, collaboration with industry, as Gibbons *et al.* (1994) assert, requires constant nurturing and support. USM's Innovation and Consultancy Centre (ICC) was constrained by a lack of funds in building on its early successes in contract work with industry.

K. THIRUCHELVAM

Holistic approach to research utilisation

The research process in the private firms surveyed was characterised by a holistic approach whereby all inputs necessary for the success of a project were identified at the outset. Inputs and participation from all relevant firm divisions, as well as from potential customers, were sought prior to any project's implementation. Such an approach ensures that the specific requirements for each phase of the project are anticipated, thus minimising delays and design changes. The research process in PRIs and universities, on the other hand, is largely implemented according to a linear or sequential approach that proceeds from an initial concept to deduce what uses the research might have. Adoption of a holistic approach involves assembling inputs from all parties involved in the project, including the end-user, at the outset. This approach implies making organisational boundaries – within the organisation, as well as between the organisation and external clients – more permeable in order to enhance knowledge flows. Such knowledge exchanges would be facilitated by management practices emphasising teamwork and partnerships. Particularly for the PRIs, a holistic approach would also imply the need to provide technical services to SMIs long after the research findings have been transferred. Providing support services would help to build credibility and confidence among SMIs in the capabilities of PRIs. Research organisations must devote specific resources to providing these services.

Leadership and commitment

The survey found the wide gaps in research management practices among PRIs and universities to reflect varying degrees of commitment among top management to the research effort. The overall performance of an organisation is likely to be better when top management displays commitment to the research effort. SIRIM's and UTM's efforts to foster partnerships with industry, to ensure discipline in research project management, and to motivate the staff to deliver their best, demonstrate the impact of strong leadership, even within a constraining operating environment. Leadership at the project level is equally important to forging commitment among the various parties, inspiring and motivating other team members, and guiding the project to fruition. Thus, project leaders must be chosen from among those able to give undivided attention to implementation. Also, top management plays a crucial role in ensuring that project teams are constituted with members of varying seniority and different disciplines as well as, wherever possible, representation from the end-user. Such project teams provide the blend of skills required to successfully undertake the project. Additionally, as Moss (1985: 15) observes, the participation of senior members in team efforts provides junior staff with excellent mentoring and practical training.

230

Policy implications of adopting sound research management practices

While various management factors can support good research management practices at the organisational level, their impact on utilisation of national research output is limited by the broader operating environment. Issues such as the incentives provided by the national research funding mechanism, personnel regulations, and flexibility in operations of PRIs and universities come under the purview of national policy in Malaysia. The policy implications emerging from the earlier discussion can be addressed in terms of conditions for research funding, scope of research funding and institutional operating environment.

Conditions for research funding

As mentioned earlier, funding for research in PRIs and universities is relatively easy to obtain.[5] Unfortunately, such a situation leads to complacency and, worse, indifference towards research quality. Notwithstanding declared policy goals, Malaysia's IRPA funding system, until recently, did not signal to researchers that industry-oriented research was being prioritised and that research proposals lacking such an orientation or industry participation should not have been funded. The failure to develop a competitive environment for research contributed to the poor utilisation of research findings from PRIs and universities.

Although some organisations have taken the initiative to improve research management, most other publicly funded institutions can be characterised as passive. In part, this is because good research management practices, such as undertaking pre-technical studies, have not been required as conditions for IRPA funding. Without the imposition of strict guidelines for IRPA funding, each institution will choose to adopt practices that reflect the commitment of its top management to the research effort.[6]

Scope of research funding

Industry's failure to adopt some promising research findings has stemmed from a lack of funds for development and other additional work as described in the case studies above. Presently, IRPA funding only covers the 'research' part of R&D and does not include activities such as development, scaling-up, engineering, prototyping, testing and marketing. Such activities are crucial to ensuring that research findings are in a form suitable for the end-user. Nor does IRPA cover pre-technical activities. Similarly, absence of funding support has limited the marketing and industrial extension activities of some PRIs and universities. These activities are essential for PRIs and universities to 'sell' their services as well as to forge partnerships with industry. The case studies also revealed that universities, in particular, have difficulty in obtaining the services of research assistants.[7] This is largely due to the unattractive salary packages as well as the uncertain career paths offered to prospective research assistants. In some cases, the shortage of research assistants has retarded the progress of promising research projects.

Institutional operating environment

PRIs and universities are constrained by existing civil service regulations from adopting more responsive and flexible management practices, particularly in working with industrial clients. For example, PRIs and universities have to follow cumbersome administrative procedures when purchasing equipment and services. Such procedures often take considerable time and invariably result in delays in implementing research projects. PRIs and universities are subject to the remuneration scale and terms of service determined by the Public Services Department (PSD), which are generally far less attractive than those offered by industry. Also, the reward system adopted by the civil service is biased towards individual performance, which undermines the teamwork essential for successful research. Additionally, civil service procedures do not encourage the mobility of researchers within and among PRIs and universities, e.g. through secondments and short-term rotation.

Financial regulations limit the authority of heads of PRIs and universities to shift funds from one budget to another in order to flexibly respond to new opportunities or to undertake additional work on promising projects. Also, existing IRPA guidelines do not allow PRIs and universities to utilise surplus project funds to finance additional activities, including training and technical services, beyond those originally approved. While control of research funding is necessary, it should not, however, stifle initiative to respond to new opportunities. Ultimately, research performance is judged by the number of projects that get utilised, rather than adherence to a pre-set budget.

This suggests that the regulations governing PRIs and universities need to be reformed to place a premium on autonomy, flexibility and responsiveness. While civil service procedures may be suitable for more routine activities, they are grossly inadequate to cope with tasks, such as innovation and research, where risk-taking and responsiveness to the client are crucial.

Conclusion

This study has outlined the vital role of management best practices in ensuring that R&D investments translate into real advantages for industry. The first section touched upon key management practices and illustrated their relevance to R&D organisations' success or failure in ensuring their research results were fully utilised. The adoption of these management practices will improve the quality of research and its utility to end-users. Their implementation would help to reduce uncertainties in project selection and enhance the likelihood of success of research efforts. However, there is no magic formula to guarantee success in research utilisation. As Twiss (1992: 24) observes, the quality of the research output is a necessary precondition for success. If this is deficient, adoption of all other best practices will be futile. Such practices, however, would help to ensure that uncertainties are reduced, thereby enhancing the likelihood of success of the research effort. Making these practices work, particularly for PRIs and universities, will involve both managerial and policy dimensions.

The discussion in the paper raised a number of managerial and policy issues pertaining to the adoption of sound research management practices, particularly in PRIs and universities. Both sets of issues must be addressed in tandem, since even the best efforts at the organisational level may be negated by unsupportive or contradictory policies. Accordingly, policies must seek to engender a competitive, yet hospitable, environment for research utilisation which permits flexibility and responsiveness in operations; encourages PRIs to meet the needs of industry; and pressures organisations to be more disciplined in R&D management. These changes are necessary so that the fruits of public R&D can contribute to the acquisition and strengthening of the nation's technological capabilities.

The need for quality management is evident in all economic activities, including R&D. No research organisation can afford to support low-quality research, however strongly it is motivated by social relevance rather than commercial profit. Given the enormous resources now allocated to R&D in Malaysia, it is critical that the benefits of R&D are not squandered on poorly defined goals. This chapter argues that adopting sound research management practices is crucial to enhanced research utilisation. Adoption of such practices, however, will not happen by chance, but must be deliberately pursued and encouraged. Fostering and implementing management change is the fundamental task of leadership at the project, organisation and national levels. Without such commitment and discipline at all these levels, pouring more resources into R&D will be futile.

Notes

Much of the material used in this chapter is based on the writer's doctoral thesis; see Thiruchelvam (1995).

1 Under the Seventh Malaysia Plan, this deficiency is being addressed with a special allocation devoted to commercialisation of research findings.
2 IRPA is the acronym for Intensification of Research in Priority Areas. It is a mechanism for funding public-sector research projects that was first used in 1988.
3 Unless specifically stated otherwise, all references to the study or survey in this chapter refer to Thiruchelvam (1995).
4 Beginning in 1996, the IRPA programme has undergone some structural modifications to ensure more stringent vetting of projects as well as competitive bidding for projects identified by the various panels.
5 This statement refers to IRPA funding prior to the recent modifications made to enhance stringency in project approval.
6 From 1996, research projects for the manufacturing sector must have industry support; otherwise, they will not be considered for IRPA funding.
7 This view was conveyed to the writer by the then Deputy Vice-Chancellor of USM.

References

Baker, N.R., S.G. Green and A.S. Bean (1986). 'Why R&D Projects Succeed or Fail', *Research Management*, November–December: 29–34.

Blackledge, J.P. (1985). 'The Potential for Contribution of R&D to the Production System', in M.P.W. Silveira (ed.), *Research and Development: Linkages to Production in Developing Countries*, Boulder, Colo.: Westview.

Business Times (1992). 'Need to Review IRPA Mechanism', 21 January.

Cooray, N. (1985). 'Knowledge Accumulation and Technological Advance: The Case of Synthetic Rubber', *Research Policy*, 14(2): 83–95.

Frumerman, R. (1992). 'Cost-effective R&D', *Technovation*, 12(3): 203–8.

Gibbons, M., C. Limoges, H. Nowotny, S. Schwartzman, P. Scott and M. Trow (1994). *The New Production of Knowledge: The Dynamics of Science and Research in Contemporary Societies*, London: Sage.

Henault, G. (1991). 'Dissemination of Research Results: A Case Study of Written Documents Based on the Producer's Perception of the User's Needs in South East Asia', Manuscript Report No. 282e, Ottawa: IDRC.

Kodama, F. (1992). 'Technology Fusion and the New R&D', *Harvard Business Review*, July–August.

Moss, T.H. (1985). 'Innovation Management in Developing Countries: Applications from the International Institute for Applied Systems Analysis (IIASA) Case Study on Innovation Management', UNIDO/IS. 566, October.

Nath, N.C.B. and L. Misra (1988). 'Case Studies in Indigenous Industrial R&D Utilisation', Manuscript Report No. 188e, April, Ottawa: IDRC.

Thiruchelvam, K. (1995). 'Utilisation of Industrial R&D Findings in Malaysia: A Case Study of Selected Public Research Institutions, Universities and Industry', D.Phil. Thesis, Science Policy Research Unit, University of Sussex, Brighton.

Twiss, B.C. (1992). *Managing Technological Innovation*, London: Pitman.

Vitta, P.B. (1992). 'Utility of Research in Sub-Saharan Africa: Beyond the Leap of Faith', *Science and Public Policy*, 19(4), August: 221–8.

10

SKILLED AND UNSKILLED FOREIGN LABOUR IN MALAYSIAN DEVELOPMENT – A STRATEGIC SHIFT?

Chris Edwards

In February 1991, the Malaysian Prime Minister, Mahathir Mohamad announced, to the newly formed National Business Council, his 'Vision 2020'. The vision was that Malaysia would become a 'fully developed country' by the year 2020 (Jomo 1994: 51). Five years later, Malaysia was on course to meet this objective. In its 1996 World Development Report, the World Bank defined a high-income (or 'developed') country as one with a per capita GNP in 1994 of US$8956 or more (World Bank 1996: 181). In that year, Malaysia's per capita GNP was US$3480, less than half the high-income cut-off point. However, over the 1985–94 period, Malaysia's per capita GNP had grown at 5.6 per cent per annum whereas the annual growth rates of the world average and the high-income average had been 0.9 per cent and 1.9 per cent respectively (World Bank 1996: 189). If we assume that the developed-country cut-off income grows at just under 2 per cent per annum over the next quarter-century, by the year 2020 it will be about US$15,000 (in 1995 prices). To reach this level, Malaysia's average has to grow at a little under 6 per cent per annum – that is, it has to continue to grow over the next quarter of a century at about the same rate that it has achieved over the past decade.

However, in recent years, report after report (both official and unofficial) on the Malaysian economy has stated that a necessary condition for achieving this high rate of growth is for Malaysia to make a strategic shift away from low-value-added activities to high-value-added activities. Thus, in its 1995 Annual Report, the Bank Negara stated that:

> The current phase of economic expansion has been driven by significant increases in factor inputs, particularly capital, with high growth being sustained in the manufacturing, construction and service sectors. . . . [To] achieve long-term sustainable growth . . . the current strategic shift towards more capital and technology-intensive activities with high export orientation, lower import content and high inter-linkages has been

stepped up in order to generate maximum value added and export earnings for Malaysia.

(Bank Negara 1996: Foreword)

Similar sentiments have been expressed in the *Review of the Industrial Master Plan, 1986–95* (MITI 1994), in the *Economic Report, 1995/96* (Ministry of Finance 1995) and in the *Seventh Malaysia Plan, 1996–2000* (EPU 1996). All of these imply that a strategic shift is needed for Malaysia to achieve Vision 2020. Thus, the consensus is that Malaysia will have to undergo an industrial revolution to achieve Vision 2020. What is needed is both

- an *upgrading* of existing sectors (from low value-added, low-skill to high-value-added, high-skill activities); and
- a *shift* out of low-value-added, low-skill to high-value-added, high-skill sectors.

In this chapter, I look at the labour market implications of this strategic shift and at the following questions:

- Is Malaysia likely to produce the quantity and quality of skills required for a strategic shift? Are the incentives for the supply of skilled labour attractive?
- Are the investment incentives in existence for such a strategic shift? More specifically, what role does the import of unskilled foreign labour play in promoting or impeding such a strategic shift?

In trying to answer these questions, I look next at the theory of skills provision and the practices in Malaysia; then, I look at the possible effects that the import of unskilled foreign labour has on the incentives for, and against, skill-intensive investments. The next section is brief compared to the following section, in which the structural role of unskilled foreign labour in the Malaysian economy is examined. The reason for looking in more depth at the effects of unskilled foreign labour is that this is a relatively neglected area in official reports and yet it is an area of considerable importance both theoretically and practically and an area of great controversy in the Malaysian newspapers. The fourth and final section of the chapter brings the threads together and draws out some possible policy conclusions.

Skill availability and the strategic shift in Malaysian manufacturing

The skill-intensity controversy

In a report dated February 1995, the World Bank caused quite a stir when it argued that the skill composition of the manufacturing labour force in Malaysia had deteriorated between 1985 and 1991. It argued that:

236

One measure of skill intensity of the work force, the ratio of skilled to total workers, has fallen from 0.43 in 1985 to 0.35 in 1991 with a sharp decline registered in electrical machinery manufactures, fabricated metal products and rubber products.

(See World Bank 1995: paragraph 8)

The World Bank admitted that the relative definition of skills might give misleading results and that all jobs might be becoming more skill-intensive, but to the extent that the categorisation of skills reflects the loss of skill intensity over time, the Bank argued that this trend needs to be reversed.

The World Bank's conclusions have been sharply criticised on the grounds that the basis of their comparison is misleading. The argument is that 1985 was a recession year, many workers were retrenched in that year, and most of the retrenched workers were unskilled. For these reasons, skill-intensity ratios in manufacturing industry were unusually high in 1985, in which case it is hardly surprising if the skill-intensity percentage fell from 1985 to 1991. Data from the Bank Negara Annual Survey of Companies suggest that between 1992 and 1994, skill intensities rose quite sharply, except in textiles and chemicals, but Table 10.1 illustrates the problems of categorising skills since the percentages vary considerably between the sources.

Table 10.1 Malaysia: skill intensity in manufacturing, 1985–94

	1985	1991	1992	1994
Total	43	35		
Food	27	31		
Textiles	27	31	69	62
Paper products	41	34		
Chemicals	28	35	56	55
Petroleum refineries	48	49		
Rubber products	30	23		
Non-metal products	27	31	49	62
Basic metals	37	38	48	54
Metal products	39	30		
Electrical m/c	64	37		
– electronics			59	60
– machinery/electrical			39	48
Transport equipment	52	39		

Sources: World Bank 1995: 8 (for 1985 and 1991 from the Industrial Survey)
Bank Negara, *Annual Survey of Companies* for 1992 and 1994

Thus, the picture is probably not as bad as suggested by the World Bank, although this is as much in spite of government policy as because of it. As elaborated later, it is only in the 1990s that policy changes have been made which offer much chance of the shortage of skilled labour being significantly eased.

In analysing the picture and the policies on skills, it is useful to divide the labour force into three groups as follows:

* existing workers in existing industries
* new entrants to existing industries
* new entrants to new industries.

If we are considering the immediate situation, then the first group is by far the most important. Thus, in the short and medium term, the training and skill upgrading of the *existing* labour force is of much greater importance than the quality of new entrants. Of course, in the longer term, new entrants for both existing industries and new industries are more important, since by the year 2020, with a rapid increase in the Malaysian labour force of between 2 and 3 per cent per annum, the vast majority of the labour force will have been replaced.

Skills of existing workers in existing industries

As already emphasised, there are acute problems of measuring skills. Nevertheless, for analytical purposes, it is useful to classify skills into three groups, namely company-specific, industry-specific and transferable skills.

This section does not discuss the provision of skills peculiar to a company while the discussion of transferable skills between industries is left to the end of this section since they raise more general educational issues. Here, the discussion is confined to skills that are *specific* to, but transferable *within*, an industry, i.e. *vocational skills*. There is some evidence that these industry-specific or vocational skills are important in Malaysia since inter-industry differences in wages are considerable (see Table 10.2).

Table 10.2 Malaysia: inter-industry wage differences, 1994

Industry	Managers, prof.	Technical, skilled	Unskilled	Others	Average
Wages (RM'000 per annum)					
Chemicals	61	26	12	25	28
Textiles	41	9	7	13	10
Non-metal products	56	19	7	18	19
Electronics	50	13	8	14	14
Basic metal	50	18	13	16	20
Machine/elec.	43	14	9	12	13
Indices (Chemicals = 100)					
Chemicals	100	100	100	100	100
Textiles	67	35	57	52	35
Non-metal products	91	71	63	73	67
Electronics	82	48	69	55	49
Basic metal	81	70	108	66	70
Machine/elec.	69	52	72	48	47

Source: Bank Negara, Annual Survey of Companies

Past policy on skill provision in Malaysia

Since the late 1980s, Malaysian government policy on skill provision has changed dramatically. In the early 1980s, government discussions of the economy contained many references to skill shortages, but skill development policy was essentially (and excessively) supply-led. The emphasis was on the *quantity* of skilled labour through a combination of manpower planning and training provision through public-sector agencies. A comprehensive survey of manpower planning was undertaken in 1973 to cover the needs of the period from 1973 to 1990. This was followed by a 1980 Master Plan drawn up on the basis of input–output coefficients. In 1986, the Manpower and Training Volume of the Industrial Master Plan (IMP) was based on a target approach using patterns of skill requirements from other countries. However, by this time, it was increasingly recognised that human development policy in Malaysia was too mechanistic and *supply-led*, and a reappraisal was taking place.

Thus, by the second half of the 1980s, there began to be some re-thinking of skill provision in Malaysia. The IMP had involved closer collaboration with industry in establishing needs, and in 1986, a sub-committee under the National Development Planning Council (NDPC) was formed to redefine and sharpen the roles of the agencies involved in skill planning and provision. In 1990, an ambitious Human Resource Development Plan Project was launched. This was followed in 1991 by a report from a Cabinet Committee on training. At about the same time, a Working Committee on Human Resource Development (HRD) was set up under the Malaysian Business Council.

Need for a levy–grant system

Gradually, there had been a change in thinking between the late 1980s and the early 1990s, with a shift from a supply-led to a demand-led approach and with the gradual acceptance of the need for a levy–grant system, which the Malaysian circumstances justified. In a recent paper (see Edwards 1996), I argued that there are ten logical steps to a levy–grant system, as summarised in Figure 10.1.

Put briefly, for a vocational training system to work well, I argue that there is a need for what neo-classical economists would label as *market imperfections*. Without some form of 'market imperfection', the provision of such industry-specific skills (vocational skills) is likely to be sub-optimal. I claim that this argument is not only theoretically sound (see Figure 10.1), but is also backed up in practice since 'market imperfections' are present in two countries that are widely considered to have among the most successful vocational training systems in the world, i.e. Germany and Japan. Their vocational training systems are summarised, along with those of a number of other countries, in Figure 10.2.

Both the German and Japanese systems work within particular political and cultural contexts and are characterised by 'market imperfections'. In Germany, the

Start with four assumptions:
* **1** Competitiveness $= f(\text{costs}) = f(\text{total factor productivity})$
* **2** For a given capital intensity, productivity (and wages) $= f(\text{skills in labour force})$
* **3** Skill in labour force $= f(\text{training, qualifications})$
    . . . and from 2 and 3 . . .
* **4** Productivity (and wages) $= f(\text{training, qualifications})$
Therefore, from 4, there is an incentive for both employers and employees to promote training and the acquisition of qualifications. But these incentives are conditional on how the particular labour market works and on *who finances the acquisition of skills/qualifications.*
Is it . . .
* **5** *the employee?*
    * by taking a 'low' wage apprenticeship
    or:
    * by paying for the training outside the workplace (assuming the qualification is widely accepted)
    . . . or is it . . ..
* **6** *the employer?*
    * this is the more likely, the lower the training costs, the more the skills are specific to the employer and/or the slower the labour turnover for the employer.
From 5 and 6, it follows that if there is:
    * no low-wage apprenticeship system, and
    * no certainty of the value of the qualification,
    and if
    * the skills are not firm-specific and there is a high rate of labour turnover
    then,
* **7** Training is likely to be *socially sub-optimal*, and there will be an incentive for free-riding, *'poaching'* or 'cherry-picking'.

Solutions?
* **8** *The government provides and pays for the training*
    * advantages: such central (supply-led) provision
        – can take advantage of any economies of scale in training;
        – may be able to 'pick winners' (anticipate new skills).
    * disadvantage:
        – the training may be 'supply-led' and not match the needs of the employers (whether in the public or the private sector).
* **9** Employers provide, but government pays for the training
    * advantage:
        – more incentive than under 8 to provide 'suitable' (demand-led) training, but
    * disadvantage:
        – problems of 'moral hazard' (the employer may over-supply at the cost of public finance) or, if the skills are employer-specific, the government may be supplying skills which the employer would have provided anyway.
So
* **10** *Is a levy–grant system the final solution?*
    * a levy–grant system is where either employers or the state (or both in close conjunction) provide the training, but where employers pay for the training through a payroll levy or tax, and are then reimbursed through grants to cover part or all of the cost of 'approved' and certifiable training.
    * advantages:
        – training is 'demand-led';
        – there is an incentive for firms to adopt a 'training culture' since they have to pay for training anyway.
    * disadvantages:
        – problems of bureaucratic expense in ensuring that the training is 'approved', that is, that the training has been provided at the right level.

Figure 10.1 Logic of a levy–grant system

Germany:
* 'Dual' system of apprenticeships, with vocational training taking place at vocational schools and at work. Reckoned to be one of the best systems of vocational training in the world. Employees know that the qualifications will matter since the system is stable and supported by strong organisations of employers and unions. Employers are encouraged to train because of low net costs (wages of apprentices are low), pressure from organisations, and the long-term context within which they operate. German employers are said to be locked into a 'high-skill equilibrium' (producing high-skill, high-value-added goods) (Casey 1991, Steedman 1993).

Japan:
* High standard of basic education, especially for 'bottom half'; vocational training builds on this; very good on-the-job training; employers encouraged to do this because of low job turnover, especially for large employers. Thus, a paradox that *the system works well only because of a major market 'imperfection', namely low job mobility* (Dore and Sako 1989).

Sri Lanka:
* State-led system of vocational training; huge proliferation of training centres with few connections to industry. Therefore, training not appropriate; large drop-out rate; levy–grant system under consideration (see Edwards 1996).

Malaysia:
* As for Sri Lanka until 1993, when a levy–grant system came into operation.

Singapore:
* Levy–grant system (Skills Development Fund) set up in 1979; provides grants for in-house and public training programmes, for training in new skills, for training for the educationally disadvantaged, and for group training schemes. Emphasis on employer-led programmes to encourage the creation of suitable skills. SDF has played a major role in restructuring Singapore into high-value-added manufacturing (see Ashton and Sung 1994; Edwards 1996).

USA:
* Most vocational training done through full-time further education following high school; highly decentralised system; high drop-out rates, large under-educated under-class. Little incentive for employers to do training because of high job mobility. Some, recent, discussion of the introduction of a levy–grant system (Lynch 1993).

UK:
* Apprenticeship system to 1964 which did not work well, partly because of high wages for apprentices; in 1964, levy–grant system, but only allowed to operate without much change until 1973; increasingly, since the 1970s, training linked to unemployment and, in the 1990s, training arranged through Training and Enterprise Councils (TECs). Many changes and considerable instability. The unstable framework discourages employees from undertaking training. Training financed by the state; little incentive for 'short-termist' employers to train with high poaching risks; UK in 'low-skill equilibrium'; paradox of the need for both change and stability (Dolton 1993; Finegold and Soskice 1988).

Figure 10.2 Alternative training systems
Sources: Edwards 1996; Lynch 1993

241

dual system is acknowledged as working well, partly because of the structure of the labour market (relatively low apprentice wages combined with a stable accreditation system) and partly because of a 'market imperfection', namely the corporate pressure exerted jointly by the organisations 'representing' the employers (the chambers of commerce) and employees (the trade unions). In Japan, the system works well because of a 'market imperfection', namely the company loyalty structure involving guaranteed lifelong employment and the seniority wage system. Employees tend to stay with the same employer for a long time in Japan so that industry-specific skills are the same as company-specific skills.

Where such 'market imperfections' are not present, it is important that a suitable one is introduced. One way is through state intervention in the form of a levy–grant system. Put simply, 'market imperfections' are inherent to skilled labour markets and vocational training (see World Bank 1995: 107, 108), so that unless another 'market imperfection' is introduced to correct this, a second-best situation will arise. Thus, in Malaysia in the late 1980s there were widespread allegations of poaching. As a result, and as the World Bank (1995) put it, 'there appears to be some support for the view that Malaysian industry generally under-invests in training' (World Bank 1995: 108).

The World Bank pointed out, on the basis of the 1988 UNDP survey, that there was little firm-based training in Malaysia (World Bank 1995: 104). It was to encourage firm-based training that the Malaysian government had introduced the Double Deduction Tax Incentive (DDTI) for training in 1987, but this did little to counter poaching. The World Bank's assessment is that the DDTI was quite ineffective (as similar schemes have been in other countries; see World Bank 1995: 114) and in 1993, it was abolished except for small manufacturing firms.

Thus, in the early 1990s, training in Malaysia was inadequate and the skills shortage continued. But what change in policy was desirable? It seemed clear that a German-style vocational training system would not work since business associations and trade unions in Malaysia were weak so that German-style 'corporatism' is absent and not feasible. Similarly, the conditions for Japanese-style firm-level corporatism are absent. Labour turnover in Malaysia is fast (see Pillai 1992: 11), so that Japanese-style company loyalty is absent.

Thus, in the early 1990s, the conditions in Malaysia seemed to be ripe for the introduction of a levy–grant system which would reduce the incentive for poaching, would inculcate a 'training culture' and would make the system more demand-driven.

The operations of a levy-grant system in Malaysia

So it was that in 1992, a levy–grant system (the Human Resources Development Fund) was set up in Malaysia under the Human Resources Development Council (HRDC). The aims of the HRDC were stated as follows:

•   to increase the supply of highly skilled workers

- to cultivate a training culture among employers
- to accelerate the process of technology transfer (see HRDC 1994: 52)

The HRDC operates the Human Resources Development Fund (HRDF), which came into operation in 1993. A *levy* of 1 per cent of payroll is imposed compulsorily on large employers in manufacturing and on small, medium and large employers in service industries and optionally on small and medium industries (SMIs) in manufacturing. The aim is to provide a floor to training.

Table 10.3 Malaysia: grants from and number of trainees assisted by HRDC, from 1 July 1993 to mid-March 1996

Scheme	1993[a]	1994	1995	1996[b]	Total (rounded)	No. of trainees ('000)	Grant per trainee (RM)
Grants (RM mill.)							
SBL[c]	2.4	37.1	73.4	16.5	129	565	229
PROLUS[d]	0.7	5.8	8.1	2.0	17	35	474
PLT[e]	0	4.9	3.5	4.9	13	197	68
PERLA[f]	0	0	3.8	0.9	5	10	470
Perantisan	0	0	0	neg.	neg.	neg.	760
Total	3.1	47.8	88.8	24.3	164	807	203
Number of trainees ('000)	25	294	320	168		807	
Grant per trainee (RM)	124	163	278	145			203

Source: HRDC interview, March 1996
Notes: (a) From 1 July 1993.
    (b) Until 15 March 1996 only.
    (c) SBL = Skim Bantuan Latihan.
    (d) PROLUS = Skim Program Latihan Yang Diluluskan.
    (e) PLT = Skim Pelan Latihan Tahunan.
    (f) PERLA = Perjanjian Latihan Dengan Penyedia Latihan.

Grants are provided (for training Malaysian citizens only) up to the amount of the levy, but they only finance part of the expenditure so that if the employers receive grants equivalent to their levy, they will spend more than their levy on training. Steps have been taken to encourage training by small companies by reducing the required form-filling, by providing help with training plans and by introducing joint training schemes. Thus, various grant schemes are in operation. The amounts granted under the various schemes are shown in Table 10.3.

The table shows that, between July 1993 and mid-March 1996, grants had been allocated for over 800,000 trainees. The number assisted has risen rapidly each year, with expenditure in 1996 running at about RM100 million a year financing about 650,000 trainees – equivalent to about a third of total manufacturing employment in 1995. By far the most important scheme, in terms of expenditure, is the SLB scheme, which is an ad hoc one under which either in-house or external (domestic or foreign) trainers can be used. The next most important scheme is the PLT (Annual Training Plan) scheme which is designed to provide grants to applicant companies within the framework of pre-approved training plans. PROLUS and PERLA are pre-approved training provider programmes and PERANTISAN is the HRDC's apprenticeship scheme.

The HRDC is widely thought to have made good progress, but the World Bank (1995: 117) complains of a low take-up rate and, according to surveys carried out for the Second Industrial Master Plan (1996–2005), there have been numerous complaints about delays in the processing of applications. The World Bank (1995: 121) has alleged that the HRDC is understaffed while others (in interviews) have alleged that a major problem is that the HRDC – like the administrators of the Skill Development Fund in Singapore – has been too cautious, is not sufficiently encouraging the adoption of computerised applications, and is generally too 'bureaucratic'. A common argument is that since the firms are merely getting their 'own money' back in grants, the HRDC should be prepared to take greater risks and to worry less about whether the training schemes are totally 'appropriate'. However, the HRDC is still in its infancy and is still changing. The pre-approved schemes were introduced to cut out some 'red tape', and at the end of 1995 the application procedure for the SBL was simplified. Also, since the end of 1995 the SLB – designed to tackle issues of economies of scale in training and labour indivisibility by providing for joint training by a number of employers – has been in operation.

It is clear that by 1992, with the establishment of the HRDF, there had been a switch in emphasis to training at the level and at the behest of the firm. The buzzwords have become 'demand-driven' and, more recently, 'clusters': 'demand-driven' to make sure that the training is what the firm wants, and 'clusters' to try to ensure that linkages and external economies are maximised.

The model is now the Penang Skills Development Centre (PSDC), and attempts are being made to emulate this in other parts of Malaysia (see MITI 1994: 100). However, reproducing the PSDC model may be difficult since Penang is something of a special case. It has a concentration of electronics companies, whereas industrial specialisation in the Klang Valley, Johor and other industrial parts of Malaysia is less marked. Nevertheless, the principle of close liaison between firms and government/business-association-inspired training initiatives is now firmly accepted, and, although the business associations in Malaysia have not been geared up to play a 'corporatist' role, some steps have been taken recently (in the plastics and the textiles/apparel industries – see MITI 1994: 86) to strengthen business associations.

The longer term: new entrants for existing industries

It is clear then that, with the formation of the HRDC in 1992, Malaysia has been making good progress with in-service training, which, in the short run, should have the highest priority. When we come to look at the longer term and at new entrants to the labour force, the issues are quite different. It is clear, from the experiences of the OECD countries and from studies of the social rate of return from education, that the lower levels of education (primary and secondary) are extremely important. In this respect, Malaysia's record would appear to be good (see Table 10.4), although the education system in Malaysia is criticised for continuing to have an excessive bias towards the arts subjects (see MITI 1994: 108 and World Bank 1995: 91).

Table 10.4 Selected Asian countries: enrolment ratios, 1985

Country	% of relevant age-group enrolled			Per capita GNP (1995) (US$)
	Primary	Secondary	Higher	
Bangladesh	60	18	5	220
India	92	41	9	320
Sri Lanka	103	63	5	640
Indonesia	118	42	7	880
Philippines	106	65	33	950
Thailand	97	30	20	2410
Malaysia	99	53	6*	3480
South Korea	96	75	32	8260
Singapore	115	71	11	22500

Source: World Bank 1995: 23 and 1996: Table 1
Note: * Malaysia's enrolment at the higher-education level rose to just under 9 per cent if students studying overseas are included

At the higher levels of education, it is clear that if the system is to be responsive to the needs of existing industries, it needs to be well integrated with them. On the other hand, if the path to this is thought to be privatisation of the higher education system, as advocated by the World Bank (1995), then the accreditation issue becomes all-important. For young people to make the necessary sacrifices in training and education, they have to be assured that their training will be recognised. This means that their training must lead to qualifications that will be accepted by potential employers. This is particularly true of vocational skills for new entrants where the recognition of qualifications becomes a major issue. In this respect, the co-ordination and accreditation bodies – the recently created National Vocational Training Council (NVTC) and Higher Education Council – play a vital role. If the policy is not right at this level, the system will be under considerable strain. In its 1995 report, the World Bank (1995: 92) argued that the NVTC needs to be given more staff and powers to be effective, and it raises the possibility that a National Vocational Training Law (similar to that in Singapore) be enacted to give the NVTC more clout.

The longer term: new entrants for new industries

When we come to consider the problem of *new* entrants for *new* industries, the situation becomes even more complicated. On the supply side, transferable skills and 'creativity' become more important, and the emphasis should be on filling the gaps at the higher end of the skills spectrum. However, Malaysia has no equivalent of the High-end Skills Programme, which was introduced in Singapore in 1993 and was designed to support the government's cluster development strategy (see SDF 1994/95: 16). Such a programme should be considered in Malaysia to more effectively support the cluster approach adopted by the Second Industrial Master Plan (published at the end of 1996). (The principles of targeting and of a selective industrial policy have been endorsed in the Review of the IMP – see MITI (1994: 29) as well as the Second Industrial Master Plan for 1996–2005.)

Summary on skills provision

In the 1990s, Malaysia has taken great steps forward in the development of institutions for the supply of skills. This is particularly true when we look at the immediate problem of the training and retraining of the *existing* labour force. Questions remain unanswered at the level of new entrants, both for existing industries and for new industries, but good progress has been made in policy on skills provision for the immediate future in Malaysia. By contrast, considerable problems are posed by the import of unskilled foreign labour, which is discussed in the next section.

Unskilled foreign labour and the Malaysian economy

Much concern, but little analysis, in official circles

As stated earlier, a drive towards industrial maturity has been in full swing since 1990 with the launching of the Second Outline Perspective Plan (see OPP2 1991; also Rasiah 1997). At the same time, there has been a heavy reliance on imported foreign labour, with most of it being semi-skilled or unskilled.

In 1997, this issue was very much in the news, but its prominent position in the newspapers contrasted with reflective neglect in official policy discussions. In the newspapers, in 1996, the issue of 'illegal settlements' being set up by or for unskilled foreign labour was particularly prominent. In March 1996, the Selangor State government was reported as identifying eight illegal settlements – covering 23 hectares – in the Hulu Langat district, south of Kuala Lumpur – which it had ordered to be torn down (*Star*, 21 March 1996). A few days later, the demolition of an illegal settlement by the Ampang Jaya Municipal Council, east of Kuala Lumpur, was given much publicity (see *New Straits Times* (*NST*), 24 March 1996). However, on the next day, the Mentri Besar of Perlis State in the north of the Peninsula was reported as saying that the state government had no plans to evict immigrants from an illegal immigrant settlement at a FELDA (Federal Land Development Authority) scheme at Mata Ayer, as FELDA settlers there were facing a labour shortage (see *NST*, 25 March 1996).

This inconsistency in the policy on 'illegal settlements' by foreign labour more generally reflects the inconsistency of government policy in the 1980s and 1990s towards the entry and role of unskilled foreign labour in Malaysia – a point which has been emphasised by Azizah (1995, 1996), Pillai (1992, 1995) and the World Bank (1995: 79). In the 1996 Budget, levies imposed by the government on the employment of foreigners were doubled, but this increase is likely to stimulate the illegal flow of workers coming into Malaysia, unless stringent penalties are imposed and enforced on the employers of such labour.

The policy inconsistency is perhaps not surprising considering how little official *analysis* there has been of the problem of unskilled foreign labour. This lack of *analysis* is in sharp contrast with the official *concern* that has been expressed about the problem. For example, the annual Economic Report on the Malaysian economy stated that:

> The labour market continues to tighten in 1995 with the economy virtually operating at full employment. This has resulted in significant employment turnover as well as pinching of staff, leading to wage pressures. While the Government has allowed the recruitment of foreign labour to ease the labour shortage, this measure cannot be sustained on a long-term basis as the size of foreign labour is already large, estimated at more than 1.2 million against the nation's total work force of about 8 million.
>
> (Ministry of Finance 1995: 39)

As we shall see, the figure of 1.2 million is probably an underestimate. However, even at this level there are seen to be major problems, as the MoF Report went on to point out:

> A prolonged reliance on foreign labour can generate social and political problems as well as give a wrong signal to industries that they can continue to rely on foreign labour without having to undertake strategic adjustments in moving towards labour-saving production technology.
>
> (Ministry of Finance 1995: 39)

Other official sources also express concern with the large-scale use of unskilled foreign labour, but there has been little detailed analysis of the role and the positive and negative effects of foreign labour (whether legal or illegal) on the economy. Bank Negara's 1995 Annual Report also expressed concern about unskilled foreign labour being an obstacle to upgrading, but again there was no detailed analysis of the problem. Similarly, the Mid-Term Review of the Sixth Malaysia Plan, issued in December 1993, described the share of foreign workers as already high and stated that 'the use of foreign labour should not be regarded as a permanent solution to overcome the tight labour market situation' (EPU 1993: 52). However, once again, no further analysis was presented. Most recently, the Seventh Malaysia Plan,

1996–2000 also expressed concern about the use of foreign labour when it stated that:

> As a short term measure the government has allowed the import of foreign labour for certain sectors of the economy to relieve the problem of labour shortages. However, the long term solution to this problem lies in utilising labour more efficiently and productively. This would require reducing the demand for labour through labour-saving techniques and processes. In this regard, the nation must move up the ladder of production from labour-intensive and assembly type of processes towards more capital- and technology-intensive as well as knowledge-based industries and processes.
>
> (EPU 1996: 7)

However, once again, there was no detailed analysis of the effects on the economy of imported foreign labour. In the remainder of this section, I attempt to do this by looking at the effects of unskilled foreign labour on the restructuring of the Malaysian economy – to see, in other words, the extent to which the import of foreign labour is an aid or an obstacle to bringing about a 'strategic shift' in the economy. However, it is important to first define immigrant labour and to discuss the growth and size of the problem.

Unskilled foreign labour

In Malaysia there is a distinction between 'expatriate' labour and other foreign labour. 'Expatriate' labour is skilled, technical and professional workers earning RM1200 more per month who are issued with Employment Passes (*Pas Penggajian*). Unskilled and semi-skilled foreign workers are issued with Temporary Visit Work Passes (*Pas Lawatan Kerja Sementara*) (see Pillai 1995: 228).

Work passes are issued in Peninsular Malaysia by the Department of Immigration, but in East Malaysia, immigration is under the responsibility of the Sabah and Sarawak State Governments, and for immigration into East Malaysia less detailed figures are available (Pillai 1992: 15). In general, work passes are valid for three years (initially, for two, and extendible for a further one) and are not renewable (except for maids). Permits are given only for individual workers, not for families (see Pillai 1995: 228). Delays by the Ministry of Human Resources and the Immigration Department in processing permit applications have been long (up to two years), and in October 1994 a one-stop Task Force was set up to speed up the process. The only regularly published data on immigrant workers in industries are in the Establishment Surveys, although the number of foreign workers is thought to be understated in these surveys (see World Bank 1995: 61).

Foreign labour in the Malaysian economy

There is a long history of the import of foreign labour into Malaysia. Under British colonialism, labour was imported to work in the tin mining and rubber estate sectors (see Edwards 1977). In general, following Independence in 1957, information on foreign labour imports was sparse until the 1990s. In 1968, the Employment Restrictions Act required employers in certain identified sectors to obtain work permits for their foreign workers, and this resulted in the removal of a 'large number' of Indian and Chinese workers (Nayagam 1992: 478). However, this had little effect on production because of the labour surplus in the economy at the time and because a switch was being made from rubber to the relatively less labour-intensive oil palm.

In the 1980s, 'labour shortages' emerged, and the 1987/88 *Labour and Manpower Report* of the Ministry of Human Resources stated that in the mid-1980s there were about half a million illegal migrants in Malaysia (see Nayagam 1992: 479). Other estimates of 'illegals' for the mid-1980s ranged between half a million and a million (Nayagam 1992: 479).

By the early 1990s, Nayagam estimated that there were more than a million immigrants in Malaysia, most of them illegal and with the total being split more or less evenly between Peninsular and East Malaysia (Nayagam 1992: 479). For 1991, the World Bank's estimate of foreign labour was 1.14 million (World Bank 1995: 59), whereas the Seventh Malaysia Plan gave a figure for 'other, non-citizen' workers in Malaysia of 407,000 in 1990 (EPU 1996: 78, 79).

The estimates of foreign labour in Malaysia in 1995/96 vary even more widely. As noted earlier the Ministry of Finance estimated the total number of foreign workers in Malaysia in 1995 at about 1.2 million. The same total, consisting of half a million 'legals' and between 500,000 and 700,000 'illegals', has been estimated by Azizah Kassim (see *NST*, 5 April 1996). Other estimates of foreign labour in the mid-1990s vary from 0.5 million to 2.5 million. The US Embassy's economic report on Malaysia in 1994 put the number of foreign workers at 2 million, with half of these being illegals (see World Bank 1995: 61, footnote). A report for the Ministry of Human Resources by consultants at the University of Malaya estimated total foreign labour in 1993/94 to be 1.04 million, or about 14 per cent of total employment, which was given as 7.6 million (see UPUM 1995: 1). It seems that the UPUM estimate is for Malaysia as a whole, rather than just Peninsular Malaysia, even though the UPUM report mainly discussed foreign labour in Peninsular Malaysia. In September 1994, the number of Temporary Visit Work Passes issued and current for unskilled and semi-skilled foreign workers was 563,000 (Pillai 1995: 228). If we add about 61,000 'expatriates', then the total number of 'legals' was about 624,000. If we further assume that the legals are about 33 to 40 per cent of the total, then the total number of foreign workers in Malaysia was about 1.7 million in 1995.

Of the 'legals' referred to by Pillai (1995: 230), a breakdown by *country* source was only available for 339,000. Of these, 66 per cent come from Indonesia, 23 per cent from Bangladesh and about 7 per cent from the Philippines (Pillai 1995: 230). A majority of the 'illegals' in Peninsular Malaysia (but not in Sabah – see Pillai 1992: 15) is thought to come from Indonesia. An analysis by *sector* is available for 490,000 foreign workers, with 30 per cent issued passes for construction, 8 per cent for manufacturing, 30 per cent for plantations and 20 per cent for others (mostly 'domestic maids') (see Pillai 1995: 229). Just over half the 'legals' had their passes issued in Kuala Lumpur (see Pillai 1995: 228). As of September 1994, just over 60,000 passes had been issued for Sabah and Sarawak, but it is estimated that the total number of foreign workers in Sabah alone was about half a million.

The Seventh Malaysia Plan gave a figure of 650,000 for foreigners in the labour force in Malaysia in 1995 (EPU 1996: 110). It is clear then that there are wide-ranging estimates of foreign labour working in Malaysia over the past decade. In this paper, I use the following estimates: for 1985, 500,000; for 1990, one million; and for 1995, 1.7 million. If these estimates are reasonably accurate, it means that foreign workers were just under 20 per cent of total employment in 1995, compared to about 14 per cent in 1990.

If the figures for the total employment of foreign labour are difficult to pin down, this is even more true of the sectoral composition of foreign labour. Within the agriculture, forestry and fishing sector, foreign labour is thought to be most prevalent in the estate sector, although there are various reports of the use of foreign labour in rice cultivation (see, for example, Ikmal 1992). For example, Thai workers are reported to migrate into northern Malaysia seasonally to work on the rice and sugar harvests, while their employers do not pay the foreign worker levy on this 'seasonal' labour (World Bank 1995: 63).

There were reports of 'labour shortages' in the plantation sector from the late 1970s as plantation owners released details of shortages they claimed to face (see World Bank 1995: 71). Labour turnover was high, with United Planters Association of Malaysia (UPAM) estates losing over a fifth of their workforce in 1985 (Narayanan 1992: 4). The shortages and the high turnover were in the face of the relatively high unemployment of the early 1980s, so it is hardly surprising that with the relatively full employment of the early 1990s, the shortages became even more acute. In the 1980s, the average wages of rubber tappers and oil-palm harvesters were not far below unskilled wage rates in industry (see Narayanan 1992: Table 3) but the wages were less assured and work conditions were considered to be inferior on the estates (Narayanan 1992: 5).

The Seventh Malaysia Plan estimated that the foreign labour in the agriculture, forestry and fishing sector in 1990 was 175,000, or about 10 per cent of the total labour force (see EPU 1996: 78, 79). In 1990, Narayanan (1992: 7) estimated that foreign labour made up about 10 per cent of the agricultural workforce, but if forestry is included the percentage is almost certainly higher. In 1995, the estimate by the Seventh Malaysia Plan of foreign labour in the sector was 273,000, or about 19 per cent of the 1.43 million total (EPU 1996: 78, 79). This seems to be an underestimate, and it is likely that the foreign labour force (including illegals) in the agriculture, forestry and fishing sector is between 30 and 40 per cent of a sectoral total of 1.8 million, with a very high 'illegal' proportion.

By contrast, in the manufacturing sector, the proportion of 'illegals' in the foreign labour force is widely thought to be relatively small, though increasing. Industries reported to be using significant proportions of foreign labour are electronics, textiles, machinery and engineering, non-metallic and mineral products and wood-based industries. A 1995 report by MITI estimated the proportion of foreign workers to be 10 per cent of the total in 1993. For 1995, the Seventh Malaysia Plan's (7MP) estimate was 7 per cent of the total (EPU 1996: 78, 79). My estimate is 13 per cent of a total manufacturing labour force of 2.2 million.

Acute labour shortages were said to be faced by the construction industry in the late 1970s and early 1980s (Gill 1988: 228), and immigrant labour was increasingly used. In 1987, the Construction Workers Union (CWU) estimated that about 60 per cent of the total workers in the industry were foreign (Gill 1988: 227), though the Establishment Survey paints a different picture, with non-Malaysians given as only 15 per cent of the workforce throughout the 1980s (World Bank 1995: 73). However, recent estimates are even higher than the proportion claimed by the CWU, with the proportion said to be as much as 80 per cent, at least of the unskilled and semi-skilled portion, whereas the 7MP's estimate for 1995 was 14 per cent (EPU 1996: 78, 79). The 7MP's estimate would seem to be far too low, and a more reasonable estimate of foreign labour in the construction industry is between 30 per cent and 40 per cent of a total workforce of just under 900,000.

The picture of the employment of foreign labour in the other sectors of the economy is even more hazy than in the agriculture, forestry and fishing, manufacturing and construction sectors. In mining and quarrying and the utilities (electricity, gas and water), the number of foreign workers is thought to be negligible. The Seventh Malaysia Plan gives the number of foreign workers in the transport, storage and communications sector as about 5 per cent of total employment in the sector. This is almost certainly an underestimate, with the truer percentage being about 15 per cent. In the wholesale and retail trade sector, the Seventh Malaysia Plan estimates foreign workers at 6 per cent, again probably an underestimate, with 15 per cent being more realistic. By contrast, the Seventh Malaysia Plan's estimate for the finance sector is probably about right at 3 per cent.

The net effect is that the number of foreign workers in all sectors other than the agriculture, forestry and fishing, manufacturing and construction sectors is probably about half a million workers – or about 12 per cent of total employment in those sectors – whereas the 7MP's estimate is about 200,000 workers (or about 7 per cent).

It is clear that there is considerable uncertainty about the number of foreign workers in the various sectors of the economy and in the Malaysian labour force as a whole. However, from my research, it seems likely that the total foreign employment figure of 1.2 million in the 1995/96 Report of the Ministry of Finance is a considerable understatement, as is the total foreign employment figure of 0.7 million given in the Seventh Malaysia Plan. As stated above, a more reliable estimate for 1995 would seem to be 1.7 million.

251

Factors determining migration

Clearly there are 'push' and 'pull' factors. As far as migrants from Indonesia (by far, the biggest source of supply of foreign workers) are concerned, the 'push' factor is the growing difference in income between Indonesia and Malaysia. In 1994, the average per capita GNP (at official exchange rates) of Malaysia was about four times as high as that of Indonesia (World Bank 1996: Table 1). The gap in average annual per capita incomes was US$2600.

Since the Malaysian economy has grown only slightly more slowly than Indonesia's during 1985–94, the absolute gap in per capita incomes of the two countries has increased by something like US$1000. The growing gap explains the 'push' factor, but the rapid growth in Malaysia and a growing labour shortage provide 'pull' factors. One indication of the labour shortage in Malaysia is the rate of unemployment, which fell from about 8 per cent in 1970 to just under 6 per cent in the early 1980s, to 5 per cent in 1990 and the 1995 figure of just under 3 per cent (see Pillai 1992: 1; Ministry of Finance 1995: Table 6.1). Equally importantly, alongside this drop in 'open' unemployment, there was probably a sharp fall in under-employment. By the mid-1990s the Malaysian economy was at full employment, with the unemployment rate representing 'frictional' unemployment.

These pressures in the Malaysian labour market mean that there is pressure in the system for employers to employ illegal foreign labour and to dodge the levies and charges incurred in the employment of legal foreign labour. And, of course, from the viewpoint of migrants, there is a similar incentive to dodge the admission procedures and authorised recruitment channels and to enter the labour force illegally – for details of levies, charges and procedures, see Azizah (1996), Pillai (1992, 1995), World Bank (1995: 38, 39) and *NST*, 5 April 1996.

However, it is worth emphasising that the figures are sketchy and the information on foreign employment unreliable. This matters not only because the import of foreign labour is an important issue, but also because the unreliability of the employment figures adversely affects estimates of productivity.

One important objective of a strategic shift should presumably be to increase labour productivity. Unfortunately, one effect that the understatement of employment figures may have is to overestimate the growth in labour productivity. For example, in the Seventh Malaysia Plan (EPU 1996: 116), it is stated that (for the period of the Sixth Malaysia Plan from 1991 to 1995): 'For the economy as a whole, labour productivity, as measured by Gross Domestic Product (GDP) per worker in constant 1978 prices, increased by 5.1 per cent per annum'. This compared with an average of only 3.3 per cent during 1986–90. Again, according to the Seventh Malaysia Plan, the productivity growth in the services sector was 5.9 per cent per annum between 1991 and 1995 compared to 1.8 per cent between 1986 and 1990.

However, as we have seen, there are good reasons to think that the figures for the employment of foreigners in Malaysia have been understated in the past decade, and, consequently, it is almost certain that the total employment figures have also been understated. If we assume that the GDP figures are accurate, then it follows that labour productivity will have been overstated. Some revised estimates are shown in Table 10.5.

Table 10.5 Malaysia: labour productivity, 1985–95

	1985	1990	1995
GDP (RM billion, 1978 prices)[a]	57.1	79.4	120.3
Employment ('000)[b]		6686	7915
Labour productivity (RM '000/employee)		11.9	15.2
Growth in labour productivity (% pa, 1990–95)			5.1
Growth in labour productivity (% pa, 1986–90)[c]		3.3	
Labour productivity in 1985 implied by 1986–90 annual productivity growth (RM '000/employee)	10.1		
Employment in 1985 implied by productivity growth	5653		
Foreign labour in official sources[d] ('000)	0	290	650
Revised estimate of foreign labour ('000)	500	1000	1700
Revised total employment estimate ('000)	6153	7396	8965
Revised labour productivity (RM '000/employee)	9.3	10.7	13.4
Revised labour productivity growth (% pa, 1990–95)			4.6
Revised labour productivity growth (% pa, 1986–90)		3.0	

Sources: (a) GDP: for 1985, see Ministry of Finance 1995: Table 2–1; for 1990 and 1995, see EPU 1996: Table 4–2.
(b) Employment; for 1990 and 1995, see EPU 1996: Table 3–2.
(c) Growth in labour productivity for 1986–90, see EPU 1996: 116.
(d) Foreign labour, 1990 and 1995 from EPU 1996: Table 3–2; estimated for 1985.
All other figures derived

The growth in labour productivity between 1985 and 1990 falls slightly to 3.0 per cent per annum (the understatements by official sources for labour totals for 1985 and 1990 to some extent cancel each other out) but the growth rate for the 1990–95 period falls from 5.1 per cent to 4.6 per cent per annum. Similarly, the Seventh Malaysia Plan's estimate of total factor productivity for 1990–95 at 2.5 per cent per annum (EPU 1996: 37) is probably between half and one per cent too high, bringing it down closer to the estimated average for 1971–90 of 1.2 per cent per annum.

Thus, the effect on total factor and labour productivity growth is considerable. This matters because the growth in labour productivity defines what I call the 'indigenous labour sustainable rate of growth' (ILSROG) in total GDP, where ILSROG is the rate of GDP growth which avoids a significant increase in the import of foreign labour. Thus, if labour productivity is running at a little over 4 per cent per annum, then ILSROG will be a little over 4 per cent per annum plus the growth in the (Malaysian-citizen) labour force. The latter is probably a little over 2 per cent per annum (see EPU 1996: 105), so that the ILSROG is probably between 6.5 per cent and 7 per cent per annum compared to the actual average growth of 8.7 per cent per annum in the Sixth Malaysia Plan period (EPU 1996: 4).

253

Every one per cent growth in GDP over and above the ILSROG will draw in foreign labour at the same proportion of the labour force, namely 1 per cent. An increase of 1 per cent in the labour force is about 90,000 workers, which is equivalent to an increase of 5 per cent in the 1995 foreign labour force. *Thus, if real GDP continues to grow at just under 9 per cent per annum over the five years between 1996 and 2000 inclusive, this will be about 2 per cent per annum above the ILSROG, and at this rate the foreign labour force is likely to grow at something like 180,000 a year, or by almost a million over the five years. At this rate, by the year 2000 foreign workers would make up over a quarter of the total labour force in Malaysia of about 10.6 million.*

Effects of foreign labour

Such a growth in the import of foreign labour is an obvious cause for concern in social, political and infrastructural terms. *Less obviously, while promoting the growth of the economy in the short run, the import of unskilled foreign labour may be an obstacle to the restructuring of the economy, and therefore an obstacle to long-run growth.* This section focuses on these effects, but, first, we look at the following more general assertions about the role and effects of foreign labour:

1   foreign labour is *harmful* because of the strain imposed on physical infrastructure and social services (housing, medical services, etc.), and because it uses these services without paying for them;

2   foreign labour is *harmful* because of its depressing effect on the wages of the poorer, unskilled households in Malaysia and the likelihood that it will increase income inequalities;

3   foreign labour is *beneficial* since it expands the domestic market for goods and services and is more likely to enable economies of scale to be achieved in the Malaysian economy;

4   foreign labour is *beneficial* because by providing cheap labour in the non-traded-goods sectors, it lowers the relative prices of these goods and therefore makes the production of traded goods more internationally competitive. On the other hand, it is considered *harmful* because by lowering the price of unskilled labour, it discourages structural upgrading of the economy;

5   foreign labour is *beneficial* because it serves as a counter-cyclical instrument in the Malaysian economy, dampening wage and price inflation during boom times, but 'exportable' during recessions, thus reducing the social and political strains associated with recession;

6   foreign labour is *beneficial* since the value-added generated by it far outweighs the remittances paid overseas;

7   foreign labour may cause *harmful* political effects in as much as it is deliberately used to change the ethnic and political 'balance' of the population.

Discussion of arguments 1, 5, 6 and 7 can be found in other sources such as Pillai (1992: 16–21), Pillai (1995: 231, 232) and World Bank (1995: 64–70). The

World Bank's estimate is that foreign workers generated something like 12 per cent of Malaysia's GDP in 1993, with their contribution being less than their proportion in the labour force because of their concentration in relatively low-value-added activities (World Bank 1995: 64). On the assumptions that 1.7 million foreign workers receive an average RM300 a month and that they remit, on average, one-third of this, their remittances overseas would amount to RM2 billion a year – see also Pillai (1995: 231). However, in connection with this, three points need to be emphasised:

- first, this does not constitute a loss to the economy since the foreign workers' contribution to value-added far outweighs this remittance total (see assertion 6);
- secondly, these remittances do not necessarily represent net savings for the foreign workers since the remittances are wholly or in part used to repay recruiting agents in the labour-exporting country;
- thirdly, even the balance of payments effects may be positive, both because of the foreign workers' contributions to exports or import substitutes and because part of the remittances may be spent on goods produced in Malaysia.

The World Bank reverses the argument that foreign workers make use of public services without paying for them (see assertion 1) by pointing out that insofar as foreign workers have received an education in their 'home' countries, it is the Malaysian economy which is not paying the full costs of labour reproduction (see World Bank 1995: 70). We are left with assertions 2 and 4, two aspects that are relatively neglected.

It is hard to see that the effect of the import of foreign workers on *income distribution* in Malaysia will be anything but harmful. The overwhelming majority of foreign workers are unskilled, and as such they are likely to depress the wages of unskilled workers in Malaysia relative to those of the skilled. This is likely to be the case even though there is evidence of some labour market segmentation, with foreign workers being paid less for the same job than Malaysian citizens (Pillai 1992: 18).[1] Indeed, there *is* already some evidence in Malaysia of widening differentials between the average wages of skilled and unskilled labour (see World Bank 1995: ii; Narayanan 1992: 31); between 1990 and 1995, income distribution worsened, with the Gini coefficient rising from 0.446 in 1990 to 0.464 in 1995.[2] These are the income distribution effects to be expected from the imports of unskilled foreign labour. However, the main focus of this section is on assertion 4 – that is, on the effects of unskilled foreign labour on the longer-term restructuring of the economy.

Effects on investment and economic restructuring

The first basic and very simple proposition is that foreign labour is used in Malaysian production because the employers employing the foreign labour make a greater rate of profit than if they did not employ them. There are two effects of this that are important to distinguish. *First*, there is an effect through the capital

CHRIS EDWARDS

investment used for capacity expansion in the economy, since it may be that the import of unskilled foreign labour raises the average rate of profit and the incentive to invest. *Second*, there will be an effect through the capital investment used to 'modernise' existing capacity, and it may be that by shifting the rate of profit in favour of low-value-added (per employee) and low-skill-intensive investments, the investment pattern will not be consistent with a strategic shift in the Malaysian economy. Neither of these two effects is easy to identify.

To bring about a strategic shift in the economy, Malaysia has to raise its international competitiveness in the higher-value-added activities. This means that higher-value-added activities have to be profitable *relative* to lower-value-added activities. This is because of the basic economic proposition that Malaysia cannot be internationally competitive in *all* goods and services. All producers in all countries produce according to comparative advantage that is revealed in the form of competitive advantage. These comparative/competitive advantages are a function of the endowments and capabilities (both natural and created) in the country. Some writers (see Wood 1994) assert that financial capital is internationally mobile so that the determining endowments/capabilities are skilled and unskilled labour. So, at any one time, we have an international pattern of comparative/competitive advantages determined by labour/technology capabilities, with the pattern tending to change over time. The pattern may be slow to change, depending on the speed of exit and entry from and to particular industries, and because of the learning (and unlearning) curves in different industries (see Krugman 1987).

It is likely that the import of unskilled foreign labour will affect relative rates of profit as well as the overall level of profit, but the nature of that change will be determined by all the various factors determining profitability, which will include the cost of finance, the cost of labour and infrastructure, and the incentive structure determined by the government. Unfortunately, there seems to be little or no analysis of the rate of profit in different sectors of the Malaysian economy (see Edwards 1995: 40 for 1987 figures for the manufacturing sector only) and of the factors determining it.

It is clear that in general, the rate of profit must have been attractive to generate a high ratio (around 40 per cent in the 1990s at least until 1997) of Gross Domestic Capital Formation (GDCF) to GDP, with most of it (about two-thirds between 1990 and 1995 – see Ministry of Finance 1995: Table 2.1) coming from private sources. And of the private investment, just over a third came from overseas between 1991 and 1995 inclusive (see Ministry of Finance 1995: 19). This high ratio of (mostly private) investment to GDP must reflect a high and sustained rate of profit, although the factors sustaining that rate of profit are not clear.

As we have seen, labour productivity has risen quite sharply in recent years, even when it is adjusted for the revised employment figures. But so has capital input, so that total factor productivity (TFP) growth is claimed to have been low. For the period between 1987 and 1993, the World Bank gives an average figure of 0.9 per cent per annum (see World Bank 1995: para. 3). (This is very much lower than the average of 2.5 per cent per annum given in the Seventh Malaysia Plan for the 1991–95 period,

256

but we have already seen that this TFP growth estimate is almost certainly overstated because of the understatement of the employment of foreign labour.)

Nevertheless, what matters more than TFP growth for the rate of profit of investors is the change in unit labour costs. According to the World Bank (1995: 6), unit labour costs seem to have been more or less constant for the manufacturing sector between 1986 and 1991, and yet, this is hard to reconcile with a comparison of wage increases and labour productivity over the same period. For example, between 1987 and 1991, the real wage rate of unskilled manufacturing workers rose by 4.9 per cent, or by about 1 per cent a year, while that of the semi-skilled rose by 9.7 per cent or about 2 per cent per annum (see World Bank 1995: 10). Such rises were slower than the rise in labour productivity over the same period. Furthermore, the Seventh Malaysia Plan talks about a trend of declining unit labour costs in Malaysia over the period between 1991 and 1995 (EPU 1996: 116).

So, declining unit labour costs may have sustained or even raised the rate of profit. What role has the incentive structure played? This is not at all clear. It seems that the government has not significantly changed the incentive structure through tariff protection and taxes over the 1990–95 period, at least for the manufacturing sector, although no study of effective rate of protection (ERP) has been done in the 1990s (see MITI 1994: 36). The average of import duty revenue to imports has declined from 10 per cent in 1980 to 5 per cent in 1990 and 1995, but, of course, this average is not a good indication of the level of protection. Changes in corporate taxation are likely to be a relatively unimportant incentive since they affect the net rate of profit and do not determine whether a profit is made in the first place.

Table 10.6 Malaysian ringgit: real effective exchange rate, 1960–95

	1965: 100	*1985: 100*	*1990: 100*
1960	125		219
1965	100		175
1970	81		142
1975	76		133
1980	82		143
1985	85	100	149
1986		84	125
1987		80	119
1988		72	107
1989		71	105
1990			100
1991			97
1992			103
1993			103
1994			100
1995 (June)			99

Sources: Edwards 1995: Table 4; IMF, *International Financial Statistics*, August 1990 and December 1995

Note: A rise in the index represents a real appreciation in the ringgit relative to Malaysia's trading partners. A fall denotes a devaluation.

Thus, the international competitiveness of the Malaysian economy in general and of the manufacturing sector in particular does not seem to have been changed much through state protection (i.e. through tax and tariff incentives) in the past decade. Nor has it been significantly affected by Malaysia pricing itself into the international market through changes in the real effective exchange rate. As Table 10.6 shows, the ringgit was sharply devalued (in real terms and with respect to trading partners) between 1960 and 1970, and again between 1985 and 1988, but since 1988 there has been little change in the real effective exchange rate. Thus, Malaysia's competitiveness in the first half of the 1990s was not achieved through a significant devaluation of the ringgit.

As stated, no detailed analysis or decomposition of the rate of profit in Malaysia seems to be available. However, it seems that unit labour costs have been important, and *it is likely that labour markets (including the import of unskilled foreign labour) have played a significant role in maintaining a high rate of profit in Malaysia. In this sense, the import of unskilled foreign labour may have been a stimulus to investment in the economy.*

On the other hand, the import of unskilled foreign labour is likely to have had a harmful effect in terms of the *direction* of investment. The import of unskilled foreign labour is probably shifting the investment incentive away from higher-value-added, more skill-intensive activities towards low-value-added, low-skill-intensive activities. Thus, it is the *relative* rates of profit which are also important, but much more research than has been possible for this chapter is needed to estimate the effects of foreign labour on the *pattern* of investment in the Malaysian economy, since the picture becomes very complicated when we consider indirect effects of the import of unskilled foreign labour, such as the effects which work through the exchange rate and through the prices of non-traded goods.

The exchange rate effect

It may be that unskilled foreign labour, if used intensively in the production of goods with a high net export or import-substitution component, will raise the exchange rate *above what it would otherwise be*, and to that extent will discourage the production of new, high-value-added goods for export. Thus, the availability of relatively low-wage, unskilled labour may have a Dutch disease effect[3] insofar as the unskilled foreign labour is in high net export-earning industries.

One example of this is palm oil, which is a commodity with a very high net export content. The availability of cheap foreign labour for harvesting the palm fruit is likely to keep the production of palm oil above what it would otherwise be, at least in the short run. This will have a knock-on effect, raising the exchange rate above what it would otherwise be.

On the other hand, in the longer run, the availability of cheap foreign labour may have a number of effects that impede the industry's survival insofar as they are an obstacle to the introduction of mechanisation and therefore higher productivity. About a third of the cost of palm oil (from the factory mill) consists of harvesting costs. These consist of the cost of cutting the fruit bunches and of transporting them to the factory. According to economists in the Palm Oil Research Institute of Malaysia (PORIM) and in the Ministry of Primary Industries, there is considerable potential for the mechanisation of fruit collection (using what are called 'mechanical monkeys' or 'grabs') and for fruit transport (using what are called 'mechanical buffaloes'), but the efficient use of such mechanisation requires more research and, in some cases, the redesign of planting on the 'inside' of terraces. The availability of relatively cheap foreign labour is likely to be a deterrent to this research and redesign.

Thus, in the short run, the availability of low-wage unskilled foreign labour may help to maintain a high rate of profit in growing oil palms but, in the long run, by discouraging mechanisation, may impede the upgrading of the palm oil industry. Thus, when the indirect effects on palm oil production through the exchange rate are considered, the picture becomes very complicated.[4]

In addition, it should be noted that if unskilled foreign labour is available to other labour-intensive manufacturing industries (e.g. electronics and textiles), it will not necessarily have the same indirect effect through the exchange rate insofar as these industries have a lower *net* export content.

The effect on non-traded goods as inputs

There is an important second indirect effect of the availability of relatively low-wage unskilled foreign labour. This works through the prices of non-tradeables that are, ultimately, inputs into internationally traded goods. A real exchange rate devaluation raises the (home-currency) prices of internationally traded goods relative to those of non-traded goods.[5] To put this another way, the relative prices of non-traded goods fall with devaluation.

However, the same effect may happen through a different path. Thus, by unskilled foreign labour being employed in non-traded-goods industries, the cost and (relative) price of non-traded goods may be below what they would otherwise be. If so, the effect may be to act as the *equivalent* of a devaluation of the ringgit.

Unfortunately, this effect is even more difficult to trace empirically than the other effects (such as the investment diversion effects). For a start, there are many different non-traded goods and services in which foreign workers are employed. Secondly, there must be considerable doubt as to whether low-wage labour actually reduces the prices of all or even most non-traded goods. The following paragraphs consider three categories of non-traded goods (construction, retail and wholesale trade services and domestic services), if only to highlight the problems rather than to provide answers.

First, as we have seen, one major sector in which foreign labour is employed is the *construction* industry. Unfortunately, this includes a diverse collection of 'goods' including the construction of housing and offices, transport infrastructure (roads, rail services and ports) and 'environmental' infrastructure (gas, electricity, water, drainage and sewerage). To trace the effects of unskilled foreign labour through each of these is difficult, but at this stage one general point can be made, namely that there is no assurance that the low wages of foreign labour will be reflected in lower *prices* of these non-traded goods, even if their production *costs* are lowered. Indeed, given the lack of competition in the production of these goods in Malaysia, there may be little or no effect on the prices of non-traded goods. For even if the construction industry itself is potentially competitive, the price of the final good may not be lower. Instead, the lower costs may simply be reflected in exceptionally high profit rates accruing to those lucky enough to get planning permission and licences, given that the market for many of the goods and services produced by the construction industry are highly 'regulated', though not necessarily in favour of national capital (see Gomez 1994 and Jomo 1994). However, it is interesting to note that Narayanan (1992: 14) has claimed that improvements in construction techniques may *not* be held back by the availability of cheap foreign labour. He argues that new techniques are stimulated by the contractors having to meet tight delivery deadlines.

By contrast, in the *retail and wholesale trade* services, it may well be that the availability of foreign labour does keep down *both the costs and prices* of the services. On the other hand, the availability of unskilled foreign labour is likely to deter the pace of reorganisation in the industry in the longer term by making self-service facilities (e.g. petrol pumps and food supermarkets) relatively less profitable and/or more risky. Thus, in the longer run, the costs and prices may be higher than otherwise.

Thirdly, unskilled foreign labour used in *domestic service* may be said to add to the labour force in two ways – partly as an addition in themselves, but also by encouraging an increase in the participation of Malaysian women in the labour force. However, two points need to be made. First, some of the labour that is recorded as coming in as domestic service is used in other services (e.g. to help in shop services – see Azizah 1996) and secondly, there are alternative methods of providing the services, particularly in the biggest household task of child-rearing. Such alternatives are crèches at places of employment and/or infant schools.[6]

Conclusions

Vision 2020 and labour markets in Malaysia

It is clear that economic growth in Malaysia up to 1997 was rapid; indeed, between 1985 and 1994, Malaysia's growth in per capita income (at 5.6 per cent per annum) was the ninth highest in the world after Thailand (8.6 per cent), China (7.8 per cent), South Korea (7.8 per cent), Botswana (6.6 per cent), Chile (6.5 per cent), Singapore (6.1 per cent), Indonesia (6.0 per cent) and Mauritius (5.8 per cent). Projecting Malaysia's growth record up to 1997 forward over the next quarter of a century suggested that Malaysia would be a developed country before the year 2020 – as envisioned by the Prime Minister in 1991.

However, the basic theme running through this chapter is that labour markets in Malaysia may prevent the realisation of this vision. It is widely recognised in both official and unofficial commentaries on Malaysian economic development that a strategic shift will be required in the Malaysian economy if a high rate of economic growth is to be maintained. What are not so widely recognised are the conditions necessary for the shift to be made. In particular, it seems that major changes in the structure of labour markets are likely to be necessary and desirable.

Changes have taken place in the market for *skilled labour* in Malaysia. There has been a major shift in policy in Malaysia away from a supply-driven, state-*managed* approach on the provision of skills towards a demand-driven, state-*guided* approach with the introduction of a levy–grant system in 1992. The levy–grant system introduced an 'imperfection' into the market for skilled labour that was necessary to overcome the imperfections embedded in the labour market prior to the levy–grant system.

However, when the market for *unskilled labour* was examined, there were fewer grounds for optimism. It would seem that, during the past decade, the role of unskilled foreign labour in Malaysia has grown enormously. Thus, it is estimated that whereas foreign labour made up about 8 per cent of the total labour force in Malaysia in 1985, by 1990 the proportion had risen to 14 per cent, and by 1995 the number of foreign workers was 1.7 million, or about 19 per cent of the total labour force. Unofficial estimates suggest between 2 and 4 million foreign workers in the country compared to the official Malaysian labour force size of less than 9 million, i.e. between 20 and 30 per cent of the total labour force.

In official circles, concern has frequently been expressed about the social and economic effects of this large and growing unskilled foreign labour force. However, there seems to have been little official analysis made of these effects. As pointed out, some, most notably Azizah and Pillai, have done valuable work on some of the effects of unskilled foreign labour. In terms of *income distribution* effects, it is likely that the large-scale import of unskilled foreign labour has had and is likely to continue to have a harmful effect in the sense that income inequalities will grow.

The difficulties of tracing the effects of unskilled foreign labour on the *structure and restructuring of the economy* are great. However, it is likely that:

- there is an investment diversion effect away from new capacity in high-skill industries in favour of low-skill industries;
- there is a discouragement of 'modernising' investment in the plantation sector, in the retail trading sector and in parts of the manufacturing sector;
- these effects are sharpened by the extent to which the exchange rate is prevented from falling by the encouragement given to the production of goods which are exports or import-substitutes.

The effects of unskilled foreign labour on the costs and prices of non-traded goods and services as inputs into the traded goods sector are very difficult to trace.

However, in general, this chapter claims that it is likely, but by no means certain, that the net structural effect of unskilled foreign labour is detrimental to the Malaysian government's stated aim of achieving a strategic shift to high-value-added, high-skill-intensive industries.[7]

Policy implications

The fact that Malaysia is not alone in experiencing widening differentials between skilled and unskilled labour should not be grounds for complacency. The OECD's *Employment Outlook* has pointed to the socially harmful effects of the growing inequalities in many OECD countries (OECD 1996). There is no reason to suppose that these effects are any the less harmful in Malaysia. Furthermore, market forces are unlikely to quickly correct these differentials and the government needs to take effective action. Not only do forces in the labour market work slowly, but the government itself has created the problem by allowing unskilled foreign labour to enter the economy in such large numbers.

Thus, on income distribution grounds alone, there is a case for much greater control on the import of foreign labour.[8] There are those who say that with increasing globalisation and with increasing links between regions of Malaysia and regions in Indonesia and Thailand, effective controls on labour immigration are not possible. However, if the government has the political will, certain measures (such as punitive fines on employers of 'illegals') would be successful. Stronger controls should be imposed alongside a planned labour policy which should put an end to the stop–go policy on immigration of the immediate past (see Pillai 1995: 234, and World Bank 1995).

With the regional financial crisis from mid-1997, the governments affected have been forced to adopt contractionary policies in response, and these are likely to result in massive lay-offs and rapidly rising unemployment. By the last quarter of 1997, there was official talk of expelling a million foreign workers from the country. Such announcements were subsequently denied, perhaps due to the rapid deterioration of the situation in Indonesia in early 1998, with growing social unrest. It seems likely that the Malaysian government was prevailed upon by its Indonesian counterpart not to expel the mainly Indonesian foreign workers in Malaysia, so as not to compound the social dislocation brought about by the anticipated lay-offs of at least 2 million workers in Indonesia itself.

Nevertheless, the crisis has driven home the fact that the previous development strategy involving labour was neither sustainable nor desirable, and reversal of the labour inflows since the early 1980s seems most likely. However, this will merely be a market development reinforced by public policy. A more pro-active labour and skills policy is long overdue, and would be a desirable outcome of the crisis.

On the grounds both of income distribution and of economic restructuring, the role of unskilled foreign labour in the Malaysian economy should be reduced and then phased out over a 5- to 10-year period. This means that the growth rate of the economy should be slowed down so as to be consistent with an 'indigenous labour sustainable rate of growth' (ILSROG) of GDP. This is estimated to be about 6 to 7 per cent per annum, by contrast with the 8 to 9 per cent per annum actual growth rate until 1997.

Thus, a slower rate of growth would have been desirable in the short run. In addition to drawing in less foreign labour and to reversing the ever-larger wage differential between skilled and unskilled labour, a slower rate of growth would have had a number of advantages:

- first, it would give the effects of the HRDC-sponsored supply of skilled labour more time to work. The World Bank report (1995: 18) argues that the supply elasticity of skilled workers is low in Malaysia. In this case, a slower rate of economic growth would give a longer time for the supply of skilled labour to respond to the HRDC initiatives;
- secondly, it would enable the government to be more selective about the type of industries into which, and the terms on which, foreign direct investment could be encouraged;
- thirdly, it might reduce the ever-tighter infrastructural bottlenecks and reduce the rising environmental costs of Malaysia's development.

Thus, a slower rate of GDP growth in the short run may be compensated by a faster long-run rate of growth of a restructured economy. In addition, a decrease in the import of unskilled foreign labour could be offset, to some extent, if the government took a number of steps to increase the growth of the Malaysian-citizen labour force, namely:

- first, by increasing the *female participation rate* (the number of females economically active as a percentage of the total number in the working age population of 15 to 64 years). This participation rate is low in Malaysia (47 per cent in 1990) compared to Thailand (76 per cent in 1990 – see World Bank 1995: 12) and has increased slowly over the past two decades (in 1970, it was only about one per cent lower than the 1990 rate). One explanation for this may lie in the low pay for Malaysian women relative to Malaysian men. Thus, there is a low gender wage ratio in Malaysia (1:2, female to male, 1990) relative to those in Thailand (1:1.1), Philippines (1:1.33) and Japan (1:1.7) (World Bank 1995: 44). The World Bank suggests that part of the explanation for this low ratio could lie in the high non-wage benefits that women receive as employees (the costs of which employers have to pay) (World Bank 1995: 44). Nevertheless, it seems likely that low wages for Malaysian women are part of the explanation for the low female participation rate. Other factors accounting for the low participation rate are probably structural and cultural;
- secondly, by raising the *retirement age* which, in public-sector employment is currently 55 years;
- thirdly, by encouraging the '*repatriation' of Malaysian labour* currently working in foreign countries. At present, this is estimated to be well over 250,000, a substantial proportion of whom work in Singapore (see Pillai 1992: 25–8). How many of these overseas Malaysians are skilled and how many unskilled is not known, but even if only half could be persuaded to work in Malaysia, this could represent between 1 per cent and 2 per cent of the existing Malaysian labour force. Most of this emigration is non-Malay and is due, it is alleged, to

'an uneven opportunity structure for non-Malays in education and other Government-related economic activities' (Gunasekaran and Sullivan 1990: 15, quoted in World Bank 1995: 84). In the past, this outflow of Malaysian labour has been said to have provided a safety valve for surplus labour, but it has also exacerbated (in 1974/75, and again in 1986) the cyclical pressures in the Malaysian labour market when recessions in Singapore coincided with ones in Malaysia (see Narayanan 1992: 27).

Unfortunately, the slower growth induced by the contractionary policies adopted by the Malaysian financial authorities since December 1997 is not likely to facilitate the reforms proposed here. With the grossly depreciated ringgit, there is also a strong temptation to revert to the earlier development strategy involving wage rate repression as the means to secure international competitiveness. This will involve competing with the neighbouring economies that have also experienced similar currency devaluations and are equally desperate to restimulate growth on similar bases. There is therefore a strong likelihood of regression to 'beggar-thy-neighbour' policies that are likely to weaken the motivation to enhance Malaysian human resources and labour productivity through greater investments in education and training.

Notes

The draft of this paper was written during March and April 1996 and presented at a seminar in mid-April 1996 while Chris Edwards was a Visiting Lecturer at the Institute of Malaysian and International Studies (Institut Kajian Malaysia dan Antarabangsa or IKMAS) in Universiti Kebangsaan Malaysia (UKM). The support of IKMAS and UKM is gratefully acknowledged, as is the help of the large number of people in government departments, companies, UKM and other Malaysian universities, and research and training establishments who gave up much of their time to discuss the issues and ideas discussed in this paper. Particular thanks go to Yusof Kasim and Rajah Rasiah at IKMAS and to Vijayakumari Kanapathy and Patrick Pillai at the Institute of Strategic and International Studies (ISIS) in Kuala Lumpur. However, none of them bear any responsibility for the views expressed in this paper; these are the author's responsibility.

1 Of course, wage rates are not the only factor of relevance to the employers' decision as to whether or not to employ foreign labour. Payroll levies raise the incentives for employing foreign labour, since employers do not have to make Employees Provident Fund contributions for foreign labour (World Bank 1995: para. 17). Non-payroll labour costs are estimated to be about 20 per cent in manufacturing, but about 40 per cent in the plantations.

2 It should be noted that in Malaysia (as in most countries), the data on income distribution are crude. Thus, there must be doubts about whether changes in the measured and published Gini coefficients (which measure the deviation between perfect equality in incomes – represented by a coefficient of zero – and complete inequality of incomes – represented by a coefficient of one) are at all significant.

3 The Dutch disease effect refers to the way in which the export of newly discovered natural gas from the Netherlands in the 1960s was said to 'crowd out' (through a real appreciation of the exchange rate) the manufacturing sector. This may be a not-easily-reversible process if there are dynamic economies of scale (through a learning curve) in the manufacturing sector (see Krugman 1987: 49, 50).

4 Similar complications are evident in the rubber-growing industry. For a discussion of these, see Nayagam (1990, 1992).

5 Conversely, if exports are higher than they would otherwise be, due to the 'support' of foreign labour to the oil palm industry, then the price ratio of traded to non-traded goods falls.

6 Here, it is worth noting that in April 1996 the Prime Minister announced that the Government was seriously considering the wider use of crèches in the public sector to encourage female participation in the labour force (see *NST*, 14 April 1996).

7 Here, it is worth noting that in Singapore foreign labour accounts for a similar proportion of the total labour force as in Malaysia (namely about 20 per cent – see *ASEAN Economic Bulletin* 1995: 119, 126), and Cheah Hock Beng has argued that: 'a second factor which slowed down the adjustment process in Singapore was a substantial reliance on foreign labour, especially large numbers of unskilled or low-skilled foreign workers for factory work, construction and even domestic services' (Cheah Hock Beng 1995: 21).

8 The imposition of stringent controls on the immigration of unskilled foreign labour might not be sufficient by itself to bring about greater equality in income distribution. Other measures are likely to be necessary and desirable (e.g. the introduction of minimum wage legislation and redistributive taxes). Such measures are likely to not only bring about a more equal income distribution, but in doing so are likely to provide the basis for faster economic growth by deepening the size of the domestic market (see Jomo 1994: 98).

References

ASEAN Economic Bulletin (1995) Special Issue on *Labour Migration in Asia*, Volume 12, Number 2, Institute of South East Asian Studies, Singapore, November.

Ashton, D.N. and J. Sung (1994) 'The State, Economic Development and Skill Formation: A New Asian Model?', Working Paper 3, Centre for Labour Market Studies, Leicester.

Azizah Kassim (1995) 'From Neglect to Legalisation: The Changing State Response to the Inflow of Illegal Labour into Malaysia', paper presented at the Malaysian Social Science Association Conference in Penang, January.

Azizah Kassim (1996) 'Foreign Workers in Malaysia; An Analysis of Sanctioned Bondage', mimeo.

Bank Negara (1996) *Annual Report*, Kuala Lumpur.

Casey, B. (1991) 'Recent Developments in the German Apprenticeship System', *British Journal of Industrial Relations*, June, 205–22.

Cheah Hock Beng (1995) 'Can Governments Engineer the Transition from Cheap Labour to Skill-based Competitiveness?', in Martin Godfrey (ed.), *Skill Development for International Competitiveness*, London: Edward Elgar.

Dolton, P.J. (1993) 'The Economics of Youth Training in Britain', *Economic Journal*, 103 (September): 1261–78.

Dore, R. and M. Sako (1989) *How the Japanese Learn to Work*, London: Routledge.

Edwards, C.B. (1977) 'Rubber in the World Economy', *Jurnal Ekonomi Malaysia*, 5.

Edwards, C.B. (1995) 'Tariff and Trade-Related Policies for Malaysian Industrialisation', in V. Kanapathy (ed.), *Managing Industrial Transition in Malaysia*, Kuala Lumpur: Institute of Strategic and International Studies (ISIS).

Edwards, C.B. (1996) 'State Failure or Market Failure? The 10 Steps to a Levy–Grant System of Vocational Training', in Martin Godfrey (ed.), *Skill Development for International Competitiveness*, London: Edward Elgar.

EPU (1993) *Mid-term Review of the Sixth Malaysia Plan, 1991–1995*, Economic Planning Unit, Kuala Lumpur.

EPU (1996) *Seventh Malaysia Plan, 1996–2000*, Economic Planning Unit, Kuala Lumpur.

Finegold, D. and D. Soskice (1988) 'The Failure of Training in Britain; Analysis and Prescription', *Oxford Review of Economic Policy*, 4(3): 21–53.

Gill, M.S. (1988) 'The Features of Labour Utilisation and the Problems of Migrant and Immigrant Workers in the Construction Industry', in *Current Issues in Labour Migration in Malaysia*, 222–31, NUPW/University of Malaya, Kuala Lumpur.

Gomez, E.T. (1994) *Political Business: Corporate Involvement of Malaysian Political Parties*, James Cook University of North Queensland, Townsville.

HRDC (1994) *Annual Report*, Human Resources Development Council, Kuala Lumpur.

Ikmal Said (1992) 'Development Cycle and Capitalist Farm Expansion', *Ilmu Masyarakat*, 22: 81–114.

Jomo K.S. (1994) *U-Turn? Malaysian Economic Development Policies after 1990*, James Cook University of North Queensland, Townsville.

Krugman, P. (1987) 'The Narrow Moving Band, the Dutch Disease and the Competitive Consequences of Mrs Thatcher', *Journal of Development Economics*, 27: 41–55.

Lynch, L.M. (1993) *Strategies for Workplace Training*, Economic Policy Institute, Washington.

Ministry of Finance (1995) *Economic Report 1995/1996*, Kuala Lumpur.

MITI (1994) *Review of the Industrial Master Plan, 1986–1995*, Ministry of International Trade and Industry (MITI), Kuala Lumpur, Malaysia.

Narayanan, S. (1992) 'Impact of International Migration on Malaysia: The Positive and Negative Aspects', The Japan Industrial Relations Research Association and The Japan Institute of Labour, Tokyo.

Nayagam, J. (1990) 'Labour Utilisation and Adjustment: A Study of the Malaysian Natural Rubber Industry', PhD thesis, University of Malaya, Kuala Lumpur.

Nayagam, J. (1992) 'Migrant Labour Absorption in Malaysia', *Asian and Pacific Migration Journal*, 1(34): 477–94.

OECD (1996) *Employment Outlook*, Organization for Economic Cooperation and Development, Paris.

OPP2 (1991) *Outline Perspective Plan 1991–2000*, Government Printers, Kuala Lumpur.

Pillai, P. (1992) *People on the Move – An Overview of Recent Immigration and Emigration in Malaysia*, Kuala Lumpur: ISIS.

Pillai, P. (1995) 'Malaysia', *ASEAN Economic Bulletin*, 12(2), November.

Rasiah, R. (1997) 'Political Economy of Malaysia', in R. Robison, Garry Rodan and Kevin Hewison (eds), *The Political Economy of South-East Asia*, Melbourne: Oxford University Press.

SDF (1994/95) *Annual Report 1994/95*, Singapore: The Skills Development Fund.

Steedman, H. (1993) 'The Economics of Youth Training in Germany', *The Economic Journal*, 103 (September): 1279–91.

UPUM (1995) 'Impact Study on the Policy of Employment of Foreign Workers', report submitted to the Ministry of Human Resources, Malaysia, December.

Wood, A. (1994) *North–South Trade, Employment and Inequality*, Oxford: Oxford University Press.

World Bank (1995) *Malaysia: Meeting Labor Needs; More Workers and Better Skills*, 28 February, East Asia and Pacific Region, World Bank, Washington D.C.

World Bank (1996) *From Plan to Market: World Development Report 1996*, Oxford University Press.

INDEX